Religious Diversity—
What's the Problem?

Religious Diversity— What's the Problem?

Buddhist Advice for Flourishing with Religious Diversity

Rita M. Gross

CASCADE *Books* · Eugene, Oregon

RELIGIOUS DIVERSITY—WHAT'S THE PROBLEM?
Buddhist Advice for Flourishing with Religious Diversity

Cascade Books
An Imprint of Wipf and Stock Publishers
199 W. 8th Ave., Suite 3
Eugene, OR 97401

www.wipfandstock.com

ISBN 13: 978-1-62032-409-7

Cataloguing-in-Publication data:

Gross, Rita M.

Religious diversity—what's the problem? : Buddhist advice for flourishing with religious diversity / Rita M. Gross.

xiv + 362 pp. ; 23 cm. Includes bibliographical references and indexes.

ISBN 13: 978-1-62032-409-7

1. Christianity and other religions—Buddhism. 2. Buddhism—Relations. 3. Religious Pluralism I. Title.

BL85 G75 2014

Manufactured in the U.S.A.

Contents

Preface: How This Book Came into Being | *vii*

Section 1: Getting Started

1 The Book's Vision, the Author's Standpoint, and a Synopsis | 3

Section 2: Useful Information for Those Thinking about Flourishing with Religious Diversity

2 Does Everyone Believe Their Own Religion Is Best for All?: Four Models from the Cross-Cultural Study of Religion Regarding How People Think about Belonging to a Religion | 21

3 Does Religion Help or Hurt?: When Religion and Politics Mix in the Wrong Ways | 33

Section 3: Others, Especially Religious Others

4 Religious Others: The Received Traditions in Christian Theologies of Religion | 55

5 Excuse Me, but What's the Question?: Isn't Religious Diversity Natural? | 81

6 Of Fingers, Moons, and Rafts: The Limits of Religious Language | 101

7 Do Others Exist? Beyond the Duality of Self and Other | 118

8 Beyond Unity and Universalism: Appreciating Uniqueness and Diversity | 135

Section 4: Identity, Especially Religious Identities

9 Who Am I? Hyphenated Identities and the Composite Self in a Diverse World | 153

10 Training the Mind: The Role of Contemplative Practices and Spiritual Disciplines in Becoming Comfortable with Religious Diversity | 174

11 Women, Feminism, and Religious Diversity | 190

12 Religious Diversity and National Identity: Pluralistic Society or Christian Nation? | 205

13 Changing Religious Identity: Conversion versus Missions | 226

Section 5: Integrity: Relating with Religious Others

14 Learning about Religious Others: The Virtues and Joys of the Comparative Mirror | 251

15 Talking with Religious Others: Dialogue and Interreligious Interchange | 269

16 Ministry in a Multifaith World: Training and Responsibilities of Leaders of (Majority) Religions | 286

17 Going Forward Together and Separately: Buddhist Proposals for Creating Enlightened Society amid Religious Differences | 304

Section 6: Conclusion: Flexibility and Comfort

18 From Religious Chauvinism to Flourishing with Religious Diversity: A Developmental Model | 325

Bibliography | *339*

Subject and Names Index | *351*

Preface

How This Book Came into Being

THIS BOOK COMES OUT of a lifelong, heartfelt project and out of my most long-lasting spiritual concern—a concern even more long-lasting than the involvement with gender, feminism, and religion for which I am usually known. Even as a teenager, discomfort with religious exclusivism led me to speculate about and contemplate how different religions could relate more harmoniously with each other—not that I had much information about other religions in those days. But it bothered me that such harsh things were routinely said about other religions, that there was so much certainty that one group alone possessed the One True Faith, and that those who said or thought anything different were in error and were most certainly condemned to hell.

The language and logic of exclusive truth claims in religion are not theoretical to me. I know them intimately and personally. That is how I was brought up. I am speaking from direct experience. I know how psychologically and spiritually bankrupting and wounding exclusive truth claims are, given the consequences (potentially lethal) not only for the others against whom they are directed, but also for the person who internalizes them, whose identity is bound up in being on the inside of an exclusive truth claim.

In most lives, a few definitive moments determine much of the course one pursues, the interests one follows up, the books one writes. It used to be fashionable, especially in theology and religious studies, for scholars to hide behind a mask of so-called objectivity, claiming that they had no personal interest in what they were studying and about which they were writing. As I have narrated many times,[1] for me, that whole supposition broke apart earlier than it did for most scholars, as I discovered, on my own and without support from mentors or colleagues, that the supposedly neutral methods I was being taught were quite androcentric and had no ability whatsoever to handle data about women's religious lives.[2] By now, thanks first to feminist methods in the study of religions, and second to postmodernism, most scholars are much more willing to admit their situatedness, their context, and their debt to certain pivotal moments. Some of the genesis for this book happened in one pivotal moment that brought many years of religious indoctrination to a head.

It is January of 1965. I am a college senior, home for a brief visit. My mother had died a few months earlier, and during her funeral service I had been subjected to an anti-intellectual sermon aimed at me. I am a philosophy student who will enter the University of Chicago the following fall to pursue a PhD in the history of religions; I have chosen that path partly because it didn't seem reasonable to me to suppose that all interesting and worthwhile religious thinking occurred in my familiar cultural context, and also because, when I become a professor, I want to help students who had been brought up like me to think more cogently about the various religions of the world. Suddenly the pastor of the church where I had been brought up (in a very conservative Lutheran denomination), and the same man who had preached the sermon at my mother's funeral, is at the door. He is surprised to see me at home in the small, wood-heated log cabin without plumbing in which I had grown up, but he wastes no time in beginning an inquisition into my articles of belief.

Now I look back with great sadness on the things that I was taught to believe as a child. According to one such belief, heaven, apparently, was going to be very sparsely populated, because unless you held impeccably to beliefs that concurred completely with those of the Wisconsin Synod of the Lutheran Church, one stood very little chance of being admitted. Having exactly the right words seemed very important. In retrospect, it seems to me that a parrot that could recite the Apostles' Creed or repeat the definition of *consubstantiation*, with every word correct, probably stood a better chance of entering heaven than a human being who asked questions, as I had always done. At some point, this pastor told to me, "I always knew I'd have trouble with you someday. You asked too many questions." We were

---

1. Gross, *A Garland of Feminist Reflections*, 23–44; and Gross and Reuther, *Religious Feminism and the Future of the Planet*, 25–47.

2. Gross, *A Garland of Feminist Reflections*, 3–22 and 55–64.

taught to make fun of and ridicule the beliefs of others. As children we were given the impression that we had a better understanding of theologically difficult issues than others who had thought about them extensively but had come to different conclusions. Foremost among those whose beliefs were ridiculed (and misrepresented) were Catholics, of course. I remember the statement "There will be Catholics in heaven, but we don't know how they're going to get there, given what they believe." Jews were also high on the list of the most confused believers. We were taught that they should not have a homeland because they had taken upon themselves the curse to wander the earth when they had Jesus executed. I was taught that "our government will be punished by God for supporting the state of Israel." Other Protestants and other Lutherans all believed in error, and we were always given the impression that they engaged in this Unbelief because, for some unfathomable reason, they willfully defied God; they chose to be in error, even though they had every opportunity to hold correct beliefs. All they needed to do was ask the Wisconsin Synod Lutheran Church what they should believe, what words they should repeat.

In any case, we children were to have nothing to do with these "unbelievers" if that contact might in any vague way involve religion. All scouting activities were forbidden because Scouts made vague statements about God. Attending a service at another kind of church was completely anathema. I imagine that attending weddings and funerals must have been reluctantly permissible, but appearing at any other kind of service in another church was not. There should be no participation of any kind in local multifaith activities, such as the local "Put Christ back into Christmas" parade. (In northern Wisconsin in the nineteen-fifties, *multifaith* meant intra-Christian.) I don't know how many times I was quoted the scriptural verse "Be ye not unequally yoked together with unbelievers" (2 Cor 6:14, KJV).

I was an obedient child and I tried to conform to these requirements about correct beliefs. As we entered our first year of high school, having just graduated from the local Lutheran parochial school, a few friends and I objected, on theological grounds, to singing an *Ave Maria* with the Freshman Glee Club. We were fourteen, mind you! Definitely old enough to have mature theological positions on such issues. I was trying. But it wasn't working. When I was asked to play the piano for the high-school baccalaureate service, I decided to accept the task. I was also the salutatorian of my class and winner of a number of scholarships, so my picture was on the front page of the local paper, and quite a bit was written about me, including my role in the upcoming baccalaureate service (a minor detail). I was commanded to report to the pastor's study and reamed out for "being unequally yoked together with unbelievers" because I was participating in the baccalaureate service. I should know better, I was told. I had been taught the One True Faith. Either at that meeting or another meeting at which I was being reprimanded for singing in the choir of the wrong kind of Lutheran church and receiving Communion there, I ventured my first theology of religious diversity:

"Weren't people of other faiths trying to do the same thing, in their own terms and their own way, as we were trying to do? Didn't all the prayers go to the same place anyway?"

"Definitely not," I was told.

Everyone else worships an idol, which, I presume, means that their prayers go unheard. God only listens to people who are completely theologically correct, and in agreement with us, whomever the *us* of exclusive truth claims may be.

It is January 1965. I am twenty-one years old, and I am facing an inquisition to determine my "eternal salvation," as the matter was put to me in the excommunication letter that followed. If I meekly said yes to whatever theological proposition was put before me, my eternal salvation would be intact, but if I asked questions or nuanced my position, that would be fatal for my eternal salvation. I was asked a number of very precise questions, to which I tried to reply with an explanation rather than with a simple yes or no. After a few sentences, I would be interrupted and would fall silent, standard female behavior, especially before feminism. I don't know where I got the courage, but after a few such encounters, I would not fall silent when interrupted, which resulted in the ridiculous situation of both the pastor and myself talking at the same time because he refused to listen to anything I might say.

Finally there was a loud and insistent demand. "I'm not interested in any of your reasoning or opinions. I want a 'yes' or a 'no' answer. Do you hold completely to the doctrines to which you swore lifelong loyalty when you were confirmed?" (At the age of thirteen, one certainly is sufficiently theologically sophisticated to take lifetime oaths about difficult theological questions!) There was a second of stunned silence.

My mind worked very fast, and I shot back, "That's what the Catholic Church demanded of Martin Luther at the Diet of Worms." How I did that I don't know, but I'm still proud of my response. The pastor turned away, storming out of my house, slamming the door so hard he almost broke the glass in its window. I was told by mail that I had "sold [my] soul for a mess of 'academic' pottage." (Note the scriptural allusion to the story of Jacob and Esau.) I was also assured that I would spend eternity in hell unless I repented and apologized. How would he know that! Wouldn't repentance be sufficient? Why the demand for an apology in addition?

I tell this story at some length because it is important to see what happens to people ethically, psychologically, and spiritually when they indulge in making exclusive truth claims. Making exclusive truth claims does not often result in people being kind and gentle; instead people become rigid, combative and defensive, brittle and very impoverished spiritually, as is so clearly demonstrated by the behavior and demeanor of the man whom I have described. I also tell the story because, though the position of this articulate and extremely conservative Christian group may be somewhat extreme, in my many years of teaching comparative religions to undergraduates, I have often encountered similar attitudes. Appreciating other religions, rather than regarding them as a mistake and a problem, was quite difficult for many of my students. One of the rules in my Introduction to World Religions class was that people needed to develop empathy for whatever point of view we were studying and to try to imagine how it would feel to be on the inside of that view. Some of my students objected, saying that their religion forbade them to think positively about other religions or to understand why they feel true to their own insiders. For a few students, even encountering accurate factual information about religions other than their own was a great challenge. Their attitude seemed to be that it is a sin even to know such information. The only thing that should ever be said about other religions is that they are Wrong, and they wanted that message to be the content of an academic course in religious studies at a state university.

I also encounter similar attitudes in my everyday life. When my next-door neighbor and her family switched churches to find a religious environment more accepting of and welcoming to gay and lesbian people and people of color, her mother reacted by saying that she hoped they would be comfortable in hell. One of the younger members of the meditation group I lead in Eau Claire is expecting his first child. But his parents are more apprehensive than excited. Why? Given that their granddaughter will not be raised as an evangelical, the grandparents fear that, for the first time, one of their family members will go to hell. For such people, even intra-Christian diversity, to say nothing of interreligious diversity, is obviously a problem. It is troubling and sad that religious institutions indoctrinate their adherents in such poisonous attitudes toward others. It causes great suffering, both to those so indoctrinated, and to the recipients of their scorn and ridicule.

Stories such as the one I have just told need to be recounted because, unquestionably, for most of their history, Christians and some other monotheists have unhesitatingly proclaimed the exclusive truth of their theologies. This position, most notoriously stated by the Roman Catholic Church in its doctrine that there is "no salvation outside the Church,"[3] historically has not been an optional belief, nor has it been stated in a low-key or tentative manner.[4] It has been proclaimed stridently and confidently in many varieties of Christianity, and was unchallenged in most official theologies until relatively recently. It fueled, and still fuels, enormous missionary efforts around the world, as well as numerous military expeditions to establish or spread the One True Faith. (Think of the Crusades or the post-Reformation religious wars.) It is impossible to calculate the harm caused by such exclusive truth claims or the way their devastating effects still linger over much of our society, despite contemporary attempts to promote dialogue and to defuse such exclusive truth claims.

I did go on to graduate school the following fall, in September 1965, and there my attention turned more to feminist scholarship. But I had already made my choice of academic specialty because of my early experiences with indoctrination to exclusive truth claims. By 1971, I was teaching classes in world religions, and I never forgot or relinquished my original motivation to provide students better tools with which to think about religious diversity than those that had been given to me or have been given to many of my students. By 1973, my own spiritual questing landed me in Buddhism, after a happy ten-year sojourn in Judaism. For reasons I do not fully understand, Buddhism was and is my true home. I am not wishy-washy about how Buddhism has brought me peace and joy.

In 1980, as soon as I was somewhat well grounded in Buddhist thought and practice, I turned some of my attention to interreligious exchange, especially Buddhist–Christian dialogue. I still remember well the single sheet of letter-sized paper I received in the mail announcing a conference on Buddhist–Christian dialogue at the University of Hawaii. Instantly I knew this was something I should do, even though I had never thought at all about inter-religious exchange before I received that piece of mail. A large part of my motivation for all the dialogue activities I have engaged in since was to work with Christians whose attitudes toward religious diversity were different from those I had previously encountered. I have been deeply involved in the Society for Buddhist–Christian Studies and many other interfaith venues ever since. As I worked in those venues, I became convinced that the prolific literature on religious diversity coming mainly from Christians working on theologies of religion could benefit from more input from Buddhist thought and from what the comparative study of religions can tell

3. See Dupuis, *Toward a Christian Theology of Religious Pluralism*, 84–109, for a thorough discussion of this axiom.

4. For a good history of the development of this position, see Knitter, *Introducing Theologies of Religion*, 64–68.

us about religions in general. Now, finally, I have written the results of my lifelong quest to help people see that religious diversity is something to be treasured rather than feared.

May it be of benefit.

Section 1

Getting Started

Chapter 1

The Book's Vision, the Author's Standpoint, and a Synopsis

As the world has become more interconnected, most people are much more aware that there are many living faiths in the world, not just the one in which they were brought up or with which they may be familiar. But by and large, human ability to accept and appreciate religious diversity has not kept up with the fact that today most living religions have a worldwide distributions and cannot avoid interacting with and affecting one another. During the past half century, as it has become clearer and clearer that religious diversity is here to stay, some thoughtful people have begun to question old assumptions about whether one of the world's religions is true while the others are false. For understandable reasons, in the English-speaking world, this discussion has been led by Christians. Christians, after all, have a long history of claiming to be the only true religion and of attempting to convert the whole world to Christianity through missionary work. Dissatisfied with this heritage, some Christian leaders have begun to rethink the relationship of Christianity to other world religions in an enterprise called the theology of religions, and others have taken the lead in promoting interreligious dialogue as a way to develop better understanding of and working relationships with other religions.

That these discussions have been so dominated by Christians also has led, inadvertently, to the fact that the issues and proposals most often discussed are those that would easily occur to people thinking within the

3

framework of a Christian worldview. While I welcome these discussions, I would also claim that their utility is somewhat limited by the fact that so few non-Christians are involved in them, though I have often participated in such discussions in my work as a Buddhist critical-constructive thinker. It is my conviction that Buddhist ideas and sensibilities have a great deal to offer in this discussion of the meaning of religious diversity, of how to accept it and flourish with it. But, to date, very little such material is available, especially when compared to the enormous Christian literature on the topic. That is why I am writing this book.

Vision

The main thesis of this book is that religious diversity is to be expected and should not be spiritually or intellectually troubling. It is inevitably, universally part of human experience. Nevertheless, religious diversity often is troubling, and often is more troubling to those who consider themselves to be especially religious. This is because they belong to one the few religions, including Christianity, that have claimed that they alone are true and able to bring benefit to their followers. The followers of such religions have conflated the notion of the religion's uniqueness and a claim that their religion is universally relevant. By universal relevance these followers mean not that the religion is available to anyone who wishes to participate in it but that all people everywhere must belong to the religion or face dire consequences in the afterlife. This belief about the meaning of the fact of religious diversity is called *exclusivism* because adherents claim that their religion is the One True Faith, excluding all others. If some religious adherents believe such a proposition, they will find continuing religious diversity to be deeply problematic rather than an interesting blessing.

But a proposal that only one religion is true and that all others false is dysfunctional and destructive, given contemporary conditions of global interconnectedness and the availability of accurate knowledge about religions other than our own. Therefore, we must find religiously satisfying alternatives to it. If exclusive truth claims were the only option available for thinking about the implications of religious diversity, there would be only two possible outcomes: either everyone everywhere would come to belong to the same religion, or we would be mired in enduring, everlasting interreligious hostility and conflict. The first alternative is not going to happen. It is inconceivable that all people around the globe will voluntarily join the same religion. The alternative of enduring interreligious hostility and conflict is extremely unattractive and violates the better instincts of all religions—that part of the teaching of every religion that promotes love and compassion over aggression and competition.

Thus, the solution is obvious. Exclusive truth claims must be given up. They are now untenable and extremely unethical and inappropriate for the world we inhabit. The present situation for exclusive truth claims is like situations religions have faced before, when newly discovered facts have forced religions to rethink previously held dogmas, such as that the sun revolved around a stationary earth or that the earth was only a few thousand years old. Thus, with some theologians and philosophers of religion, including John Hick, I join the call for a Copernican revolution in how religious people think about religious diversity, though my ways of thinking about the issue are somewhat different from Hick's. My thinking is informed by Buddhist practice and thought on the one hand, and, on the other hand, by what the discipline of religious studies tells us about religions—information that we cannot ignore. I am completely convinced that spiritually valid and satisfying alternatives to exclusivism can be found in each religion. In other words, I claim that believing one's own religion to be the only valid and valuable religion among the world's many religions is not necessary to a deep and profound spirituality. I will claim even more: such an exclusivistic belief may actually be harmful to the quality of one's religious life.

Religious diversity, like almost every other difficult issue, is really about the relationship between the self and the other, and about how to deal gracefully and skillfully with both. Thus, my discussion about how to flourish with religious diversity will concern three main topics: first so-called others; second, identity or self; and, third, integrity, or discerning what are helpful and healthy interactions between religious others and oneself.

For many people, the most disconcerting fact about religious diversity is the mere existence of other religious perspectives. Though I claim that the much deeper problem is how we ever came to be the kind of self that is uncomfortable with diversity, we must begin with pertinent discussions about religious others and how we think about them. This is the starting point of current Christian theologies of religion, and I also claim this is a more appropriate starting point than is a call for interreligious dialogue. Dialogue can only be fruitful when we have thought through our presuppositions about other religions, at least to some extent.

Why are people uncomfortable with diversity, whether religious diversity or other kinds of difference, among human beings, given its omnipresence? I locate the answer to this question in conventional psychology, which finds others who are different to be disrupting or threatening to our identity; those who are different elicit a reaction different from our reaction to those whom we perceive to be similar, like us. When we encounter others who are different from us, we mainly experience that difference and separation as threatening to us and our group. Our identities seemed secure and safe, but then others come along and make us less sure of our own identity in many ways. One of the great motivators in the inevitably failed quest for religious uniformity is the question that religious others present to our own orthodoxies: "I was told that this is most certainly true, that this is the one true faith, so why are *they* there and what does their existence say about my one true faith? They must be infidels, because I am faithful to the truth." It seems to us that the world would be a simpler, safer place if only *they* weren't here to begin with. On one level this very typical reaction to the perception of religious difference may seem to reinforce security in our own identity, but at another, more subtle level it also betrays anxiety.

These reflections lead us to the realization that to learn how to flourish with religious diversity, we have to reconceptualize simultaneously how we think about religious others and also who we think we are. In the linear medium of language, however, we must do those tasks sequentially. Because it is the disruptive perception of different others that initially raises questions for most people, we will begin by discussing religious others. One of my chief claims is that much current thinking about religious differences makes the mistake of translating the simple *phenomenological experience* of encountering others into the *metaphysical construct* of otherness. In other words, the simple experiential duality of self and other is turned into metaphysical dualism, a belief in the real and enduring existence of both self and other. Metaphysical beliefs about dualism are then taken to be more real and relevant than our experience.

This, however, is only how things seem conventionally. We need to ask: Do others exist? In what sense do they exist? We need to ask: Is identity really a singular thing? Is identity not already internally differentiated? If it is not a singular thing, how can it be so affected by the perception of external difference? We have serious questions to ask about our conventional ways of constructing self and others and about our own sense of being a centered, permanent entity. There are other, more compelling ways to imagine others, ourselves, and our interactions.

After a somewhat lengthy discussion presenting (on the one hand) a critique of conventional ways of thinking about others and self-identity, and (on the other hand) more penetrating ways to think about each, we come to the point of being able to find more graceful and skillful methods of interaction between self and other. The section on integrity will deal with these topics. In it, I will suggest that the person of integrity who wishes to follow the moral code found within each religion encouraging kindness and compassion to all beings, not just those whom we like or happen to agree with, has two tasks.

The first is easier, more neutral, and more basic. I claim that given the interconnected world in which we live, every person has an ethical responsibility to learn something about religions other than their own. There are many benefits to such knowledge—not the least of them being a more accurate understanding of one's own religion. This kind of learning is best accomplished in the most neutral possible environment. It goes far to undo a great deal of interreligious hostility, simply because through it, people usually learn that they have a great many mistaken, incorrect, inaccurate impressions of what adherents other religions actually believe and practice. Such knowledge has two elements. First is simple, factual accuracy: What does each of the religions teach? We are not asking whether or not the religion is true. We are only asking what its teachings are. Second, it is important to explore each religion using one's own imagination to empathetically enter into it, attempting to understand why that religion feels true to its adherents.

Some more committed and curious people may wish to also take part in the second way to defuse interreligious hostility and misunderstanding: interreligious dialogue, a method highly recommended and very popular at present. However, I believe that some self-training is necessary before one attempts to engage in interreligious dialogue. One must be sufficiently comfortable with the inevitability of religious diversity that one can enter the dialogue able to listen and learn. If the dialogue devolves into debate or into covert attempts to convert others to one's point of view, dialogue can be counterproductive.

Thinking about religious diversity can be challenging because serious, rigorous, and logical thought about the topic often requires that one give up previously held beliefs. That can be challenging and temporarily disruptive. As I end this brief overview of my vision for how to flourish with religious diversity, I want to present examples from the Buddhist tradition that are personally inspiring to me.

The Dalai Lama has stated that if science (which includes empirical, Western-style historical studies) can definitively demonstrate that some traditional Buddhist claim does not make sense, then Buddhist thought will have to adjust. A spiritually mature religious practitioner is flexible, not rigid, in her stance toward newfound information, even if that information is disconcerting. Ken McLeod, Kalu Rinpoche's translator, tells a story about a lama who had been traditionally educated in Tibet. McLeod accompanied him to northern Canada during the summer. They arrived in the afternoon and settled in for the night, as usual. The next morning the lama was very troubled by the fact that it had not become dark during the previous night. McLeod used apples and oranges to show him that the sun does not set in the summer in the far north because of the earth's roundness, because of the way it tilts on its axis, and because of the way it rotates around the sun. The lama said that he had heard people say the earth was round when he came out of Tibet, but he had dismissed such claims as more Western nonsense. Such a claim seemed too contrary to everyday sense perceptions to him, and also contradicted his traditional training. After a few days of gloom, he conceded that his traditional position must have been wrong, and his usual cheerful manner returned. The lama's *knowledge* about nights without darkness proved more powerful than inherited *beliefs* about the flatness of the earth, even though changing his worldview caused the lama some depression.[1] I like to think of this traditionally trained Tibetan lama as a good model for those encountering novel ideas about religious diversity. A period of disorientation or depression is a small price to pay for more accurate knowledge, especially when flourishing with conditions of inevitable religious diversity is at stake.

Thinking about Religious Diversity as a Buddhist Scholar-Practitioner

A book so centrally focused on *religious diversity* has to begin by defining what I mean by each term. Given that it is impossible to define *religion* satisfactorily, I should at least explain why I consistently opt for the term *diversity* rather than *pluralism*. The usual distinction between the terms is that *diversity* refers to the fact that there are many religions, whereas *pluralism* refers to a theological evaluation of that fact—usually the positive evaluation that other religions besides Christianity are "true," whatever that might mean, a usage well established in Christian theologies of religion. Many commentators concerned with how we might flourish with religious diversity prefer the term *pluralism*—not least among them Diana Eck, the esteemed scholar of American religious diversity. She writes, "*pluralism* is not just another word for diversity. It goes beyond mere plurality or diversity to active engagement with that plurality."[2] While flourishing with religions diversity (my vision) obviously involves and includes "engagement" with that diversity, I prefer the term *diversity* to *pluralism*. The need to accept, accommodate, and live well with that diversity overrides any theological evaluation of that diversity, including my evaluation that religious diversity is not only a blessing, but

1. McLeod, *Wake Up to Your Life*, 353–54.
2. Eck, *A New Religious America*, 70.

God's will (to put the matter in Christian terms). It is simply a reality that even those who are initially uncomfortable with religious diversity have no choice but to learn how to accommodate themselves to that fact, just as they have had to accept the heliocentric view of the solar system. Eventually, the existence of religious diversity should cause them no greater disturbance than the heliocentric view of the solar system now causes them, no matter how disruptive it may have once been. In the meanwhile, the greater need is address people's discomfort with religious diversity and overcome it, rather than to make theological assessments of that diversity.

I also prefer the term *diversity* for another reason. Some pluralist theologies of religion are so interested in the commonalities of religion that they gloss over the irreducible distinctiveness of each tradition, looking for lowest common denominators among the traditions. One quite frequently hears even well-informed people claim that all religions are essentially the same. But I don't think it's that simple. There are real differences among religions, especially at theological and philosophical levels. Flourishing with religious diversity cannot be bought at the price of denying or undercutting the distinctness of traditions. I do not think that such distinctiveness in any was diminishes our ability to flourish with religious diversity. The term *diversity* makes that point much more clearly than the term *pluralism*.

As for the term *religion*, no generally accepted definition of religion has ever been devised, and I do not hope to be successful in this context. Nevertheless, a few comments guide my discussion and my usage. First, as a Buddhist, I find definitions that turn on transcendence, the purported existence of higher or supernatural beings, or the presumption of an otherworldly orientation unsatisfactory. I prefer more sociological or psychological descriptive definitions to theological definitions of religion. I also seek a definition that is as nonrestrictive as possible, a definition that could include many things that would not be included in the class called religion according to many traditional definitions. Thus, I have always found Tillich's definition of "ultimate concern" to be relatively adequate. If we need a more complicated definition, I prefer Clifford Geertz's definition: "a system of symbols which acts to establish powerful, pervasive, and long-lasting moods and motivations in men [*sic*] by formulating conceptions of a general order of existence and clothing these conceptions with such an aura of factuality that the moods and motivations seem uniquely realistic."[3]

The virtue of such definitions, as I see it, is that they could envelop any deeply orienting system of beliefs and behaviors, including atheism, secularism, Marxism, communism, or what have you. I am especially suspicious

3. Geertz, "Religion as a Cultural System," 168.

of the opposition between the so-called secular and the so-called religious. The category called secular is particularly troublesome, and, I think, very unclear, but it is important to be able to include secularism within our understanding of "ultimate concerns," not outside it, as a widespread alternative to traditional religions, not as some demonic antireligion. Some people, including the Dalai Lama in his book *Beyond Religion*, embrace the term *secular* and mean by it a political neutrality in which all religions can find their place, an understanding he attributes to how secularism is practiced in India, at least in theory. Thus, rather than being antireligious, secularism makes space for all religions, and for no personal religion, as well. However, the term *secular* is not routinely used in this fashion in the West, where it has more connotations of being antireligious, rather than religiously neutral.

But in the West, being anti-religious is often synonymous with hostility to traditional religions. Many people in the West have been deeply wounded by intolerant, xenophobic, antirational, and extremely dogmatic religious education, but they long for the things religion provides when it is more in tune with the current ethos. I would claim that many orientations usually called "secular" by their holders and by others provide as profound and deep an orientation towards life as traditional religions do, even though those who hold so-called secular orientations may find traditional religions deeply dissatisfying. This is important especially for discussions of working together despite religious differences. Regarding that subject, I always mean working together across the secular/traditional-religions divide, not only across and among the various traditional religions.

This book has two intellectual-spiritual foundations: my forty-some years of thinking, practicing, and teaching as a Buddhist, and my nearly fifty years of studying and teaching comparative religions. To speak first of Buddhism, it is already clear from some of the ways I talk about these issues that my approach to the topic of religious diversity owes a great deal to the Buddhist practice, which informs who I am and how I am, how my relationship with the world of apparent duality feels, and how I verbalize my insights. I believe that these insights are a missing ingredient in current discussions of comparative theology and theology of religions, and would do much to enrich that discussion. Therefore I offer this book simply to inform and enrich others who also think about religious diversity and long to live in a world in which religious diversity ceases to trouble people.

It is critical that readers understand that I am not advocating for Buddhism and against other religions in this book, claiming that Buddhism has all the answers to questions about religious diversity, or that Buddhism has a perfect or stellar record of dealing with such issues. In fact, in its institutional forms, Buddhism has committed the same errors regarding religious diversity as every other religion. In this book, I am *offering* Buddhist insights, not advocating for Buddhism. I am also convinced that while the insights I will offer concerning how to flourish in situations of religious diversity came to me as a result of contemplation and meditation practices I learned in Buddhist contexts, these insights are available to anyone regardless of religious orientation because of their rationality and humaneness. I will especially be emphasizing the deep psychological and spiritual wisdom of Buddhism, much of which applies universally and does not require adherence to Buddhist doctrinal systems.

This book rests on much more than a doctrinally correct appropriation of Buddhism or a scholar's knowledge of Buddhist history, culture, and texts. I have been practicing various Buddhist spiritual disciplines quite deeply for a long time—for more than half my life, for nearly forty years. I have never been a "closet Buddhist," as are so many other Western scholars who write about Buddhism. Buddhist spiritual and meditative disciplines have been deeply transformative and liberating for me, first providing relief from the grief and rage stemming from my early feminist awareness of all the injustices routinely done to women,[4] and I have always tried to acknowledge my debts and my sources. Study and contemplation of Buddhist thought, especially the profound and subtle doctrinal systems of Indo-Tibetan Buddhism, also have had a major impact on me. The difference is that I do not merely know *about* these systems. Because I have spent so much time in contemplative and meditative practices, the words have become mine, and I use them in my own idiosyncratic way. I also teach them, these days more often as a *dharma* teacher than as a university professor. I am not presenting abstract theories about which I can speak fluently; I am speaking from my own experiences.

Much of what I will have to say that is Buddhist-inspired is not explicitly found in extant Buddhist texts. Instead, it is born of endless hours spent contemplating how *Buddhadharma* might be applied to our current situation of religious diversity and the anxiety it causes for so many. Thus, I write and speak as a Buddhist critical and constructive thinker, a.k.a. a *theologian*,[5] a label with which I am quite comfortable, despite the anxiety it causes many Buddhists. I am also writing as a *Western* Buddhist, which makes a real difference in how I approach and present Buddhism. While I do affiliate with a specific form of Buddhism and am an authorized *dharma* teacher within that form of Buddhism, I do not think or speak only within the limitations or the orthodoxy of that form of Buddhism, or even within the limits of Buddhism altogether. I do not hesitate to criticize and disagree with conventional

4. Gross, *A Garland of Feminist Reflections*, 235–44.
5. Gross, "Buddhist Theology?" 53–60.

Buddhism as it has constructed itself to date. This is clear from the work I have done on Buddhism and gender, especially in my book *Buddhism after Patriarchy: A Feminist History, Analysis, and Reconstruction of Buddhism*. In the contemporary world, very few Buddhists, whether Western or Asian, have undertaken such critical and constructive Buddhist thought.

Furthermore, everything I say *as a Buddhist* is informed by my life-long immersion in the comparative study of religions. I always characterize myself as a scholar-practitioner, which is one word with two components. Integral and essential to the *scholar* part of that word is the cross-cultural, comparative study of religions, which is the second major intellectual-spiritual foundation of this book. This allegiance to the cross-cultural, comparative study of religion is actually older than my immersion in Buddhist study and practice. After an undergraduate major in philosophy, I decided that philosophy did not really get at the central, existential issues of meaning, life and death, and that a discipline dealing with religion would be a far better fit for me. But even in the mid-1960s at the age of twenty and in the midst of a rather provincial education, I concluded that it would be shortsighted of me to assume that the religions that predominated in my culture were the only ones with cogent, thought-provoking comments on those issues. Why would anyone interested in theological or religious questions confine themselves to the answers given in only one religion? Furthermore, as a future professor, I wanted to help students who were struggling with repressive and intolerant views about religious diversity into which they had been indoctrinated. With that combination of interests and convictions, I resolved to study religion cross-culturally and globally in graduate school. Clearly, I did enter that field with religious or theological motivations, though in those days one could not speak openly of such things. Fortunately, very fortunately for a *female* graduate student in those days, and for one as poor as myself, I received scholarships to attend the then-famous "Chicago school" of the history of religions.

One of the most important *religious* developments of the past century is the development of *religious studies* as a discipline independent of confessional religious allegiances, a discipline able to illumine the phenomenon of religion in global context. Today to be a credible theologian, one needs accurate and empathetic knowledge of traditions other than one's own. Such knowledge is no longer a luxury or an optional add-on for theology, especially for those theologians who construct their traditions' comments on how to live in a world characterized by religious diversity. The days when it was acceptable to think about religious diversity by focusing on ourselves and denying the worth of others while knowing almost nothing about them are over. We can learn a great deal about what is true of religion in general by studying, in comparative context, how religions actually work on the ground, as opposed to by merely repeating theories about how things should work according to our own theological perspective. Whatever our tradition and practice may be, we do not exist in a vacuum, and what is true of religions in general will be true for our own traditions.

Therefore, what we learn from the cross-cultural and historical study of religions is of utmost spiritual and theological significance. This piece has been largely absent from current discussions of the theology of religions, though it is becoming more prominent as the field of comparative theology gains credibility. The comparative, global study of religions entails certain conclusions about what religions are and how they work, which traditional religions do not usually propose. But traditional religions must take into account the knowledge about religion garnered from religious studies. Religions always have to stay current with advancing human knowledge if they are to remain relevant. Some of religions' most devastating failures have to do precisely with refusing to accommodate such advancing knowledge.

I will make an even stronger argument. I will argue that knowledge learned from the cross-cultural and comparative study of religions about how religions work trumps theological claims when the two are in conflict. It may sometimes take religious authorities and religious people a long time to accept conclusions that superficially are at odds with their received dogmas, but these days, few people would still argue that the sun revolves around the earth because the Bible seems to make such a claim. This paradigm shift is a model that should be taken seriously by all religions and religious people.

As for my own hyphenated identity as a Buddhist scholar-practitioner, let me say immediately that I live by rules I am suggesting for others. Sometimes what I learn as a scholar of religions or as a feminist scholar conflicts with what Buddhist teachers whom I revere think is the case. There can be no question about how to resolve such conflicts, at least in my own mind. Religious authority cannot trump knowledge, as should be obvious from the example of the Tibetan lama who gave up his belief in the earth's flatness when presented with more convincing information. But apparent knowledge is also subject to never-ending, ongoing refinement. Willingness and ability to live with hypotheses, rather than demanding infallible conclusions, is also a critical component of learning how to live well and flourish with religious diversity. We will hear much more about this tentative, flexible, questioning state of mind when dealing with difficult issues in this book. I believe that unless we learn to live with much less certainty about many religious issues than we have previously demanded, we cannot learn to flourish in conditions of religious diversity—and religious diversity is here to stay. That much is certain!

Synopsis/Overview of the Book

In chapters 2 and 3, we consider information essential for anyone trying to think theologically and normatively about religious diversity. Chapter 2 discusses various models of religious belonging found in the world's religions. In that chapter we learn that contrary to many assumptions in cultures where monotheistic religions dominate, it is not common for followers of most world religions to think that in an ideal world everyone would belong to the same religion. Chapter 3 turns to questions of what can happen when religious and political institutions become too closely intertwined. Sometimes, religions seek to suppress religious diversity by convincing governments to support only one religion or its policies, and sometimes religions betray themselves and their vision by supporting problematic government policies. A secondary thesis of this book is that for religious diversity to be maintained, governments and religious institutions cannot be intertwined. Too close an identification of any religious claim with an ethnic or political group is deadly. I look at the post-Reformation religious wars in Europe, Japanese Buddhist support of Japanese militarism before World War II, and the Sri Lankan Civil War as examples of how dangerous it is to collapse religious and political/state institutions, despite a long-standing tendency to do so.

The third major section of this book, comprising chapters 4 through 8, takes up the crucial topic of *others*, especially religious others. These chapters, relying heavily on my knowledge of Buddhism and my Buddhist practice, begin the major discussions of this book, and take up new approaches to questions of how to live with and appreciate diversity. Chapter 4 consists of an analysis and critique of the received traditions in the Christian theology of religions for thinking about religious diversity. Chapter 5 begins the discussion of overcoming our own uncomfortableness with others, especially with religious others and religious diversity. That task requires a paradigm shift from regarding religious diversity as a flaw or a mistake, as something that has to be explained, to regarding religious diversity as something natural and normal. It suggests that the various religions are different skillful means for coping with diverse human needs in diverse situations, rather than monolithic prescriptions relevant for all human beings everywhere. Chapter 6 discusses the inevitably metaphoric, symbolic, and *provisional* nature of religious language. It also suggests that open curiosity about what we believe is the most fruitful attitude toward any truth claims. This chapter relies heavily on Buddhist teachings about the dangers of clinging to ideas, ideologies, and concepts—especially our ideas about what truth is. Chapter 7 suggests that most of our ideas about religions others are not founded on any secure knowledge about those others but only on our own projections and fantasies. We do need to discuss whether and in what sense others exist. This chapter will suggest that the phenomenological experience of duality does not warrant the construction of a metaphysical Other. It will also suggest that when we harden our experience into metaphysical constructs such as Otherness, we create much of our uncomfortableness with diversity and difference. So we need to undo that construction. Chapter 8 concludes our discussion of religious others by addressing some of the ways religious diversity is a great gift that helps us understand the specificity of our own tradition and appreciate it, not because it is universally valid, but because it is, specifically, what it is. This chapter will also entertain a question that has long been discussed by Christian theologians and is the basis for some of their claims for exclusive truth: does something's *uniqueness* make it *universally* relevant? I will answer that question negatively.

From questions about religious others, we move on to a discussion of religious identity. A primary claim of this book is that most of our problems with being able to flourish in situations of religious diversity have more to do with our own issues about ourselves than with the others with whom we interact. Thus, we need to clarify many questions about identity, which is the task of chapters 9 through 13. In chapter 9, we begin discussing the serious question of who we really are and suggest, agreeing with standard Buddhist assessments, that we are not an entity or a self, but that we are a composite put together out of many different experiences, inevitably leading to a hyphenated identity. When we acknowledge the hyphenated nature of our identity, we are much less likely to fixate on any one element of our identity, such as a religious identity, and, as a result, we can be much less uncomfortable with diverse others. Chapter 10, on the role of spiritual and contemplative disciplines in becoming comfortable with religious diversity, is in many ways the lynchpin chapter of the whole book. Appropriate mind training or spiritual discipline has everything to do with developing the skills required to be comfortable with religious others and religious diversity, as well as with our own hyphenated identities. We return to a discussion of flexibility and openness, rather than conviction and firm belief systems, as the most spiritually healthy attitude one can have—which is also the attitude most conducive to flourishing with religious diversity. Chapter 11 discusses the inattention of one of my primary identities—feminism—to religious diversity. In chapter 12, we deal with one of the most critical issues for North American discussions of religious diversity—to what extent, if any, should the United States be identified as a Christian nation? In chapter 3, we will learn how dangerous it can be for political and religious institutions to be too closely intertwined. It is ironic that descendents of those who sometimes left their home countries to escape unacceptable religious pressures are now seeking to impose their values and in some cases their religious affiliations and teachings on public space and public institutions in the United States. I will suggest that while religious people naturally will want to express their values in public forums, it is always inappropriate for religious people to try to impose their own values and norms on society as a whole. Finally, in chapter 13, I turn to another important issue about religious identity—changing religious identities (a.k.a. conversion). As a convert myself, I should not avoid dealing with the issue of inappropriate proselytization versus the need and right to join the religions of one's choice. In such discussions other rights and needs are often forgotten: the need not be pestered by missionaries and the right to remain in one's birth religion.

In conclusion, chapters 14 through 17 address more specifically and concretely how self and other can interact with more integrity in situations of religious diversity. Another way to put the matter is to ask how persons of integrity would deal with inevitable religious diversity. Chapter 14 argues that in contemporary circumstances, it is the ethical responsibility of every person to acquire a basic working knowledge of the world's religions and suggests how to go about acquiring this knowledge in nonthreatening and effective ways. I suggest that neutral classes on world religions taught in secular institutions by well-trained instructors are the easiest way to begin to acquire this important knowledge. Chapter 15 discusses what interreligious dialogue actually is and under what circumstances it might help us deal with the inevitability of religious diversity. In my view, dialogue is an advanced and difficult task, not to be put forward as a Band-Aid solution for discomfort with religious diversity. Chapter 16 discusses the responsibilities of the religious institutions of the majority religion (in this case Christian institutions, especially seminaries) to take non-Christian religions seriously. It suggests how they can fulfill those responsibilities better, and advocates that such institutions should always hire experts and practitioners of non-Christian religions to teach about them. Chapter 17 then discusses how people who have trained themselves about the world's religious options could then work together across sectarian lines. Not being upset about lack of theological agreement among themselves, such people can work on the mutual task of improving the world in which we all live. Even though the world's religions do not have identical ethical outlooks either, enough is shared across sectarian guidelines that we can work together on many projects and not argue about those about which we will not agree. This is the answer to the often-asked question of how to dialogue with people with whom we disagree.

The book ends with a final chapter sketching the typical spiritual journey of someone who begins with relative ignorance about religious others and some degree of discomfort with religious diversity, thinking that their own religion is best. This is the default setting for most people who have not reflected deeply about religious diversity. However, as the whole book shows, such a position is inadequate for flourishing in the world we now inhabit. What are the stages of moving from our initial discomfort about religious diversity to appreciation for it so that we can flourish in a religiously diverse world?

Section 2

Useful Information for Those Thinking about Flourishing with Religious Diversity

Chapter 2

Does Everyone Believe Their Own Religion Is Best for All?

Four Models from the Cross-Cultural Study of Religion Regarding How People Think about Belonging to a Religion

O NCE A REPORTER WHO was interviewing me declared that religious people necessarily think their own religion is the best and should be adhered to universally. Another way of saying the same thing is to claim that all religions necessarily make exclusive truth claims. This assumption is indeed widespread in many parts of the world. However, there is a very persuasive counterargument. It simply is not true, if one investigates religious communities globally rather than relying only on culturally familiar information. To make exclusive truth claims about one's own religion is not the only position regarding religious diversity, or even the most common position. One of the great liberating and sobering effects of the cross-cultural, comparative study of religion is the discovery that human beings do not always do things in the ways that are most familiar to us. In fact, others may even have some more adequate and compassionate ways of proceeding. We can learn about and adopt those customs and practices, and we can critique our own common assumptions (including the assumption that everyone makes exclusive truth claims) on the basis of those alternate practices and understandings.

In this chapter, I will consider one of the more useful ways of classifying the world's religions: a sociological rather than a doctrinal classification. After laying out these major types of religion, I will discuss the various models or styles of religious belonging practiced in these different kinds of religions. We will find that only one model of religious belonging involves exclusive truth claims or views the ideal situation as one in which everyone would belong to the same religion.

Classifying religions broadly into two categories—ethnoreligions and universalizing religions—is helpful for gaining insights into why some religions think it is important to seek converts and others do not. Ethnoreligions are very closely tied to their culture, whereas universalizing religions are portable wanderers that can be practiced in any cultural context.[1] This classification is useful in part because it does not follow the superficial, but usual classification of religions as Eastern and Western. There are Eastern and Western religions in each category.

An ethnoreligion is truly a way of life in which it is almost impossible to separate religion from culture. Customs and behaviors are far more important than beliefs, which can be quite flexible. Typically, matters that are considered secular in the context of many universalizing religions, such as diet, dress, marriage and divorce, and laws regulating society and politics are far more important than doctrines, beliefs, and creeds. The only way to convert to an ethnoreligion is to join the society and be adopted by its members. Ethnoreligions are usually quite localized and usually have no dreams of empire or universal relevance.

Universalizing religions, by contrast, are based on a set of ideas that transcend culture. These must be portable, abstract, and general enough to attract followers from a wide variety of cultures, and to attract followers away from their cultures of origin. A very detailed code for daily living is usually not as important to a universalizing religion as are its core beliefs and doctrines, but it must believe that its message is universally relevant, and that all people would benefit from hearing and absorbing that message. Almost by definition, a universalizing religion has spread widely from its point of origin. A portable religion, of course, must have porters, people, usually men, who have good reasons to travel extensively and little to tie them to any specific location. Merchants, monks, and soldiers are the best candidates, and they have had a lot to do with the spread of the universalizing religions.

---

1. Sernett, "Religion and Group Identity," 217–30, first introduced me to this classification.

There are three major universalizing religions: Buddhism, Christianity, and Islam. Each claims to have a message that would be relevant and useful to everyone, no matter what their culture or daily lifestyle might be. Though difficult issues often arise, each religion tries not to disrupt the daily lifestyle of their new converts too much. However, Islam does impose a fairly strict code of daily living; Buddhism does prohibit certain occupations, such as butchering, hunting, and soldiering; and Christianity usually insists on monogamy and other aspects of its code of sexual behavior. Christianity and Islam both have vigorous missionary movements and have often spread through conquest. In many parts of the world, one of them holds almost a monopoly on religious affiliation. They also both claim to be the religion that God has given to humanity, thus making exclusive truth claims for themselves. Both have justifiable reputations for engaging in wars of religion,[2] though there have always been significant voices arguing against religious use of violence in each tradition.

Buddhism has also spread widely, and its current transmission to the West is arousing both concern and interest. Buddhism makes universal claims but, though exclusive truth claims have appeared in some Buddhist sects, they are not characteristic. To explain, Buddhists say that their description of the human condition and how to work with it applies to all people. But usually Buddhists have not insisted that solving the riddle of human existence, finding peace or salvation, can only be done through Buddhist methods or that all people would need to express their realization in Buddhist words and concepts. Buddhism has typically been quite accommodating to indigenous religious traditions, and in many of the places to which it spread, it did not become the dominant religion. Typically, it has not engaged in the large-scale imperial conquests, whether economic or military, accompanied by mass conversions in which religions sometimes participate. Monks and merchants play a much greater role in its spread. The Chinese adoption of Buddhism is the only premodern instance in which the religion of one major culture area (South Asia) has been adopted in another major culture area (East Asia). Most of this adoption came from Chinese rather than Indian initiative. Tibet's adoption of Buddhism is actually a reverse missionary movement! Tibetans traveled to India to find teachers and texts, and to take the religion back to Tibet. So this case of a universalizing religion seems to be rather different from those of Christianity and Islam. To discover that a religion could make universal claims without also making

---

2. For two accounts of monotheism's linkage with religious violence, see Schwartz, *The Curse of Cain*; and Stark, *One True God*.

exclusive claims adds a great deal to the discussion of religious diversity and theologies of religion.

The division between ethnoreligions and universalizing religions is not always so sharp. A universalizing religion can take on many local features when it has been established for a long time in any particular culture and has lost touch with other forms of that religion in other parts of the world. This happened to Buddhism to such an extent that some suggest that Buddhism is not a single religion[3] and that if we regard Buddhism as a single religion, we could also regard Judaism, Christianity, and Islam as different sects of an overarching monotheistic religion—a claim I find quite cogent. A religion that was once a universalizing religion can become an ethnoreligion due to historical circumstances and hardship, as happened to Judaism. A religion that has not become universalizing because it has not spread widely could become so in different circumstances. There is no reason why Confucian or Daoist ideas could not appeal widely. They have as much general relevance as Buddhist, Christian, or Muslim ideas, but they have not had the historical fortune to spread widely. Even a stereotypical ethnoreligion can have widespread appeal. Followers of indigenous Native American religions are very reluctant to open their practices to outsiders, but a few teachers do. As I watched blond Germans who traveled to South Dakota every year dance in the annual Sundance, I also watched the categories "ethnoreligion" and "universalizing religion" collapse before my eyes. Nevertheless, they are useful general categories.

Among the world's religions, we can isolate at least four distinct ways of negotiating religious diversity, four ways that individuals who belong to one of the religions are encouraged to think about the diversity of the world's religions. In only one of them are believers encouraged to think that they alone possess religious truth and that the world would be a better place if everyone belonged to their religion.

In ethnoreligious contexts and in some other situations, believers may erect barriers against outsiders rather than trying to lure them into religious participation. These adherents clearly do not believe that it is necessary for the salvation of outsiders that the outsiders begin to think and act like the insiders. As has already been noted, ethnoreligions are characterized by a close intertwining of religion and culture, which helps explain adherents' attitudes toward religious others. To practice the religion, an outsider would have to join the culture completely, and there is little reason to promote or accept such conversion. While members of an ethnoreligion obviously

3. This argument is made in the fifth edition of a classic textbook on Buddhism: Robinson et al., *Buddhist Religions*.

prefer their own religion and culture to any other, they do not regard it as categorically superior in the same way that those who make exclusive truth claims proclaim superiority for their religions

Ethnoreligions and some others present another interesting counter-example to the expectation that everyone should practice the same religion. Even within a single ethnoreligion, people may not know the details of one another's religious experiences or the specifics of their beliefs and practices. This secrecy is simply accepted, and no one feels deprived because they are not privy to the religious practices of others. People feel that it is simply inappropriate to share one's own religious experiences with anyone except one's teacher or closest companions. Though as a Buddhist I belong to a uni-versalizing religion, many aspects of my particular path as a practitioner of Tibetan Vajrayana Buddhism predispose me to be very sympathetic to this ethnoreligious approach. There is a great deal of secrecy in Vajrayana Bud-dhism. The view is that too much information too soon could be destructive rather than helpful because the path of spiritual development is long and complex. Profound secrets disclosed too soon are usually either dangerous or easily trivialized. For Vajrayana Buddhists, the preferred practice is to introduce basics to those who request such instruction and gradually intro-duce other aspects of the tradition when appropriate.

Such reticence to share one's beliefs and practices may well be a useful counterposition to those who are feel that it is their supreme duty to share their religious beliefs and practices as widely as possible, and in that pro-cess to wipe out alternative visions of the real, the good, and the beautiful. Instead, in some contexts, such as in North American indigenous religions, extreme reluctance to share religion with outsiders has developed, and those who teach outsiders some of the more esoteric and important aspects of religious belief and practice are accused of selling the religion. This attitude is the exact opposite of the notion than one should send missionaries to the ends of the earth to bring all people into a correct belief system.

Multiple religious belonging is another possibility not explored or imagined by those who assume that all religious people make exclusive truth claims. In East Asia, people typically belong to several religious tradi-tions, using each one to meet specific needs. Or one could say that ordinary people belong to no specific religious tradition because they utilize them all, either simultaneously or sequentially. Only religious specialists belong to a specific tradition. Usually such specialists acknowledge and promote the multireligious context in which they operate, though examples of sectarian rivalry and exclusive loyalty, both among laity and religious specialists, are not unknown. The most striking demonstration of the reality of East Asian multiple religious belongings is that Japanese census figures routinely turn up nearly twice as many religious affiliations as the population of Japan.[4] Most people participate in at least Shinto and Buddhist activities, and it would not occur to them to choose one set of activities over the other. Instead, Shinto specializes in religious events pertaining to birth and fertility, whereas most people turn to Buddhism to deal with death and the afterlife. Thus, New Year's celebrations occur in a largely Shinto context, but death anniversaries are memorialized at Buddhist temples. A person taken to a Shinto shrine soon after birth will probably have a Buddhist funeral. Though the practice is dying out, traditional homes would have both a Shinto shrine for the *kami* (Shinto divine beings) and a Buddhist altar, where the family ancestors are remembered, and both would be used regularly.

Much the same situation prevailed in traditional China regarding the Three Traditions—Buddhism, Confucianism, and Daoism. Where early Western scholars had seen competing, distinct traditions, the Chinese saw cooperating traditions. Confucianism governed public life, etiquette, and the state, while Daoism inspired poetry, the arts, and private contemplation. Buddhism was often the favorite religion of women, who played little part in public life, while Confucianism was the preferred outlook for upper-class men. As in Japan, so in China most people participated in more than one religion during their lifetimes.[5] The plurality of religious perspectives was built into the architecture of pilgrimage sites. One observer of Chinese culture narrated her growing understanding of the plurality of Chinese religious perspectives as she participated in a pilgrimage up a mountain. The lower reaches of the mountain were dedicated to temples for various deities of Daoist folk religion and other aspects of popular folk religion, including vivid portrayals of the many tales of popular religion. As the pilgrimage route wound further up the mountain, the imagery changed from Daoist and folk religions to Buddhist imagery.[6] One should not think that the three traditions did not compete with each other—they did, and Buddhism especially often faced disapproval because of its foreign origins. But the competition resulted in ensuring that no one tradition ever became too dominant rather than in the elimination of one or more tradition. To reduce religions to one to be adhered to by everyone does not seem ever to have been a goal, and competition for power rather than doctrinal conflict seems to have motivated much interreligious rivalry.

Things changed, however, with the introduction of Christianity. Martin C. Yang's classic account, *A Chinese Village: Taitou, Shantung Province,*

4. Berling, *A Pilgrim in Chinese Culture*, 43.
5. Ibid.
6. Ibid., 12–13.

narrates not only how Chinese Christians separated from the rest of village, regarding everyone else as sinners and themselves as the "chosen people," but also how Catholics and Protestants mutually regarded each other as sinners while each group regarded itself as the chosen people. Neither group celebrated the overarching practices of Chinese religion such as ancestor veneration and veneration of the kitchen god and the earth god, which all other Chinese would observe even if they personally were more devoted to the Buddhist, Daoist, or Confucian perspectives.[7]

Negotiating religious diversity by encouraging multiple religious belonging clearly promotes a cultural situation in which different religions will flourish side by side, often in healthy competition with one another, but without the rancor generated when one religion really regards itself the One True Faith and its competitors as misguided mistakes. Such a solution also allows individuals to tailor make their religious paths to fit their own needs, at least to some extent.

A third way of negotiating religious belonging is common in Hinduism. *Hinduism* is actually an umbrella term that covers a multitude of religious options—many deities, many paths, many practices, many religious groups. The abundant plurality of what is called Hinduism defies neat classification. But Hinduism does not solve the issue of religious belonging by advocating exclusive loyalty to one religious path regarded as the most appropriate path for everyone. One introduction to Hinduism tried to orient students to this diversity by suggesting that no matter what facet of Indian society one observed, one would see diverse, ever shifting patterns. For example, regarding a typical family:

> The mother, a widow, is a devout worshipper of Shiva; her sister-in-law, equally devout, follows the teachings of Ramakrishna; the eldest son is an engineer trained in England, a worshipper of Shiva, but not as knowledgeable or dedicated . . . as his mother and younger brother; his wife's father worships Krishna, as does all her family.
>
> . . .
>
> The family worships Shiva in the home; they go to a temple of the Goddess . . . or special occasions; they visit a temple and teaching center dedicated to Vishnu; they sing devotional songs to Krishna.[8]

Because Hinduism is so diverse, it is hard to make generalizations about it. Certainly in some ways, Hindus make sharp divisions between

7. Yang, *A Chinese Village*, 158–61.

8. Hopkins, *The Hindu Religious Tradition*, 1.

themselves and others, especially in the dictum, not always enforced and somewhat controversial, that it is difficult or impossible to convert to Hinduism. Nor, except with a few modern forms of Hinduism, has there been any attempt to spread Hinduism outside Indian ethnic populations. In this regard, Hinduism contrasts strongly with its Indian cousin, Buddhism.

But regarding religious beliefs and practices, the dominant motif in Hinduism is unquestionably pluralistic. Many versions of Hinduism would claim that salvation is available to all, no matter what path they follow, what deity they worship, or what their station in life may be. Hinduism is the one religion that traditionally has advocated the pluralist position, which claims that there are many true paths to the same goal. However, this theological pluralism should not be mistaken for a lack of vigorous theological and philosophical debate, both among Hindu schools of thought and with competing religions. Thus, holding a pluralistic theology about the existence of many religious options does not preclude normative claims being made or the validity of these various claims being debated and discussed.

The confusing pluralism of Hinduism is perhaps best illustrated by looking at a typical Hindu temple. A temple will be dedicated to a main deity, but there will also be icons of most other major deities of the Hindu pantheon in the same temple. For example, one prominent temple in Delhi displays icons of Krishna and Radha in its center, an icon of Shiva to the right, and an icon of the goddess Durga to the left. These are the three major contenders for loyalty in the vast Hindu pantheon, but they are only rarely pitted against each other. In this temple, as in many others, a devotee can approach any one of them or all three of them. Hindu literature includes many instances of particular individuals who are intensely devoted to one of the deities, but there are also stories of deities rejecting the offerings of a devotee who wants to acknowledge only one of the deities.

This Hindu model is not like the East Asian model of multiple religious belonging. Instead, it presents a model of shifting centers, with no teaching and no deity, holding or claiming ultimate authority and loyalty. Unlike the East Asian situation, in which indigenous participants identify with multiple religions, Hindus do not regard devotees of the various deities or various teachings as members of different religions. Yet Hindus also did and do differentiate themselves from followers of other religions such as Buddhism and Islam. In most cases, Hindus would agree that members of those religions may gain salvation, whatever that might be, but they also recognize them to be different religions, or, alternatively, distinct sects within Hinduism. I have been told many times that, because I am Buddhist, I am really Hindu.

This model of religious belonging presents yet another option. It is possible for religious believers to recognize sharp divisions among themselves and others, either within their own broad umbrella or among those clearly recognized as outsiders, and still not consider those outsiders to be in need of conversion. This model of diversity is not like the East Asian model, in which indigenous participants participate in several different religious traditions and report multiple belongings. In this Hindu case, people can have very specific loyalties and yet do not claim exclusive relevance for their particular chosen path. They also recognize a difference between their own internally diverse tradition and other outside traditions. Buddhism and Islam are definitely recognized as separate traditions, but they are recognized too as valid spiritual paths, contemporary Hindu-Muslim tension not withstanding.

These models all contrast with the position of the reporter, cited at the beginning of this chapter, who was sure that all religious people think that their own religion is the best religion for everyone, and that any one person can only have one religious affiliation at a time. The models also present alternatives to the tendency of some religions to engage in deliberate missionary activity and to seek converts. Thus, we see that most of the world's religious traditions do very well without claiming exclusive truth for themselves or seeking to bring all humanity into their fold. In all cases, these are old, well-established religious traditions that have served their followers well for millennia. This fact undercuts the claim of some advocates of exclusive truth claims that anyone who really takes his religion seriously and is accomplished in it would naturally and inevitably desire to spread it, not only universally, which is unproblematic, but also exclusively, which creates many problems and great suffering.

This fourth model for negotiating religious diversity—making exclusive truth claims for one's own religion—is found only in universalizing religions and is especially prevalent in some but not all monotheisms. A universalizing, monotheistic religion almost faces double jeopardy for making exclusive truth claims. Any universalizing religion will see its claims as relevant for everyone, no matter their cultural background. It is also understandable that monotheists would, in addition, claim exclusive relevance for their religions because of their belief that the sole, universal deity communicated its recommendations for religious belief and behavior in revealed texts. If such claims could be verified, the cogency of exclusive truth claims would be very high indeed. The difficulty of taking exclusive truth claims seriously, however, is the fact that several monotheistic religions make identical exclusive truth claims about several different scriptures and theologies.

As we explore these questions further, it is important to look at two other pieces of information—the historical reluctance of the earliest monotheists to seek converts, and the fact that only those monotheisms successful in creating empires and attaining great political domination continue to claim exclusive and universal relevance for themselves.

The early history of Jewish monotheism is quite instructive in this regard. Early Israelite monotheism was essentially an ethnoreligion that emphasized that Israelites should worship only Yahweh, their specific deity but none of the deities worshiped by other people. (The existence of these deities was not denied in early times. They simply were not to be venerated by Israelites.) Even the Hebrew scriptures record that for Israelites, learning to worship Yahweh alone with singular commitment was a gradual process that took place over a long period of time. The breakthrough seems to have occurred after the destruction of the first temple, when Israelites chose to remain loyal to Yahweh despite their own defeat and exile. They could do this because of a theological revolution; their deity, they determined, was actually the universal ruler of history, and the defeat and exile experienced by the Israelites was due, not to the weakness of Yahweh, but to his universal rulership. He had chosen to allow defeat and exile to the Israelites and victory to their conquerors because of Israelite apostasy, but he was still in charge. Israelites in captivity proclaimed Yahweh to be the universal deity in charge of everything. This is probably the first time such a claim was made.

When Israelites returned to Palestine and rebuilt their temple, they became players in the kaleidoscopic competition for religious adherents that prevailed in the Roman Empire. They proclaimed the reign of a universal deity, and many outsiders sought entrance. After all, a universal deity who accepted only a very small segment of humanity was an oxymoron. But for some Israelites, Yahweh was their deity, and outsiders were not welcome, despite his universal rule. This debate was won by those who accepted converts, and this battle over whether or not to accept converts is usually said to be the lesson of the Book of Ruth in the Hebrew Bible. After a certain point, Judaism became a religion that readily accepted converts. It was quite successful in gaining converts well into the late Roman Empire, until a newly ascendant Christianity made it illegal for Jews, among others, to accept converts. Then Jews reverted to a more ethnoreligious perspective; though they worshiped a deity who was the universal sovereign, that deity had established multiple covenants with the peoples of the earth, which ensured that the "righteous of all nations" would inherit "the kingdom of God." Judaism was for Jews; others did not need to join, but they were not damned because of their different perspectives.

Thus we see that even monotheism, which is theologically predisposed to claim both exclusive and universal truth, can cope with a situation in which it becomes improbable to assert that all people would be better off if they only would join up. Christians and Muslims usually have not come to that conclusion, mainly for one reason. They have been too successful politically. Both religions became the favored religions of large empires very early in their histories. From those favored political positions, both religions have been able to use their influence to undercut and destroy competing religions and to enforce an orthodoxy of belief within their own ranks.

The problems inherent in situations when large religions also hold great political power are not limited to monotheisms, of course. They would occur in any situation in which powerful religions cooperate with powerful empires and could probably be documented in many East Asian and South Asian contexts, in addition to European and Middle Eastern contexts. For example, such cooperation between Japanese Buddhist organizations and the Japanese government in pre-World War II Japan has been well documented.[9] The only remaining question is whether nonmonotheistic religions also use political power to enforce religious orthodoxy internally.

Making exclusive truth claims for one's own religion is only one among four main ways of negotiating religious diversity. Such a way of dealing with religious diversity, if successful, would eventually eliminate religious diversity. Thus, anyone who values religious diversity should find this way of negotiating religious diversity extremely problematic. It has none of the virtues of the other ways of negotiating religious diversity discussed in this chapter. The world's many ethnoreligions demonstrate that one can value one's own religious tradition but not wish to share it with outsiders. The possibility of multiple religious belongings allows believers to participate in all the religious options found in their culture, whether simultaneously or sequentially. Hindu pluralism demonstrates the possibility of the co-existence of many strongly argued theological and philosophical positions with a pluralistic acceptance of this variety as normative.

At this point in our discussion and for the remainder of this book, it will be helpful to make a subtle distinction between universal truth claims and exclusive truth claims. Universal truths are about things that are true whether or not a specific person agrees with that claim or even knows about it. For Buddhists, any universal truth claim would only apply within the limits of what language can accomplish in expressing truth and would be very minimal. The best candidate would be Interdependence

---

9. Victoria, *Zen at War*.

(*pratityasamutpada*), often translated as "dependent arising," and all its implications. This is not a metaphysical claim in any way. Anyone can easily see that everything about our lives is interdependent with everything else, even if we sometimes do not like to live out the consequences of such interdependence.

By contrast, those who make exclusive truth claims assert that not only are these claims true universally, but that they alone constitute the truth and that those who do not hold those claims will suffer as a result. Furthermore, most often when religions make exclusive truth claims, they make them about things that are metaphysical and nonempirical—which means that those truth claims would be very hard to validate by any universally acceptable methods.

This distinction between universal truth claims and exclusive truth claims is not meant to apply to empirical realities such as gravity. Individuals will suffer if they defy the law of gravity by attempting to fly when they are not in an airplane, whether or not they believe in gravity. The distinction between universal truth claims and exclusive truth claims applies to non-empirical, metaphysical issues about which there has not been and cannot be agreement or proof, such as the existence of a Supreme Being or that there are unmediated, therefore, infallible revelations. One can claim that they believe a certain position to be universally valid and can adduce reasons for holding that belief. But it seems extremely unwise to assert that such a position is so exclusively true that it is necessary for everyone to hold the same belief, and that those who disagree with it will suffer the same kind of fate as those who try to defy the law of gravity by jumping off tall buildings in the belief that they can fly.

Even though making exclusive truth claims may not be an appropriate response to religious diversity, it is also important to remember several other points. Though it is inappropriate to make exclusive truth claims, this does not mean that people are disallowed from proclaiming their faith or seeking converts to it. They are only asked to proclaim and promote their religion without claiming that it alone among all religions is exclusively true and deserves universal adherence. Separating claims of universal relevance from claims of exclusive relevance is not difficult and should be expected of all participants in our religiously diverse world. Finally, though historically monotheism has been more prone to make exclusive truth claims than other types of religions, the problems are with the exclusive truth claims, not with monotheism as a religious system. Monotheism certainly has adequate theological resources to free itself from entanglement with exclusive truth claims.

Chapter 3

Does Religion Help or Hurt?

When Religion and Politics Mix in the Wrong Ways

Many people, especially those to whom spiritual practice and religious understandings of the world are important, regard religion as a beneficent, positive force in their lives and for the world. But when one considers how easily religions can be used to motivate people to violence and ethnocentrism, how often such manipulation has been engaged in by both political and religious leaders, and how much current and past suffering, both physical and psychological, has religious roots, one has to wonder whether humanity might not be better off without religion. It is maddening, sorrow-producing, and incomprehensible that so often people who claim deep faith in a specific religious system end up killing or harming people who adhere to a slightly different version of that same religious system or to a different religious or cultural systems with completely different names for ultimate reality and a different set of creeds. To those harmed or killed, it matters little whether their attackers belong to a completely different religious system or to one that is only a slightly different variant of their own faith. The damage is the same and is equally incomprehensible. How can something touted as so life giving end up dealing death or harm instead, simply because those doing the killing and those being killed use different words and symbols to express their understandings? Even more incomprehensible is the fact that religious people will often justify their violent actions against other religious people by claiming that they seek the ultimate good of those whom they pressure to abandon one religion in favor of another.

One major thesis of this book is that exclusive truth claims in religion serve no useful purpose, are very harmful, and are easily dispensed with without harm to serious and meaningful religious commitment and spiritual life. Another major claim of this book is that religion can be most harmful when both religious and political power and authority reside in the same institutions: in other words, in situations of insufficient separation of church (or religious authority) and state (or political authority). The worst of all possible worlds occurs when exclusive truths claims are combined with a situation in which both political and religious authority are collapsed into one institution. In such situation, no matter whether religious leaders or state officials take the lead in enforcing exclusive truth claims, it is much easier for them to succeed. Thus, wherever and whenever exclusive religious truth claims are made, strict separation of church and state becomes mandatory for the safety and protection of those who belong to alternative religions. Even if exclusive truth claims are not being put forward, it is always safer to divide religious and political authority. When these major loci of power are invested in different institutions and held by different people, each can hold the other in check, and each is less likely to be able to control or seriously harm individuals or society at large. While this book makes no attempt to deal comprehensively with church-state relations, I do claim that a workable approach to religious diversity is impossible when religious leaders are too involved in affairs of state or vice versa. Therefore it is important to study a few examples of what can happen when religious leaders become too involved in state affairs.

Sometimes this urge to collapse religious and political authority into one set of institutions takes of form of trying to force religious and political boundaries to correspond, so that most or all people living in a political state share the same religion. In such situations, those who refuse to join the favored religion are often subjected to various forms of social, economic, and religious discrimination. Various forms of so-called ethnic cleansing sometimes result from this "anti-vision." The European religious wars following the Reformation are good example of this kind of attempt to exterminate religious diversity, though they are by no means the only such example. It is also important to note that while, at least in most of the Western world today, few people dream of imposing a uniform religion on everyone, some religions practiced in the West still seek to have elements of their religious view imposed on everyone, whether or not people belonging to other religions assent to or agree with those views. Examples of such impositions abound in the United States—from including "under God" in the

Pledge of Allegiance to advocating specific practices surrounding sexuality and reproduction important to some but not all citizens.

At other times, religious uniformity is not at issue. Neither religious nor state authorities are pursuing religious uniformity, but religious authorities are nevertheless eager and willing to do the bidding of the state, often compromising central values of their religion in the process. Such collusion occurs either because religious leaders would like to experience the additional prestige and power that can come from having state support, or because political authorities seek the legitimacy that endorsement by religious leaders might give them. The fact that freedom from exclusive truth claims, by itself, does not protect a religion from undue and inappropriate entanglement with political authority is demonstrated by two of the three examples to be discussed in this chapter. They involve different forms of Buddhism whose leaders became quite invested in political and military outcomes in their respective states and lent the prestige and authority of their religious institutions to furthering the state's objectives.

Wars of Religion in Post-Reformation Europe

For virtually all people of European descent living in the Western world, as well as for many non-European people who have immigrated to Western countries, the relative freedom of religion that most of us take for granted and that some of us prize is the hard-won result of a century and a quarter (1524–1648) during which the peoples of Europe fought over religion almost constantly. These wars involved virtually all the countries of Europe— especially Germany, France, the Netherlands, and England—and were devastating in their effects. During the Thirty Years' War (1618–1648), by some estimates, 30 percent of the population perished, famine and disease were widespread, and political entities were bankrupted by their constant war effort. Why focus on these wars among many others? As one author puts it, though warfare had been endemic in Europe, "the fighting in these years had its distinctive features . . . The common denominator was Protestant-Catholic religious strife."[1]

The facts are reasonably well known and easily summarized. In 1517, the Protestant Reformation began when Martin Luther nailed his Ninety-Five Theses to the church door in Wittenberg, Germany. Unlike with previous heresies that had sprung up, the Roman Catholic Church was unable to contain this protest, which grew rapidly and soon involved other nonconforming theologians and church leaders as well. Protestants were no

1. Dunn, *The Age of Religious Wars*, 1.

more willing to tolerate Catholicism than Catholics were willing to tolerate Protestantism. Each church viewed itself as the only correct and true representative of the Christian religion. In response, kings allied themselves with one or the other version of Christianity and fought with each other and their own people over which religion would be practiced in their territory. Not only was this a period of Protestant-Catholic conflict, but this was also a time when the Inquisition flourished, especially in Spain, hunting out Jews and Muslims who secretly practiced their own religions after being forced to make a show of conversion to Christianity. Adding to the misery, during this period, both Protestants and Catholics tried and executed large numbers of people, the majority of them women, whom they determined to be witches: people who were accused of having made a pact with the devil and of secretly practicing pagan rites. Estimates of the number of people killed as witches vary from thirty thousand to one hundred thousand. No wonder this era is routinely called the age of religious wars.

For this book, it is not important to narrate many historical details of this time period. They are easily available in encyclopedias, including online versions, or in standard historical surveys. What is important in a book about how to flourish with religious diversity is to understand and critique the religious justifications for this continual and devastating warfare over religion.

It is obvious that both Roman Catholics and Protestants routinely made exclusive truth claims in the post-Reformation era; each claimed that the other was heresy, a dangerous misrepresentation of the Christian faith. Christianity, of course was said to be the only true and valuable faith among world religions, though knowledge of and interaction with members of other world religions was quite limited in this period. European Christians avoided Jews and Muslims when they could, which was most of the time, even if such minority communities lived nearby. Today many Roman Catholics and Protestants still have similar attitudes toward each other, but they manage to live together without open violence. What is the difference? For Christians of the immediate post-Reformation period, religious diversity, especially intra-Christian diversity, was a completely new phenomenon. As one scholar of this period put it,

> Before the reformations, from the boot of Italy to the fjords of Norway and from the Emerald Isle to the plains of Lithuania, Europe had formed a single spiritual community—a "catholic" one, in the sense of universal—united, if only loosely, under the aegis of Rome.[2]

2. Kaplan, *Divided by Faith*. 2.

Christendom had experienced heresies earlier in its history, but the Roman church had been able to suppress them or keep them very local. The Protestant heresy was different. It spread widely and quickly, and the Protestants themselves soon split into numerous factions. "This process shattered Western Christendom, destroying a religious unity that stretched back for over a millennium."[3]

The reaction to this new phenomenon was to fear it intensely and to regard it as a situation that should not be tolerated because it presented an extreme danger. But what is so dangerous about religious diversity *within* a single community or political entity? Kaplan explains the matter well. Heresy, and any diversity was defined as a heresy by those who held different views, was seen as "a species of sin—a particularly heinous one—and as such threatened the *Heil* of entire communities." It threatened the health of the entire community in at least two ways. Unless silenced, a heresy might gain more adherents as others came to be convinced by the heretic's logic, causing the heresy to spread like a cancer (that word was used) through the community. It was also taught that God punished communities that did not root out sin in their midst but let it go unchecked or even spread. Thus, fighting heresy was an act of "communal self-defense."[4]

Not only was it felt that God would punish communities for allowing the sin of heresy to persist. It was also thought that a coherent, well-ordered, peaceful community was impossible unless all its members shared the same religion. There had to be uniformity of lifestyle, calendar, social customs, manners, and values, all of which were provided by religion, if the community was not to be torn apart. Whatever the boundaries of the community or political unit might be, all within it must conform to the same religion so that overall uniformity would prevail. Because religious diversity could not be tolerated, violent suppression of the diversity introduced by these heresies was the only option. But for a century and a half the attempts to suppress heresy and diversity simply failed. It is not so amazing that they ultimately failed but that they went on for so long. In the meanwhile, the interim solution most often adopted was for the ruler of a territory to determine which religion, Protestant or Catholic, would prevail in his state. Various treaties and edicts were promulgated during this period, which attempted to apply precisely that solution or to provide limited legal sanction to non-conforming religions in limited geographic areas within a political unit. Complete identification of church and state was seen as the only way to build and maintain a well-ordered society. Thus, the religious

3. Ibid., 3.
4. Ibid., 70–71.

wars of Europe were due not only to the exclusive truth claims abundantly made by both Catholics and Protestants. The wars were made much more intense and long-lasting because the only solution to conflicting exclusive truth claims that people could imagine was to force political and religious boundaries to correspond, so that to be a citizen of a political entity was also to be a believer in the religion of the political ruler. In some situations, people might be able to emigrate if their political ruler confessed a different religion, but coexistence was not thought possible. Or, as one author put it, "Everyone agreed that religious toleration was intolerable."[5]

Eventually the forces that brought these religious wars into being and allowed them to endure for so long played themselves out. Scholars disagree as to precisely what changed and why. Did people simply become too exhausted to continue the warfare and opt for tolerance as the second best, for tolerance in the sense of putting up with what one cannot overcome? Did religion altogether loose its potency in the face of emerging secular values? Did new ideas about freedom of religion and human rights take the foreground over old ideas about the need for religious uniformity? Did covert tendencies to find ways for differing Christians to live together, which had always been engaged in by ordinary people, become more dominant? For my purposes, it is less important to answer that question than to realize that eventually, ideas of freedom of religion and separation of church and state replaced the fear that tolerating religious diversity would bring down the wrath of God.

That period now seems very far away and long ago, very different from the conditions we expect to live under today. Nevertheless, as I said at the beginning of this unit, there is a causal connection between those difficult times and the ease with which today we can change religious affiliations and the ease with which foreign religions can be practiced in our world. The absurdity of allowing so much misery to arise because people held different religious views and kept different religious practices is at least partially responsible for the modern value of freedom of religion, which developed soon thereafter. But also, when we look a bit beneath the surface, we see lingering remnants of attitudes that had prevailed during the age of the religious wars, not so much among variants of Christianity anymore, but towards practitioners of other religions. We see such lingering intolerance in frequent popular claims that the United States is a Christian nation, which means, to those who make the claim, that Christian folkways and values should dominate public space, laws, and values.

---

5. Dunn, *The Age of Religious Wars*, 8.

But why was it so difficult for Christians of all stripes to learn to tolerate religious diversity? The difficulty was increased immeasurably because of a lack of any experience with religious diversity in Christian Europe. The long period of Christian uniformity across the large European territory was anomalous, perhaps unique, in world religious history. In the previous chapter we discussed four basic models of religious belonging, one of which was the ethnoreligious model, in which religion and culture are closely identified. Pre-Reformation Christian Europe approached that model, but was spread over a very large territory, which is quite unusual. The ethnoreligious model is more characteristic of a small-scale society, not of a state or an empire. Pre-Reformation Christian Europe also differed from the ethnoreligious model in other significant ways. Followers of ethnoreligions do not promote their religions universally beyond their own community, as adherents of Christianity did, even with little knowledge of religions beyond Europe. Furthermore, ethnoreligions often exhibit significant internal diversity, which was the very thing that Christians of the period found so intolerable.

Unlike Europe, other large geographic areas such as South Asia and East Asia, which were home to other major religions, had long since transformed away from the ethnoreligious model. For millennia already, people in those areas had become familiar with religious diversity within their political units and had managed to cope with that diversity without large-scale religious wars, perhaps because exclusive truth claims were not characteristic of the religions practiced in them. Additionally, compared with the other religions making exclusive truth claims, Christianity was at a disadvantage because of its long period of hegemony and uniformity. Jews lived on the peripheries in many societies and had long since made the accommodations to their claims to exclusive truth—accommodations discussed in the previous chapter. Judaism was indeed exclusively relevant—but only for Jews. Islam, which was also dominant in a large geographical area and which often prefers to collapse religion and society into a seamless unity much like ethnoreligions, had devised ways to accommodate religious minorities within Muslim societies. Established non-Muslim religious communities were allowed to exist as communities in their own right, with their own laws, customs, and places of worship, though their members were not regarded as full citizens and were required to pay special taxes. Non-Muslims could not proselytize, convert (except to Islam), or intermarry (except that Muslim men could marry non-Muslim women). Thus, different religious communities were strictly segregated from one another, and their members did not interact very much.[6] While this method of accommodating religious diversity does not provide true equality among religions or seem very satisfactory to those of us who value individual freedom of religion and the separation of church and state, it certainly has advantages over a situation in which the state decides what religion all its subjects will practice—on pain of a penalty worse than special taxes!

Thus one conclusion that could be drawn from this brief discussion of the European post-Reformation religious wars is that while many people think that uniformity of religion is an ideal and would promote peace, the opposite may well be true. This would be the case, especially if religious diversity rather than religious uniformity is the normal situation, as I will claim throughout this book. European Christianity's long period of hegemony and dominance in the delimited world of which it was aware made it ill-prepared to cope with the religious diversity that had, in fact, always been present in its world. When that diversity came knocking on its doors in the form of upwellings of intra-Christian diversity, the Christian churches were unable to cope with diversity, whereas if religious diversity had always been present and acknowledged, presumably more effective methods of dealing with diversity—rather than simply trying to suppress it—would already have been in place.

In this mix, the exclusive truth claims caused the most difficulties, and made the mix of religion and politics so deadly. Because religious people naturally have opinions about political and social issues, it can be extremely difficult to completely disentangle religious authorities and state institutions. Instances of church-state entanglement, sometimes with beneficent results, sometimes with less favorable results, are common. The practice of separating church and state as much as possible is a modern idea, after all, and came into existence after, and probably due to, the European post-Reformation religious wars. Throughout history, most religions have sought government favor and patronage, but few have ever used their alliance with the government to try to exterminate religious diversity so consistently or for such a long period of time as did the various Christian groups after the Protestant Reformation.

Buddhist Interventions into State Affairs

To make accurate generalizations about relationships between Buddhisms and state institutions is difficult, both because the topic has not been studied much by modern scholars, and because Buddhism is such diverse,

6. Kaplan, *Divided by Faith*, 239–45.

long-lasting, and widespread religion. But one could safely claim that nothing like the century and a half of religious warfare endured by post-Reformation Europe has even occurred under Buddhist aegis. Some generalizations may help explain this situation. First, a single form of Buddhism has never been dominant over all the Buddhist world. Second, in both South and East Asia, Buddhism has always existed in a religiously diverse environment and often was not the dominant religion. Even in Southeast Asia and Tibet, where Buddhism became the dominant religion, it coexisted with indigenous traditions that while institutionally less powerful than Buddhism, continued to be practiced. Thus, Buddhists have always been familiar with religious diversity and never experienced anything like the millennium-long period when a single form of Christianity completely dominated all of Europe. This observation lends more credence to my claim, stated in the previous paragraphs and to be repeated many times in the coming pages: religious diversity, both internal and external, is actually a more normal and healthy condition than uniformity of religious belief and practice, whatever proponents of exclusive truth claims may tell us.

In addition, frequently told legends about the Buddha clearly indicate stringent limits against collapsing political and religious authority into one person or one office. At some point, a relevant incident became part of the standard narrative about the Buddha's life. The newborn Siddartha Gautama was taken to a soothsayer who examined the child and told his father that if he remained a prince, eventually he would become a *cakravartin*, a wheel-turning monarch, which is usually taken to mean a universal emperor in the political sense. But if he renounced his social station to become a monk, he would become a Buddha, the foremost teacher of this world age. This story sets the stage for all the stories about Siddartha's protected childhood and the four sights on his first journey outside his protected palace, which led to his departure from worldly life, eventually to his enlightenment and to the founding of Buddhism. But as I interpret this story, it makes another point, which has not been noticed, at least in modern Western commentaries. It makes very forcefully the point that the same person or the same institutions cannot and should not hold both supreme political power and supreme religious leadership, that it is not possible to be truly accomplished in both endeavors at the same time. Exactly how this insight would take form in legal and religious practices is not completely clear, though it did give rise to the concept of the two wheels of *dhamma*: one pertaining to religion and the other to the state, in both ancient and modern Theravada Buddhism.[7] The basic point

---

7. Obeyesekere and Reynolds, *The Two Wheels of Dhamma.*

seems clear. The church should not run the state and the state should not run the church, whether or not the religion in question makes exclusive truth claims.

Siddartha Gautama became a Buddha, not a *cakravartin*. Though he often gave political advice to kings, he did not try to combine supreme political leadership and supreme religious leadership in his own life and work. Though his life and work present an ideal model of how a religious leader interacts with the state, this model does not answer all questions for Buddhists of future times. As Buddhism became a popular religion with many adherents, inevitably political leaders were Buddhists, and, as political leaders, they had to deal with difficult issues of defense, military, and economic policies. What are the guidelines for them? What are the guidelines for religious leaders who are asked to advise political leaders or to lend their support to and approve of policies promulgated by political leaders? We move again from the relatively clear-cut topic of the relations of church and state, of political and religious institutional authority, into the much more difficult topic of the intersection between religion and politics—an intersection with which all participants in any religious tradition must deal. When reading Asian history, especially East Asian history, one hears constantly of interactions between Buddhism and state institutions. Buddhists frequently tried to gain recognition or favor from the government or to influence state policy (though not to have Buddhism declared the sole legitimate religion of the state), and the state often controlled or tried to control Buddhist institutions. It is clear that the modern ideal of separation between church and state was not on anyone's minds—Buddhist or non-Buddhist in these contexts.

Emperor Ashoka and Religious Diversity in His Empire

Any discussion of Buddhism and the state must include some consideration of Ashoka (ca. 304–232 BCE; reigned from 269 to 232 BCE), the great Indian emperor who ruled most of the Indian subcontinent and has been fondly remembered by Buddhists of all persuasions. In fact, especially in Southern (Theravada) Buddhism, he is often considered a counterpart to the Buddha. He provided the second model necessary for the two wheels of *dhamma* to actually function. If the Buddha was the ideal monk or religious figure, Ashoka was the ideal layman and Buddhist king.[8]

Ashoka was undoubtedly a historical figure, but the sources we have for his life and thought present rather different pictures. Probably the most

8. Ibid., 29.

reliable source is the famous Rock Edicts, more that thirty shorts statements intended for widespread edification and consumption that Ashoka had inscribed on pillars and rock faces throughout his vast kingdom. Most of them are addressed to the populace at large; a smaller number is addressed specifically to the Buddhist *sangha*. However, the script in which these edicts were written did not long remain a recognizable script. Thus, while the presence of the edicts was known for centuries, people could no longer read them accurately.[9] Their meaning was not deciphered again until the nineteenth century, when an Englishman became intrigued with the pillars and managed to decipher the long-forgotten script. Because the content of the Rock Edicts was not known to Buddhists in ancient India, they relied on literary sources and legends about Ashoka that were collected many years after the life of Ashoka. A widely used Sanskrit source is the *Ashoka-vadana*, which was probably in circulation by the second century CE.[10] The Sri Lankan chronicles, another important source, are even later. They were written in Pali in the late fourth or early fifth centuries, CE.[11]

All sources agree about a few points. First, Ashoka converted to Buddhism after he inherited his empire, though they differ about what occasioned his conversion. The Edicts attribute it to remorse about the suffering caused by his conquest of Kalinga, the one part of his empire he did not inherit. Because the Edicts are the oldest source, they are probably more reliable on this point. Second, Ashoka promoted a tolerant and humane policy toward all religions found in his empire. He also sponsored many public works that benefited all members of society. Ashoka is also portrayed, in all sources, as being especially interested in what went on the Buddhist *sangha* and as intervening in its affairs, though the degree of that intervention differs significantly in the various sources.[12] For our purposes, only two questions about these sources are germane: what were Ashoka's policies towards the various religions that flourished in his kingdom, and what were his policies toward his own favored religion—Buddhism?

In his Rock Edicts, Ashoka is very clear about the policies of his state concerning religious diversity. The twelfth edict is quite remarkable.

> Beloved-of-the-Gods, King Piyadasa, honors both ascetics and householders of all religions and he honors them with gifts and honors of various kinds. But Beloved-of-the-Gods, King

---

9. Strong, *The Legend of King Ashoka*, 5–13.

10. Ibid., 26–27.

11. Obeyesekere and Reynolds, *The Two Wheels of Dhamma*, 31.

12. For a thorough presentation of the different accounts of Ashoka's policies regarding religion, see Lamotte, *History of Indian Buddhism*, 223–55.

Piyadasa does not value gifts and honors as much as he values this—that there should be growth in the essentials of all religions. Growth in the essentials of all religions can be done in different ways, but all of them have as their root restraint in speech, that is not praising one's own religion, or condemning the religion of others without good cause. And if there is cause for criticism, it should be done in a mild way. But it is better to honor other religions for this reason. By so doing, one's own religion benefits, and so do other religions, while doing otherwise harms one's own religion and the religions of others. Whoever praises his own religion, due to excessive devotion and condemns others with the thought "Let me glorify my own religion," only harms his own religion. Therefore, contact (between religions) is good.[13]

I see no reason to doubt that this rock edict represents Ashoka's actual policy. Unfortunately, the later, literary sources, whether in Sanskrit or in Pali, present a less ideal picture. In some of those later sources, Ashoka is represented as having been quite cruel to heretics on some occasions.

Regarding Ashoka's intervention into intra-Buddhist affairs, the records are far more varied. In a minor Rock Edict, addressed specifically to the Buddhist *sangha*, which in this case means Buddhist monastics, Ashoka affirms his faith in the Buddha, *Dharma*, and *Sangha*, and then recommends specific texts that all monks and nuns should study.[14] Another edict states that any monk or nun who caused a schism in the *sangha* should be returned to lay status.[15] The *Ashokavadana* stresses Ashoka's Buddhist piety. He opened the original stupas that held the Buddha's relics and redistributed them in 84,000 stupas he had built; he went on pilgrimage to all the many sites important in the Buddha's life; he was especially devoted to the Bodhi tree; he was extremely generous to the monastic *sangha*, in the end giving the whole earth to that Buddhist institution. But he does not try to intervene in the monastic *sangha*'s affairs or to control it.[16]

By contrast, in Pali records from Sri Lanka, Ashoka is portrayed as convening a Buddhist council, declaring what the true doctrine should be, and defrocking sixty thousand monks whom he deemed to be heretics.[17] In other words, Ashoka is here portrayed not only as the head of state but also as the supreme religious authority. The Pali chronicles also claim that

13. Dhammika, *The Edicts of King Ashoka*, 8.

14. Ibid., 15.

15. Ibid., 22.

16. See note 12 above.

17. Tambiah, *World Conqueror and World Renouncer*, 165–68.

Ashoka sent missionaries to all regions of the then-known world, including Sri Lanka itself.[18] In the Sri Lankan chronicles, the council that Ashoka is said to have convened was called the third Buddhist council. This event is recorded only in Pali or Southern Buddhist sources, and most historians doubt that it occurred as the pan-Buddhist event that it is represented to have been in those chronicles. The Sri Lankan chronicles also give pride of place in the Buddhist world to Sri Lanka and in other ways reflect Sri Lankan rather than general Buddhist interests. Certainly they present, in an approving way, a portrait of Ashoka as an extreme meddler in religious affairs!

Which of the many portrayals of Ashoka is the actual Emperor Ashoka? The rock edicts, forgotten in Buddhist legends about Ashoka, present a picture that is much more palatable to people of the twenty-first century seeking models of flourishing in situations of religious diversity than do the literary sources, whether in Sanskrit or Pali. These sources are also undoubtedly later. It is discouraging that later Buddhists, reworking records and legends of Ashoka, preferred a partisan promoter of their own specific viewpoint to an Ashoka who patronized and encouraged religious diversity in his empire.

Twentieth-Century Buddhist Interventions in State Affairs

In the twentieth and early twenty-first centuries, Buddhists have faced many challenges regarding interactions between Buddhist institutions and the state. The two most dramatic concern Japan leading up to World War II and the Sri Lankan situation, which culminated in 2009 with a "total war" in which the Sri Lankan government, largely controlled by Buddhists, definitively defeated its long-term challenger, the (largely Hindu) Tamil Tigers of northeastern Sri Lanka. For most commentators, the issue at stake has been Buddhist participation in military ventures. Buddhism had enjoyed a widespread reputation as a nonviolent religion that never engaged in warfare, so many were outraged by the participation of Buddhist leaders and institutions in these and other violent confrontations. But Buddhists have often been involved in military engagements and only certain assumptions made by sympathetic commentators have protected Buddhists from linkage with warfare.[19] Because Buddhist teachings

18. Lamotte, *History of Indian Buddhism*, 292–310.

19. Jerryson and Juergensmeyer, *Buddhist Warfare*, was one of the first books to discuss warfare in Buddhist societies in general, rather than in one particular form of Buddhism.

unequivocally reject violence and harming—not only with regard to humans but also with regard to all beings—and also because Buddhists have never engaged in anything like the Crusades or the religious wars of post-Reformation Europe, many had assumed that Buddhists had a clean record regarding participation in military ventures. But one could as easily assume from reading the New Testament that Christians would not support warfare. Rather than focusing on Buddhism and militarism, I am more interested in the ways that Buddhists, especially Buddhist monks and religious leaders, were involved in government in prewar Japan and in Sri Lanka. To what extent did Buddhists follow the example of the Buddha in not seeking to combine political and religious leadership in one person or institution, and in what ways did they deviate from it?

Sometimes when I give presentations on Buddhism to church groups and talk about the Buddhist preference for nonviolence, an older gentlemen, a World War II veteran, will challenge me. "Then why did the 'Japs' attack us!" he will demand. Usually, I explain that at that time, the Japanese government was dominated by Shinto, which was the state religion, not Buddhism. Technically, that is correct, but such information does not satisfy anyone who looks a little more deeply into Japanese Buddhist attitudes about Japan's attempted empire building before and during World War II.

In 1997, Brian Victoria, who has trained extensively at Eiheiji, one of Japan's foremost Buddhist training centers and is an ordained Soto Zen priest, published the first edition of *Zen at War*.[20] In it, he details the extensive support given to the war effort by all Japanese Buddhist sects, by Japanese Buddhist intellectuals such as D. T. Suzuki, who was well known to and beloved by many Western Buddhist practitioners, and by some well-known Japanese *roshis* who had begun to teach Zen Buddhism in the West. At that time, at least among Westerners, Buddhism still basked in the inaccurate opinion that, alone among world religions, it had never supported warfare. Needless to say, Victoria's book unleashed a firestorm of disbelief, hurt, and disillusionment. The information in his book had been little noted by either Japanese or Western commentators before Victoria released his book. The sole exception had been a Japanese commentator, Ichikawa Haguken (1902–1986), whose work had been ignored in Japan and had not yet been translated into English. An extensive English summary of his work is now available.[21] Based on Victoria's and Ichikawa's research and their extensive quotations from Japanese Buddhist comments from the period between 1930 to 1945, it is impossible to doubt that Buddhists vied to add their

---

20. The second edition is now available. Victoria, *Zen at War*.

21. Ives, *Imperial-Way Zen*.

support to official government policies and offered no significant contrary advice. For many Westerners, especially Buddhist practitioners, the stinging question was, how could Buddhists, whom I respect and whom I had assumed were pacifists, have done this?

As I already stated, for me the primary concern is not about Buddhists and warfare but about attempts by Buddhist institutions to exercise significant political power, whether by controlling the government themselves or by advancing their own prestige and influence by supporting government policies. Japanese Buddhist reasons for supporting war were quite different from what drove European Christians into unending warfare after the Protestant Reformation. Japan was already religiously diverse and had been so for centuries. Many competing versions of Buddhism were also well tolerated. And though the various Buddhist sects did establish overseas missions in lands that Japan had conquered, instilling Japanese religions outside Japan was not a primary concern for anyone. Rather than religious beliefs and exclusive truth claims, this conflict was about power and empire. And Buddhists were out of power in Japan. Until 1868, they had been, at least nominally, the established religion of the state, in that all citizens were required to be registered with a local Buddhist temple. That all changed with the Meiji Restoration, which transferred power to the emperor and to the Shinto religion. Japan then set out on a very successful mission to modernize and to compete with the Western powers in building an empire in Asia. Nationalism and militarism were the necessary tools for that enterprise.

Now out of power, Buddhists responded that Buddhism could be useful to the state as it modernized and militarized. "They portrayed Buddhism as an essential component of Japanese culture, as a loyal supporter of the emperor, as a constructive social force that could contribute to the building of a strong, modern Japan."[22] To gain or retain institutional power and prestige, Buddhists of all sects rushed to support what came to be called "Imperial Way Buddhism." According to Victoria, this meant "the total and unequivocal subjugation of the Law of the Buddha to the Law of the Sovereign. In politics, it meant subjugation of institutional Buddhism to the state and its policies."[23] Both Ichikawa and Victoria provide extensive demonstrations of how Japanese Buddhists interpreted Buddhism as supporting whatever the government was doing, including initiating military conflicts. Many Japanese Buddhist commentators claimed that the wars of aggression being waged against China were, essentially, acts of compassion that

22. Ibid.,18.
23. Victoria, *Zen at War,* 79.

benefited China and would eventually eliminate warfare.[24] That all Buddhist institutions wholeheartedly supported a position that seems so at odds with Buddhist principles indicates how much Buddhists longed to be part of prevailing political institutions and how little thought was given to maintaining an independent voice that might have moderated or questioned government policies. Granted, many have claimed that Japan was a totalitarian state at that time and that independent voices would not have been tolerated. Nevertheless, Japanese Buddhist institutions went far beyond passive, powerless acceptance of the situation to actively promote nationalism and warfare. In other words, Buddhist religious institutions and Japanese government institutions became virtually indistinguishable, at least in their views and recommendations. As had been the case throughout its history in Japan, Buddhism played the role of "'Buddhism for the protection of the realm,'" functioning to "pacify and protect the nation."[25]

To modern Western Buddhists, this Japanese situation seems extreme, but it should be realized that there is little, if any, tradition in East Asian Buddhism of Buddhist institutions being independent of state control. State control of Buddhism prevails, whether Buddhism is the favored religion or is out of favor at any specific time. In other words, East Asia presents one extreme of how church (so to speak) and state can be collapsed, with the state being totally dominant. This generalization also helps us understand the situation for religions in China today and for Buddhists in Chinese-controlled Tibet.

In China, Buddhism was a foreign religion that entered another already highly developed culture, and, as such, it always had to defer to already established political powers, both in China and later in Japan. Buddhism could be useful to the state, as Japanese Buddhists tried so hard to demonstrate, and it often was useful to the state. But it did not control the state, nor were Buddhist institutions truly independent from the state. Very early in the history of Buddhism in China, Buddhist monks tried to maintain their independence vis-à-vis the government, but they were soon forced to give up. During the Sung dynasty (960–1280) in China, the Buddha's law and the law of the land came to be identified with one another and the emperor was regarded as an embodiment of the Buddha's truth-body (*dharmakaya*).[26] We know which one prevailed as the dominant partner.

Thus, the situation for Buddhism as it developed in East Asia and prevailed for centuries is very far from the model presented in the story

24. Ibid., 86–94.

25. Ives, *Imperial-Way Zen*, 108–9.

26. Seiko, "Zen Buddhist Attitudes to War," 6–8.

of infant Siddartha, the future historical Buddha, and the soothsayer. He predicted that the child could be either a Buddha or a Universal Emperor, but not both. The separation of those roles and functions was lost in East Asian Buddhism, with eventual results that are all too evident in Japanese Buddhist militarism and nationalism.

What about the Buddhist participation in the Sri Lankan civil war? Sri Lankan Buddhism is a very different Buddhism with a very different history. It is much closer to the traditions of Indian Buddhism and the historical Buddha. Furthermore, Buddhist reactions to the Sri Lankan civil war are very complicated and not yet fully analyzed. However, one important factor is that like most of Asia, Sri Lanka was dominated by European powers until well into the twentieth century, a fact that surely colors its ways of dealing with civil war and terrorism on its soil.[27]

In modern Sri Lanka, though Buddhism constitutionally is given "the foremost place," all religions are constitutionally protected, and freedom of religion is guaranteed.[28] Nevertheless, a long-standing and deeply rooted feeling prevails among Sinhala Buddhists: there is a special relationship between Sri Lanka and the *dhamma*. Sri Lanka is to be an "island of *dhamma*," charged with protecting and preserving that *dhamma*. This feeling is intensified by Sinhala belief that the historical Buddha had magically visited the island three times, destroying forces that would be inimical to the eventual introduction of Buddhism, thus consecrating the entire island.[29] In the long run, these beliefs heavily colored Buddhist reactions to the civil war. Partly because Hindu Tamils have lived in Sri Lanka for many centuries, these beliefs did not result in the view that there must or should be religious uniformity in Sri Lanka, but it did lead to identification of Buddhism as a religion with the Sinhala people and language, which then led to significant involvement in Sri Lankan politics by Buddhist monks. Among many other Buddhist political activities, some monks vociferously promoted warfare against the Tamils, who were demanding an independent homeland in regions where they were in the majority.

One observer suggested that partly as a response to the repression of Buddhism during British colonialism and partly as a reaction to Tamil protests against a Sinhala-only language policy, there was a significant shift in the role that Buddhism played in Sri Lankan life, beginning in the 1960s.

27. In this brief discussion of Buddhism's involvement in government in Sri Lanka, I will not attempt to trace the history leading to the current situation. Readers interested in that history can consult Tambiah, *Buddhism Betrayed?*; Seneviratne, *The Work of Kings*.

28. Bartholomeusz, *In Defense of Dharma*, 5.

29. Ibid., 20–23.

> Substantively soteriological, ethical, and normative components
> of Buddhism were weakened, displaced, and even distorted,
> while the religio-political associations of Buddhism . . . which
> bound it with the Sinhala people, with the territory of the entire
> island, and with a political authority dedicated to the protection
> of Buddhism, assumed primacy.[30]

Another observer was more forceful in his assessment of what happened
when religion, language, and ethnicity were fused into a single identity by
Sri Lankan Buddhists. "The Buddha's universalism and the complex, compassionate discernment at the heart of his message are fatally annexed to
the passionate intensities of ethnic competitiveness."[31] According to recent
research completed by Elizabeth Harris, this kind of collapsing of Sinhala
ethnicity and the Buddhist religious identity continues in postwar Sri Lanka
as the government uses images of the Buddha as symbols of its dominance
over Tamil areas of the island.[32]

Eventually, such intertwining of civic and religious affairs led to the creation, in 2004, of a monk-only political party (the JHU or National Sinhala
Heritage Party) which fielded over two hundred monk-candidates for election to the parliament and succeeded in electing nine of them. Monks held
all the key positions in this political party, and it was formed specifically so
that monks would not divide their loyalties between various political parties
but would contest the election as a unified group.[33] This event was evaluated
as a "watershed in the entire history of Theravada monastic world in South
and South-east Asia"[34] because Buddhist monks had historically been passive agents in the political history of Sri Lanka.[35] This monks' political party
represents itself as the result of long-standing "non-representation of Sinhalese Buddhists in the Sri Lankan political system." The monks' party charged
the government with political corruption, with ignoring threats to Buddhism
(including threats to its very survival), with unwillingness to ban or restrict
"unethical" conversions on the part of Christian missionaries, and with unsatisfactory negotiations for peace with the Tamils to end the civil war.[36]

In their manifesto, the JHU called for Sri Lanka to be ruled by
Buddhist principles, "as it was in the past and [for] the protection of the

---

30. Tambiah, *Buddhism Betrayed?*, 58.

31. Grant, *Buddhism and Ethnic Conflict in Sri Lanka*, 116.

32. Harris, "Buddhism and Post-War Reconciliation in Sri Lanka."

33. Deegalle, "JHU Politics for Peace and a Righteous State," 234.

34. Ibid.

35. Ibid., 233.

36. Ibid., 243–48.

Buddhasasana [to be] the foremost duty of any government." The state, however, was to be identified as Sinhala, rather than Buddhist, and the rights of other religions to practice were to be safeguarded, though unethical conversions should be disallowed. Culturally, "the hereditary rights of the Sinhalese should be granted while protecting the rights of other communities who inhabit the island." The national economy should follow Buddhist principles, and education should promote "a righteous society in which the five precepts are observed." As part of this "righteous society," traditional hierarchies, including those between men and women, should be introduced, and women should have their "moral rights," including the "nobility and dignity of motherhood restored."[37] While this manifesto does not call for privileging Buddhism as the state religion or for Buddhist religious and Sri Lankan political boundaries to coincide, certainly under its aegis the interests of conservative Theravada Buddhists would be promoted far more than those of other citizens because the government would enforce a conservative Buddhist agenda if it followed JHU principles. As of this writing, the JHU is still active and holds a few seats in the Sri Lankan parliament. One can follow its exploits on the Web to some extent. Many consider the JHU to be an extremist party.

The creation of the JHU could be seen as the most extreme manifestation of the common tendency to collapse Sinhala ethnic identity and language and the Buddhist religion into one fused unit. While at its inception the JHU did not promote quite the same kind of identity between political and religious boundaries that was seen as the ideal in post-Reformation Europe, eventually this fusion of Buddhist religion with Sinhala ethnicity and language on the part of Sri Lankan Buddhists did lead to very problematic results.

Conclusions: When Religion Becomes Evil

As terrorist acts that are at least partially religiously motivated have become more common today, many have sought to explain and understand religious violence.[38] One especially insightful book, *When Religion Becomes Evil*, investigates five "warning signs" that a religion is about to become evil, that is, to endorse and perpetrate acts of violence or warfare. The author, Charles Kimball, states that when one or more of these warning signs is occurring, "history suggests that serious trouble lurks just ahead."[39] According to him,

37. Ibid., 247–48.

38. Selengut, *Sacred Fury*; Girard, *Violence and the Sacred*; Juergensmeyer, *Terror in the Mind of God*; and Kimball, *When Religion Becomes Evil*.

39. Kimball, *When Religions Becomes Evil*, 6.

the first and most dangerous sign is *absolute* truth claims (what I am calling *exclusive* truth claims, which do need to be distinguished from *universal* truth claims). Kimball asserts that "when zealous and devout adherents elevate the teachings and beliefs of their tradition to the level of *absolute* truth claims, they open the door to the possibility that their religion will become evil."[40] Absolute truth claims then manifest in individual behavior as "blind obedience" to authority, the second of Kimball's five warning signs.

The remaining three warning signs are all variants of the problems that ensue when religious leaders and institutions become too closely allied with political institutions. The third danger signal involves zealous adherents of a tradition trying to force the divinely ordained future society to begin *now* by engaging in violent acts. Kimball writes, "Those who narrowly define ideal temporal structures of the state and determine that they are God's agents to establish a theocracy are dangerous."[41] They are dangerous because they often believe that the "end justifies the means," Kimball's fourth warning sign that a religion could easily commit evil, violent acts or become involved in warfare. Fifth and finally, such zealous adherents are willing to declare a "holy war" against any and all others to force their vision of an ideal future to happen now. Clearly, we have seen all five of these signs in this chapter. We have also seen how they crystallize into two major factors: exclusive truth claims and the identity or close collaboration of religious and political institutions.

We have now set the stage for a Buddhist-inspired discussion of how we might flourish in situations of religious diversity rather than be intimidated by them. We know that the common, knee-jerk reaction in our culture—that everyone believes their own religion is the best for everyone—simply is not true. In the world's religions we find significant alternatives to that position. We have also investigated several situations that demonstrate how devastating it can be when religious institutions become too deeply intertwined with state institutions—a grave warning signal for the religious Right in the contemporary United States. Such sober knowledge about the ins and outs of religious diversity is a necessary foundation for exploring how one might flourish in situations of religious diversity. Now we are set to begin an exploration of how we might think about *others* and otherness, and about our own *identities* in situations characterized by religious diversity. In turn, those explorations will set the stage for how we live with *integrity* in the midst of religious diversity.

40. Ibid., 44.
41. Ibid., 125.

Others, Especially Religious Others

Chapter 4

Religious Others

The Received Traditions in Christian Theologies of Religion

A S I SEE IT, religious diversity is simply a given. Therefore, it need not elicit the amount of discussion it currently receives. Nevertheless, especially in the last half century, since Vatican II, an emphasis for Christian academic theologians has been how to relate to the inevitable display of religious diversity among human beings. Two closely allied subdisciplines in this discourse are called theology of religions, which discusses questions about the truth of various religions, and comparative theology, which was founded by Christian theologians who claim that theologians should not evaluate the truth of religions before undertaking detailed comparative study of them. It is noteworthy that the vast majority of those who engage in such discussions, and for whom the issue seems to be of utmost priority, are Christians by confession. Very few non-Christian religious thinkers or unaffiliated scholars of religion participate in these discussions.[1] This chapter will present something more unusual: a somewhat thorough discussion of this literature by someone who is not a Christian but nevertheless identifies as a religious person.

1. One of the few deliberate exceptions was a conference that resulted in the book, Knitter, *The Myth of Religious Superiority*. However, despite the claim of comparative theologians that their discipline should not be limited to Christian commentators, a book intended to highlight comparative theology as an emerging discipline includes only one entry by a non-Christian author. See Clooney, *The New Comparative Theology*.

55

It is interesting to ask why this particular topic, which could be relevant to insiders of every religious tradition, is so much discussed by Christians and so little discussed by commentators from other religions. I suggest that it is simply an extension of the shock Christians experienced when they lost their uniformity and insularity after the Protestant Reformation—a shock that intensified as Western explorations of the world began to demonstrate that there were many vital and vibrant living religions in the world. Christians fought among themselves in the wars of religion discussed in chapter 3. But at the same time, they also discovered the existence of other, very different religions as European explorers began to colonize the world as best they could. Before that, Christians, in their own vast and uniform world, were only dimly aware of the world beyond their boundaries. Thus, at the same time, Christians were dealing with both the breakup of their own religious uniformity and the discovery of many other living ways of being religious. I cannot suppress the impression that because they had been so uniform and so isolated for so long and had believed so intently that their religion was the universal norm against which everything else should be evaluated, Christians have never recovered from shock and indignation at having to coexist with internal and external religious diversity. Thus, what is normal and natural for most other religions—religious diversity—is a problem for them.

The reaction by both Catholics and Protestants to the discovery of external religious diversity was ever stronger insistence that there could be only one true religion—the exclusivist position. They subscribed heartily to some version of the dogma that there could be no salvation outside the church, however *church* might be defined. During the age of exploration, Christian missionaries followed closely on the heels of explorers and traders. While missionaries often did compile accurate ethnographic accounts of the peoples whom they sought to convert to Christianity, their main agenda was conversion, not dialogue and mutual understanding.

Though many Christians did not agree with the official exclusivist positions of the various Christian denominations, official church policies did not begin to change until the loss of European empires occurred after World War II, as country after country in Asia and Africa that had formerly been a colony gained its independence. A possible link between this loss of empires and a softening of the "no-salvation-outside-the-church" position on the part of both Catholics and Protestants has not been explored, but I would suggest that there could well be a causal relationship between these two events. As Westerners lost or gave up political dominance over the world and began to respect the aspirations of other peoples, perhaps Christians also began to doubt what they had told themselves for so long:

that they alone, despite the fact that they could not agree among themselves religiously, nevertheless had a "monopoly on salvation."[2] In any case, these two major changes did coincide.

Most historians chronicle the beginning of a shift in official Christian attitudes towards other religions with the Second Vatican Council, which took place from 1962 to 1965. Its official conclusions include an often-quoted statement about other religions:

> The Catholic Church rejects nothing which is true and holy in these religions. She has a sincere respect for those ways of acting and living, those moral and doctrinal teachings which may differ in many respects from what she holds and teaches, but which none the less often reflect the brightness of that Truth which is the light of all men [sic].

But the document immediately moves on to proclaim "Christ, who is 'the way, the truth and the life.'" The relevant portion of the text ends by speaking of the church:

> She therefore urges her sons, using prudence and charity, to join members of other religions in discussions and collaboration. While bearing witness to their own Christian life and faith, they must acknowledge those good spiritual and moral elements and social and cultural values found in other religions and preserve and encourage them.[3]

This position, which was also accepted by many Protestants, came to be called the inclusivist position. The main thesis of this position is that non-Christians can also be included in salvation. This differs from the more common exclusivist position, which declares that non-Christians could not be included in salvation. From the inclusivist perspective, Christianity was still evaluated as the only truly adequate religion. Followers of all other religions, whether they realized it or not, were incomplete and needed what was fully available only through Christ and only fully available to Christians. But such people might nevertheless be "saved," whereas the exclusivist position declares that only those who actually confess Christ would be saved. Or, as I was taught as a child, "good people who had never heard of Jesus could go

2. This phrase comes from a letter written in 1609 by Roberto de Nobili, a Catholic missionary in India who had debated with local Hindu religious authorities. De Nobili reported in his letter that the Brahmin with whom he debated declared about him to his fellow Hindus "Has this man alone the monopoly on salvation?" (Fletcher, *Monopoly on Salvation?*, 42).

3. Vatican Council II, "Declaration on the Relation of the Church to Non-Christian Religions," 81–82.

to heaven, but if ever you heard of Jesus, even once, and did not become a Christian, eternal damnation awaits you."

Eventually a third position, the pluralist position, which claims that salvation and truth might also be *fully* present in other religions, not merely *partially* present, was developed by Christian theologians. Of course, there had always been people who believed that people of all religions could be saved. The difference is that people who wrote and spoke as church theologians were now making such claims. John Hick, a British theologian and philosopher, comes up most frequently as an innovator and major thinker in the world of Christian pluralist theology. Other prominent Christian pluralists include Raimon Panikkar, Stanley Samartha, Paul Knitter, and Diana Eck.

Since Alan Race introduced this typology of Christian theologies of religious diversity in 1983,[4] it has been widely utilized and commented on, though Paul Knitter, a prominent commentator on Christian theologies of religion, has continued to use the term "replacement model" instead of the word *exclusivist*. Indeed, his language has some real merits; whatever name this view goes by, Christians of this stripe believe the Christianity should *replace* any and all other religions. Knitter also calls the inclusivist model the "fulfillment" model instead, because these Christians claim that while there are some worthwhile elements in non-Christian religions, Christianity, especially the person of Jesus Christ, *fulfills* them all. Knitter also replaces the term *pluralist* with *mutuality* because, according to this model, rather than there being only one true religion, we live in a world characterized by "many true religions called to dialogue."[5] In his second survey of Christian theologies of religion, Paul Knitter has added a fourth option, which he calls the "acceptance model." Thinkers in this camp are less concerned with judgments about the truth of any specific religion. He includes in this model those who wish to disassociate themselves altogether from theology of religions and to call themselves "comparative theologians."[6] However, in a recent, closely argued article, Perry Schmidt-Leukal has argued that there can only be three models in the theology of religions and has sought to answer objections that had been made to this tripartite typology.[7]

---

4. Race, *Christians and Religious Pluralism*.

5. Knitter, *Introducing Theologies of Religion*.

6. See Clooney, *The New Comparative Theology*; Clooney, *Comparative Theology*. In his second survey of Christian theologies of religion, Paul Knitter also includes a fourth model, which he calls the "acceptance model," which is less concerned about whether any of the religions are true. See Knitter, *Introducing Theologies of Religion*, 173–91.

7. Schmidt-Leukal, "Exclusivism, Inclusivism, Pluralism," 13–27.

Very interesting is that most of the Christian theologians who write frequently on the theology of religions or comparative theology do not discuss the exclusivist position very much, even though it is the one that causes the most problems. These academic theologians debate whether or not there should be a moratorium on the theology of religions, and they debate the pros and cons of inclusivism versus pluralism, but they do not dismantle the Christian exclusivist position in any thoroughgoing way. They have moved on themselves, but they have left many—perhaps the majority of—Christians behind. Many Christians, including most evangelical Christian still make exclusive truth claims, and Christian theologians of religion are not addressing this audience. This is frightening for the rest of us, for non-Christians who are still the objects of Christian exclusive truth claims, missionary efforts, and attempts to impose conservative Christian values on whole societies.

Given my uncompromising criticism of the exclusivist position, I am often asked by more liberal Christians about whether and how I would dialogue with exclusivists. My own answer to that question does not belong in this chapter but will be discussed in chapters 15 and 16. In any case, it is other *Christians*, not someone like myself, who have the most responsibility to dialogue with Christians making exclusive truth claims and to wean them from the dangerous and oppressive aspects of their theological position. I do fault the inclusivists and pluralists for being more eager to lift up elements of the exclusivist position they acknowledge as authentically Christian than to clearly and insistently demonstrate that exclusive truth claims are dangerous and demeaning to others. This task is especially urgent today in an interconnected world in which at least half of humanity belongs to religions that historically have made exclusive truth claims—Christianity and Islam. These two religion are spread across the globe and often try to interfere with or dictate local or national policies.[8] Clearly, Muslims must take the lead in the discussion as it pertains to Islam. Westerners often criticize Muslim moderates, claiming that they do not speak out against their own extremists. But that claim sounds hollow if inclusivist and pluralist Christians are not as critical of Christian exclusivists as they want Muslim moderates to be of Muslim extremists. In my view, Christian exclusivism is also an extremist position.

8. Kimball, *When Religion Becomes Evil*, 6.

The Moral and Religious Deficiencies of Exclusivism

The most obvious deficiency of exclusive truth claims in religion is that for the vast, vast majority of people, religious identity is a matter of birth, not choice. How can most people be asked or expected to affirm an identity and belief system different from the one into which they were born? That is what most people would have to do to belong to the One True Faith, whichever one that may be. Most people do not choose their religious identity; they inherit it, along with their ethnicity, culture, and language. Changing their religious identity is just as difficult and unlikely as changing any one of those other identities. The percentage of converts among the world's major religions is actually very small, and only converts can truly claim to have chosen their religion. No matter how much people may come to affirm what they have been indoctrinated into, that belief is not really a choice on their parts. John Hick likes to make this point in arguing for his version of the pluralist model. He tells an amusing story. "The point is well made by a twelve-year-old boy I've been told of, born into a Christian family in Cairo who remarked one day, 'You know, if I'd been born next door, I'd be a Muslim.'"[9]

Nevertheless, it is important to acknowledge an inevitable tendency towards a prereflective, garden-variety exclusivism. Well-adjusted, contented people appreciate their own way of being. My own spiritual teacher, who certainly does not countenance sectarianism, once said, somewhat spontaneously, in a discussion with me about religious diversity, "But it's hard not to think your own is the best."

This prereflective preference for what is familiar is not the problem and need not lead to eventually making exclusive truth claims. Everybody roots for the home team. Children and teenagers long to fit in, to be like everyone else and not be ostracized. People who are happy with their life circumstances often express profound love for the home place—their city, their country, their family, their spiritual path. Sometimes that enthusiasm includes making fun of the other team. During my first trip to India, I was a bit puzzled that North Indians made so much fun of how South Indians eat, and that South Indians expected me to join them in their distaste for North Indian food. To me, the difference between North American food and any variety of Indian food was much more striking than differences between North and South Indian food and I was amazed at, but also amused by, their mutual dislike of each other's food. (Now the two cuisines do seem quite different to me.) But, while we root for the home team and love our country and our familiar cuisine, if we

9. Hick, "The Next Step beyond Dialogue," 7.

are sane, we recognize that everybody else also roots for their own home team and loves their own place. We do not regard their enthusiasm for their world as a problem for us. Why do exclusivists treat religions so differently, regarding others' religions as a problem, both for them and for us?

Perhaps the most basic human psychological reaction is dichotomizing, noticing this and that, most commonly perceived as self and other. This dichotomy easily morphs into the familiar and safe versus the different and threatening. How this plays out religiously has been identified by the great twentieth-century historian of religions Mircea Eliade in his classic handbook, *The Sacred and the Profane: The Nature of Religion*. He speaks of "a dichotomy between . . . inhabited territory and the unknown and indeterminate space that surrounds it." He goes on to discuss how (religious) people always feel that they live at the center of the universe, which is the best place to be—in the cosmos as opposed to in the demonic chaos beyond their boundaries. People who live in those places are viewed as barbarians or nonhuman.[10] This evaluation is probably the first and most basic human view of religious diversity, and indeed such ethnocentrism is still quite common. However, such evaluations are not theological analyses, and they do not include an assumption that those outside the boundaries should imitate our ways so that they can transcend the category "barbarian." As we saw in chapter 2, ethnoreligions do not seek converts from outside. Rather, the basic point is that to create duality is simply how humans typically construct their worlds, how the conventional mind works. What is familiar and near is sacred; what is outside the boundaries is profane and scary.

For most religions, and for most people much of the time, dualistic consciousness is taken as a completely factual and accurate description of what is real. It is assumed that there is nothing more basic or real than duality. However, according to most schools of Buddhism and some strands of other religions, this assumption about the ultimate reality of duality is highly questionable. Duality feels real, but when subjected to analysis and to meditative experience, this assumption may not hold up. Perhaps all the grief that has resulted from discomfort with religious diversity comes from mistaken beliefs about how real duality is? This is a question to which we shall return many times and especially in chapter 7. Conventionally, people do operate with dualistic consciousness. Buddhism recognizes the human need to work with dualities in the relative world. But it also claims that though dualistic reactions are inevitable, they are only a relative view of things, not how things really are at an ultimate level. (For those not familiar with Buddhism's Two Truths, it is important to state that relative truth is not

10. Eliade, *The Sacred and the Profane*, 29.

wrong or inadequate. Rather, it is not the whole picture, but when taken as the whole picture, that is to say, when absolutized, it becomes quite destructive.) Thus, it is important for us to realize that while we conventionally operate with dualistic consciousness, we cannot definitively separate sacred from profane, good from evil. They are interdependent, defined only relative to each other, not absolutely.

Buddhists recognize that dualistic consciousness is practical for negotiating the everyday world, and they recognize that at that level, such dichotomizing is unproblematic. In many situations, it is necessary to differentiate this from that and to evaluate the relative utility of each. However, when people solidify their inevitably dualistic everyday perceptions and patterns of loyalty into fixed metaphysical and moral declarations about what is real and unreal, good and bad, worthy and unworthy, major difficulties arise. This move from ordinary, fleeting reactions to dualistic ideological systems is extremely common and is, in my view, the basis for exclusive truth claims in religion. Dividing the world into good and evil is extremely attractive to many people. Fixed, rigid ideologies, held to desperately and unreflectively, then replace fluid and shifting common-sense ways of negotiating everyday experience. These become doctrines and prejudices, fixed systems pitting *us* against *them*.

Such ideologies, without exception, are destructive both internally and externally. They poison the psyches of those who cling to them. They also make life difficult for those on the receiving end of such ideologies, as those whose ideology is dominant try to control others whose belief and value systems may differ. These hardened and inflexibly hostile dualisms are most likely to occur regarding race, ethnicity, culture, political or social systems, sometimes gender, and most especially religion—at least in those contexts in which mere religious differences are hardened into exclusive truth claims. It is important to locate the roots of exclusive truth claims in ordinary, conventional psychological processes that are inevitable and, therefore, not to be demonized. As Buddhists often say, perceived duality is not the problem; it's what we do with the perception that makes all the difference. It is not necessary for perception of difference and duality to morph into exclusive truth claims used aggressively against those who use different words and concepts to understand the world we share.

Because once people have become addicted to exclusive truth claims, they are usually very resistant to giving them up, it is important to analyze carefully exactly which parts of an exclusive truth claim are problematic and which are not. Giving up the claim that any certain idea is an exclusive truth necessary for all humanity to accept does not mean giving up most of one's core beliefs. This is a very important point, and it is crucial to be clear about it. Those of us who argue against exclusive truth claims are not asking people to give up their beliefs but only *the manner in which they hold those beliefs*. I am largely indifferent to religious beliefs that I do not find convincing. I see no need to criticize them or to explain why I do not find them cogent. Only when exclusive truth is attributed to these same ideas do I find them dangerous and problematic. It is that claim for exclusive relevance that I criticize, *not the belief itself*.

For example, I don't find the claim "Jesus saves" to be very cogent or appealing, but I also find it unproblematic in and of itself and wouldn't try to convince others to give up such a belief. Nor do I find it problematic when someone says about themselves, "Jesus is *my* only savior." Perhaps I don't even find it too problematic when that belief somehow mutates into the claim, "not only is Jesus *my* only savior, but he is also *your* only savior," though the cogency of such a belief completely escapes me. However, that belief usually has another clause: "and it is *necessary* for *you* to believe that Jesus is *your* only savior." Only then do I raise objections. Mainly I ask how you could possibly know that. I can recommend certain Buddhist sensibilities and practices for wider consumption because I know from my own experience that they work—for me. But how could I possibly know that they will work for you? I can't, and therefore I only recommend them. I don't insist that they are also necessary for you. Regarding the claims of the exclusivist, Christian or otherwise, not only do I raise objections. I also become frightened—very frightened. Exclusivists *do* need to give up that tiny part of their belief system because of its ethical consequences. Notice how little exclusivists would actually have to concede to be able to flourish in situations of religious diversity. Their core beliefs are in no way threatened—only their wish to have a "monopoly on salvation."[11] Believers who have found their own belief system to be comforting and cogent, are, understandably, reluctant to give up their whole belief system in the face of a counterclaim to (exclusive) truth. Why is it so difficult for believers to understand that, say, Muslims or Buddhists find the same cogency and comfort in their beliefs that Christians do in theirs?

The ethical consequences of holding onto that part of a belief system that claims to be the best religion, not only for oneself, but also for everyone else, make exclusive truth claims completely untenable and unacceptable. What about others who feel the same way about their religion and make the same claims for it? Or what about others who do not make exclusive claims for their religion but nevertheless treasure it and don't want to abandon it? The deep problem with exclusive truth claims about religion is that

11. See note 2 of this chapter.

in a religiously diverse world, it is *impossible for a religion to hold such a claim about itself without creating conflict and causing harm.* Exclusive truth claims are untenable because such claims cannot be universalized. If every different religion claimed exclusive truth for itself, the result could only be mutual aggression and competition. It is unreasonable and inhumane to demand a position for oneself that, if taken by others as well, would only lead to suffering and mutual hostility. It is unreasonable, unethical, and mean-spirited to claim for myself something that I adamantly deny to others—the prerogative to treasure one's own religious worldview and regard it as true, whatever that might mean. (In religious matters, truth is more likely to be about subjective preferences than about objective accuracy.) There has to be a more cogent and ethical way of dealing with this situation than the mutually entrenched claim, "I'm right and you're wrong!" On the basis of exclusive truth claims, religions cannot be a force for peace, wholeness, and healing. And if religions don't provide peace, wholeness, and healing, what good are they? One would think that lesson should have been thoroughly engrained by the European religious wars of the sixteenth and seventeenth centuries, but apparently it has not.

In situations of geographic isolation and homogeneity, such claims may be understandable, even acceptable. But in the very diverse, highly interconnected world we live in today, it is untenable and dangerous for any religion to proclaim its exclusive truth. This conclusion should be completely obvious and completely convincing. Since it is dangerous in a religiously diverse world for there to be any religion claiming exclusive truth and relevance for itself, and since there is more than one religion in the world, no religion should claim exclusive truth and relevance for itself. Every religion's internal ethical demands concerning kindness, compassion, and nonharming should trump its pre-reflective tendencies toward self-universalizing. As I have said on more than one occasion, exclusive truth claims in religion do not lead to salvation; they lead to suffering. No religious dogma should have such weight that it would override the logic of this simple fact—especially when it would be so easy to give up the claim to have the exclusive truth for everyone else while retaining one's belief system intact.

Embedded in these questions is another very serious question. How is one's own spirituality improved or strengthened by claiming that it is also right for everyone else? In fact, there is no evidence that such claims improve the quality of one's own religious life at all. Those who claim that it is necessary to hold one's own religion to be the One True Faith in order to be faithful or to feel secure totally misunderstand what religion is about and how it works. Making exclusive truth claims does not improve the spiritual well-being of a believer in any way, despite centuries'-old claims that it does.

If we look around us, we see that many who hold exclusive truth claims about religion are not calm, peaceful, relaxed, cheerful, or happy. They are often rigid, lacking in confidence, defensive, and aggressive to others. Nothing so fuels aggression towards others as a self-righteous belief that one knows what is best for everyone. Only remember the story I told in the preface to this book. Such scenarios are quite common, I suspect.

It is their actual attitudes and behaviors regarding religious others for which I most fault those who hold exclusive truth claims. Sometimes it seems that claims of religious superiority are the only form of prejudice that people openly express today. Many may still think privately that whites are superior to people of color, that men are superior to women, that heterosexuality is normative for all people, or that Western culture is superior to any other. But most people are careful where they express such prejudices. I see little difference between such claims to superiority and claims for the singular, universal validity of one religion among many. Yet in many quarters it is quite acceptable to express scorn and hostility for religious others. In more than one discussion, I have claimed that expressing negative attitudes about a religion is no more acceptable than expressing negative attitudes about race, ethnicity, gender, or sexual orientation. If we remember that the vast majority of people inherit their religion as part of a package that includes language, culture, and ethnicity as well, that argument becomes even stronger. But the people with whom I was discussing the matter disagreed, claiming that because religious truth was at stake, the situation was completely different from racial or ethnic prejudice. My interlocutors claimed that their negative attitudes about others' religions were actually an expression of concern for them; if people are marching towards a precipice, any ethical and compassionate person should hold them back by any means. We are back to the one part of any exclusive truth claim that must be rejected: the part that says, you must accept my claim, for your own good.

Such a claim is one of the most touching aspects of exclusive truth claims. Those who hold and promote exclusive truth claims are often genuinely concerned for others in a certain way. They claim to be motivated by compassion. And I am sure that their own conviction about their own compassion is genuine. However, as a Buddhist, I have been trained to always look carefully into my own convictions, into any belief in which I am too invested, especially if it involves my prescriptions for others. Compassion is a very tricky matter, something that must be informed by intelligence and insight if it is to be more than my ego-invested project and the projection of my version of how things are onto other people. Feeling called or needing to change people or situations "for their own good" is often quite aggressive and self-centered. Furthermore, in a world characterized by multiple diversities, the greatest compassion of all is to *stop interfering so much with others, to stop claiming to know what everyone else should do and think, and to let them be who they are, just as we want to continue being who we are without exclusivists badgering us to imitate them.* This is wisdom that those who are eager to make exclusive truth claims would do well to acquire, and wisdom that will be repeated many times in this book.

Because the exclusivist model is still so dominant in so many quarters, contemporary Christian theologies of religion need to proclaim messages about the downside of exclusive truth claims and about their inappropriateness for our times and our historical moment much more commonly and forcefully. That message, proclaimed from seminaries and pulpits everywhere, is much more urgent than deciding the relative merits of pluralism versus inclusivism. The same applies, of course, for any other religion that still persists in claiming its exclusive relevance for everyone. That message also requires a clear proclamation that belief systems as such are not being criticized; under criticism is only the claim that everyone else needs to accept the same belief system. Those of us who dislike being on the receiving end of exclusive truth claims have no quarrel with what other religious people believe—only with their need for us to believe the same thing they do.

A Quick Look at the Inclusive or "Fulfillment" Model

The inclusive model became the official Roman Catholic position after Vatican II, and the document from Vatican II quoted earlier in this chapter is often cited as something of a charter for inclusivists. Most liberal Catholics and liberal Protestants now probably adhere to some version of inclusivist model.[12] The World Council of Churches, the organization of mainline Protestants and Eastern Orthodox Christians, also adopted a similar position. Beginning in the 1970s, it vigorously promoted "respectful dialogue" with people of other faiths, though, according to Paul Knitter, its theological position is unclear and it may actually remain within the exclusivist model.[13]

The most frequently cited inclusivist theologian is Karl Rahner, a German Catholic who did his most important work in the mid-twentieth century. According to Paul Knitter, Rahner's theology of religions "took standard Catholic doctrines and used them as building blocks for a truly revolutionary theology of religions."[14] According to Rahner, God's grace is such that non-Christians can be "saved," not *in spite of* their non-Christian

12. Knitter, *Introducing Theologies of Religion*, 63.

13. Ibid., 42–44.

14. Ibid., 68.

religions, as had been previously taught by some theologians, but *because of* their non-Christian religions. Thus, the Christian deity saves even non-Christians because it is the nature of the Christian deity to do so. In fact, practitioners of non-Christian religions are actually *anonymous Christians* by virtue of experiencing the "saving love of God" in their own religions.[15]

On the one hand, such a teaching goes far beyond anything that most Christian exclusivists would allow. But on the other hand, for all of Rahner's generosity and for all the improvement his position represents over hard exclusivism, his theology still is inadequate, in that it can understand and account for my religion only in terms provided by his religion. A phrase such as the "saving love of God" means nothing to a Buddhist and cannot, to a Buddhist, begin to account for the felicity and contentment I experience due to Buddhist practices and teachings. Thus, Rahner's theology of religions remains a *Christian* account of other religions, which may be helpful to Christians but does little to account for or value religious diversity in more neutral and widely applicable ways. I have always reacted particularly negatively to Rahner's assertion that I am an "anonymous Christian," even though I understand the magnanimity of his intentions, and even though I completely accept Knitter's apology for Rahner's language:

> We must immediately remind ourselves that Rahner proposed this vision of anonymous Christians only for his fellow Christians. He did not write for Buddhists and Hindus. His purpose was to liberate Christians from their negative views of those outside the church and to enable them to realize that God is much greater than they are.[16]

This is well said, but shouldn't the pith of Rahner's views be obvious to any deeply practiced follower of any religion, no matter what specific language they use? Why did we wait until the mid-twentieth century for such a position to become widely proclaimed in Christian circles? That, apparently, such grace and wisdom isn't obvious to those who make exclusive truth claims only deepens my criticism of that particular model of thinking about religious diversity.

Different kinds of inclusivism have also been employed by other religions, especially Islam and Hinduism. In those cases, it is not a modern innovation but is long-standing. However, for those who experience Muslim or Hindu inclusivism, the results may be no more satisfactory than in the Christian case. Muslims take pride in the fact that in societies they rule, they

---

15. Ibid., 73. See pages 68–75 for Knitter's summary of Rahner's theology of religions.

16. Ibid., 73.

have freely tolerated Jews, Christians, and anyone else whom they could determine had a scripture and thus could be called "people of the Book," the category within which one needed to be included. But such people, nevertheless, had to pay special taxes to protect their property rights and personal safety. In addition, they could not participate in government or hold civic positions. Some strands of Hinduism follow the classical model of an inclusivist religion. Hindus have long justified internal diversity with the motto that there are many roads up the mountain but the view from the top is the same, no matter how one gets there. That same logic is easily and often applied to other religions as well. Other Indian religions in particular have been declared to be simply different versions of Hinduism. For example, the Buddha is said to have been one of Vishnu's incarnations, thus making Buddhism a sect of Hinduism. I have often been told by Hindus that because I am a Buddhist, therefore I am really a Hindu. But that inclusion also erases the specificity of Buddhist identity. I have often been in dialogue situations with Hindus who simply refuse to take Buddhism seriously as an independent religion rather than a knock-off of Hinduism. Without any serious study of Buddhism, *qua* Buddhism, they assume they understand Buddhism and can speak for it. Such inclusivism is really irritating to those who are "included" but also erased in that process.

So are there any redeeming features to the inclusivist model? For many, it seems to be a way to step out of exclusivism, a way of focusing on what we share with religious others rather than what differentiates us from them. For those who are initially uncomfortable with religious diversity, who think that in an ideal world everyone would practice the same religion, such a step is helpful and necessary. It can be a bridge to *becoming comfortable* with religious diversity and *valuing* it. A conversation with Paul Knitter about this issue really touched my heart and taught me a lot. I was expressing my own impatience with the claim that non-Christians are anonymous Christians. Paul said to me, "You don't understand the *relief* it provided for us Christians who had been trying to be faithful to the church's teachings but found them ethically problematic." His face said even more than his words.

I also remember Hindu or Muslim students in my world-religions classes hearing neutral accounts of the other religion for the first time. With tremendous relief and surprise, they would say, "They *are* just like us!" It did not seem to me like good skillful means in that situation to reply that Hindu and Muslim theologies and practices are actually very, very different from one another. For those students, acknowledging those differences and being comfortable with them would be a later step in the process of beginning to appreciate the other religion and no longer regarding genuine religious diversity as a problem to be overcome.

To someone outside this Christian discussion, inclusivism feels like a softer form of exclusivism. Other religions are no longer wholly condemned. It is admitted that they may have many good features, but they are, nevertheless, not adequate or sufficient. "They're okay, but we're the best" seems to be the motto of inclusivists. We are back to the everyday, garden-variety exclusivism—the exclusivism of preferring what is familiar to what is unfamiliar, of preferring, say, North Indian cuisine to South Indian cuisine because one is more familiar. This "soft exclusivism" has already been discussed in a previous section of this chapter. It is unproblematic in everyday conversation among friends. It may also be useful and helpful in intra-Christian conversations. Christians and other exclusivists who may be unable to comprehend a statement that other religions are worthy in and of themselves may be able to assimilate the claim that the deity they think they believe in actually is okay with Hindus and Buddhists. Perhaps, contrary to what they had previously been taught, their deity may not want all Hindus and Buddhists to become Christians. But as a theological position taken into public, multifaith conversations about serious matters such as religious diversity, it is disrespectful, inadequate, and undignified. There has to be a better way to talk about these matters.

The Turn to Pluralism

By the late twentieth century, some Christian theologians had begun to find inclusivist theology of religions inadequate. Whatever else they may claim, pluralist theologians all agree that it is inappropriate and incorrect to claim the absolute superiority of one religion over all others or that one religion is *really* true, whereas other religions are only partially true. They want to find ways to value other religions in their own right and to claim that followers of those religions are not somehow dependent on the Christian deity for whatever well-being they experience, but find it directly through the practices of their own religions. Put another way, pluralists want to *disprove* claims made by their own religion (or any other religion) that it alone is worthwhile because it has unique access to truth. When that claim is disproven, there is no need for any one religion to seek to be the world's only religion. Multiple religions can coexist peacefully on one planet. Many pluralist theologians are fond of quoting Hans Küng: "There will be no peace among nations until there is peace among religions; and there will be no peace among religions until there is greater dialogue among them."[17] Paul Knitter adds another clause to Küng's statement. "There will be no real and effective dialogue among religions if each religion continues to make its claims of superiority."[18]

17. Küng, *Global Responsibility*, xv.
18. Knitter, *The Myth of Religious Superiority*, ix.

In any case, the bottom line of pluralist theologians is that there is no way, theologically or empirically, to cogently argue that one of the world's religions is truer than and superior to all the rest. Whatever else pluralist theologians may go on to say, this minimal position makes pluralist theologies of religion quite different from either exclusivist or inclusivist theologies in very important ways. Without this move, it is difficult to imagine how religious diversity could be understood as anything but a mistake or a problem, something that would not be present in an ideal world. This minimal position of being unwilling to declare that any one of the world's religions is superior to all the others would seem to be necessary for human flourishing in situations of religious diversity. This minimal statement is also all that unites pluralists.

Because pluralists will not pick out one religion as true, many immediately rush to accuse them of relativism, by which these critics seem to mean that unless a person picks one thing in a group as the best, one has no standards, that anything goes. That this is not a good definition of the relationship between relative and absolute does not matter. The accusation of relativism is the fastest cheap shot made against anyone who finds it unethical and uncompassionate to elevate one religion (always one's own, of course) above all the others. Except in the most easygoing of New Age contexts, pluralists are not saying that all religions are the same or that all paths lead to the same mountaintop. Nor are they saying that mistakes and bad choices cannot be made religiously. To say that we can't isolate one religion as clearly superior to the others does not mean that every religious idea or practice is as good as any other religious idea or practice, nor is any pluralist theologian making such a naïve claim. The important question of how to evaluate competing religious beliefs and practices will be dealt with more fully in the next chapter.

Pluralist theologies of religion really don't need to go further than the minimal position that no neutral, universally acceptable criteria can be found by which to declare that one of the world's religions is truer than and superior to all the rest. This part of their work contains their truly revolutionary, innovative, and valuable insight. But many of them do try to go further and often get into difficulty in that enterprise. Pluralist theologians agree that religions are very different from one another, but they often want to find a more abstract lowest common denominator to religions, something that all religions, despite their differences, share in common. That common root than becomes the Truth that all religions refract or reflect in different ways. Inevitably, of course, theologians find it difficult to resist the temptation to name that abstract source or force accounting for all the different religions. This move from declaring what *isn't* the case—that one among the many religions is uniquely valuable and true—to trying to declare what *is* the case—that we can isolate accurately a common denominator underlying all religions, is the difficult point on which many a pluralist theology of religions breaks down.

There are two places to locate this underlying source for all the diverse religions in the world. According to one position, the world's differing religions could be different ways of discussing the same transcendent Ultimate Reality, which cannot be fully understood by human beings but whose existence can be intuited by them. This position approximates my teenage question to the exclusivist pastor who later excommunicated me for heresy: different ways of speaking about this reality are due to linguistic and cultural differences. According another position, the world's differing religions could be grounded in the same ineffable human experience. Because this experience is beyond language and because language divides people, inevitably, once they start talking about this experience, people will talk about it in diverse ways, and cultural differences will accentuate their differences even more. Both options are attractive, and both present problems.

John Hick, one of the great names in pluralist theology of religions, has elaborated the first option in his many books. He puts it this way. "One . . . sees the great world religions as different human responses to the one divine Reality, embodying different perceptions which have been formed in different historical and cultural circumstances."[19] My immediate response is that a Buddhist seeking to name what is common to all religions would probably not use the phrase "one divine Reality." A Buddhist would probably not even use Hick's much more recent terminology.

> I suggest that the best religious account we can give of the global situation of a single ineffable Ultimate Reality whose universal presence is being conceived and experienced and responded to within the different human religious traditions.[20]

There is not necessarily anything objectionable, wrong with, or inadequate about Hick's terminology. But it clearly shows its origins and is much more at home in a religious universe oriented to oneness and to substantive terms like Reality than in a religious universe more attuned to impermanence and process, which is why a Buddhist would probably not choose that language for self-expression.

Pluralist theologians of this stripe are, by and large, still consumed with the question of *truth* in religion and with finding adequate words and concepts to convey that truth. Furthermore, they are mainly concerned with

19. Hick, *God and the Universe of Faiths*, 131.
20. Hick, "The Next Step beyond Dialogue," 12.

truth claims about metaphysical, transcendent "realities" made by the various religions. Thus, one can question how much progress they have made on the question of how to *flourish* in situations of religious diversity. They have simply shifted the focus from defining the One True Religion, whether in exclusivist or inclusivist ways, to finding an underlying truth shared by all religions beneath their apparent diversity, to proposing that there is truth in every religion, or at least in more than one religion. Schmidt-Leukel's definition of *pluralism* makes this clear.

> Pluralism: Salvific knowledge of a transcendent reality is mediated by more than one religion (not necessarily by all of them), and there is none among them whose mediation of that knowledge is superior to all the rest.[21]

Knitter's subtitles for his final two models of theologies of religions, both of which Schmidt-Leukel would classify as pluralist models, also betray this overriding concern with the truth of religions. He calls them "the Mutuality Model: Many True Religions Called to Dialogue" and "The Acceptance Model: Many True Religions: So Be It." Even the comparative theologians, who recommend a moratorium on theologies of religion and simply want to compare religious ideas carefully, only recommend *deferring* questions of religious truth. At a later time, when more is known about the various options, questions of religious truth could be discussed more adequately.[22]

But what if *truth* about metaphysical, transcendent realities is not the primary issue for religions? In my view, there could never be a *verbal* account of a common metaphysical reality pointed to by the differing religions that we can all agree upon. As I will claim in chapter 6, it is impossible for language even to communicate fully what any *one* religion is talking about, so religious ideas expressed in language are a poor candidate for talking about underlying religious unity. Does locating a common, universal source for religions in *experience* rather than in words about metaphysics and underlying truth work any better? This attempt to find a unity underlying religious differences is quite popular and venerable. Perhaps the most classic expression of it is the Perennial Philosophy espoused by Aldus Huxley, among others.

In contemporary Christian theologies of religion, the work of Raimon Panikkar is often cited as an example of such a position. His work and life represent a fascinating internal dialogue as he moved between Hinduism, Christianity, and Buddhism, to a lesser extent, without ever leaving one for

---

21. Schmidt-Leukel, "Exclusivism, Inclusivism, Pluralism," 20.

22. Knitter, *Introducing Theologies of Religion*, 212–14.

another, even though he was also an ordained Roman Catholic priest. He grounds his speaking about religions in experience rather than in thought, though to move out of the silence of experience at all, he has to use language. The name he uses to bring his experience out of silence into language is "cosmotheandric experience,"[23] a mystical experience uniting the divine, the human, and the material. According to him, whatever is said theologically will come out of and be grounded in this experience, which means that the inevitable *linguistic and cultural* diversity of religions is not a problem, and that the various religions, having a common experiential source, can mutually enrich each other through dialogue and interaction. He also claims that any mystic, or anyone with deep religious experience, would know what he means by the term he coined: "cosmotheandric experience."[24]

This more experiential way of talking about the unity underlying the world's diverse religions and vouching for their truth is cogent and attractive in many ways. Clearly, if there is an *unmediated* basis for religions, it is more likely to be in experience than in logic and language. Unmediated language is impossible. To claim that there is such a thing amounts to a claim that God speaks Hebrew rather than Arabic, or some other version of a similar, nonsensical claim. It is much more likely that beneath language, we do share experience. The problem is, how would we ever know that for sure, given that the only way we can connect with each other is through *expression* of some sort, whether it is verbal or not? It is impossible to prove, either empirically or theologically, that it is actually the *same* experience grounding different religions because that experience is said to be *ineffable,* or beyond language. It is difficult to use the words *same* and *ineffable* together, as is done when appeal is made to the "same ineffable experience" grounding the different religions. If the experience is truly ineffable, how would we ever know that different individuals experience the *same* thing, or even that I experience the same thing on different occasions? Between even religious languages as similar as those of Buddhism based on Nagarjuna and of Advaita Hinduism, it is difficult to ascertain if we are really talking about the same religious experiences. If the theologies are as different as those of Buddhism and Christianity, it is even harder to ascertain if the underlying experiences are the same or different, simply because the languages are so different.

A third way of reaching across religious boundaries has been developed more recently by pluralist theologian Paul Knitter and others. His writings are more about what interreligious dialogue should focus on and who should be dialoguing together, not on a theology of religions per se.

23. Ibid., 127.
24. Ibid., 126–34.

Knitter focuses more on how religions can and should work together rather than whether there is a lowest common denominator or root underlying all religions and from which they stem. Drawing heavily on Latin American liberation theology, his answer is that religions should work together on alleviating the suffering of the world, especially the suffering of the poor. In his discussions of theologies of religion, Knitter has developed the language of various "bridges" between religions and also claims that people can use these bridges to "pass over" to another religion and "cross back" to one's own, enriched with interreligious insights. He calls this particular bridge (the bridge of alleviating suffering and mitigating poverty) the "ethico-practical" bridge, thus picking up a theme that many find cogent: there is much more convergence between religions ethically than theologically or metaphysically. Somehow, despite vast theological differences, religions nevertheless come up with relatively similar, *though not identical* ethical teachings. This bridge has been extensively used by the Dalai Lama as well. In fact, as he details in his book *Toward a True Kinship of Faiths: How the World's Religions Can Come Together*, he regards it to be the main point of significant convergence among the religions.

Especially in his article in *The Myth of Christian Uniqueness*, Knitter laid out his thinking about this bridge. He claims that the two pressing problems for contemporary Christin thinkers are the many poor and the many religions. He then proposes that progress on both fronts could be made if religions dialogued and worked together on both issues, but especially on the economic issues resulting in the many poor. He writes that the Latin American liberation theology movement "needs not just religion but *religions*! Economic, political, and especially nuclear liberation is just too big a job for one nation, or culture, *or* religion."[25] He then challenges those who engage in interreligious dialogue not only to engage in pleasant tea parties in pleasant resorts or retreat centers on mountaintops overlooking the suffering masses, but to engage with those who are suffering. We should "encounter other religions, not *primarily* to enjoy diversity and dialogue but to eliminate suffering and oppression,"[26] a value judgment that might not be agreed upon by all those devoted to the cause of flourishing with religious diversity. It's not so much that we *enjoy* diversity as that we have no other choice than to learn how to live successfully with religious diversity on all levels—and especially on those levels where we are much less likely to agree, such as conflicting truth claims. Knitter then makes a strong case, drawn from Latin American liberation theology, for a "preferential option for the

25. Knitter, "Toward a Liberation Theology of Religions," 179.
26. Ibid., 181.

poor," which means they must be listened to first and their needs given priority, especially because they have been so completely ignored heretofore.

In one of the most important claims in this article, Knitter proposes a new standard by which Christians might evaluate other religions. In his earlier book, *No Other Name?*, he had proposed that Christian thinking about other religions had evolved from ecclesiocentrism (no salvation outside the church) to Christocentrism (Rahner's "anonymous Christianity") to theocentrism (Hick's Ultimate Reality). But it needs to evolve further, to "soteriocentrism." By this, Knitter means that "that which unites the religions in common discourse and practice, is . . . to what extent they are engaged in promoting human welfare and bringing about liberation with and for the poor and nonpersons."[27]

Any assessment of the contributions of Paul Knitter to Christian theologies of religion must also acknowledge his example (perhaps unparalleled among other theologians), his honesty and courage in truly encountering other religions, especially Buddhism. His account of his "passing over" to and "crossing back" from Buddhism, *Without Buddha I Could Not Be a Christian*, is especially moving for his telling how much his Christian activism was tempered and transformed by his encounter with Buddhists, who insisted that dualistic confrontation with and denunciation of others, even when their behavior is problematic, do not really result in peace or significant social change, a theme to be much emphasized in this book. After narrating his encounter with Thich Nhat Hanh's book *Being Peace*, he tells us that "we're really not going to be of much help in making peace for the world unless we are seriously committed to making peace and being peace with ourselves."[28]

All Christian pluralists are quite severely criticized by more conservative Christians, but this move towards "ethico-practical" concerns was heavily criticized by Gavin D'Costa. He complains that soteriocentrism is also a normative position vis-à-vis other religions and that Knitter is aware of this. But he "seems to find 'imperialism' on behalf of the poor and marginalized more acceptable than 'imperialism' on behalf of correct doctrine."[29] "'Promoting human welfare' is an unhelpful common denominator, as it specifies nothing in particular until each tradition defines the terms."[30] While D'Costa is correct that there is not 100-percent convergence among religions on what constitutes human welfare, nevertheless there certainly

27. Ibid., 187.

28. Knitter, *Without Buddha I Could Not Be a Christian*, 196–97.

29. D'Costa, *Christianity and World Religions*, 17.

30. Ibid.

is more convergence among religions on ethics than on metaphysics. Furthermore, "human welfare" is certainly more discernible and ascertainable than "correct doctrine." And unless we want to be total relativists and postmodernists, human welfare is a much more relevant place to be "imperialistic" than correct doctrine. For example, it is far more relevant to work for changes so that girls are educated rather than married off at the age of twelve than it is to insist that Christianity (or any other religion) is the One True Faith.

Buddhism is always oriented toward reducing suffering rather than towards metaphysical abstracts. Thus, I am positively disposed toward the development of this "ethico-practical" bridge. Nevertheless, I would suggest that Knitter is too single-mindedly focused on the poor, to the exclusion of other marginalized groups, and even the oppressed planet. For example, Knitter draws much inspiration from largely Catholic liberation theology. But many, perhaps even a majority, of the poor are women. How much has liberation theology focused specifically on women? How much has it focused on the major causes of female poverty—lack of education and reproductive freedom? How much does this lack of focus on the causes of women's poverty increase not only poverty but also environmental degradation, which further increases poverty? It easy to overlook the interconnected nature of oppressions by focusing on the one that commands one's own attention. This is a minor criticism, for those of us who focus on justice and equality often focus most on the group we are most identified with or are most concerned with. It can be argued that none of us can develop equal competence in so many areas. Thus women are focused on sexism, people of color on racism, gay and lesbian people on homophobia, and the like. Nevertheless, when this so-called race to the bottom (this competition to be the most oppressed) occurs, it is detrimental to all causes for justice and equality. We need to avoid rhetoric that claims, in my paraphrase, *I am more oppressed than thou, and therefore thou owest me.*

A Critique of Current Forms of Pluralist Theologies

I have two major criticisms of Christian pluralist theologies of religion. The first is that in many cases, they remain overly concerned with the question of whether a religious claim is *true* or provides salvation, which are essentially Christian questions. Discomfort with Christian claims that only Christianity could provide salvation was the starting point of the whole enterprise of theology of religions. But even though pluralists want to answer that question in the negative, much of what they have to say is still deeply dependent on Christian categories and norms. An example is Schmidt-Leu-kel's arguments, quoted earlier in this chapter, about why there can be only three models: the exclusivist, inclusivist, and pluralist models. He defines what is at issue among these three models as whether "salvific knowledge of ultimate/transcendent reality" is mediated never, once, or more than once in the various religions, claiming these are the only possible options.[31] But both "salvation" and "ultimate/transcendent reality" are terms that don't come easily in many religious contexts, Buddhism included. In other words, many Christian pluralists are still operating from within a Christian para-digm, judging other religions by Christian standards, except that they are now willing to evaluate the other religions positively rather than negatively. If other religions can mediate "salvific knowledge," they are on a par with Christianity. But what if "salvific knowledge" isn't even at issue for some of the religions? What if philosophical or theological truth, expressed verbally and propositionally, isn't the main concern of a religion?

Students of comparative religions routinely note that Christianity is unique in its concern with correct creedal beliefs and its search for the one correct version of that creedal belief. Other religions that do enjoy complex philosophical arguments, such as Hinduism and Buddhism, also allow for and expect internal diversity of practices and claims. For many other religions, creedal belief is much less important than correct practice or simple group membership. Furthermore, though we can *understand* religious others some-what adequately across religious lines, it is much trickier to *evaluate* religious others across religious lines, and especially to adjudicate conflicting truth claims, such as theism versus nontheism, or monotheism versus polytheism. Understood in their own terms, each position makes sense. They can be fruit-fully compared. A person who stands within one of the positions could decide to adopt some features of another position. But to decide on their *truth*, what-ever that might mean? Even when stated in propositional form, religious ideas are primarily *symbols*, not something independently verifiable. I don't see any grounds by which symbols can be evaluated cross-culturally. Or, if there are such grounds, evaluation would be on the basis of what effect the symbol has on those who take it seriously. As John Hick argued, and as I will argue in the next chapter, when the criterion of the effect of a symbol on believers is applied, no religion stands out as superior to all others. Thus, even the titles Knitter gives to his last two models—the mutuality model ("many true reli-gions called to dialogue") and the acceptance model ("many true religions: so be it")—are questionable.[32]

---

31. Schmidt-Leukel, "Exclusivism, Inclusivism, Pluralism," 19.
32. Knitter, *Introducing Theologies of Religion*, ix.

A much more adequate way of going about answering the question of how the presence of many diverse, even conflicting, religious claims is not an ultimate problem is to recognize that they all work for their adherents—whether or not they would work for us. As the Dalai Lama puts it,

> Regardless of how one may feel about specific doctrines of other faith traditions, this fact alone—their service to millions of fellow human beings—makes them worthy of our deep respect. Their profound benefit to others is really the ultimate reason each of us, believers and non-believers alike, must accord deep respect to the world's great faith traditions.[33]

Thus, our own reactions to doctrines found in other religions are somewhat beside the point. We don't need to determine whether they are true or false. "It is . . . undeniable that the teachings of the great religions provide great benefits to their adherents."[34] Our job is then to understand those teachings as best we can, and perhaps to learn something from them. The only point at which our evaluations might become relevant is if those doctrines lead their adherents into ethically untenable behavior—violence, oppression, sexism, and so forth. This issue will be discussed more fully in the next chapter.

Within this first main criticism of Christian pluralism, I also have another quibble with the tendency of some Christian pluralist theologians to continue to claim unique and universal relevance for Jesus Christ, which pulls them back into the inclusivist camp in some ways. To an outsider, this tendency is rather strange. Though they willingly recognize the profundity and worth of our religions, they still seem to expect us to personally incorporate reverence for Jesus into our practices, rather than simply to rejoice that their relationship with Jesus is profoundly meaningful for them. I cite Paul Knitter's challenge to me in his remarks at an American Academy of Religion session celebrating my lifework. Among the things he asked me to consider was whether "some rafts, some events, and some persons represent a unique or distinct discovery or expression of truth that cannot be found elsewhere and that is universally important. Christians believe this about Jesus."[35] Knitter has said something similar on other occasions. "So as a Christian, I would witness to what I have discovered in my religion, through Jesus Christ, and why I think it is true, important, powerful and meaningful, not just for me but also for you."[36] But how does Knitter know that, somehow, Jesus is or should be meaningful to me? That is for the non-Christian, not

33. His Holiness, the Dalai Lama XVI, *Toward a True Kinship of Faiths*, 149.

34. Ibid., 148.

35. Knitter, "Rita Gross," 83.

36. Stewart, *Can Only One Religion Be True?* 41.

the Christian, to decide. The question here is whether something's uniqueness, which is inarguable, not only for Jesus, but also for many religious symbols, makes it *universally* important, that is, important for everyone. In chapter 8, I will argue that it does not.

My second major reservation about much pluralist theology of religions is more basic. As we have seen, many pluralist theologians justify their claim that many religions are "true" on grounds that the religions actually share basic similarities. This is the case for all three major forms of pluralist theologies (the philosophical, the mystical, and the ethical). I have raised questions about the adequacy of all three claims of commonality. Simply put, I find it much more cogent to declare that Christianity, or any other religion, is *not* the only true religion than to claim that many or all religions are at least partially true. Faithful to my Buddhist sensibilities, I always prefer negative to positive language about ultimates.

However, I have a more basic question: do followers of religions need common ground to be able to live together, peacefully sharing the same earth? What happens if there is no common ground that all religions could agree is indeed a common ground that at the same time speaks accurately to the specificity of each religion? Why is unity so important? What is wrong with radical difference? Why is difference so troubling to people? How do we learn to be comfortable with difference, untroubled by difference? Why can't we simply drop the whole question of whether any of the world's religions is superior or inferior in any definitive way? Can't we agree that there are no criteria or grounds by which we could come to such a conclusion, and get on with understanding each other and living together peacefully? To me, these are the real questions, the real issues concerning religious diversity. The quest for a lowest common denominator among religions that everyone, or at least most serious religious thinkers, can agree with has proved to be extremely elusive. I do not want our ability to live together peacefully to be jinxed by failure in the quest for a common truth or a common ethic uniting all religions. Suppose religions are just *different*, radically diverse, at least as far as theological and metaphysical claims go. Suppose they *are* incommensurable, not in the sense that one cannot understand the different religions somewhat adequately, and perhaps even learn something valuable from religions not one's own, but that they cannot be made commensurate with one another, either theologically or ethically. Should that undo our ability to live together peacefully?

In other words, to flourish in conditions of religious diversity, we do have to stop elevating one religion above the others as somehow truer or better. That basic step taken by pluralists is necessary. But can we go any further? Would it even be helpful to try to do so? About religious matters, it is always easier and safer to eliminate bad options and unhelpful views, to say what is not the case, than it is to describe what is the case in positive language. I would suggest that the pluralist quest for a common denominator among religions, whether found in a more abstract metaphysic, in common mystical experience, or in ethical convergence, is still mired in a traditional quest, especially dominant in the West, for correct propositional statements. As a student of comparative religions, I would suggest that this quest for correct propositional statements is only one aspect of religion, and perhaps not even the most central one. Furthermore, I will always suggest that what prevents us from flourishing with religious diversity is never the other religions and what they propose, but our own psychological and spiritual limitations and immaturity. We need to learn how to accept and flourish with religious diversity rather than hoping against hope that diversity is illusory, that everyone else is just like us after all.

Negative theology is always more accurate than positive theology. Beyond that, I will suggest in chapter 8, we could well find that manyness and diversity are more adequate expressions for what is at the heart of reality than the unity and universality so longed for by monotheists. But then, it is not surprising that, as a Buddhist, I would prefer a minimal language of negating untruths to trying to articulate any single truth. That task is less likely to deviate us from the wordless truth found in silence. With that statement I recognize and admit that it is impossible to say anything that all religious people will find adequate. There is no such speech. We have to find ways to flourish with religious diversity anyway, because religious diversity is not going to disappear. It is both normal and natural! But to live together peaceably we do not have to create a system into which we can fit all the world's religions—not even a pluralist system that tries to find lowest common denominators linking all religions. Thus, while the pluralist model is by far the least inadequate of the Christian models for thinking about religious diversity, it is also not without problems. I will now try to move forward from that conclusion, always trying to suggest, from my Buddhist practice and my knowledge of the comparative study of religions, ways that are more fruitful for flourishing with religions diversity, always trying to maintain for theists and monotheists as much of their received system as possible. In fact, as I have already demonstrated, the one and only part of those systems that fails all tests for providing an ability to flourish with religious diversity is the claim to possess propositional creeds that must be adhered to by all people everywhere for all time.

Chapter 5

Excuse Me, but
What's the Question?

Isn't Religious Diversity Natural?

To tell the truth, I have no idea which element of my hyphenated identity as a Buddhist practitioner and a scholar of comparative religions is more prominent in my conviction that religious diversity, which also includes indifference to organized religions, is simply a normal, natural aspect of life. I have regarded religious diversity as a fact of life that presents no genuine problems for so long now that I can't imagine thinking anything different, can't imagine being troubled by the fact that people believe very different things religiously. Yet I was brought up to think that it was a huge problem. So how did the transformation happen? At some point, fairly early in my life, it just became ludicrous to me to think that of all the people on earth, only a relatively small group of very conservative German Lutherans had their heads on straight and had all the correct answers to every difficult problem or existential issue. Truly, how much sense could that make! I did not have many resources with which to come to that conclusion—very little lived experience encountering much diversity, no like-thinking friends or mentors, and few books or other intellectual stimulation. But it just didn't make sense to think that the group into which I was born was so superior to every other group on earth, or that other people didn't feel affection for their own lifeways, whatever they might be. Given the ease with which I thought past the indoctrination I was given, I am somewhat impatient with people who buy into religious chauvinism—or chauvinisms of any kind.

John Hick is fond of talking about adopting a pluralist outlook regarding religious diversity as a Copernican revolution regarding religion that is necessary in our time. While I basically accept his idea, I would add that *overcoming* our *discomfort* with that diversity is critical in that Copernican revolution required for religious believers at this time. There are two parts to my claim. The first is that religious diversity is a fact, and it is also a fact that religious diversity is here to stay. There simply are no grounds to dispute those facts. The second part of my claim is that we need to find the resources and means to become comfortable with and untroubled by the fact of that diversity.

The sun does not revolve around the earth, and one's own religion cannot be declared the One True Faith. These are equivalent statements, of equal obviousness and clarity, no matter what previous religious dogmas may have declared. It is as useless to hang on to the dogma that one's own religion is the best because that is what one was previously taught as it would be to hang on to the dogma that the sun *literally* rises and sets because it appears to and because the Bible seems to say so. Religions always get into the most trouble when their dogmas lead them to deny facts on the basis of authority; but dogmas die slowly. I was amazed in the fall of 2011 to discover that some Jain pundits still declare that the earth is flat because that's what Jain scriptures state. When empirical evidence is presented to them, they respond that some day science will catch up with their scriptures.

Exclusive truth claims and religious diversity are mutually exclusive; they *cannot* survive together in any harmonious, peaceful, and respectful way. Surviving religious diversity involves coming to a deep and profound realization that religious diversity is not a mistake or a problem. It does not have to be overcome, and there is no need to suggest that other traditions may have partial truth or to try to find some deeper, overarching or underlying truth that encompasses the many religious traditions. To accept this truth often requires profound inner adjustments, but they are not very hard to make in the face of obvious evidence. Remember the Tibetan lama we met in chapter 1 who adjusted his views about the flatness of the earth in a few days when presented with incontrovertible evidence.

What is such incontrovertible evidence regarding the naturalness of religious diversity? From the comparative study of religion, we learn that, no matter where or when we look in the history of humanity, people have devised a great variety of religious practices and beliefs. This diversity is both internal and external. That is to say, not only are there many religions around the world; each religion also contains a great deal of internal diversity. Even those religions that proclaim they are the One True Faith are internally very diverse. How could they imagine that someday there will be one universal global religion to which all people will adhere when they cannot even secure internal agreement about their own religion's essentials? Why should we expect that in the future, such diversity would disappear and the religious outlook of one group of people would prevail over all others? That has the same cogency as expecting that most people would give up their native tongue to adopt another language for the sake of an ability to communicate universally. And, as I have argued in the past, having a universal language would actually be very helpful and make communication easier, whereas having a universal, common religion would not significantly improve anything. In fact, it would rob us of a lot interesting religious and spiritual alternatives, a lot of material that is good to think with, in the felicitous phrasing of anthropologist Claude Levi-Strauss. It would be helpful if we could all talk about all those alternatives in a language we could all understand. It does not seem that we are likely to have that common language anytime soon. But diminishing the number of religious alternatives, per the vision of religious exclusivists, does nothing to enrich our human community.

However, the vast variety of data available from the cross-cultural comparative study of religion does not provide *theologically* the incontrovertible proof regarding the normality and naturalness of religious diversity that I am seeking. Those data are simply a fascinating kaleidoscope. They present us with facts but say little about how to value those facts. There would seem to be an obvious, simple theological justification for religious diversity available to theists and monotheists. I used to suggest to my Christian and theistic students that the deity they believed in had obviously created a world in which religious diversity rather than uniformity prevailed. One would think that for those to whom belief in a creator deity is important, the manifest world that the deity had created would be acceptable. But my students objected to that logic, saying they knew that God wanted them to stamp out religious diversity. Factual information is often unconvincing to those with settled theological opinions. Unfortunately for them, one of the most famous monotheistic justifications of religious diversity was from the wrong revealed scripture, so it didn't matter to them. The Quran states:

> To every one of you we have appointed a [sacred] law and a course to follow. For, had God so wished, He would have made you all one community. Rather He wished to try you by means of what He had given you; who among you is of the best action. Compete therefore with one another as if in a race in the performance of good deeds. To God shall be your return, and He will inform you concerning the things in which you had differed (Q. 5:48).[1]

1. Quoted in Ayoub, "Religious Pluralism and the Qur'an."

Take out the theistic language, and this advice is not too different from what I shall propose.

Begin with Human Beings, Not with Ultimate Realities

On the other hand, what I shall propose is quite different from what the Quran says in one significant way; for I locate the rationale and need for religious diversity, not in what unseen and unknowable metaphysical entities such as deities might decree, but in how human consciousness operates. If we are to speak of Copernican revolutions in how we view religious diversity, I would suggest that we shift our focus from how we think of God and instead put much more emphasis in thinking about how and why we construct and accept the theologies we do. In other words, shift the gaze from theology to spirituality. Shift from looking to something external, even an external as abstract as Ultimate Reality, as the source of our religious ideas. Instead look to our own quest for meaning and coherence. As I am fond of telling my fellow Buddhists who want to believe in strange, nonhuman origins for some of their texts, sacred books do not fall from some other world into our sphere, neatly bound between two covers.[2] They are the products of cultural evolution and are accepted only because they seem coherent and helpful to humans. For those who are or want to remain theists, such a move does not jeopardize their belief system. Belief in an external deity is such an attractive alternative that most people prefer it to nontheism. In fact, in some forms of Buddhism, it can be hard to detect how Buddhists have remained true to their nontheistic origins, though more sophisticated exegesis of such forms of Buddhism can always rescue a nontheistic core. However, thinking there could be an *unmediated* text, creed, or religious practice—something independent of human agency—is not only a strange idea but also an idea that is devastating to flourishing with religious diversity, as we shall see.

Moving from theology to spirituality and human consciousness would be a realistic and very helpful move. It is also a typical non-theistic and

2. Despite alleged Buddhist nontheism, some of my Buddhist colleagues, especially in Tibetan Buddhism, like to believe literally in many stories about supernatural origins of beloved but "new" Buddhist texts and teachings that were not part of the legacy of the historical Buddha. They believe literally that somehow these texts fell into the human world, intact and fully formed, unmediated by human cultural creativity. Usually, it is explained that the Buddha set aside these teachings, to be revealed later when humans would be more receptive to them and more able to put them into practice. Starting with the Mahayana *sutras*, which began to be written and circulated some four hundred years or so after the life and death of the historical Buddha, most major developments in Buddhist thought have been explained by means of such essentially supernatural intervention into human history.

Buddhist move. According to Buddhism, human minds create our worlds, both their problems and their possibilities. This is probably the biggest difference in the claims made by theistic and nontheistic religious, though a nontheist Buddhist would argue that theistic religions are actually created by their adherents, not by the deities they worship. (Interesting is that both Buddhists and students of comparative religions agree on the point that religions are products of human history and culture, not of direct divine intervention into history.) We have created our problems, and only we can solve them. That becomes something of a bottom line for Buddhists. We need to train our minds to be less attached, less mistaken, less shortsighted, and, most of all, less self-centered. After all, discomfort with religious others is a form of self-centeredness.

How do we take that perspective into solving the "problem" of religious diversity? *First*, consistently, I will argue that religious diversity exists because it is psychologically and spiritually impossible for all human beings to follow one theological outlook or spiritual path. We are not built that way. That's just not how we are. Religious diversity, which is inevitable, natural, and normal, flows from our different spiritual and psychological inclinations. Therefore, inevitably, we will encounter religious others. *Second*, I will also consistently argue that the acid test of a religion's worth lies with what kind of tools it provides its adherents for coping gracefully and kindly with their worlds and the other beings who inhabit them. Discomfort with religious diversity and the wish to abolish it is a psychological and spiritual deficiency arising in an untrained human mind, a mind that does not know how to relax and be at ease with what is, with things as they are, as Buddhists like to say. Solving the "problem" of religious diversity has much more to do with human beings' attitudes toward one another than with somehow adjudicating their rather different theological and metaphysical views. Thus, I am suggesting that we should start, not with religious creeds and questions about religious or metaphysical truth, but with questions about how people are—different from one another—and about how well religions function to help them live with how they are.

Religion: Not a One-Size-Fits-All Phenomenon

At least regarding internal diversity, some religions, especially Buddhism and Hinduism start with the premise that people have very different religious and spiritual needs and capabilities, which means that a religion has to provide different options for its members. It is foolish and foolhardy to try to force all members into conformity, into a common mold, lifestyle, and belief system. Different capabilities and needs are, in the long run, simply different and should not be evaluated hierarchically, though it is easy to slip into such evaluations. Two traditional Buddhist phrases praise this internal diversity: the "eighty-four thousand *dharma* gates" and the "variety of skillful means like the rainbow." This multiplicity has not been regarded as a flaw either in the religion or in the people who need methods different from one another. I find no hint in Buddhist thought that in an ideal world there would only be one *dharma* gate and everyone would practice and think in the same manner. Nevertheless, Buddhists have argued about whose list of eighty-four thousand *dharma* gates is better. Though Buddhists of all stripes do expect internal diversity, they still can and do succumb to disagreements and rather nasty conflicts about which diversities are acceptable and which are not. In other words, internal sectarianism is quite alive and well within Buddhism. However, that sectarianism exists within the *expectation* that there will be religious diversity rather than with the judgment that the diversity itself is a failing. In an ideal Buddhist world, there would be religious diversity; it's just that some things are off limits nevertheless—a topic to which we shall return soon.

There are several prominent examples of how Buddhists handle internal diversity. Buddhism is a highly monastic religion, and, according to many, a monastic lifestyle is almost required for serious practice of this religion. Attaining Buddhism's goal of enlightenment is not easy, and there is no deity or vicarious means of salvation to make the path and the goal more lightweight. It takes time and effort to walk that path, and monastic institutions are designed precisely to provide an environment conducive to making that effort. Nevertheless, it is also recognized that though the monastic lifestyle might be ideal, it simply is not appropriate for everyone. Many people would be miserable and unsuccessful if that were the only option available. They may well not have the talent for celibacy, for intensive textual study, or for intensive meditation. It would also be difficult for lay practitioners if they were consistently told that they are less worthy Buddhists because of their lack of talent for a monastic lifestyle. Instead, Buddhism has developed a vision of symbiosis and mutual interdependence between its monastic and nonmonastic communities. The lay community is essential for the survival of the monastic community; without its economic support, monks and nuns could not survive. Nor is the role of being a serious Buddhist practitioner limited to the monastics. Most forms of Buddhism have developed traditions of serious nonmonastic practice as well. Western Buddhism is almost entirely nonmonastic, which is something of an experiment, but an experiment that seems to be going relatively well. As the Buddha said many times in the Pali *suttas* (among the oldest Buddhist records and those most likely to contain some teachings from the historical Buddha), the normative Buddhist society consists of monks, nuns, laymen, and laywomen. Religion simply cannot be a one-size-fits-all phenomenon.

One might reply that all religions provide for such differing aptitudes and talents with specialized institutional roles. But the matter of religious diversity is really about different religious *teachings, views, or doctrines.* Can there really be diversity on such matters, which most religions regard as of utmost importance? In fact, the Buddhist path always begins and ends with *view,* and it is frequently said that without right view, any progress on the path to enlightenment will be very difficult. However, counterintuitive as it may sound, in Buddhism view is fundamentally not a matter of doctrine, belief system, or creed. As will be dealt with more extensively in the next two chapters, those must all be left behind for real insight to dawn. Right view, which is fundamentally equivalent to enlightenment, transcends word and concept. But in the meanwhile, just as different lifestyles work better for different people, so different doctrines, teachings and practices may be needed for different people or at different stages of the path. Some people have a tremendous appetite for devotion, essentially a dualistic practice even in nondualist Buddhism, while others find devotion distasteful and much prefer the rigors of philosophical analysis. Similarly, some people thrive on very demanding regimens of meditation while others handle administration well. Some people find theism the only belief that makes sense to them while others find it completely distasteful, utter nonsense.

The Primacy of Methods over Theory

The need for religious diversity even regarding teachings and practices is handled within Buddhism with the concept of *upaya,* usually translated "skillful means," or "methods." I will mainly use the translation "methods." Though perhaps more prevalent in Mahayana forms of Buddhism, it is important in all forms of Buddhism. About *upaya,* three points are essential. First, any *upaya* is a tool, to be used to accomplish something else; it is not an end in itself, which means no *upaya* is an ultimate. Second, methods are necessarily plural. One-size-fits-all does not work in the delicate task of birthing nonaggressive, compassionate, wise people, and no one tool works for all the different tasks that need to be done. Needles and screwdrivers are not interchangeable. Third, the criteria by which methods are evaluated is their usefulness and effectiveness in getting the required job done.

It is also important to understand at the outset that I am not suggesting that Buddhists have historically used their notion of *upaya* to think about external religious diversity. It has mainly been used as a tool with which to think about internal religious diversity, and even in that usage, there are some problems, which will be noted later in this chapter. But, working as a Buddhist critical and constructive thinker (a.k.a., a theologian), I am extending the way this concept has been used historically because I think that it offers very fruitful avenues of approach that have not been explored heretofore by Buddhists or by other theologians to the question of how to flourish with religious diversity. Though this model of acceptance of internal religious diversity has not been consistently applied to discussions of worldwide religious diversity across deeper intellectual or theological divides, I believe that boundary could easily be crossed, provided that it is truly understood what *upaya* is and what it isn't. It is especially important to understand the relationship between religious doctrines and *upaya*, which will be discussed extensively below.

Discussions of *upaya* begin with the observation that in the Pali *suttas*, the historical Buddha is portrayed as having taught different things to different people or in different circumstances. *Upaya* (Methods) is essentially the skill to give teachings and practices appropriate to the students—teachings and practices that will actually help them. This skill is highly prized in Buddhism. This understanding of Skillful Methods, by definition, includes the claim that profound teachings may be useless if students are unprepared to assimilate them, for whatever reasons. It would be much better to give them other teachings instead. Thus, teachings are contextual rather than timelessly abstract and universally applicable. Because contexts will be diverse and varied, skillful teachings must also be diverse and varied—that is to say, multiple rather than singular.

In Mahayana Buddhism, teachings on *upaya* expanded significantly and became much more important. In part, *upaya* offered a ready explanation of why so many different versions of Buddhism had developed. The earlier explanation found in the Pali *suttas* that the Buddha had taught differently to different audiences simply expanded to cover much greater variety. Mahayana sutras, all composed somewhat later than the Pali *suttas*, all portray the Buddha either teaching or approving of the teachings being given in the sutra. Most Mahayana sutras also portray the Buddha as revealing a new teaching that he had withheld previously. But given that Mahayana sutras do not merely repeat one another but teach very different points of view, and that all of them purport to be the word of the Buddha, therefore the skillful means employed by the Buddha would have expanded considerably. Many versions of Mahayana Buddhism suggest how to classify or arrange these different sutras, all of which are deemed to be authentic teachings of the Buddha, even though they led to the formation of a number of diverse Buddhist sects or denominations. At the head of the list, of course, is always the sutra upon which one's own school is founded.

As part of our considerations of *upaya*, it is helpful to discuss more fully two dyads very common in Buddhist expression. One is the dyad of Wisdom and Compassion, and the other is the dyad of Wisdom and Methods. One really can't elevate either of these dyads over the other as more important, nor can one reduce either dyad to a unity. The relationship between the elements of a dyad is easier to understand through symbolism or analogies than through linear logic. For both, their relationship is said to be like that between vowels and consonants, female and male, left and right hands. In all cases, Wisdom is the one first mentioned in the pair. In both cases, each element of the pair is inseparable from the other and both are equally necessary in the dance of life, but the members of the pair do not melt into one. It is not emphasized that the two hands are on one body or that vowels and consonants together form an alphabet, though, of course, that is also true. This is one good example of how, when talking about truth or how things are, Buddhists always prefer both/and logic to either/or logic. The relationship between the elements of either dyad is nondual, as is the relationship between the dyad and the phenomenon of which they are parts. In Buddhism, nonduality is considered to be far more profound than unity or oneness, which often obliterates difference and diversity.

One may wonder why Wisdom is paired sometimes with Methods and sometimes with Compassion. Is it because Lady Wisdom is fickle? No. It is because while Compassion should flow from true Wisdom, conventional compassion is often not very wise and easily becomes misguided and aggressive because Methods are lacking, undeveloped, or monolithic. So in order for Wisdom to act compassionately rather than stupidly, she must act in concert with Skillful Methods. In the exercise of true Compassion, Skillful Methods are equally as important as Wisdom. One without the other is quite ineffective and inept. Wisdom without compassion can be cold and indifferent while compassion without wisdom can be both stupid and aggressive. It is the presence of Skillful Methods, the rare ability to assess a situation accurately and then have the discipline to act appropriately, within the limits of that situation, that determines whether or not Compassion and Wisdom are acting in concert.

Partly as a response to the increased role of *upaya* in portrayals of the Buddha's teachings in Mahayana sutras, Skillful Methods becomes a *paramita*, the seventh *paramita*, in Mahayana lists of the ten *paramitas*, or transcendent virtues. These are skills or virtues the bodhisattva must perfect in her or his long journey to the kind of enlightenment experienced by a Buddha, that is to say, by one who discovers the teachings in a time and place in which they have not yet been discovered. In this list, *upaya* is far down the road to full enlightenment, being placed after *Prajna* (Wisdom), which is considered to be the highest of the *paramitas* attainable by an ordinary human being. This is because, in a sense, possessing good skills is more difficult than attaining some wisdom, and also because it is Skillful Means that enables Wisdom to become effective and relevant. I think this is quite easy to illustrate. On many complex issues, it is not so difficult to have the right answer. How hard is it to determine that gender equality and equity are superior to patriarchy and male dominance? How easy is it to get that point across to both women and men who still prefer the privileges male dominance brings them? One can easily illustrate this relationship between Wisdom and Skillful Means with reference to almost any difficult and tense political or religious discussion. Skillful Means will require great verbal skill, whereas Wisdom is much more intuitive, even preverbal. It takes the right words said at the right time and in the right manner to be effective in getting others to assent to one's wisdom. Furthermore, there is no one right verbal formula that is going to work in all situations. Remember that one of the three defining characteristics of Method is that Methods are necessarily *multiple*. Needles and screwdrivers are not interchangeable. Because people are so different spiritually and intellectually, one-size-fits-all does not work regarding religions.

Religious Teachings as *Upaya*, not *Prajna*

Where do religious teachings fit into this dyad of Wisdom and Method? The usual expectation is that religious teachings would have to do with Wisdom rather than Method because religious teachings purport to be about reality, which would be in the domain of Wisdom. But this is not accurate. Religious *teachings* as well as religious practices are essentially in the realm of *Upaya*, not in the realm of *Prajna*, as Buddhists see it. They are essentially a Method that helps one approach Wisdom, which transcends word and concept, but they are not the content of Wisdom itself. Without such methods, one would be lost, but one is equally lost and mistaken if one confuses the tool with accomplishing the task for which the tool is designed—in this case, the task is developing wisdom. Religious teachings are meant to be contemplated until their meanings are so internalized that one's acts are infused with those meanings and are truly compassionate. Religious teachings are utterly ineffective when they are only memorized and clung to. If religious teachings are understood in this way, as a means of approaching clearer insight into the nature of reality, rather than as claims about what reality is, appreciating religious diversity and flourishing with it are much more possible. There would be no reason to expect verbal agreement at the level of doctrine, and, thus, no discomfort about doctrinal diversity. According to this way of understanding the role of teaching or doctrine in religions, doctrines are necessary, but they do not have the finality that is often attributed to them in many religious systems. I suggest that it could be very useful to Christians, who have been so overwhelmingly concerned about correct doctrine, to think about doctrines as tools rather than truths.

Buddhists would agree with most religious believers that some doctrines can be mistaken or unwise. What would that mean? Either that they lead their adherents in a demonstrably wrong direction, or that they simply do not accord with anything discoverable through analysis or meditative investigations. In either case, unwise or unskillful doctrines should obviously be abandoned. However, the goal is not to eliminate all doctrines except for one. Even in Buddhist systems that do talk of the "highest view," it is also argued that many doctrines and practices have proximate value and therefore are necessary and should be retained rather than eliminated. They will be more helpful to some people than a more refined or elevated doctrine that they cannot understand, an analysis they cannot follow, or a meditation practice they cannot do. Religions cannot be a one-size-fits-all phenomenon.

Recognizing that doctrines are essentially tools that help people attain greater insight also means that we can account for and respect their cultural situatedness, which deeply affects their content. One of the reasons doctrines are so varied is the cultural distinctiveness that is another aspect of the variety that makes it impossible for religion to be a one-size-fits-all phenomenon. We can make sense of almost any doctrine if we take its own time and place, its own cultural context, into account. It we pay attention to its cultural context, we can appreciate the doctrine, even if it does not appeal to us at all—so long as its adherents are not trying to coerce us into accepting it. For example, of all Christian theologies, none is so irritating to me as that of Karl Barth. But when I understand the specific situation it is addressing I can understand more of its rationale. Though Barth probably thought he was making comments relevant for all people in all times and places, if we understand his thought more in its own time and place, it makes more sense. If a doctrine's relevance is limited to its own time and place, it is more understandable and acceptable to those in other times and places. Regarding doctrines as culturally specific tools also helps us understand that it is nearly impossible for a teaching or a doctrine couched in words and concepts to be so abstract that it applies to and appeals to all people everywhere.

I once heard a wise Buddhist teacher whom I respect a great deal state that the reason for religious diversity is that each group of people ends up with the religion that can tame it—in other words, with the one religion among the many that they could actually hear and respond to, the one religion that could actually make them more disciplined and loving. For example, she said, Buddhism would not have been able to tame the people of the Middle East, which is why it doesn't flourish there.[3] Other methods are more suitable to those cultures.

So to flourish amid religious diversity, set aside, simply bracket, questions about the truth of various religious doctrines. Those are very interesting and fruitful questions for interreligious dialogue and mutual learning, but that is not the foundation on which a theology and ethic that fosters flourishing with religious diversity can be built. It seems to me to be a mistake to begin with the standard questions considered thus far in theologies of religions: questions about whether there is a universal religious truth, about the truth of various religions, about other religions' partial truth in relation to my religion, or about how there could be more than one true religion. Instead of wondering about how to parse out or think about the different truth claims contained in religious doctrines, put those questions aside as unresolveable and therefore somewhat useless for thinking about how to flourish with religious diversity. Any possible truth value of religious doctrines is elusive and evanescent. People simply don't agree on it. Even a single individual doesn't usually espouse the same religious truths for their entire lifetime; I certainly haven't. Within the various religions, theologians have never been able to agree about their truth claims, and ideas about what is true theologically change radically from generation to generation. Given that religious doctrines are conceptual tools attempting to articulate experience and to respond to ever-changing and varied cultural-historical situations, that is not surprising and should not cause emotional difficulty to religious believers. Given how people are, that is to be expected. Like methods or *upaya* in general, religious teachings or doctrines—a specific kind of *upaya*—are necessarily multiple and plural.

Therefore, a theology of religions does not really need to deal with questions of the truth of the various religions, or worry about the fact that religions teach very different things. If you say something different from me about deity, ultimate reality, what happens after death, or any other such weighty matters, where does the problem lie? If you say that my views, different from yours, endanger my ultimate well-being, how can you possibly demonstrate that? If your views promote hostility and hatred, that is a

3. Jetsun Khandro Rinpoche, Oral teachings given at Lotus Garden Retreat Center, Stanley, VA, August–September 2011.

problem, and must be dealt with. But if you believe that Jesus Christ is the only savior for all people, and I can't make any sense of that view, what's the problem? The only problem would be your trying to impose belief in Jesus on me in any form, however subtle, or my doing the same regarding my views. If agreement on what to do with all these differing beliefs is necessary for us to flourish in the midst of religious diversity, we are more likely to struggle than to flourish. What all these claims could share is that they are skillful methods that promote more appropriate religious sensibilities in those who think with them and adhere to them.

The one warning I would sound about this solution to the question of how to think about religious diversity—to regard doctrines as tools with which people think and through which they develop spiritually, rather than as anything that actually captures the content of Wisdom—is that it can easily slide into a species of inclusivism. Granting that many doctrines may be useful and relevant, it is then very tempting to line them up relative to one another, ranking them from lower teachings to the highest teachings. When that happens, of course the doctrinal system that winds up at the top of the heap is that system to which the list maker happens to adhere. In such cases, the inevitability and naturalness of religious diversity is not really acknowledged. This has often happened within Buddhism, which is more likely to find some relevance to most doctrines than to reject any of them outright, though the category of heretic does exist in Buddhist thought.[4]

Much of my own work inside the Buddhist tradition and especially within the particular lineage to which I belong is bound up in critiquing this inclusive use of the notion of skillful means. Many of the Buddhists who use it to classify various denominations within Buddhism are genuinely unaware of how offensive it can be to "include" others as having less adequate forms of one's own understanding. They claim that they mean no offense at all and are acknowledging the relevance, even the necessity, of these more preliminary doctrines and practices. The problem occurs when the same name is applied to both a preliminary stage of the path, as understood in one's own system, and also to another historical form of Buddhism with its own understandings of how mature spirituality develops. This has happened extensively in Mahayana Buddhist polemics, especially in the way Mahayanists use the derogatory term *hinayana*, but this way of using the concept of skillful means to understand religious diversity is not at all what I have in mind.[5]

4. Kiblinger, *Buddhist Inclusivism*, demonstrates some of the ways that Buddhists have sometimes developed inclusivist rather than pluralist views of religious others.

5. See Gross, "Buddhist History for Buddhist Practitioners," for a preliminary discussion of some of these issues.

What I propose taking from Buddhist understandings of skillful means into discussions of how to flourish with religious diversity is the modesty with which religious doctrines and verbal teachings can be taken. We do not have to claim timeless truth for them. It is sufficient that they are relevant and helpful to their own believers in the time and place of their own situatedness. If we concede the limitations of what any verbally stated religious doctrine could ever do (be true for all people for all time), the existence of religious diversity is unproblematic. Theological *differences,* even those as big as the difference between theism and nontheism, are *not important*—at least not for purposes of solving the "problem" of religious diversity, though they may be very interesting for interreligious dialogue and mutual learning. This understanding of the limitations of religious doctrines also has the virtue that unlike many proposals for learning how to negotiate religious diversity peacefully, to accept the limitations of religious doctrines, no one needs to change currently held doctrines for different doctrines. All that needs to be conceded is that whatever doctrine may be our current favorite, it is not the final, really true doctrine among the many contenders for that title. As we saw with exclusive truth claims in the previous chapter, the content of the beliefs is not the problem. It is the way those beliefs are held that causes all the suffering that results from making exclusive truth claims. What other people believe and whether it is true or not, whatever that could possibly mean, should be irrelevant to me, *so long as others' beliefs do not lead them to engage in conduct that is harmful to others*, which includes aggressive missionary activity. That is the acid test that should be applied to every and any religious belief.

Beyond the Specter of Relativism: Evaluating Religious Ideas as Tools to Promote Living Well with Religious Diversity

I suggest that the focus of discussions in theologies of religion should change from concern about truth in religion to discussions of usefulness in religion, defining usefulness as that which enables us to live more comfortably in an inevitably diverse world. Then the primary question becomes, not the *truth* of religions (mine or others), but their *effectiveness* at encouraging their/our ethical treatment of ourselves and others. This could also be phrased as a concern with religions' *usefulness*, by which I mean their ability to effect meaningful transformation toward kindness, compassion, and nonaggression in their adherents. Are their methods, their *upayas*, including their various doctrines, working or not? What *upayas*, what tools, including what doctrines, would promote true kindness and compassion in those who utilize them? This arena, *method*, is the arena in which it is relevant to discuss religious differences and their consequences—not the arena of non-empirical metaphysical or theological truth claims.

For it is not the case that if we don't evaluate whether specific religious ideas are true, then we fall into the specter of relativism and have no standards at all. We have a very high standard: the ethics of those who hold the various ideas. It is not the case, of course, that if we evaluate religious ideas in terms of their ethical impact rather than in terms of their metaphysical accuracy, we will come to agreement easily. But uniformity is not the point. My claim is that we have to learn how to flourish with religious diversity, not to find some common ground that we all agree upon. Or perhaps it would be more accurate to say that the common ground we need to find is the agreement that religious diversity is here to stay, and it would be better if we could live well with that reality rather than resisting it or fighting over it. Then what is up for discussion is *how best* to do that. The claim that the ethical implications of doctrines are much more relevant to that discussion than their metaphysical truth follows easily.

It doesn't really matter what religious views people espouse if they mistreat themselves or others. No matter how lofty or orthodox their views may be, or how sophisticated their understanding of emptiness may be, their religion is not working properly, is a false religion, if it does not result in kindness and compassion. Thus, people who engage in strong-armed, forceful missionary tactics, such as terrorizing people about what will happen to them if they don't convert, are not preaching a true religion; it is not a true religion at least as it is being preached and practiced by those particular adherents. Another example of such ethical misconduct in the name of religion concerns those who insist on trying to make everyone in society adhere to their values—for example by trying to outlaw sexual behaviors disapproved of by a particular religion. This kind of attempt on the part of followers of one or more of the existing religions to force universal religious behavior in a religiously diverse world is the only truly negative aspect of religious diversity. The mere existence of differing ideas about religious truth cannot be harmful; only the attempt to do away religious diversity is harmful.

If people are kind and compassionate to each other, to strangers, to animals, and to the environment, why should I worry about whether or not they believe in Jesus Christ as their only savior, regard the Qur'an as the deity's final revelation to humanity, meditate correctly on emptiness, or don't adhere to any of the traditional religions? Would their kindness be improved if they changed their theology? Or, as I was told in my youth, is their kindness irrelevant because they will go to hell for having incorrect theological views and ideas? Mother Theresa and Albert Schweitzer were both headed there, I was assured. Thus, we see how bizarre religion can become when doctrinal truth expressed in words takes on ultimate importance. Let us put aside, once and for all, the question of truth in our discussions of how to live well with religious diversity. Let us center on questions of ethics, not metaphysics; let us focus on the impact our theologies have on our lives rather than searching for a generic theology we can all live with or some wiggle room in our own doctrines that allows for the legitimacy of other religions. It is more important that we learn how to live together than that we all think alike religiously. And since we are never going to all think alike religiously, we must not pin peace and security on theological agreement. Theological agreement is irrelevant to building a better, more peaceful world.

What Methods promote decency and kindness? Which Methods detract from decency and kindness, and perhaps even promote hatred and discord? Since all religious beliefs, doctrines, and teachings are in the realm of Method, not the realm of Wisdom, we can now have a discussion of religious doctrines focusing, not on whether they are true, but on whether they are useful.[6] Such a discussion would be long and fruitful, and would probably lead to the conclusion that most or all religions have some useful methods, and most or all religions have at times fallen into methods that promote suffering. When we put the debate on this plane, which is where I think it belongs, I doubt we will find absolute winners or losers. Using these criteria, we will find that all major, long-lasting religions are both true and false. We will also find that there is no criterion whatsoever by which we could possibly evaluate and rank whole religions, as if they were monolithic entities.

This empirical demonstration of both ethical success and failure on the part of all major religions demonstrates in another way that exclusive, or even inclusive, theologies of religion do not have merit. As pluralist theologian John Hick, who also argues that the truth of religions turns on "the observable fruits of religion in human life" likes to argue,

> And what has made me, personally, come to doubt the unique superiority of my own Christian faith is that these observable fruits do not seem to be specially concentrated in the Christian church, but, on the contrary, seem to be spread more or less evenly around the world with its different cultures and religions.[7]

Then he reverses the argument. If Christianity (or any other religion that makes such claims) does, indeed, have a "uniquely full revelation of God and a uniquely direct relationship with God," then,

6. Kimball, *When Religion Becomes Evil*, is a very helpful discussion of which religious methods promote hatred and discord rather than peace and harmony.

7. Hick, "The Next Step beyond Dialogue," 8.

Surely this ought to produce some noticeable difference in our lives. Christians *ought* to be better human beings than those who lack these inestimable spiritual benefits . . . We either have to claim, against the evidence of our experience, that as members of the body of Christ, Christians in general are better human beings than non-Christians or we are going to have to rethink those of our traditional doctrines that entail that.[8]

Because Hick spent his early life as an enthusiastic and quite fundamentalist evangelical Christian who did take Christian exclusive truth claims very seriously, his movement away from that position is noteworthy. He narrates how moving to Birmingham, England, a city with great racial, cultural, and religious diversity changed him.

And occasionally attending worship in mosque and synagogue, temple and gurudwara, it was evident that essentially the same kind of thing is taking place in them as in a Christian church— namely human beings opening their minds to a higher divine Reality known as personal and good and as demanding righteousness and love between man and man [*sic*]. I could see that the Sikh faith, for instance, is to the devout Sikh, what the Christian faith is to the sincere Christian; but that each faith is, naturally enough perceived by its adherents as being unique and absolute.[9]

In an older, pioneering article first published in 1976 and arguing against the plausibility of knowing by revelation that other religions are false, Wilfred Cantwell Smith reports that he has encountered people who are troubled by empirical evidence that people in non-Christian religions are good, decent people.

Instead of being overjoyed that some Hindus and Buddhists and some Muslims lead a pious and moral life and seem very near to God, . . . I have sometimes witnessed just the opposite: an emotional resistance to the news, men [*sic*] hoping firmly that it might not be so, with a covert fear that it might be.[10]

8. Ibid.

9. Hick, *God Has Many Names*, 5.

10. Smith, "The Christian in a Religiously Plural World," 99.

Beliefs and Practices That Harm or Help

The topic of what beliefs and practices might be *upayas* useful to promoting flourishing with religious diversity cannot be dealt with exhaustively in this context. In fact, that is a topic better suited to multifaith inquiry and a full book of its own. However, to better demonstrate the kinds of suggestions that can fruitfully be made, and also to demonstrate that these are trends or tendencies found in many religions, rather than a matter of some religions being true as wholes and others being false as wholes, I will make a few suggestions.

First on the list of harmful beliefs and practices would be any that promote the superiority of the in-group, whatever it might be, against others. Thus, exclusive truth claims rank high as beliefs that are completely counter to living peacefully and flourishing with religious diversity. The cruelty that so easily results from exclusive truth claims should be contradicted by the basic impulse toward kindness and compassion that is part of every major religion, even though religions do disagree on some particularities about compassion. Part of that whole package includes not encouraging people to hold their beliefs aggressively or defensively. Unless one is being aggressively challenged, there is little reason for one to feel combative, threatened, or undermined when encountering someone who holds quite different views and opinions. Even then, someone well versed in Skillful Methods would refrain from polarizing the situation by replying in kind, but would seek ways to defuse the confrontational nature of the interaction.

When I was thinking about this question of harmful beliefs and practices while preparing to write this chapter, my mind repeatedly moved to a phenomenon that very few theologians of religion have taken up, probably because most of them are men. One of the things held in common by most religions is male dominance, with a good deal of sexism and misogyny often thrown in as well. In some religions, this male dominance is exacerbated by exclusively male language used to speak of the deity. Perhaps this male dominance is the often-sought lowest common denominator that all religions can agree upon, given that this practice bridges even the wide gap between theistic and nontheistic religions! But there is also hardly any other facet of religions that has caused as much suffering as male dominance. Such a negative lowest common denominator is hardly a healthy basis on which to build an overarching theology of religions. However, it could serve as a unifying element for religions as a common problem that all religions could work to solve separately and together.

Finally, when discussing beliefs that may not be useful *upaya*, though I will not develop the arguments in any way in this context, I have long been puzzled by the doctrine of original sin in Christianity. One of the greatest contrasts between typical Christian and typical Buddhist beliefs concerns the working basis of our human potential. Buddhists regard having a human birth as something to be celebrated and rejoiced in, as the best possible circumstance one could have. Buddhists also regard human nature as basically good, fundamentally okay, capable of enlightenment. Fleshing out this proposition would require many pages and cannot be undertaken in this context. Nevertheless, I suggest that it offers a significant contrast to Christian notions of original sin, which seem to predispose people to negativity, and to have many other unfortunate consequences. The utility of this Buddhist teaching about peoples' Buddha-nature, or inherent potential for enlightenment and compassion, will be relevant at many points in this book. Such questions are fruitful topics for interreligious dialogue, one of the main topics to be taken up in this book's final section.

What about candidates for practices and beliefs that help, that work well as an *upaya* promoting flourishing with religious diversity? I will name only two at this time. The first is to encourage rigorous analysis of everything one has been taught by anyone. For Buddhists, the *locus classicus* for this practice is a *sutta* in the Pali canon called the *Kalama Sutta*. The context is that the Buddha has come to visit a town on his wanderings through north India. The residents of the town tell him that they are visited by many wandering religious teachers and that each of them insists that his teachings alone are true and that all the others are false. The Buddha's reply is a ringing recommendation of uncensored analytical, critical thought.

> It is right that you should be doubtful, Kalamas, right that you should be uncertain. Your uncertainty concerns something that is indeed a matter of doubt.
>
> Kalamas, you should not go along with something because of what you have been told, because of authority, because of tradition, because of accordance with scripture, on the grounds of reason, on the grounds of logic, because of analytical thought, because of abstract theoretical pondering, because of the appearance of the speaker, or because some ascetic is your teacher. When you know for yourselves that particular qualities are unwholesome, blameworthy, censured by the wise, and lead to harm and suffering when taken on and pursued, then you should give them up.[11]

Then the Buddha reverses the language, saying that one should take on what one has found for oneself to be wholesome, not leading to harm and suffering, or the like.

---

11. Gethin, *Sayings of the Buddha*, 252.

My second recommendation for *upayas* that promote flourishing with religious diversity is a deep spiritual life of one's own based on meditation, contemplation, and contemplative prayer according to the practices of one's own tradition. This recommendation might seem quite the opposite of the previous recommendation of rigorous critical analysis. But, as someone who engages in both, I can affirm that they actually work together very well and complement each other. When I talk of such religious practices, I am not talking about perfunctory ritual performances merely following directions by rote. I am talking about deep introspection, so that one truly understands the basic teachings of one's religions. Such practices have a great deal to do with developing internal mental attitudes and abilities to flourish with diversity rather than being made uncomfortable by difference.

Summary and Conclusions

This chapter is central to my overall argument. In it, I claim that we should begin our considerations of how to deal with the "problem" of religious diversity by shifting our gaze from Ultimate Realities conceived of as largely external to religious human beings. Religious diversity is necessary because of how humans are—different in their capabilities and inclinations, and also in their cultural and historical situatedness. Then, I draw heavily on Buddhist notions of *upaya*, or skillful methods: the necessarily multiple tools that religions use to train and tame their members. An important part of the argument suggests that religious doctrines are better understood as tools for human transformation than as propositions whose truth or falsity we can ascertain from the outside. We leave aside the question of conflicting truth claims among the many religions as not central to the task of learning how to flourish with religious diversity. Instead, we should ask whether a religion's *upayas* are working to transform its members in positive directions, toward greater kindness and compassion. In other words, "by their fruits you shall know them." Using that criterion for evaluating religious doctrines, we find that all major religions have both succeeded and failed. It is especially important to note that religions with the most extensive and explicit claims that all humans need to accept their exclusive truths do not have especially good track records in this regard. I end with a few suggestions about religious views and practices that hurt or help people develop towards being comfortable with and appreciating religious diversity.

Chapter 6

Of Fingers, Moons, and Rafts

The Limits of Religious Language

ONE RESULT OF MY interreligious interactions is that I have come to the conclusion that no issue is more central to flourishing with religious diversity than overcoming the tendency of some participants in those discussions to rely too much on words and concepts. As I see it, nothing so inhibits flourishing with religious diversity as overestimating what religious language can do. This can take the form of believing that one's own religious language is not humanly created at all but is an unmediated revelation from a transhuman realm. Or it can take the form of excessive attachment to one's own specific religious language, to the words and creeds that one has studied, cherished, and assimilated into one's being. To be sure, those specific words, creeds, and practices have been very helpful to oneself. But why assume that they will be equally effective for everyone else? Can one not realize that words that may mean a great deal to oneself do not impress another in the same way, and that the other person is, nevertheless, not necessarily any poorer? I propose that some Buddhist methods of working with words and ideas, which are applicable outside the Buddhist context, can help us to a genuine appreciation of religious diversity and take us well beyond any desire to smooth out the differences between religions, to search for some basic convergence of views, or to dream of a "good-parts" version composed of all the available materials.

Those most uncomfortable with religious diversity have a very high opinion of what words and concepts can accomplish, so this discussion is vital. They often claim that for them some words and concepts are non-negotiable. They attribute to words and concepts more accuracy and finality than they could possibly have, regarding them as somehow conveying ultimate truths. But in actuality, such clinging has led to a great deal of suffering. I make this claim both against more conservative religious people, who seem to think that holding correct verbal doctrines is a matter of life or death, and against more liberal/pluralist commentators, who think that we can find a verbal formula underlying religious difference upon which we could all agree.

It is not that I dismiss words and concepts in favor of pointing and grunting. As a highly verbal person who made my livelihood through verbal communication, who has written many books and articles, and who now specializes in *dharma* teaching—a highly verbal enterprise—I love and respect words and concepts a great deal. One can do a lot with them. I would also argue that one can do more with them if one respects their limits as well as their potential.

The Impossibility of Unmediated Words

One of the more common ways religions ignore the limits of words and concepts is by claiming that their own words are not the result of human cultural creativity but that they dropped, unmediated and fully formed, from some other realm into our human world and are, therefore, unblemished by human bias or error. This claim is not limited to the Western religions, all of which claim that the deity spoke directly to them but to no one else, at least not as completely. Even nontheistic Buddhism has found ways to attribute its texts to something beyond mere human authorship, though not all forms of Buddhism make such claims. That such claims exist at all in Buddhism demonstrates how reluctant human beings can be to claim and own their own religious innovations.

Such claims first came into Buddhism with the rise of Mahayana Buddhism and its new scriptures, which purport to be, like the older scriptures preserved in the Pali language, dialogues between the Buddha and his disciples. Except that they are vastly different from the earlier dialogues. Anyone with any minor skills in critically assessing texts who reads the two sets of texts side by side could not fail to come to such a conclusion. How could they actually be the words of the Buddha? Mahayanists claimed that these sutras had been hidden by the Buddha because his disciples were not yet ready to understand what he was teaching in them, and that they were later retrieved from the realm of *nagas*, water-dwelling spirits popular in Indian mythology, by Mahayana teachers who journeyed there to get these texts. Not quite divine revelation but certainly not owning the words of the Mahayana sutras as the creations of Mahayana Buddhists living some hundreds of years after the death of the historical Buddha! Obviously, if these texts could be passed off as the actual words of the Buddha, their authority would be greatly increased.

Tibetan Buddhists have developed an even more ingenious strategy that amounts to continuing revelation. Certain respected teachers, called *tertons* or "treasure revealers" either compose texts or "find" texts that had purportedly been hidden by Padmasambhava, the eighth-century Indian teacher largely responsible for first bringing Buddhism to Tibet. Just as it is taught about the Mahayana sutras, so it is taught that these texts too would come to light when circumstance were such that their message was appropriate and they could, therefore, be heard. Tibetans believe that these newly revealed texts are more reliable than older texts because there are fewer links between them and their reliable source and thus much less chance for corruption to have entered the process of their transmission. This process continues to the present day. During my lifetime a Tibetan teacher discovered some "mind *terma*," texts composed in the present rather than having been hidden centuries ago, in northern Wisconsin, about fifty miles from where I grew up! It is not clear whether these texts are considered to be completely unmediated, and thus free of human input, though I have heard Tibetans claim that they are completely reliable because their source is nonhuman and thus much more trustworthy than anything authored by a human being. A scholar of religion evaluating this phenomenon could regard it as an ingenious device for keeping religions more up to date and introducing needed changes into them. Sometimes one really wishes that those who believe so ardently in the Bible also allowed for *terma* to be discovered in contemporary times! But, unfortunately, such a process could also reinforce conservative as well as progressive elements in any religion.

Certainly the way revelation is presented in the monotheistic religions goes much further than these Buddhist examples of quasi-revelation. In these cases, there is no question that the text, the words, are regarded as being completely unmediated and, therefore, completely reliable. Though I am skeptical about Buddhist claims about their texts, the possibility of unmediated divine words found in the Bible to the extent claimed by biblical literalists strikes me as incoherent, an oxymoron. As anyone discovers when we try to put into words either what God is really like or what is the natural state of mind, or whatever else a religion may point to as ultimate, words are very limited. They just don't go there, a fact readily admitted by all theists in certain contexts. So how could scriptures be unmediated words having nothing to do with the historical, cultural context in which they were received? Even if human beings do have unmediated experiences in which they encounter deity or ultimate reality directly, the second they come out such direct experience and try to communicate about it, they would be back in the historical and cultural limitations of their own context, quite far from the transcendent or the nondual. They would find themselves unable to fully communicate whatever they had experienced or heard. Language can only express duality well; at the nondual it can only hint. This simple fact has always seemed to me to indicate that it is simply impossible to have fully authoritative, unmediated, reliable texts (i.e., revealed texts). To claim otherwise is to try to make words do what they simply are incapable of doing.

Even stopping short of regarding words as revealed and, therefore, unmediated, religions and religious people often attribute to words and concepts far more ability and relevance than they actually can have, in my view. On this point, Buddhists are nearly unanimous, and I think this skepticism about words and concepts is something very helpful to flourishing with religious diversity.

Fingers Pointing to the Moon: Words—What They Can't Do

In the fall of 2010, the Society for Buddhist-Christian Studies, with which I have been involved for most of my career, held a session on my lifework during the annual meetings of the American Academy of Religion. One of the commentators was Paul Knitter, a colleague whom I respect a great deal and from whom I have learned a lot. He commented on my frequent citation of Buddhist claims about the limitations of words in the following way. *"Isn't it true that Buddhists do not—because they cannot—throw away their rafts?* I am asking whether Rita may be running the risk of neglecting the importance of religion and of religious doctrine."[1] In my reply, I wrote,

> "Oh yes, we do throw away our rafts." This does not mean that we disregard the various relative practices, but that we understand that they are *relative*. It seems strange to suggest that someone who spends as much time as I do on religious practice doesn't understand the value of such relative practices.[2]

1. Knitter, "Rita Gross," 83.
2. Gross, "Thank You, Friends and Colleagues," 96.

As I see it, there is a huge difference between *valuing* a set of religious teachings and practices for their skill and helpfulness, and claiming that they are *true* under all circumstances for all people for all time—the kind of claim that is so often made by religious believers about their doctrines. In other words, it seems to me that theses believers confuse usefulness with abiding truth. Easily and quickly, I remember learning verbal formulae as a child. They were always followed by the firm declaration, "This is most certainly true." I remember being told, in no uncertain terms, that I would spend eternity in hell for not repeating the correct words, as if salvation, whatever that might mean, were a matter of having the correct words and concepts floating around in my head, whether or not I understood them. It would be very difficult indeed to regard religious diversity as anything but a huge mistake if we accorded that level of adequacy to our words and concepts. That is why I regard being more modest about what words and concepts can do as so central to the project of flourishing with religious diversity.

Of course, assertions about the need to recognize both the utility and the relativity of religious words and concepts do not depend on my authority. I can quote far more reliable and definitive authorities, including the historical Buddha himself and the great thinker Nagarjuna, regarded by many Buddhists as a second Buddha. But I will begin by quoting a traditionally trained, twenty-first-century Asian teacher, Dzongsar Khyentse, writing in English, about the relationship between methods and enlightenment.

> These infinite methods are the path. However, the path itself must eventually be abandoned, just as you abandon a boat when you reach the other shore. You must disembark once you have arrived. At the point of total realization, you must abandon Buddhism. The path is a temporary solution, a placebo to be used until emptiness is understood.[3]

Later in the same book, the same author writes, "If you still define yourself as a Buddhist, you are not a Buddha yet."[4] These are very strong words. The fact that they come from a contemporary but traditionally trained Asian teacher corrects for any liberal, postmodernist, or Western preferences of which I might be accused in making my selections from traditional texts.

Traditionally, Buddhists use two main analogies, one about rafts and shores, the other about fingers and moons. The raft analogy, to which Dzongsar Khyentse referred above, is attributed to the historical Buddha.

---

3. Khyentse, *What Makes You Not a Buddhist?*, 77–78.
4. Ibid., 106.

Though it is impossible to demonstrate definitively which teachings found in the Pali canon come from the Buddha himself, this analogy is very old.

> O bhikkhus, even this view which is so pure, so clear, if you cling to it, if you fondle it, if you treasure it, if you are attached to it, then you do not understand that the teaching is similar to a raft, which is for crossing over, and not for getting hold of.[5]

In this analogy, the raft stands for classic Buddhist teachings, such as the Four Noble Truths, which are a method for getting to the other shore. The "other shore" represents enlightenment or truth, about which nothing is said because nothing can be said definitively, though figurative language can be somewhat helpful in pointing to that so-called shore. As was pointed out in chapter 5, this relationship between methods (*upaya*) and wisdom or truth (*prajna*) is standard in Buddhism and explains why someone like Dzongsar Khyentse can claim that in the long run, Buddhism itself as a specific set of teachings is a placebo that must be transcended.

Another very famous analogy is common in Zen Buddhism. This analogy is about someone trying to teach someone else what the moon is by pointing to it with her or his finger. The pointing finger obviously refers to Buddhist (or any religious) teachings and practices, while the moon represents enlightenment or realization. The person who would mistake the words of the teachings for enlightenment itself is like someone who only looks at the finger and confuses the pointing finger with that to which it is pointing. Such a person misses realization completely while also misunderstanding the teachings. Religious teachings and practices are relatively helpful methods, but they cannot contain ultimate or absolute truth. They are only a placebo, only pointers to the moon, about which nothing is said because words and concepts do not go there. This analogy is very forceful and strong. One wonders how a person could be so stupid as to put all one's attention on the tip of a pointing finger, rather than beyond the finger on that to which it points. Yet the analogy suggests that people often make this mistake, which is done whenever a relative set of teachings, useful and good in and of themselves, are made into more than they could possibly be: the truth itself.

The point made in these analogies is worked out very forcefully in more philosophical, discursive texts. It is the main point of the most important Buddhist teachings that are not attributed to the Buddha himself—Nagajuna's *Mulamadhyamikakarika*, or "Verses on the Middle Way." Nagarjuna, however, claims that his teachings are simply what was taught by

5. Attributed to the historical Buddha, and quoted in Rahula, *What the Buddha Taught*, 11.

the Buddha himself—that no philosophical position or set of teachings can be maintained as definitive or final. When subjected to rigorous analysis, all positions turn out to be untenable. In both the prologue and the last verse of his famous work, Nagajuna claims that he is only reiterating what the Buddha taught. The prologue reads:

> I prostrate to the Perfect Buddha,
> The best of teachers, who taught that
> Whatever is dependently arisen is
> Unceasing, unborn
> Unannihilated, not permanent,
> Not coming, not going,
> Without distinction, without identity,
> And free from conceptual construction.[6]

Many pages later, the conclusion of his text reads:

> I prostrate to Gautama
> Who through compassion
> Taught the true doctrine
> Which leads to the relinquishing of all views.[7]

On the pages between these two comments, we are told that every teaching of the Buddha, as well as the Buddha himself, are dependently arisen and without enduring essence or inherent existence. The religious life itself only makes sense if change is possible, but change and inherent or true existence are incompatible.

Most Buddhists, however, do not read and study Nagarjuna. Mahayana Buddhists get their understanding of the distinction between their most prized teachings and wisdom itself or realization from the Heart Sutra, a short text, often recited daily, about the transcendent wisdom of emptiness. This text is famous for its enigmatic declaration that "form is emptiness and emptiness is form," but much more to the point for this discussion is the culmination of a long string of denials it sets forth. After declaring the identity, equality, inseparability and interpenetration of form and emptiness, the Heart Sutra proceeds through a long string of statements negating all the categories delineated in earlier Buddhist texts. The list culminates with "no suffering, no origin of suffering, no cessation, no path, no wisdom, no attainment and no non-attainment," which is, of course, a negation of the Four Noble Truths, the content of the Buddha's first sermon and the

---

6. Garfield, *The Fundamental Wisdom of the Middle Way*, 2.

7. Ibid., 83.

supposed bottom line of all Buddhist teachings.[8] It is not being said that the Four Truths are false. What is being said is that they are a raft, not the shore, the pointing finger, not the moon (to return to our analogies). So Buddhism is, with very few exceptions, consistently modest in what it claims about the finality of its teachings.

Naming the Culprit: Attachment to Views

Spiritually and religiously, the importance of such teachings is that they protect practitioners from the arrogance and intolerance that are so problematic for religious people. In fact, the more pious and religious people are, the more they need such protection. So many religious leaders encourage too much fervor and too much conviction among their followers. Paul Knitter claimed that we Buddhists don't throw away our rafts because we can't. Perhaps he is right. We don't exactly throw our rafts away, but we are very aware that someday we will, and we don't exactly cling to them in the meanwhile either. Few Buddhists claim that they are enlightened or know everything that is worth knowing. *But we do know, and know definitively that the teachings and practices we love and cherish are only a raft, not the other shore, a means, not the end.* That knowledge is vital and would be salutary for every religious and nonreligious believer in any cause or position. Such knowledge protects us from thinking that we know best what everyone else should think, what's wrong with their religion, or that they should convert to ours. We easily see the great danger in absolutizing the relative and strenuously avoid doing so. That is a lesson that all people, religious and nonreligious, would do well to take to heart. This is what has allowed Buddhism to be the only religion to spread around the world without ever once doing so by means of military or economic conquest of the people who adopted Buddhism. There is a great deal to recommend such modesty about our words and concepts.

Clearly it is not the views people hold that are the problem, but their *attachment* to those views. Consistently throughout this book, I have been arguing that changing one's attitudes about religious diversity from regarding it as a mistake or a problem that would not persist in an ideal world to regarding religious diversity as a blessing that makes life more interesting does not require changing one's core religious beliefs. It only requires changing *how* those views are held. At this point, it is easy to see

8 There are many translations of the Heart Sutra. The one with which I am most familiar can be accessed online: http://nalandatranslation.org/media/Heart-Sutra.pdf/. Because the text is only a page long, page numbers are not given.

why attachment to views is considered to be such a serious problem by Buddhists. As is well known, attachment or clinging is considered be the root of suffering in Buddhism, and attachment to views is even more problematic than other attachments. The Second Noble Truth is quite clear; the cause of suffering is attachment rooted in ignorance. When more detailed teachings on the Second Truth are given, it is commonly noted that people become attached mainly to four things: sense pleasures, rituals and other religious observances, *beliefs and opinions*, and a supposed eternal self or soul. It makes little difference whether the beliefs and opinions concern politics or religion. People easily become quite attached to either. It is also noteworthy that attachment to views and opinions is considered to be just as harmful as something more usually condemned by religions—attachment to sense pleasure.

Incalculable human misery is caused by people's attachment to their views, their belief that their ideas are *correct*. In fact, it is commonplace in Buddhism to say that all human suffering is ultimately traceable to a thought, a view in someone's mind, which is why it is important to purify one's mind. But purification has much more to do with not being attached to views or doctrines than with getting the right words in our heads or out of our mouths. In the lore of meditation teachers, there are numberless anecdotes about how much spiritual progress is impeded by views, ideas, and concepts, and by the conviction that they are important and true. It usually takes significant time on the meditation cushion just to begin to see how painful, imprisoning and useless our thoughts, beliefs, and ideas can be when we take them too seriously, how much relief there is experiencing our thoughts fully and completely without having to believe in them.

Instead of a state of mind that clings tenaciously to received views and opinions, Buddhist teachers recommend a state of mind that is flexible, curious, and open, because it is so much more workable and causes so much less misery, both to self and to others. Many attempts have been made to describe this state of mind, but one of the most successful, in my view, is to call it the mind of "only don't know," a phrase much used in Zen Buddhist circles. This is not a "don't know" of ignorance or stupidity, but of lack of fixation about what currently seems to be the case, combined with willingness to go further and deeper in one's knowledge and understanding. Important is that this state of mind is not dualistic; it never says, I'm right and you're wrong. About any assertion made to one, especially if it is made very forcefully, one responds, "Is that so?" This state of mind is not at all enervating but gives one sufficient energy to keep working on issues long after one's more self-righteous friends have burned out and given up. It is not passive or dull, but awake, curious, flexible—and very clear about one's own values without any dogmatism.

I can illustrate this with a personal story. In the winter of 2011, the whole state of Wisconsin, where I live, was in turmoil over actions taken by its newly elected governor. There were demonstrations against him in the state capital, and the Democratic members of the state senate left the state to try to forestall a damaging vote. I teach a small meditation group in Eau Claire, where I live. Many who participate in that group were state employees who were seriously affected by the governor's actions. They were very fired up, held very clear opinions about the matter, were very angry, and were quite miserable as a result. One evening when I arrived for our weekly meeting, everyone eagerly asked me, "And where do you stand?" I replied that I knew what my opinions were, but I wasn't letting them make me miserable—a statement that many found startling but also refreshing. By the fall of 2011, passions were high again as petitions to recall the governor circulated. However, the meditators, who had become somewhat more adept at meditation in the intervening months, responded differently. They knew their minds, knew where they stood on the issues and what actions they would take. But they were not so miserable, so burdened by their beliefs. They were much more cheerful, but realistic at the same time.

There is a middle path between being aggressively angry, and thus miserable, about injustice or other problems, and just caving in or giving up entirely. It involves being less attached to one's views, which in no way involves less clarity about what needs to be done in any given situation. It would be so helpful if only more people could approach discussion of difficult issues concerning religion, politics, and economics with such flexibility, such softness and gentleness. It is so helpful to learn how not to take whatever emotions or thoughts may be in our minds at the current moment quite so seriously, as if they will be true for all time. Not taking ourselves and our views quite so seriously is essential for the flexibility I am praising so highly. It is also the opposite of the dogmatism—the fixed, rigidly held beliefs—that so often mars religion and politics. Nothing is gained by rigid polarization or by demonizing those who think differently. But unless all parties in a discussion are willing to be less ideological and more flexible, the situation is very difficult. Flexibility is not something easily practiced unilaterally. But I can think of nothing that would more improve the quality of civic discourse in our society.

What Words Can Do

The strong Buddhist condemnation of words and concepts only applies when words and concepts either become objects of attachment or when they are mistaken for experience. When either of those things happens, we become the slaves of our words and concepts. But once we understand what they can and cannot do, then words and concepts become our delightful companions, the means for communication and community. Words and concepts can perform two very useful functions. They can help us *eliminate dead ends*: ideas and practices that are not useful. And they can *point us in the right direction*. Verbal communication, after all, is the mainstay of much human interaction and is vital for teaching, exchanging, and refining religious ideas.

When it comes to working with what words and concepts can do, several useful distinctions are frequently made by Buddhist commentators. I don't think there is anything specifically Buddhist about these distinctions, and that they can easily be transferred into a broader discussion of how to flourish with religious diversity. It is useful to distinguish between provisional and definitive teachings, and it is critical to distinguish between words and meaning. As was demonstrated in chapter 5, religious teachings need to be appropriate to the audience, which is why there is a distinction between more provisional and more definitive teachings. For example, a beginner might not be able to make much sense of the teaching, considered in the next chapter, that self and other co-arise interdependently. But eventually, we do have to come to terms with the fact of interdependence and the lack of objective perceptions of others, which is a more definitive teaching than what is given by our everyday perceptions and reactions. Nevertheless, as was demonstrated earlier in this chapter, words, which in the long run include all doctrines, creeds, and texts, are themselves provisional rather than definitive—though at times some Buddhists disagree with this assessment, in spite of the raft parable, the Heart Sutra's statement about the Four Truths, and the clarity of the final comment in Nagarjuna's text.[9] The definitive meaning cannot be captured in words, formulae, creeds, doctrines, or texts.

This does not mean that words are useless, that anything goes, that all beliefs are equally valid, or that there is no point in trying to use one's intellect and trying to refine one's understanding. There are provisional teachings that point one in the right direction and other teachings that are

---

9. For an interesting discussion of this issue, see Garfield, *The Fundamental Wisdom of the Middle Way*, 352–59.

less useful, perhaps even harmful.[10] Intellect, analysis, and careful use of words all help sort out these various levels of provisional meaning. The pith is that, however skillful our words may be, in the long run they can only be pointers, only fingers pointing to the moon, not the moon itself (to refer once again to the famous Zen analogy). But, on the other hand, it is equally important to recognize that words and concepts, skillfully used, *can* definitely point us in the right direction. For that to happen, we must go beyond the *words* to ferret out their *meaning*. This distinction is one of the most important of all. Words, when taken literally, can easily deaden, but when one intuits the meaning behind the words, they are completely life giving. Any other conclusion, such as that words are without value if they can't be taken literally, would be nihilistic.

The first task when working with words is to eliminate false or unhelpful beliefs. What is left after this process will be more trustworthy, more likely to point one in the right direction. This part of working with words and concepts to eliminate some of them as pointing in the wrong direction is especially applicable in the framework of the raft analogy. If we are going to trust ourselves to a raft, before we get into it, we should thoroughly check it out to make sure it isn't going to sink in the middle of our crossing. This process, which is essential to Buddhist methods, often puzzles people. Most of us have conventionally approached religious ideas with the question, is this true? rather than the question, is this false? Yet no method is more useful than eliminating options that won't work. Strange as it may sound initially, though enlightenment or Truth is not a matter of intellectual content, beliefs, words, or ideas, nevertheless one can specify some intellectual, doctrinal content for error. Thus, though there can be no absolutely true verbal doctrines or formulae (not even in something as basic as the Four Noble Truths), there can religious beliefs that are definitely false, especially if they are also harmful.

It is easy to isolate some religious claims that cannot be true, and most of them deal with claims about *exclusive* truth. When multiple religions make exactly the same claim about different but very similar entities, it is more likely that all claims are false rather than that all the claims are true. For example, Jews, Christians, and Muslims (and Mormons as well)

10. In chapter 5, it may be remembered, I argued that the criterion for more and less useful provisional teachings is their effect on the ethical sensitivity and responsiveness of those who adhere to the teachings. Thus my primary argument against literalist or fundamentalist interpretations of religious traditions is not that they are intellectually flawed, though I believe that they are, but that their adherents so often cannot tolerate religious diversity, or other kinds of diversity and seek to destroy, in one way or another, those with whom they disagree.

all believe that their own scripture is a revelation from the deity while the other scriptures either are not revealed at all or are incomplete. There is no method of adjudicating between these claims that all parties making very similar claims could agree upon. How could anyone possibly demonstrate that one of these claims is true while the other three are false, given that the same claim is made about four relatively similar books? One can understand how such claims for exclusive relevance could be made in relative isolation and given a lack of knowledge of other traditions. But surely they become completely untenable once one has accurate knowledge about the other traditions. The existence of these four utterly conflicting exclusive truth claims discredits the very notion of making exclusive truth claims about nonempirical matters for which there can be no proof. There is no way to pick definitively between these beliefs, and they cannot all be *exclusively* true. While in such a situation, the frustrated skeptic may be inclined to reject all four scriptures as irrelevant because of excessive claims made on their behalf by adherents of all four religions, there are many ways to find value in all the scriptures. But none of them involve accepting any of the claims for exclusive relevance or truth. This specific example can be extended to any other similar cases. Probably the least trustworthy religious claim, the one we should avoid at all costs, is any claim that contains the phrases "only way" or "One True Faith."

As we have already seen, the evidence of the world's religions is that people who are equally moral and learned may hold very different religious beliefs—beliefs about metaphysical realities or other things that cannot be verified outside the circle of that faith. The only viable conclusion is that things that must be matters of faith or belief are weak candidates for also being exclusively and ultimately true for all people, which is not to say that one should not have faith and beliefs. It only means that one should be modest and humble about what one declares about one's beliefs. One should be modest and humble for at least two reasons. First, such demeanor is more becoming and persuasive than zealous, self-righteous certainty about claims that cannot be verified. Second, thoughtful believers realize that other, equally thoughtful and dedicated religious practitioners can find different beliefs and practices convincing. Different teachings would be a problem only if one believes that the finger (words, doctrines) could actually grab the moon, rather than merely point to it. The moon can be pointed to by many fingers at once, and the fingers could look rather different from one another. To say they are all pointing at the same moon, so there must be one ungraspable truth is to miss the point of the analogy. Some of the fingers could be pointing at a moon reflected in water, others at a moon in the sky, and still others at a picture of a moon.

Thus, I am suggesting that the Buddhist insight that words, thoughts, ideas, doctrines, teachings, and so forth are only and nothing more than fingers pointing to a moon is extremely useful in learning how to flourish with religious diversity. In one sense, words and doctrines are very limited in what they can do. They should never be regarded as bearers of truth but only as possibly useful methods for human transformation towards kindness and compassion. In another sense, however, as methods, they are very useful and their potential should not be underestimated. Paradoxically, the more we try to dignify our words and concepts by insisting that they have great or ultimate significance, the more we actually diminish their scope and relevance.

Pointing in the Right Direction

The moon is an experience, not a set of teachings or doctrines, and Buddhist tradition is consistent in saying that while reality can be experienced, there are no words for that experience. Nevertheless, Buddhist tradition is also consistent in claiming that Wisdom or truth can be pointed to, that words can catch some glimpse of what is experienced. Though the language is evocative rather than precise, many Buddhist traditions talk of the experience of the moon as nakedly seeing the mind as it is in something like the following manner:

> When you rest in this experience of the mind, which is beyond extremes or elaborations, what is the experience of that like? It is characterized by a profound state of ease, which means an absence of agitation or discomfort. Therefore, the experience is comfortable and pleasant. The term comfortable does not indicate pleasure in the sense of something you're attached to, or the pleasure of acting out an attachment or passion. It's simply the absence of any kind of discomfort or imperfection in the nature of the mind itself. Therefore, the experience of that nature is characterized by comfy blissfulness. This is as close as we can come in words to what you experience when you look at your mind. You can't actually communicate what you experience. It's beyond expression . . . [it] is inexpressible, indescribable and even inconceivable.[11]

Note the absence of any metaphysical or theological language when the moon of reality is pointed to by language. Conceptual, propositional, verbal Truth, as such, really isn't the issue. The issue is what methods get

11. Thrangu, *The Ninth Gyalwa Karmapa's "Pointing Out the Dharmakaya,"* 90.

one from point A to point B, from the confusion of duality to experience that is not confused or mistaken. Though this particular expression comes from a Vajrayana Buddhist context, I can recognize much the same moon in different words coming from other Buddhist traditions. There isn't much more that can be said.

In much less sure ways, I can also recognize something of the same moon in some theistic language. When theists proclaim that God is hidden, unknowable, and indescribable, my ears perk up. To regard human speech about deity as truly accurate is a confusion of linguistic orders, a confusion of what can be spoken about with that about which only silence is accurate. Human speech is relative and deity is ultimate. I always wonder why there is so little apophatic God-talk in most theistic religions, because such talk seems so much more accurate than the endless parsing of arcane doctrines about three persons, two natures, transubstantiation versus consubstantiation, and so forth.

Other Disciplines as Analogies for Religion

I have long felt that it can be helpful when attempting to understand what religion is and why there is so much variety in religions to compare religions to other, more mundane and perhaps less controversial disciplines. In the West, where propositional, discursive, doctrinal truth has historically been so central, especially since the European Enlightenment, many think that if religion is valid or valuable, it should provide the kind of information and factual accuracy provided by the study of modern science or history. There are many problems with such a view of religion, not the least of which is that, by that analogy, it would be very difficult to accommodate religious diversity as anything but a problem. Even more serious problems with an Enlightenment-influenced view of religion are that many of the most valued assertions made by many religions cannot be verified by the methods of modern science or historical investigation and also that many assertions previously made by religions have been definitively disproved by modern study of science and history. This fact has led to a major crisis for many contemporary people and has resulted in the rise of fundamentalism as an attempt to hold onto literal meanings of the words of revered texts despite their incompatibility with modern methods of knowing. This fundamentalist tactic has been called the only modern heresy; traditionally religions focused much more on various analogical, metaphorical, and symbolic meanings encoded in their texts, and less on the literal words.

But as factual, empirical knowledge alone has come to be valued, as a result of the success of modern study of science and history, people find it more and more difficult to appreciate nonempirical, metaphorical, or symbolic truths. Even Western Buddhists fall prey to this modern heresy, not so much regarding science as regarding history. I have been amazed to discover how troubling accurate modern histories of Buddhism are to many Western Buddhists, and how little they know about Buddhist *history*, as opposed to pious insiders' traditional accounts of how Buddhism came into being and developed.[12]

Obviously, I do not hold the view that religious claims are analogous to the empirically demonstrable claims of modern history or science, or that to be meaningful and valuable, religious claims have to be verifiable as empirical facts. However, because so many modern people demand that kind of truth value for religions if they are to be worth pursuing, I want to take on their science envy head-on. Science envy has been endemic in both religions and religious studies for some time now. Many especially religious people seem to want their religious claims to be true in the way that they think science and history are true—with certainty for all time, both factually and literally. But that longing involves a serious misunderstanding of these modern disciplines. Both disciplines deal in *hypotheses*, not *certainties*, and the content of both disciplines is in process, constantly changing. For example, much of the science I learned in high school is now obsolete, and our knowledge of history has grown exponentially in the last hundred years. I fully expect that some of the conclusions I have derived from my studies of Buddhist history will be outdated and outmoded before the end of my life.

If the disciplines of modern science and history were properly understood by religious people with science envy, as ever evolving hypotheses rather than as static, unchanging certainties, these disciplines would be very good analogues for religions, as religions actually work. Any given religious outlook at any given time is the best hypothesis available at the current time, given current knowledge. It will change—or die. I always used to tell my university students who decried changes to the "old-time religion," such as gender-inclusive liturgies, that if they wanted to practice a religion that would never change on them, they should find a dead religion and practice that one. But I also warned them that their own understanding of it would probably change during the course of their lifetimes and that it would be very sad indeed if their understanding did not grow and develop. So, if

12. Gross, "Buddhist History for Buddhist Practitioners," 83–85, 118–20; and Gross, "Why We Need to Know Our Buddhist History," 7–8.

properly understood, the disciplines of modern science and history could be very good analogues for what religions are and for how they work.

However, even though many people think of religions as sets of propositional, discursive truth claims, many of the most central features of religions are more like the arts than like modern science or history. Stories and symbols are much more basic to most religions than are abstract quasi-philosophical metaphysical claims. Many more people rely centrally on rituals than on creeds and doctrines. Many religions have more often communicated their message through visual arts than through texts, whether through storytelling texts or more discursive texts. We should not forget the importance of chant, dance, and music in communicating much of what religion is about for many people. For these reasons, I have long thought that the arts are also a very good analogy for what religions are and how they work. I also think it is only the low prestige accorded to arts in our society that makes this analogy less appealing and less obvious to most commentators.

However, another feature of the arts makes them even more appealing as analogues for religions. No one condemns variety in art, and most of us can easily appreciate a wide variety of artistic styles and media. We can appreciate Paleolithic art from thirty thousand years ago as readily as contemporary music. It seems like sheer nonsense to imagine there could be One True Poem. It would be very helpful if people were equally skeptical about One True Religion. Given the limitations of words and concepts to portray reality, it is completely unsurprising that there are many different verbal attempts to somehow express what those who have seen deeply have experienced. To expect them all to use the same words or eventually to give up the words they have used all their lives in the face of a missionary's exhortations is like expecting that all artists would draw the same thing or write the same poem. We simply wouldn't expect such a thing to happen and would be unnerved if it did. While we may disagree about which poem, painting, or piece of music we like best and can have vigorous arguments about the relative merits of various pieces of art, few of us worry about the long-term, after-death fate of someone who does not share our tastes in art, even though we reject their art by not buying or displaying it. Because the analogy of religions as somewhat like the arts could so easily accommodate the diversity of religions, I find the analogy of religions as artworks to be very appealing. I think that seeing religion as similar to art is also truer to how religions actually work than seeing religion as about propositional systems. Even the great systematic theologies seem, in comparative perspective, to be more like grand stories than like propositional, metaphysical statements. And the point of stories is not their propositional or empirical truth; they teach in other ways that are no less meaningful or relevant.

Chapter 7

Do Others Exist?

Beyond the Duality of Self and Other

Buddhist thought and practice offer a sharp criticism, which then becomes a helpful suggestion, concerning one of the major intellectual and spiritual bases of many discussions of religious diversity. This chapter was first written to fulfill an assignment from an interfaith group in which I participated for many years—an assignment to write an essay on "the other" as thought about in my religious tradition. Participants from other religious traditions had the same assignment. Intuitively I knew immediately upon receiving the assignment that something about the topic made me quite uncomfortable. Yet because of the naturalness and inevitability of religious diversity, we do live in a world where we must interact with religious others, and to do so sanely and humanely, we must have some understanding of the category of the other.

The problem is that much interreligious discussion simply assumes that the other exists as a metaphysical entity independent of my perceptions of and ideas about her or him. We often talk is if religious others are simply there, objectively given, apart from how they appear to me, as if my own subjectivity, beliefs, and assumptions had nothing to do with how they appear to me. As a result, frequently in such discussions, I have seen the much simpler term *other* morph into *the Other*, or even *Otherness*, while the simplest term, *others*, is left behind altogether. When that happens, a simple phenomenological experience is turned into a metaphysical proposition setting forth the hardened, solid, rigid, enduring existence of both self and other. Though in interreligious circles, such discussions are usually well intentioned, in that people want to take the other seriously and stop dismissing the other as simply misguided and in need of conversion, this move often further confuses the matter. It some cases, it can also polarize the situation, especially when hostility develops between self and other. A hard sense of Otherness as a metaphysical entity can as easily support a hostile *us/them* dichotomy as curiosity and friendliness. In the past, the former reaction probably prevailed much more often than the later. The metaphysical assumptions cloud rather than clarify the situation, launching us immediately into the realm of duality, without our even considering the adequacy of perceived duality as the bottom line for our discussions of religious diversity.

From a Buddhist perspective, all questions about the other are secondary questions, not the primary question or the primary reality. When we perceive and talk about others as if they are fixed, enduring realities, we are already in the realm of duality and have bypassed a more fundamental situation. We are already once removed from the clear, basic awareness that surrounds and supports our projection or creation of the seeming reality of self and other. I am not questioning that in many conventional perspectives, nothing seems more real than the duality of self and other. I am suggesting that it is worthwhile to look more introspectively and with more curiosity into what is really going on in this interaction, and especially to question the metaphysical assumptions imputed to the experience of interacting with another or with any field of experience. While this point may seem subtle and esoteric, it is actually completely basic. If we assume the existence of self and other as separate, metaphysically real entities and take that as the starting point of our discussions, our discussions will be limited and unsuccessful. We are starting our discussions at a point well into a process, without ever becoming grounded in the underlying realities.

We need to look into what precedes duality, not as a temporal absolute beginning, but in the moment-by-moment flickering of consciousness. We need to understand that there is an other only in the experience of a self, that self and other are cocreated, or, in better Buddhist language, arise together and interdependently. However they may be perceived or conceptualized, they can arise only dependent on one another, experientially at least. And the question of what exists independently of perceptions and conceptions is abstract and unanswerable. Furthermore, it is irrelevant to the matter at hand—becoming competent at flourishing with religious diversity. We need to understand that duality, when reified into a metaphysical absolute, is based on a secondary and somewhat mistaken account of our perceptions. While it is important and useful to talk of self and other, such talk needs to be put in proper perspective. That proper perspective is at least threefold. First, such talk should be grounded in fleeting awareness of the vast space in which self and other co-arise. Second, we should question the metaphysical assumptions that often harden such talk into the conviction that there is an independent, separately existing self and an independent, separately existing other. Third, it is always important to check how accurate our perceptions of others actually are, and how much is simply our own projection and fabrication.

Not Taking Duality for Granted

I understand that these claims run very much against the grain of everyday assumptions about the nature of reality. Usually, we take ourselves to be the center of the world and experience others as momentary, sometimes pleasing, sometimes unpleasant or painful, arisings in our consciousness. But we also assume that others, like ourselves, are separate, fixed, and metaphysically real entities. The profundity of the Buddhist message is to challenge as fundamentally erroneous these views about the substantiality of self and other, and about the ultimate reality of duality to which we are so habituated. Buddhism also challenges us to recognize that these fundamentally mistaken views are the source of our misery, much of which arises from our unsatisfactory relationships with the other.

Not only have I received training as a Buddhist, but I have also been deeply influenced by other streams of thought that are very suspicious of duality. Especially in the early literature of the second wave of feminism, sexism and male dominance were often analyzed as the results or the expression of the othering of women, of the way in which men, who created culture and thought, experienced and saw women as the others, as the ones who are different, and perhaps not even completely human. This was a powerful explanatory tool for many of us, helping us understand why we so often felt like outsiders and victims in a world that was male dominated despite a superficial rhetoric of equality. We were always associated with the downside of a long list of hierarchical dualities. *Duality* quickly became the code word explaining what was wrong with conventional ways of thinking and acting.[1]

1. The classic source for this analysis is Simone de Beauvoir's *The Second Sex*. Problems with and correctives to the othering of women in androcentric thought and scholarship were important themes in my early work as well. See Gross, "Androcentrism and Androgyny in the Methodology of History of Religions," reprinted in Gross, *A Garland*

I will claim, as a Buddhist and as a feminist,[2] that whether or not we consider duality to be ultimately real as the underlying fact of our existence could make a great deal of difference in how we understand otherness and in how we relate with others. It will be harder to solidify and demonize the others if we recognize that duality is only apparent, that all persons and all things live and move and have their being in an interdependent matrix of nonduality. It will be harder to categorize them as subhuman and to set artificial limits to their humanity and their achieving.

Even if nonduality is not seen as more logical and persuasive than some form of dualism, which will probably be the case for most theists and monotheists, they do nevertheless important to realize that in any immediate, discrete event or moment, self and other, *as actually experienced apart from any theory or metaphysic later imputed onto the experience*, are interdependent and co-arising, not separate and independent. In other words, who I am partially determines how I see others. When we are interacting, I do not see others objectively, independent of my assumptions. And who I am is also partially determined by my interactions with others. They have formed me. I am not independent of them. Thus, rather than being objectively given, others and the world, at least as we encounter them, are formed by human minds, as has also been said in other contexts in this book.

When Buddhists say that phenomena are like dreams and illusions or that the world is mind created, these statements are very confusing to outsiders. It does not mean that there is no material world external to our minds and bodies. It means that how we apprehend that external world, including other human beings, is in accordance with how our human minds work, and also in accordance with specific cultural norms to which we have become conditioned. If our minds and sense organs operated differently, or if we operated with a different set of cultural presuppositions, we would apprehend a different world. This insight is extremely important to conversations about religious diversity and religious others. Contemporary discussions about theology of religions and comparative theology grow out of a recognition by monotheists, most of them Christian, that monotheistic and Christian claims about their own uniqueness, universal relevance, and supremacy, which resulted in missionary activities of religious imperialism, may have been arrogant. This recognition was accompanied by another— that these activities may well have been based on mistaken assumptions about the Other. Religious others had been construed as heathens, pagans,

---

of Feminist Reflections, 55–64.

2. At this point in my explorations, I would claim that the Buddhist analysis of duality and nonduality is far more profound than the feminist analysis. Nevertheless, feminist analyses of the ethical implications of dualism remain illuminating.

idol worshipers, and with a whole host of other labels that justified forcibly interfering with them and trying to fix them. But where did these labels come from? Did the Others arise independently, in and of themselves, as heathens? Are they heathens independent of Christians' labeling them as such? Would others who did not operate with monotheistic or Christian presuppositions also see them as heathens? Undoubtedly not! The heathen is co-arisen as a Christian perception rather than as a heathen in and of herself apart from perceptions and labels.

That is why Buddhists say that one of the more mistaken ways to apprehend the world or others is to superimpose upon the experience of interactions between self and other a theory or metaphysic that both self and other actually exist, as opposed to accepting that self and other may appear in each other's fields of awareness. Such a statement will require some explaining, but first, it is important to understand that such claims are not mere speculation but are utterly relevant to the problem at hand—how to flourish with religious diversity. It is much easier to appreciate religious others rather than being threatened by them if we regard them as interdependently arisen coinhabitants of our nondual matrix than if we regard them dualistically, as fixed entities completely independent of our interactions with them.

This is the way it always is. This is why people of integrity need to learn to mistrust the accuracy of their automatic but unreflective assumptions about the Other, who does not exist independently of our construction of that other. That is why I am so suspicious of making Otherness the chief focus of our discussions of how to flourish with religious diversity. Buddhists also say that there are more mistaken and less mistaken ways for human minds to perceive the other, the object of perception. We can gradually purify our minds of the tendency to project mistaken views onto both other and self. That is where introspective disciplines of contemplation and meditation come in. But we are getting ahead of ourselves. That topic will be discussed more in chapter 10.

Setting the Stage: Buddhist Antimetaphysics

Early Buddhist texts such as the Pali suttas are famous for their disavowal of metaphysical or speculative thought. The Buddha is represented as having repeatedly declared that the only thing he taught in his long career was suffering and the cessation of suffering, the content of his first teaching on the Four Noble Truths. He is also represented as consistently refusing to entertain speculative or metaphysical questions because, he claimed, such questions cannot be answered, and such inquiry is not conducive to the cessation of suffering because answering such questions does not alleviate suffering. This refusal to discuss metaphysical matters reached its climax in his answer to the frequently asked question about the status of a Tathagata (fully enlightened one) after the death of his or her physical body. The common understanding was that rebirth was inevitable except for those who had fully realized "things as they are," but that for an enlightened one, the current rebirth was their last rebirth. Furthermore, the Buddha did declare that his current rebirth was his last. This led to intense and urgent questioning of the Buddha as those still mired in dualistic thinking demanded an answer to their question. In one case, a disciple threatened to abandon the Buddha as his teacher unless he got an answer to his question, to which the Buddha replied that he had never offered him answers to such metaphysical questions but only advice on how to overcome suffering. To those who were less demanding, the Buddha frequently explained that there was no adequate verbal, logical, or conceptual answer to such questions. One simply could say nothing at all, at least in positive language, about such matters. The most one can do is eliminate incorrect, untenable assumptions. After his or her physical death, one could not say that the formerly living being existed or did not exist, could not say that the being both existed and did not exist, and could not say that the being neither existed nor did not exist: this formula becomes known in English-language discussions of Buddhist thought as the *tetralemma*. The *tetralemma* figures heavily in Madhyamika, the most important of later Mahayana Buddhist systems, which made clear that the *tetralemma* actually describes the mode of existence for all things, not only for a Tathagata after physical death. Contrary to many assumptions, however, this insight did not originate with Nagarjuna, the founder of that system but is implicit in early Buddhist scriptures.

The *tetralemma* baffles discursive, conceptual, logical mind—that is to say, dualistic mind, and that is the whole point. Buddhism is frequently known as a middle way, and that middle way is often said to be a middle way between sensual overindulgence and strict asceticism, but it is also a middle way between eternalism and nihilism. This later form of the middle way is more important, especially for our discussions. Discursive and dualistic mind wants to declare that if we do not affirm the existence of something, then the only remaining option is the nihilistic option, that it does not exist at all. But in an important discourse, later picked up and amplified by Nagarjuna,[3] the Buddha declares that

---

3. In chapter 15 and verse 7 of his major work, Nagarjuna cites this passage from the Pali texts (Garfield, *The Fundamental Wisdom of the Middle Way*, 40).

> This world, . . . for the most part depends upon a duality—upon
> the idea of existence and the idea of non-existence. But for one
> who sees the origin of the world as it really is with correct wis-
> dom, there is no idea of nonexistence in regard to the world.
> And for one who sees the cessation of the world as it really is,
> with correct wisdom, there is no idea of existence with regard
> to the world.
>   . . . "All exists": this is one extreme. "All does not exist":
> this is the second extreme. Without veering toward either of
> these extremes, the Tathagata teaches the Dhamma by the mid-
> dle. With ignorance as condition, volitional formations. With
> volitional formations as condition, consciousness . . . Such is the
> origin of this whole mass of suffering. But with the remainder-
> less fading away and cessation of ignorance comes cessation of
> volitional formations. With the cessation of volitional forma-
> tions, consciousness . . . Such is the cessation of this whole mass
> of suffering.[4]

To clarify for those not used to the style of early Buddhist scriptures, the Buddha is saying that he teaches a middle way between the extremes of eternalism and nihilism, between the assertions that things truly, inherently exist or, if that is not the case, then that they are utterly nonexistent. Rather than assuming either inherent existence or nonexistence, the Buddha teaches *interdependent arising*, which is to say that insofar as things exist, they only exist interdependently, not independently. Therefore their existence is temporary and contextual. The phrase "with ignorance as condition" introduces the famous formula of the twelve links of interdependent arising, which, when proceeding forward leads from ignorance eventually to old age and death; and, conversely, as one eliminates each preceding cause, finally, upon eliminating ignorance completely, "this whole mass of suffering" collapses, never to arise again. We do not need to understand the details of the twelve links of interdependent arising to understand that self and other arise interdependently, or to reap the benefits of such understanding for learning how to flourish with religious diversity.

A basic understanding of interdependence, perhaps the most central of all Buddhist teachings, is vital, however. Interdependence is an alternative name for and the source for one of the most famous and potentially confusing of all Buddhist teachings: emptiness or *shunyata*. Much is clarified by understanding that teachings on interdependence or emptiness simply assert that no phenomenon, without exception, can exist by itself, apart from its matrix, without causes that lead to its formation and upon

---

4. Bodhi, *In the Buddha's Words*, 356–57.

which it depends. Furthermore, because all phenomena are the results of causes and conditions, they are impermanent and evanescent, ever changing. Therefore, it is said that they do not exist *inherently* but only *interdependently*. This distinction is crucial for understanding how the existence of self and other can be questioned. The tendency of confused human beings who misperceive their world is to assume that things exist inherently, that they are truly real, and therefore we either cling to them or ward them off, thinking that such actions will bring happiness and satisfaction. Except that they never do, for the long run, in any truly satisfying way, because phenomena do not really exist in the way we think they do or in the way we want them to—permanently and constructed in such a way that they could bring lasting happiness. In Buddhist language, because the word *exist* is so confusing and so prone to being used inaccurately, we talk instead of appearance and reality. In reality, things do not exist inherently because they have no enduring, uncaused essence, which is to say they do not *truly* exist. But they definitely do appear temporarily, arising interdependently and falling apart again. How we relate with such appearances will be very different if we do not reify them but instead remain fully and steadily aware of their contingency and impermanence.

There is no quarrel with appearances, and they must be dealt with. But they should not be *reified* or *absolutized*. That imputes to them more reality than they can possibly have, with often disastrous consequences. When an interpersonal interaction morphs into a theory of how to deal with Otherness, experiencer and experienced have both been reified. Then it is very easy for theory and projections to overwhelm direct experience, which often happens in interreligious interactions, whether of the positive or the negative kind. Better is to remain in the fluidity and openness of interdependent arising out of basic space than to solidify self and other by reifying them.

The Interdependent Co-arising of Self and Other from the Ground of Basic Space

That which is pointed to by the *tetralemma* is often called in Buddhist thought basic space or the basic ground. In Madhyamika thought, it is accorded nominal existence but not ontological reality. Nevertheless, it points to an experience that is universal to introspective people and to those who engage in contemplation and meditation, though no words that can be agreed to by all to describe that experience have ever been found. In discussions of flourishing with religious diversity, however, the primary point of these discussions is to demonstrate that neither self nor other are fixed entities. They are contingent and relative, and therefore their/our ideas and belief systems are also contingent and relative, context dependent, historically and culturally conditioned. Thoroughly absorbing and assimilating this point will protect us from reifying Otherness and greatly improve our flexibility and ease with diversity in general, not just religious diversity.

A brief discussion of how self and other appear moment by moment in or from this basic space could be based on many texts, but I especially want to refer to a liturgy used by the Nyingma lineage of Tibetan Vajrayana Buddhism called "The Aspiration of Samantabhadra."[5] I will rely on two translations, one published[6] and the other unpublished. The beginning of this liturgy talks about the relationship between space and form; background and foreground; the unconditioned ground and the play of conditioned, contingent, relative phenomena; absolute truth and relative truth. To say that they are an inseparable nonduality, rather than a monistic unity or a truly existing dyad is as close as language can come to expressing the inexpressible in Buddhist understanding. As the "Aspiration" says,

> The ground of all is uncompounded,
> An inexpressible, self-arisen expanse.
> Without the names "samsara" and "nirvana."
> If it is known, buddhahood is attained.
> Not knowing it, beings wander in samsara.[7]

It is important to notice that while this ground of all cannot be adequately conceptualized, verbalized, or theorized, it can be experienced. It

5. Aspiration prayers are quite common in Buddhism, despite Buddhism's lack of any concept of a supreme being to whom one could pray. They could be understood as pep talks one gives to oneself, expressing one's deepest longings or aspirations. For more discussion of prayer in Buddhism see Gross, "Prayer and Meditation ." Samantabhadra is the primordial Buddha of the Nyingma lineage, a personification of enlightened mind. Despite his anthropomorphic form, he is not a deity in the sense of deity as an externally existing being separate from oneself. For a translation and commentary on the Aspiration of Samantabhadra see Ponlop, *Penetrating Wisdom*. The translation that I use and with which I am most familiar is privately circulated and is not generally available. However, because my understanding of this text is colored by the translation with which I am most familiar, I will sometimes quote from it.

6. See note 5.

7. Ponlop, *Penetrating Wisdom*, vii. *Samsara*, or the pain of cyclic existence, and *nirvana*, or the cooling and cessation of turmoil, are the fundamental *duality* of our experience, when the focus of Buddhist analysis is on duality. Notice that in this text it is said that the fundamental ground is without those names, and that knowing or not knowing that fundamental ground means the difference between Buddhahood and the pain of cyclic existence.

is experienced continuously in silence and space, which are all pervasive, but because the habits of dualistic thinking are so deeply and habitually ingrained in us by now, we consistently overlook or fail to notice this basic ground. The easiest analogy for this consistent mistake may be that of a piece of paper with some text on it. The paper is the background and the writing is the foreground. They are, in fact, inseparable; the text definitely could not exist without the paper, and the paper is useless without the text. Pristine awareness takes in both background and foreground without preference or prioritizing. But we consistently tend to ignore the background, the paper, and fixate on the foreground, the text. It is this *fixation* itself that gives rise to duality. The *contents* upon which one fixates are not the problem or the mistake. It is not that distinct phenomena do not appear (often a point of misunderstanding) but that distinct phenomena are assumed to be more real and important than the matrix of space.

This pristine awareness, which is always available in all circumstances regarding any experience, does not hold, however. If there is a mysterious First Cause in Buddhism, this is it. However, it is crucial to realize that this loss of awareness is not considered to be a temporal First Cause in Buddhism. In other words, it did not happen once upon a time long ago; it happens moment by moment and is, therefore, reversible in every moment. But often awareness gives way to ignorance, dualistic consciousness takes over, and things spiral downward. I quote from the unpublished translation.

> First, deluded sentient beings,
> Not seeing awareness at the ground,
> Fall into a trance of thoughtless oblivion.
> Not realizing this is itself the cause of delusion.
> This sudden stupefaction causes
> Bewilderment, fear, perception, exhilaration and grasping,
> From this arises 'self' and 'others,' the enemy is born
> And habitual tendencies gradually develop.
> Thus samsara becomes an established system.[8]

With awareness diminished or lost, "a trance of thoughtless oblivion," itself the problem, ensues. Beings experience extreme agitation, and from this arise both self and other. As I noted previously, the key point is that self and others co-arise. They are interdependent. It is not that a previously established independent self then perceives others, who are also there independently; the sense of self arises only in interdependence with consciousness of others. Nothing has really changed fundamentally, but *allegiance has switched* from nondual, pristine awareness to focus on oneself, which automatically

8. Unpublished translation made by Jetsun Dechen Paldren.

includes a focus on others. As Ponlop Rinpoche's translation of some of the same lines puts it, from "terrified, blurry cognition, self-other and enmity were born."[9] In this case, "self-other" becomes a hyphenated word—an extremely accurate and brilliant translation that brings out this vital point in Buddhist understandings of otherness. And once dualistic consciousness dominates, enmity is inevitable, even though in pristine awareness, both poles of experience, called self and other in dualistic consciousness, coexist peacefully and harmoniously.

The operative word in this description is *process*. As I already stated, this text is not a creation myth; it does not describe what happened once upon a time long ago when the world was permanently set up. It is a description of a moment-by-moment process in which allegiance switches from pristine awareness of all-pervasive ground, which includes myriad phenomena in continual flux, to belief in a separate underlying self reacting dualistically to others, or in even more static language, to the other. An ongoing flickering stream of processes is frozen into belief in independent, truly existing, separate selves. But since separate selves do not truly exist but only appear to exist, the freezing is only illusory. That is the saving grace in Buddhist analysis. Not only is thawing possible; it is inevitable and is, in fact, more real and more powerful than the freezing.

Appearances and Their Interdependence

Of course, Buddhists also find it necessary to talk about the relationship between self and others in practical, everyday terms. Self and others may not truly exist, but they do appear. How do we negotiate the world of appearances? This question can be answered in a single word—*interdependence*, or as Thich Nhat Hanh likes to put it, "interbeing." Perhaps no contemporary Buddhist has written or spoken more eloquently of interbeing in English, and it is worth quoting him at length both on the spatial and the temporal dimensions of interbeing. He is fond of saying that the self is composed of only nonself elements, that a human being is composed of only nonhuman elements, and that living beings are made of nonliving things.

He frequently uses a flower as an analogy for the self we attribute to ourselves. In his words:

> Let us look again at the example of a flower. It is a manifestation
> of reality. If we look deeply into the flower and touch it deeply,
> we touch everything in the cosmos: the sunshine, a cloud, the

---

9. Ponlop, *Penetrating Wisdom*, viii.

earth, time, space, everything . . . The flower cannot exist by itself alone. The flower inter-is with a cloud, the sunshine, and the earth. If you remove the cloud, the sunshine and the earth from the flower, it will collapse. Our true nature is interbeing. Interbeing applies to everything. Look into your body. Your body cannot exist alone, by itself. In has to inter-be with the trees, the earth, your parents, and your ancestors. There is nothing in the cosmos that is not present in your body.[10]

Regarding the temporal dimension of interbeing, which also involves the fact that birth and death are not as real as we habitually assume, his favorite analogy is a piece of paper, and its prelife and afterlife.

When you look at this sheet of paper, you think it belongs to the realm of being. There was a time when it came into existence, a moment in the factory it became a sheet of paper. But before the sheet of paper was born, was it nothing? Can nothing become something? Before it was recognizable as a sheet of paper, it must have been something else—a tree, a branch, sunshine, clouds, the earth. In its former life, the sheet of paper was all these things . . .

The paper's story is much like our own . . . We usually think that we did not exist before the time of our parents, that we only began to exist at the moment of our birth. But we were already here in many forms . . .

If I burn this sheet of paper, will I reduce it to nonbeing? No, it will just be transformed into smoke, heat, and ash. If we put the 'continuation' of this sheet of paper into the garden, later, while practicing walking meditation, we may see a little flower and recognize it as the rebirth of the sheet of paper. The smoke will become part of a cloud in the sky, also to continue the adventure.

After tomorrow, a little rain may fall on your head, and you will recognize the sheet of paper, saying "Hello." The heat produced by the burning will penetrate into your body and the cosmos.[11]

10. Nhat Hanh, *The Path of Emancipation*, 172.

11. Nhat Hanh, *The Heart of Buddha's Teaching*, 137–38.

Beyond the Duality of Self and Other

Nevertheless, despite interbeing, the appearance of self and other is inevitable in our experience as human beings, and that separation is easily foregrounded. It is not that if we had been raised properly or lived in an ideal society, we would never fall into dualistic consciousness. To function in the world, we have to interact with others who do seem to be separate from us. That everyday sense of separateness can lead to conflict and difficulty as well as to closeness and love. Why, if the ground is a nondual matrix of interdependence, do we so often forget that and revel in duality, objectifying others and seeing them as enemies? In Buddhist terms, the simplest answer is that this is the karma we are born with as human beings. As sentient beings within the human realm, we have inherited a predisposition or habitual tendency to solidify self and other, to regard them as separate, and to regard the others mainly as dangerous. We can't do anything about what we have inherited, but we certainly can do something about how we work with that heritage. Contrary to popular misconceptions, concepts of karma are not about predestination; it is not at all predestined what we do with our inheritance. In fact, usually Buddhists would say that pristine awareness is our birthright, far deeper in our karmic and genetic makeup than the two veils of confused emotions and mistaken views and beliefs.[12] Nor are we left without resources for overcoming these two veils and dwelling more frequently in pristine awareness. Buddhism relies primarily on two resources: intellectual reasoning and the kind of direct experience resulting from contemplation and meditation. This chapter grows out of such contemplation and meditation, and represents a small example of intellectual reasoning verbalizing these claims as best they can be verbalized. These techniques are freely available to anyone who wishes to learn them and use them.

After one has thought through, contemplated, and realized the truth of the fact that self and other arise interdependently, a subtle but profound shift occurs. In addition to being aware of distinctiveness, separation, and difference, one becomes aware of the fundamental equality of all beings—an equality more profound than political equality, though not incompatible with concern for political and social equality. If ever one were to use a metaphysical term in a Buddhist context, this is the place for it. Deeply realizing that all beings have the same *nature*—which is to be empty of inherent, independent existence—brings home very forcefully the point that we are all in this together, all in the same boat. *Sameness replaces otherness as the chief*

---

12. This is a reference to a widespread Buddhist analysis, which says that two things, the two veils of confused emotions and mistaken beliefs about reality, keep us from realizing our birthright and must be slowly eroded or corrected.

headline for how we are. This is a fundamental sameness that does not in any way undercut or undermine distinctiveness and difference. Nothing could be more salutary for learning how to flourish with religious diversity and for the quality of interreligious interactions than coming to such a realization. *Otherness, the Other,* and so forth are all objectifying and distancing terms that do not really help.

Furthermore, though I have presented this analysis in nontheistic, Buddhist language, I believe that same insights are readily available in theistic contexts. This analysis of how self and other co-arise is essentially psychological, not theological. I do not believe that theological beliefs regarding theism and nontheism fundamentally alter or change these human-to-human perceptual processes. This is not a matter of theological belief systems but of taking the time to slow down and then doing the introspection required to examine how things actually arise in our consciousnesses. Furthermore. Though theists and monotheists usually find the language of emptiness strange and confusing at first, nevertheless, in theistic perspective, phenomena are also equal in a fundamental way. All are *created,* not creators; all are creatures. Therefore they are also dependently arisen, dependent on the creator deity for their existence. Monotheists do not usually affirm independent existence for themselves either, especially when the full implications of such an assertion are contemplated. Phenomena certainly are not independent of the creator deity, and they are not really independent of each other either. It is hard to argue against the proposition that phenomena deeply affect and alter one another.

The practical implications of regarding self and other as fundamentally equal and interdependent with each other and with the whole cosmos are too numerous and profound to explore in depth in a few brief comments. For starters, it is more difficult to have enemies when one understands that the others who temporarily seem to be enemies are also ever-changing, context-dependent processes. It is not that we will not have to deal with difficult people and difficult situations when we internalize the insight that others do not actually exist independently. They will still seem to be difficult, annoying, and irritating. But instead, we will be less driven by conventional reactions to provocation, such as anger, resentfulness, and a desire for revenge. Our own responses will be much less reactive, much less driven by others and their actions. They will derive much more from our own values and discipline, a kind of relative independence that is well worth pursuing. Aware of others as fluid processes, interdependent with their matrices, it is much more difficult to respond with anger, fear, and hatred to aggressive provocation. Rather, the response is sorrow and compassion, but not a debilitating, enervating sorrow. When the twin towers came down, my response was never anger but always sorrow for the vast confusion that drives such actions, combined with resolve not to become mute and passive in the face of such actions. I have the same response to situations in Iraq and Afghanistan (or anywhere else where such confrontations occur) and to the patriarchal, racist, or homophobic oppression faced by so many. Anger, aggression, hatred, and fear never accomplish anything of any enduring value. Any immediate changes they might bring are cosmetic in nature. This attitude about enmity is inevitable with a nondualistic view of self and other.

Furthermore, it is sobering to reflect that we always perceive the other as they arise in our consciousness and can never perceive them as they are apart from our consciousness. That too is an implication of the reality of interdependence beyond the duality of self and other. Therefore, it would be wise not to jump to conclusions about how the other is, free of our preferences, preconceptions, and reactions. Friends turn into enemies (and vice versa) extremely quickly. Just think of a former friendship or romantic relationship now in shambles. How can we be sure which impression of our former friend or lover is correct? Did the other change, or did we? Do the other's other friends and relatives still feel affection for that person? Then it is likely that our own certainties have changed, as least as much as the other changed, and our own certainties about the other could change again. As John Hick[13] and many others have discovered regarding religious others, when we actually encounter such others, they are usually rather different from the doctrines about them that we have been taught to believe. Rather than being certain that religious others fit our projections of them and beliefs about them, we should always be less opinionated, holding our own certainties about religious others loosely, rather than tightly. Such a mental outlook causes less suffering for both self and other.

This flexible state of mind also promotes the kind of compassion prized in Buddhist ethics, which always foregrounds spontaneous, unpremeditated nonfabricated compassion over any compassion based on obligation, command, or unhealthy enmeshment with others. Compassion arising out of a vision of the fundamental equality of self and other is not directed for or against a specific object. It is not directed only at those whom one likes or with whom one is related. Dropping the illusion of separate selfhood frees up the boundaries between self and others, so that well-being flows throughout the matrix of interdependence. The other is fundamentally no different from the self in that neither of us is an object among objects. One does not need commandments or external codes of ethics to tell one how to treat another who is no different from oneself, though there are Buddhist

13. See chapter 6, above.

codes of ethics for the level of provisional teachings and understandings. Furthermore, true compassion is never forceful, unlike some versions of ethics of obligation and commandment. When one truly realizes that self and other do not exist independently but only interdependently, compassion arises spontaneously.

It is especially important to separate true compassion based on insight into our inseparability and coequality with others from the unhealthy *enmeshment* with others often called codependence in much self-help literature. Often mistaken for compassion by those who are codependent, their caring for the other is actually a form of neediness and a way of living through others rather than living one's own life. The codependent subject's sense of well-being depends on getting those with whom one is enmeshed to change or on protecting them or on taking charge for them. Because of their enmeshment with the other, they often cannot actually be present to and for the other, especially if the other happens to be suffering; instead they want to fix the situation and change others so that they will feel more comfortable themselves. As a result, their concern is often more harmful than helpful, even if it is based on good intentions.

Another pitfall to true compassion in addition to enmeshment with others is what often passes for concern for social reform. But that kind of so-called compassion is often a dualistic project. One thinks that one knows what others need. They need to be more like me or my group, to think or act more like us, so I am going to work very hard to change things on their behalf, motivated by my compassion for them. It has taken me a long time to realize that one of the kindest and most compassionate things one can do is to let things and people be as they are, even if one thinks they are making mistakes, rather than trying to force one's version of things onto them. This point is easily demonstrated by remembering how irritating it is to have someone else aggressively push their agenda onto oneself. It is made even more clearly by remembering how many atrocities began as an idea about how to fix or improve the world or other people. This insight applies forcefully to religious others. So long as we regard them dualistically, seeing them mainly as *others* to our *us*, we do not have much to offer them. Under those conditions, it is a mistake to think that we have the solution.

This ethic of not interfering with others may appear to outsiders as lack of sufficient concern for justice and social change. Many have long criticized Buddhists for a seeming lack of sufficient social engagement. This is not a book about Buddhism and social justice, and I cannot adequately consider those issues in this context. However, I will say two things. The first is that projects for social change are often heavily dependent on aggression and self-righteousness in the psyches of those promoting the social change.

They feel that they need their self-righteous anger to keep them going. But this self-righteous, aggressive stance is actually quite counterproductive. The situation is becoming fully polarized as those on the other side fight back against the aggression and anger directed at them. Those whose motivation to work for social change is fueled mainly by self-righteous anger often also face serious burnout. Anger, even when used in the service of a just cause, is corrosive for the one who indulges in it. The second thing I will say is that regarding the primary social-justice cause in my life, feminism, purifying my concerns of their aggressive self-righteousness has greatly improved my ability to continue to maintain a lifelong involvement with feminist issues and has greatly improved my ability to communicate about the issues in a way that others can hear. In fact, I would say that no change in my whole life has been as welcome and salutary. I have often written about how important these changes have been for me.[14]

Understanding self and others as interdependent also promotes another nuance that I think is critical for more successful interactions in a religiously diverse world. Understanding self and other as fluid, interdependent processes compels us to think of neither as static, singular, or unchanging. Though in this chapter, I have mainly applied the implications of interdependence and going beyond a rigid duality of self and other to what we conventionally call the other, the same logic applies to oneself as well. This insight will be essential to our discussions of identity in the next section of this book. Standard English usage, growing, in my view, out of a substantialist, dualistic worldview tends to talk of self or identity as if it were monolithic, fixed, and independent. This view of self helps promote a rigid dichotomy of self and other, even *the Other*, which easily and imperceptibly morphs into the *us/them* mentality so characteristic of conflict and war. But if we think about our experience at all carefully, we must concede, whatever our metaphysical views about duality and nonduality, that our sense of ourselves, of who we are, of our identity, is ever changing, context dependent, fluid, and multiple. We do not always identify with the same groups, and our primary identities change over time. Most of the time, it is difficult to separate out a single identity that trumps all the others. Truly, identity is a hyphenated matter, not just for so-called minority groups, but for all of us. And what is true for us is also true for others. For this reason, I think that the subtle linguistic change from talking about the other to talking about others is key and would promote much better discussion of religious perceptions of the so-called other. In any case, it is crucial to question what we mean by the term *other* and to question how others exist.

14. Gross, *A Garland of Feminist Reflections*, 235–44.

Chapter 8

Beyond Unity and Universalism

Appreciating Uniqueness and Diversity

Because I am writing in a cultural context in which the existence of religious diversity has previously been regarded as a flaw to be corrected by the eventual universal acceptance of one religion (always one's own, of course), this book had to begin by demonstrating the inadequacy of such a view of others and of diversity, not by discussing the flourishing that is possible with diversity. The very suggestion that religious diversity could be a resource and a blessing rather than a flaw and problem could not make sense until the impossibility and undesirability of religious uniformity could be understood. To get to that point, it was necessary to spell out several steps in detail, to clear away some underbrush so that we could get a clearer view of the valleys and mountains, so to speak.

In chapter 5 we needed to demonstrate that religious diversity may be necessary, natural, normal, and useful, simply because of the diversity of human beings—their diversity of spiritual and intellectual aptitudes, their diversity of temperaments and inclinations, and also the diverse cultures they have evolved. When we regard religious diversity as inevitable and unproblematic, then the primary question becomes whether religious ideas and practices *work*, whether they are useful tools for transforming human beings in beneficent ways. The question of the truth of religious ideas, whatever that might mean, recedes into the background. For whatever else religious truth might mean, it can't mean simply repeating formulae, as if repeating the same formula or creed often enough somehow makes it true. Conversely, if people hold firm religious convictions but are aggressive, belligerent, and intolerant of those who are different, their behavior and attitudes are not a recommendation for their beliefs and makes one question their possible truth very deeply.

Then in chapter 6, we explored the difference between words and meaning, seriously questioning the ability of words and concepts to capture the kinds of truths religions deal with. I think nothing has so fueled the conviction that religious diversity is a flaw to be stamped out than the deep-seated belief that *our* words really do the trick, that they are so accurate that they really are unsurpassable. The belief easily follows that therefore everyone else needs to use the same words that we do, even if they are translated into a different language. As we earlier had suggested the modesty of regarding doctrines and practices as tools rather than as the truth, so in chapter 6 we suggested that modesty about how much words and concepts can do is intensely liberating. Yes, we can definitely rule out some words and concepts that don't work very well—chief among them the notion that we can identify one exclusive truth among many competing religious claims. For example, how can one find a neutral basis on which to determine which scriptures actually is revealed, given that the same claim in made about a number of such texts? And, yes, if we are modest enough to regard words and concepts as rafts or pointing fingers, then, but *only* then, words do work quite well. In fact, they work splendidly.

Finally, digging deeper, in chapter 7, we needed to question the usual assumption that those whom we call "other" are simply there, independently, and that the labels and characterizations that have been attached to them by us are independently accurate rather than created by us. Looking more deeply into reality, we questioned whether self and other are as real and independent as they often seem to be. We explored the possibility that it may be more accurate to think of them as co-arising interdependently than it is to think of them as independent of each other or to think that we apprehend them accurately. If that is the case, the whole project of relating to Otherness, the supposed task of much theology of religions, needs to be reevaluated. The great advantage, in terms of flourishing with religious diversity, of making such a move, is that we could then drop objectifying and distancing terms such as *Other*, and instead mutually explore our diverse, cocreated worlds of meaning. Using language as agreed-upon conventions, which Buddhists do, we would continue to use the terms *self* and *other* without all the metaphysical baggage that has been imputed onto them in contexts in which duality is accorded more reality than it actually has.

Unity, Universality, Manyness, and Nonduality

Where does all this clearing away leave us? Not bereft and adrift, but free to appreciate both uniqueness and diversity. We begin to understand that they go together. We begin to understand that just as the wrong kind of conviction is actually imprisoning attachment, so unity and universality, focused on wrongly, can really become death dealing, both to ourselves and to others. *Unity* and *universality* are appealing slogans, but if they do not include diversity and manyness within the unity, but seek instead to unify everyone through conformity to a universal norm, they turn out to be oppressive. Those who are different do not disappear; instead they are suppressed and oppressed, as has been the case in many pursuits of ideals. Single standards for the ideal gender, race, sexual orientation, or culture have amply shown how easily a pious ideal becomes an oppressive norm, as women, people of color, people with different sexual orientations and members of foreign cultures can vibrantly attest. People who like to shout about unity and universality rarely stop to think about their oppressive underside, about how impossible it is for everyone to be the same as everyone else, or about how undesirable that would be.

It is the same with religions. We do not help others, nor do we dignify our own religion by regarding it as the One True Faith, so wonderful that everyone else should adopt it. It is even worse when various pressures are brought to bear on those with a different or with no religious identity. If we value our own religion, if we find it life giving, then, rather than regarding it as the norm for everyone else, we need to recognize that others find their religions to be as life giving as we find ours to be. That simple contemplation would short-circuit all exclusive truth claims. Such claims become one of the few unacceptable positions in a religiously diverse world because they are so harmful. We have already shown the logical and ethical bases for declaring them unacceptable. Exclusive truth claims defy both the golden and the silver rules because they cannot be universalized. If others were to do as we do when we make exclusive truth claims, the only result is conflict (or if one side has enough power, the suppression of other religions). Christians rightly resent that Christians cannot easily practice or worship in some Muslim countries. But these same Christians then try to ban Muslim or sometimes even Buddhist or Hindu religious centers in the United States, and calls for banning Muslim centers have become quite vociferous in the United States in some cases.

Rather than idealizing unity and oneness, religions deriving from Indian cultures, including Buddhism, assume that manyness, and thus diversity, is natural and normal. Things are, or to be more precise, appear *only* because they are different. In the natural world and in the realm of form, of phenomena or appearances, manyness is necessary. It is impossible to imagine it being any different. How could there be individuality if there were not many? How could there be individuality if the unity of universal norms prevailed? This is why, when we try to talk about how things are beyond the relative level, Buddhists always use language of nonduality rather than language about unity and oneness. Forcing language to point to reality as best we can, Buddhists always talk about nonduality rather than about oneness or unity. What is being denied with this term is the ultimate reality of the cosmic dualisms so popular in so many religions. The assertion of a truly real opposition between good and evil, light and dark, right and wrong, and, most important and devastating of all, the independent and ultimate reality of self and other, were put to rest in chapter 7.

Peace to all who want immediately to jump to the conclusion that then we must be thoroughgoing relativists at all levels, having no standards at all. Obviously, we have relative ethics. What is being claimed here is that things such as good and evil are not ultimates, not truly real, because they exist only *relative to* each other, in *interdependence* with each other. They are not dual or Not Two because they cannot really be separated. That is how things are. That ultimate nonduality leaves plenty of space for many things to appear, to arise. Sometimes they are in harmony and other times not. Some of them are worthy of being nurtured and some of them are not. But they cannot and should not be reduced to a single standard, to uniformity, to norms thought to prevail universally. That such a position may also be compatible with monotheism and Christianity is indicated by the Indian Christian theologian Stanley J. Samartha. In his suggestions for formulating Christian theology that may be more appropriate for a Christian pluralist theologian, he writes, "The Mystery . . . cannot even be described as 'one.' It is 'not-two' (*advaita*), thereby indicating that diversity is within the heart of Being itself and therefore may be intrinsic to human nature itself."[1]

Ironically, once when I made this case to a theologically conservative colleague, he said, as a criticism of me, that I seemed to be claiming that Buddhist or Indian ways of thinking about unity and manyness were "better" than Western or Christian ways. He seemed to think, as do so many, that because I value diversity and manyness, therefore, I am disallowed from claiming that some positions are problematic, even wrong. Perhaps I would prefer the term *misguided* to the term *wrong* because it is less absolutistic. But clearly some theological positions are misguided, and as I claimed in chapter 5, the criterion for making such judgments is the impact they have

---

1. Samartha, "The Cross and the Rainbow," 75.

on the ethics of those who hold those theological views. I definitely would claim that theological and philosophical views that can accommodate difference and diversity in religion are superior to those that cannot, for both ethical and philosophical reasons. I will rest my case by quoting a Christian theologian making a passionate case for affirming diversity in religion.

> Denial of diversity, refusal to entertain alternatives, avoidance of disjunctions and ruptures in the human fabric and insistence on oneness result in idolatry. Idolatry is the insistence that there is only one way, one norm, one truth. It is the refusal to be corrected or informed by the "other."[2]

I actually find it quite amusing that the second anyone suggests that it is possible and even worthy to develop theologies that undercut exclusive or inclusive positions in Christianity and other religions, someone immediately worries loudly and vociferously that "there are things we can't tolerate."[3] One such theologian wrote:

> Ecumenical tolerance represents a moral and religious gain, a step toward love and acceptance. But it has its own deep risks and one of them is the specter of relativity, this loss of any place to stand, this elimination of the very heart of the religious as ultimate concern.
>
> Plurality, as we have seen drives in the direction of ecumenical tolerance. Plurality, however, has another face than this, a face fully as terrifying as the relativity just described. For within the plurality of religions that surround us are forms of the religious that are intolerable, and intolerable because they are demonic. Toleration is here checked by the intolerable; and plurality means *both*.[4]

I simply cannot follow the logic behind the fear that if we do not elevate one of the world's religions as solely true, that would result in wholesale, thoroughgoing moral relativism. Furthermore, some of the greatest atrocities, such as Nazism, to which this author was referring, as well as sexism, racism, homophobia, and economic disparity have been tolerated precisely in religious contexts that have also proclaimed very loudly that theirs is the One True Faith. In an interesting follow-up to the passage quoted above,

2. Driver, "The Case for Pluralism," 216.

3. For a very interesting example of a Christian theologian just beginning to think about religious diversity in a new and much less exclusivistic way and his immediate upwelling of concern about "relativism," see Gilkey, "Plurality and Its Theological Implications" 37–50; see especially 44–48.

4. Ibid., 44.

which was given at a Christian symposium on pluralist theologies, one of the Indian Christians commented to the author of that passage, "Intolerable? Did you say intolerable? But you do tolerate them—for they exist . . . Oh yes, my friend, you do tolerate them."[5] So much for any protection from ethical lapses if one makes exclusive or inclusive claims for one's religion. There seems to be no correlation at all between ethical uprightness and regarding one's own religion as the One True Faith!

In keeping with a principle I have been advocating throughout this book, I suggest that it may be much more fruitful to isolate the few concepts and practices that *don't* work well, that are unfruitful, rather than trying to find one better or correct relative language among the many examples found in the world's religions—not only among the many religions, but within each one as well. I think we can rest the case that the most suitable candidate for a religious idea that does not work well is the idea that there could be one religious claim to which all people in all cultures must adhere. As Indian Christian theologian Stanley Samartha said, "diversity is within the heart of Being itself and therefore may be intrinsic to human nature itself."[6]

Does Uniqueness Equal Universal Relevance?

We are moving away from idealizing unity and universality to recognizing the value, the life-giving qualities, of diversity and uniqueness, and also to recognizing that they go together. In a diverse world, there are many unique things. It would seem that uniqueness is at the opposite end of the spectrum from universality. To my ear, *uniqueness* connotes singularity, that there is only one such phenomenon, whereas *universality* connotes that there is one norm or ideal for many specific phenomena, something that is claimed to be relevant or applicable to one and all. They seem to be quite opposite to me. The *Oxford English Dictionary* seems to agree. It gives the first definition of *unique* as "of which there is only one, single, sole, solitary." It further defines the term: "that which, or he who is, the only one of a kind, having no like or equal: unparalleled, unrivaled." But it goes on to say that "the loose sense 'unusual, remarkable' is widespread but is often regarded as incorrect: since *unique* means 'being the only one of its kind' it is either unique or not."[7] But the *Shorter Oxford English Dictionary* doesn't suggest that uniqueness implies universal relevance. Something can easily be unsurpassed at being what it is without being universally relevant for everyone.

5. Driver, "The Case for Pluralism," 206.

6. Samartha, The Cross and the Rainbow," 75.

7 Brown, *Shorter Oxford English Dictionary*, 2:3442.

Nevertheless, recent Christian commentators have tried to have it both ways, to argue that because Christianity has *unique* perspectives and teachings, it therefore must be universally relevant. In his comments about my lifework, referred to in chapter 6 as well, Paul Knitter suggested that perhaps I should concede "that some rafts, some events, and some persons represent a unique or distinctive discovery or expression of truth that cannot be found elsewhere and that is universally relevant. Christians believe this about Jesus."[8] Notice what has happened. The argument is quite slippery. A claim that one could hardly disagree with (Jesus and Christian teachings about Jesus are unique) slides into a claim that this unique phenomenon is universally relevant (something that I *must* therefore find relevant for myself), a claim I can't easily concede. It is not that I want to dispute with Christians that they are mistaken about what Jesus means to them or to suggest that their theology is inappropriate for themselves or that they should change their views about Jesus. I don't even want to dispute the claim that Jesus *could* be universally relevant, in the sense that anyone, Christian or not, *might be* inspired by his example. But is that required of everyone? The *possibility* of universal relevance is quite different from a claim of *inevitable or necessary* universal relevance. Buddhism is also universally relevant, in the sense that anyone might choose to follow some of its precepts and could benefit from doing so. However, I would never claim that such is required of all decent human beings, or that everyone would benefit from doing so. It is quite different to suggest that anyone could benefit from something than to claim that everyone will. Thus, it seems frightfully easy for Christians to slip into old claims about Jesus and his universal relevance. Paul Knitter would not expect me to accept the old kind of Christian claim (that Jesus in my only savior and that I must confess him as such). But I suspect he does want me to see Jesus as a unique example of human virtue and, therefore, as someone who should be relevant to me in some way. It is easy to concede that he is *an* example of human virtue, but unique in the sense that we are missing something absolutely vital and necessary if we don't pay much attention to him? I simply do not see the grounds by which one can derive from the conclusion that something is unique that it is also universally relevant. It is logically possible, of course, but by no means a necessary conclusion.

Some pluralist Christians still say a lot about the uniqueness and universal relevance of Jesus. Pluralist theologians John Hick and Paul Knitter organized a major project involving a conference with a great deal of discussion and feedback for paper presenters that resulted in the book *The Myth of Christian Uniqueness*, which strongly argued that traditional claims about

8. Knitter, "Rita Gross," 83.

Christianity's exclusive truth were outmoded in a world in which many religions need to coexist. In their introduction, they explained that what they were calling a myth was not the simple sense of the uniqueness of Christianity (that it is different from other religions) but "the unique definiteness, absoluteness, normativeness, superiority of Christianity in comparison with other religions of the world."[9] The book argued very forcefully against exclusivist and inclusivist positions, and there was quite a vociferous reaction to it. A rebuttal, *Christian Uniqueness Reconsidered: The Myth of a Pluralistic Theology of Religions,* was published in 1990. Its authors all wanted to argue, not just for the uniqueness of Christ, but also for some kind of universal relevance for him. I want to suggest, however, that part of the problem is linguistic unclarity. Are all these Christians arguing about the *uniqueness* of Christ or for his *universal* relevance? Returning to dictionary definitions of *unique* cited above may be helpful. We can easily concede the one without granting the other.

Somehow, even Christians who are very sympathetic to other religions, who have promoted interreligious dialogue and pluralist theologies, and who have learned a great deal from other religions seem to have some urgency that members of other religions develop appreciation for Jesus. I must admit that I find this urgency strange. But I do find it as a thread in the thinking of two men, both of whom I admire greatly and with whom I have worked closely in Buddhist-Christian dialogue and in discussing pluralist theologies of religion—Paul Knitter and John Cobb—and I must admit their claims are surprising to me. Or perhaps, given my personal history, I am hypervigilant to any tendencies toward exclusive truth claims.

I would like to discuss John Cobb's position first. Few if any Christian thinkers have contributed more to our understanding of the importance of interreligious dialogue, and few have been better exemplars of that art. His contributions to dialogue will be considered more fully in chapter 15. As cofounder of the International Buddhist-Christian Theology Encounter, better known as the Cobb-Abe group, he led that group, of which I was a member, for many years. I have known and admired him for years, and respect him as a wonderful colleague, and as someone who has been supportive of my own work while providing many helpful questions that prodded me to think more deeply and clarify my own thinking. Very early on, he asked me to think more deeply about whether my work as a Buddhist feminist might owe a great deal to my Western roots and whether it would be difficult or impossible for an Asian Buddhist to do similar work? While I am somewhat skeptical of Western claims that Buddhism and Indian religions in general

9. Hick and Knitter, *The Myth of Christian Uniqueness,* vii.

lack a sufficient social ethic, I admit that I remain immersed in my Western roots to some extent and regard that immersion as helpful. Western Buddhism is not and should not be a carbon copy of any extant version of Asian Buddhism.

John Cobb has made many statements throughout his long career concerning whether or not Christianity or Christ has universal relevance, and they are always characterized by thoughtfulness and nonarrogance. Earlier in his career, in a statement published in 1984, more towards the beginning of his discussions of pluralism and dialogue, he made the following rather remarkable statement:

> In faithfulness to Christ, I must be open to others. When I recognize in those others something of worth and that I have not derived from my own tradition, I must be ready to learn even if it threatens my present beliefs . . . I cannot know that when I have learned what I have to learn here and been transformed by it, I will still see faithfulness to Christ as my calling . . . in faithfulness to Christ, I must be prepared to give up even faithfulness to Christ. If that is where I am led, to remain a Christian would be to become an idolater in the name of Christ. That would be blasphemy.[10]

This statement summarizes much of his thinking about what interreligious dialogue implies. However, such openness to change one's religious perspective to the extent outlined in the quotation is more than what is needed to learn how to flourish with religious diversity. That goal only requires that we learn to relax about religious diversity, not that we have to completely alter our inherited views. It is inspiring, however, to see such genuine curiosity and openness to growth and development.

As Cobb continued learning about and dialoguing especially with Buddhists, he made new claims and clarified his thinking further in his essay in *Christian Uniqueness Reconsidered*, the rebuttal book to *The Myth of Christian Uniqueness*. Cobb had refused to contribute an essay to that book because he did not think the proper goal of pluralist theologians was to try develop a metatheology beyond and independent of the various current religious perspectives. Instead, he advocated that each religion should concede that its members couldn't possibly know everything there was to be known currently, but could "in faithfulness to its past . . . be enriched and transformed in . . . interactions with other traditions."[11] He wants the separate traditions to remain true to their own past norms but also to continue

10. Cobb, *Transforming Christianity and the World*, 45–46.
11. Cobb, "Beyond 'Pluralism,'" 92.

to develop within those norms and in interaction with other traditions; and Cobb especially wants Christians to do so, claiming that Christianity is well equipped to develop in this way. Cobb concedes that he cannot prove that other traditions are less well equipped to develop in contact with other traditions, but he is sure of Christianity. Graciously, he says he hopes he is proven wrong that Christians have an advantage in this competition—and he does call for competition. He then makes a sweeping claim for Christianity.

> I am making a claim for Christian superiority. It is not a claim that Christians are better people or that Christian history has made a more superior contribution to the planet than have other traditions or that Christian institutions are superior. The claim is only that a tradition in which Jesus Christ is the center has in principle no need for exclusive boundaries, that it can be open to transformation by what it learns from others, that it can move forward to become a community of faith that is informed by the whole of human history, that its theology can become truly global.[12]

This is a very sweeping proposal and in many ways quite unclear. In some ways, it seems to be a mirror image of more common pluralist proposals suggesting that there is a metareligion beneath the specifics of the various named traditions of the past. But this metareligion would still be Christianity—a Christianity that had absorbed everything worthwhile from all other traditions. Is this the ultimate Christian triumphalism? And, most problematic, Cobb still finds claims to Christian superiority attractive, even if it is a call for superiority at something in which most traditional Christians would be utterly uninterested. Why the call for competition among religions, and why is it so important to be *the* best, to be superior? Isn't a simpler uniqueness sufficient? What would happen to religious diversity if his vision were fulfilled? This sounds a great deal like a proposal of which I have always been suspicious: what I call a "good parts" religion, made of all the available materials. Such a proposal actually wants to eliminate religious diversity by creating a new universal religion. Still, this universal religion would have all the problems of any traditional religion making exclusive truth claims—a lack of sufficient diversity to meet human needs for options.

Finally, in a still later comment, Cobb expressed his deep wish that all religions would find a place for Jesus Christ within their own traditions, without becoming Christian. He claimed that Judaism (at least in the Jews for Jesus movement), Islam, and Hinduism already have such niches for Jesus. But he would like to see Jesus have a place in Buddhism, the religion

---

12. Ibid., 92–93.

with which he has had so much interaction. In a somewhat long discussion, he suggests that though Buddhism has great wisdom and many virtues, "from the Christian perspective, Buddhism is incomplete."[13] He continues for a number of pages to detail what he sees as Buddhism's inadequate approaches to justice and social criticism, a comment familiar to Buddhists who interact with Christians, and in line with Cobb's very early, and useful, suggestions to me about my own work as a Buddhist feminist. I would say several things in reply. First, while the language of justice and rights is foreign to Buddhism and may well have relevance for Buddhists, I do not think that Cobb fully understands or acknowledges the centrality of compassion language in Buddhism, or how much that language fulfills the same role in Buddhist speech as justice language does in Abrahamic traditions, but without the stridency and self-righteousness of justice language.

In much earlier writings I have called for a dialogue of Christian justice language and Buddhist compassion language.[14] However, especially regarding issues of gender and feminism, my later work is much more wholly immersed in Buddhist categories (without appeal to the language of Western feminism), but it is even more radically and thoroughly feminist than my earlier work. I regard this as a positive development because *Buddhists* are much more likely to hear what I am saying if I do not sound like an interloper from the West to them. Whatever the complex, multireligious personal genesis of my own concern with gender equity in Buddhism is, I am most concerned that Buddhism change. For that reason, I have always tried to present my case in authentically Buddhist ways, and I have finally succeeded.[15] But it has taken me thirty years of full-time study and practice to learn Buddhist sensibilities to this extent, which should clearly indicate how subtle and difficult these interreligious transformations are. Fortunately, however, learning simply to flourish with religious diversity, without going further, is much easier.

Paul Knitter is another person who has greatly enhanced the cause of interreligious understanding—more by his clear writings on the various options within theology of religions than by interreligious dialogue. His own most impressive interreligious dialogue is his own internal dialogue, which finally led him to the conclusion that *Without Buddha I Could Not Be a Christian*, to quote the title of his book.[16] Towards the end of his book, Knitter reveals that he finally did formally become a "dual belonger" by taking

---

13. Cobb, *Transforming Christianity and the World*, 155.

14. Gross, *Buddhism after Patriarchy*, 134–35, 169–70.

15. Gross, "How Clinging to Gender Subverts Enlightenment." 18–19, 32.

16. Knitter, *Without Buddha I Could Not Be a Christian*.

the triple refuge in the Buddha, *Dharma*, and *Sangha* without renouncing his affiliations with Christianity.

How does such a Buddhist Christian (for Knitter says he is Buddhist Christian rather than a Christian Buddhist[17]) deal with all the claims about Christian superiority and Christ's uniqueness? I have already narrated his challenge to me in his comments on my lifework and have begun to articulate my response. He also dealt with this question more formally and in more depth in *Without Buddha I Could Not Be a Christian* and in his most recent survey of Christian theologies of religions, *Introducing Theologies of Religion*. In both cases, he wants to hold onto claims for Jesus's uniqueness, which, as I have already stated, is not disputed. He makes a similar case in both books: that Jesus is not only unique but universally relevant because his message "does not seem to be found as clearly or as powerfully in most other religions or religious leaders."[18] (I think that claim would be very difficult to demonstrate definitively.) According to Knitter, Jesus's central message has to do with what liberation theologians call "the preferential option for the poor," a cause that ties in well with Knitter's lifelong involvement with Latin American liberation theology and issues. Knitter seems to believe that Jesus's life and message teaches, as no other, that it is mandatory for us, not only to be concerned about the poor and about victims, but to regard this as the most important social issue of our day. Therein lie both the uniqueness and the universal relevance of Jesus's message, as Knitter sees it. And he communicates well his sense of urgency that others come to see it that way.

> What makes Jesus unique for me is not simply something only "for me," something that only I or my fellow Christians can appreciate. There's a universal quality about it. I want others to see in him what I see in him; I want Jesus to make a difference in their lives as he has made in my life—perhaps not as deep or as sweeping, but still a real difference.[19]

What of my reaction? I suspect that it might be easier to be more enthusiastic about Jesus if so many claims about his exclusive and universal relevance had not been made so forcefully for so long. Living in a Christian culture in which the power of the evangelical religious Right seems to be growing yearly, in which the money says "In God we trust," and where every year I have to go through an orgy of Christmas extravaganzas, there is still a quality of being force-fed something I don't want to swallow. Moreover, the social-justice cause with which I identify is women's oppression, much more

17. Ibid., xiv.

18. Knitter, *Introducing Theologies of Religion*, 146.

19. Knitter, *Without Buddha I Could Not Be a Christian*, 123.

so than poverty, given that all women, not just poor women, suffer under male domination. Not that issues of justice, peace, equality, and ecology should ever be pitted against each other. Granted, there are some materials in stories told about the life of Jesus that could be lifted up to speak to issues of gender justice, but they would not be unique in the world's religions, and don't seem to have made much difference in Christianity. But for me to catch any fever of enthusiasm about something uniquely relevant that was really going to make a difference for me, gender justice would have to be more prominently part of the mix. As I already said, it's not that in any way I want to undercut Christians' enthusiasm for and love of Jesus. It's just that for their enthusiasm and love to be genuine, life-giving, and life-saving for them does not require that he mean the same thing to the rest of us. If he did, we'd probably be Christians! As I have already said, I do find it odd that even Christians who are very sympathetic to other religions and have learned a great deal from dialogue with them still have such urgency that non-Christians find a place for Jesus in their religious lives.

The preceding reflections leave me with a question that is also urgent. Given that I resist taking on what my beloved Christian colleagues find so meaningful, I must question whether I feel the same urgency about any-thing Buddhist that I really want my Christian colleagues to take on? Am I practicing a double standard? That is a difficult question. Certainly Bud-dhist practice, especially meditation, has been life giving and life sustaining for me. More than anything else, it has helped diminish all the sources of greatest pain in my life and has been instrumental in fostering whatever peace, joy, and contentment I now feel, which are considerable. Certainly I would want those same benefits for my Christian colleagues.

But to experience those benefits, do they have to do as I have done and think as I think? I think not. Do I think my Christian colleagues could benefit from meditation? Definitely, yes. But do I, therefore, want everyone to meditate? I doubt that they would all take up meditation practice, no matter who recommends it. It would be just as unrealistic for me to hope or expect that my Christian colleagues would take up religious practices that Buddhists find life giving as it is for Christians to hope and expect that everyone else will take up what they find most life giving—Jesus's life and teaching. So I only want them to take up Buddhist meditation practices if it seems to them that they could benefit from them, and if they freely chose to do so. Wanting us all to be the same has been the problem. It would not be solved by getting everyone to meditate any more than it is solved by getting everyone to find a place for Jesus in their religious lives. What people think religiously and what practices they do are not that important to me. What people are like is much more important. Are they compassionate, kind, generous, able to refrain from anger and aggression, able to cheerfully let others be different from them? Those qualities are much more important than what methods people use to attain them. What seems important to me is that we figure out how to differ, even to differ profoundly. To be able to differ peacefully, we need to become peaceful, gentle people familiar with equanimity. Whatever belief system and religious practices support that state of mind are to be promoted, and whichever ones militate against it are to be discouraged. Thus, there is one thing I most definitely do want from all of us. Whatever else we value, we must value uniqueness and diversity rather than enforcing unity and universality.

Uniqueness and Diversity

Having set aside oneness and universality in favor of nonduality and diversity, we can turn again to *uniqueness*. And uniqueness fares much better in world that fosters diversity than in a monochrome world in which there is a single universal ideal supposedly open to all but only at the price of great conformity. Even then, for many, it is impossible even to attempt to attain a universal ideal that is also quite specific. Single racial, gender, ethnic, and even class ideals are unattainable by many, both biologically and emotionally. Recognizing and appreciating uniqueness is such a blessing, especially after having been burdened by worries about needing to find religious claims so cogent that everyone would or should be compelled to accept them.

A very simple linguistic change demonstrates what is at stake in the acceptance of uniqueness and diversity. As one advocate for the comparative study of diverse religions has put it, "Our own world, instead of being taken for granted, becomes exposed *as* a world, its contents held up to the comparative mirror and we become a phenomenon to ourselves."[20] These words and the experience behind them are very powerful and transformative. The burden of assuming that our perspective is normal, normative, and universal falls away. We realize that our perspective is *a* perspective, one among many, and we are no longer indifferent to it because we no longer take it for granted. Our world is *a* world, one among many others, not *the* world that we had taken for granted and that we ignored. Our world is *interesting* because it is specific and unique, not because it is the only possible outlook we could have. In the process of moving from thinking of our outlook as *the* truth about the world to thinking of it as *a* worldview, one among many, we see and understand ourselves much more clearly. Part of that seeing includes seeing strengths and weaknesses in the perspectives

20. Paden, *Religious Worlds*. 165.

we take for granted, and making appropriate self-corrections in the light of what we learn from the diversity all around us.

One of the implications of living in a religiously diverse world is that one's own perspective and the perspective of the religion with which one identifies is unique, exquisitely itself: not generic, not a universal norm, and not identical with any other. Nor does one wish it were otherwise. If one has accepted religious diversity as normal and natural, one can then rejoice and delight in one's own specificity without competitiveness or defensiveness. We no longer have to worry about whether our religion is the best or fear that another religion's might be truer and wonder what changes that would require of us. Having long ago given up the rather strange notion that one religion could be uniquely true (along with the quest for an abstract truth undergirding all religions), having realized that religions are more about facilitating human well-being than about metaphysical truth, and even having given up on the idea that whatever truth and virtue religions may have could be adequately expressed in words and concepts, we happily and cheerfully relax. Religious others and ourselves simply are as they/we are—coinhabitants of the same planet on a level playing field. Comfortable with who we are, we are also comfortable with how they are.

However, for all those benefits to become real, we actually do have to live in a religiously diverse world and interact with religious others who co-inhabit that world. In nature, monocultures, such as forests with only one species of trees or something like lawns, are not considered viable, healthy environments for living organisms because they are so fragile and so subject to mass extinction when any adversity hits. I suggest that for humans, living in cultural monocultures, where everyone is more or less like everyone else, and especially where there is no diversity in religious outlooks, value systems, and cultural practices, is similarly stunting and debilitating. Humans may initially prefer to stay in flocks or herds where there is little diversity, but that does not mean such a situation is ideal. Intellectual and spiritual inbreeding and isolation are just as problematic as the physical variety. Everyone needs interreligious education and exposure so that the world can be a safer place and we can finally flourish with religious diversity. In the final section of this book, in chapters 14 through 17, we will look into the practicalities of such interreligious learning.

But to become comfortable in the religiously diverse world, to flourish in it, we must train ourselves properly for membership in it. The real impediments to flourishing with religious diversity have nothing to do with the religious others; they have to do with us and are of our own making. For all the attention given to *others* in exclusivist, inclusivist, and even pluralist theologies of religion, they are not the paramount issue. We are. Buddhists always say that suffering, in the long run, is not due to others; it is due to us, and especially to our attitudes toward others. We also say regularly that one can't do much about external conditions, about what the others are doing and saying, but we certainly can do something about ourselves, our reactions, our expectations, and our own ability to flourish, including about our ability to flourish with religious diversity instead of regarding it as a mistake or a problem. It is our own *discomfort* with religious diversity, our wish for religious uniformity, that is the real problem, not the existence of religious others. I cannot emphasize this point enough. Thus, we turn next to the topic of how to work with our own minds as we discuss identity and religious identities in the next section of this book.

Section 4

Identity, Especially Religious Identities

Chapter 9

Who Am I?

Hyphenated Identities and the Composite Self in a Diverse World

IN THIS SECTION OF the book and this chapter, we move from considering religious others to discussing identity—the subjective pole of the interdependent matrix in which both self and other dwell. As we saw in chapter 7, in this interdependent relationship, the leader is actually our own subjectivity, not the other, despite naïve, prereflective impressions to the contrary. Prior to serious reflection, most people assume that their opinions and reactions are governed by what others do and say. But deeper reflection demonstrates that we always have a choice in how we evaluate and react to others. "You made me do x" is one of the most inaccurate and misleading sentences in any language. We are not simply pawns or puppets of others whose activities and opinions dictate our reactions.

Thus, it would actually be more appropriate to begin our discussions of others, identity, and religious diversity with considerations of identity. But the conversation thus far has always begun with comments about *others*, whom most commentators consider to be the problem. Furthermore, in the linear medium of language, it is impossible to simultaneously discuss interdependent phenomena. Therefore, I am also following that convention. However, recollection of the issues already discussed about religious others will quickly bring to mind how many issues of identity and subjectivity have already been discussed. We have already made many comments about the kind of subjectivity that can flourish with religious diversity and the kind that is uncomfortable with religious diversity. But we have not yet addressed directly what identity or subjectivity is and how it is constructed. As is well known, Buddhists attribute all suffering to mistaken identity, to profound mistakes in understanding who we are and what we are not.

The Buddhist View: Separate Selfhood and Oppositional Duality as Mistaken Identity

For ordinary people of any religion or ideology, Buddhists included, a large component of their identity is based on their sense of being separate from and different from others. By adulthood, if not much earlier, this sense of oneself as a separate entity is so entrenched that it seems incontrovertible. This identity is formed out of contrast, out of difference. "Me" is "here." "Me" is "not that, not them." Whatever is not "that" is "me," and that boundary seems very clear. It is not just Western psychology that approaches basic identity formation in this way. Buddhists agree that the ordinary, conventional ego, the ego that Buddhists would call samsaric (basically confused about reality) is formed in that fashion. In his famous book *Cutting through Spiritual Materialism*, Chogyam Trungpa discusses how ego, or the sense of being a separate self, develops. Fairly early in the process, the nascent sense of being a separate self begins to rely on the others out there. "By doing so we reassure ourselves that we exist. 'If I can feel that out there, then I must be here.'"[1] So it is easy to see how much ordinary identity depends on duality. Duality actually undermines the reality of the separate self because the sense of being a separate self cannot exist in the absence of perceived duality. But the imputation of truly existing duality becomes so strong that its reality is accepted unquestioningly and, thus, the separate, real self is also accepted unquestioningly. So the first step in building the mistaken identity that results in the suffering of conventional cyclic existence is creation of the imputed separate self by reference to the other—what is called the basic split in some more advanced Buddhist literature.

Reflection and contemplation reveal how this process works to form an individual's sense of separate identity, but in group formation the process can really become intense and dangerous. Identities as part of a group are integral to most people's sense of who they are as individuals: "I am who I am because I'm not one of them." But identity formation does not stop at this level. It usually goes on to make the judgment, Not only am I who I am because I'm not one of them, but we are better than them, which makes me

1. Trungpa, *Cutting through Spiritual Materialism*, 126.

one of the superior people. Thus, much ordinary identity is not only dualistic; it is also oppositional.[2] The ease with which people accept claims about the superiority of their own group, which includes exclusive truth claims in religion (or in any other endeavor) and the tenacity with which folks cling to them against all logic and comfort indicate how important such claims are to maintaining identity. Many people argue that such group identities are inevitable and even helpful, at least in some cases. Without deep spiritual training, many people seem unable to drop the oppositional dimension of their identities, which is usually trained into them when they are children. But an oppositional identity will always include elements of discomfort, anger, and fear. It can never really be at ease. Thus, it could hardly be the result or the goal of spiritual maturity or the greatest level of insight that the human mind can achieve.

Buddhist claims that this separate ego is illusory initially seem incomprehensible to most people. Yet from one perspective, we have already demonstrated in chapter 7, that the duality of self and other is not as real as it seems without examination and introspection. That is one level of Buddhist deconstruction of our common ideas about identity. But we have to go further. For many people, even if it is accepted that the self exists only in interdependence with the others but not by itself, it is thought that at least that self is singular and lasting. We still think we are an *entity* that *lasts*. But Buddhist introspection also questions both these suppositions, with significant implications for the expectation that a strong religious identity would, of necessity, entail exclusive truth claims.

The Buddhist View, Part II:
Identity as Composite, Not Monolithic, as Changing, Not Static

Whereas in contemporary identity politics one aspect of identity significantly trumps all other aspects (as if that aspect were the only thing about oneself that really mattered), in Buddhist thought the sense of self is always composed of many parts, no matter how singular the self may feel to us. Thus, from a Buddhist point of view, severely pronounced identity politics would be a mistake, and as we will see, the same thing applies to religious identity. A tightly held religious identity that overrides all other aspects of one's identity is actually quite fragile and brittle, not strong and secure, despite how often some religious believers are told the opposite. Buddhists would say that taking any identity as one's whole or real self is actually a

---

2. For a recent Western psychological account of this process, see Berreby, *Us and Them*.

serious mistake, one of the most serious mistakes one can make. It is also the source of much of the suffering in the world, especially the suffering of conflict. Conflict, after all, always results in suffering, and much conflict is a result of people with tightly held identities fighting with each other, each trying to convince the other that only one of them holds a cogent position— a very common scenario in both religion and politics. When we acknowledge the hyphenated nature of our identity, we are much less likely to fixate on any one element of our identity, such as a religious identity, and, as a result, are much more comfortable with diverse others.

The Buddhist terms for the composite self are *anatman* in Sanskrit and *anicca* in Pali. Often translated as "egolessness" or "no-self," these terms are notoriously difficult to render accurately into English. Although these translations sound negative, egolessness *does not* mean that one does not exist. It only means that we do not exist in the ways that we conventionally assume we exist. Nevertheless, these teachings are often extremely confusing to outsiders and to those just beginning to study Buddhism. They are also the most difficult aspect of Buddhism for inexperienced teachers of Buddhism to present successfully. Many university professors of comparative religions who are not Buddhist practitioners simply fail. Even more telling, many who identify as Buddhists cannot explain this concept cogently to their friends and family. It must be noted in passing that this concept is unique in world religions. Nor it is helpful to draw upon most Western psychological systems, especially Freudian or Jungian systems, to try to understand Buddhist teachings about egolessness. What Buddhists mean by egolessness has nothing to do with having what is often called a "weak ego" or a "strong ego" in Western popular language. These teachings must be approached in their own frame of reference, on their own terms.[3]

In technical language, Buddhist egolessness is the claim that a permanent (i.e., immortal, unchanging, independent, singular) self cannot be found, no matter where we look, no matter how long or how hard we search. It is simply *lacking*, and this lack can be frightening. One reaction to this *lack* is to project our discomfort with it outwards, onto others, whom we either blame for our discomfort or expect to fill up our sense of lack. Either way, hostility and suffering are the outcomes. Note carefully: this is not a philosophical or metaphysical assertion but a claim about what we experience, a phenomenological claim. Buddhists have arrived at the conclusion that our sense of self or identity is composite rather than monolithic, by deconstructive analysis grounded in experience. From its beginnings, Buddhism has

---

3. For a recent Western account that is quite similar to some Buddhist thinking, see Hood, *The Self Illusion*.

insisted that what feels like a unitary self is actually a composite made of many parts. To demonstrate this claim, it asks people to find that assumed unitary self in their own experience—in their direct experience, not as a theory, belief, or dogma. In other words, to be certain that the assumed unitary self actually exists, it could not be a matter of faith but must be a matter of knowledge. Buddhists of all schools then suggest that, upon examination, what feels like a unitary self is found to be, in fact, composed of many smaller units, and that in none of those can an abiding, permanent self be found either.

One of the earliest and most enduring deconstructive analyses suggests that there are five components in our composite self—(1) form or body, (2) positive, neutral, or aversive feelings the body experiences, (3) perceptions that are the bases of those feelings, (4) numerous tendencies or habitual ways of dealing with body, feelings, and perceptions, and (5) consciousness of all these experiences. This analytical pattern is called the five *skandhas,* often translated as the five aggregates. Another common deconstructive analysis focuses on consciousness itself, which is divided into twelve discrete elements. Consciousness depends on the six sense organs and the six sense objects. (Mind is the sixth sense, and its object is thoughts.) Another analysis divides consciousness eighteen ways, adding a sense consciousness between each of the sense organs and sense objects. Analysis done by the various *abhidharma* schools[4] is even more minute and refined, but the basic point is always the same. Looking directly into our experience fails to reveal a unitary, eternal, independent or unrelated ego or self.

According to these claims, no basis for personal immortality can be found, which makes for a significant doctrinal contrast between Buddhism and Christianity. But that is not what I wish to emphasize concerning Buddhist ideas about identity as a composite rather than a monolith. The mundane sense of personal identity I am discussing in this chapter is not what Christians and others mean by an immortal soul, which is not apparent and empirical in any case. Personal immortality is not proved by finding a basis for it in everyday experience. This difference between Buddhism and Christianity is rooted in other major differences between those religions—differences about the reliability of metaphysics and revelation. For someone who

4. *Abhidharma* schools of analysis developed in Indian Buddhism several centuries after the Buddha's death and reached their highest point of development by about the fourth and fifth centuries of the common era. Though the various schools differ in details, all attempt to deconstruct what appear to be singular entities into their component parts. For Buddhist spiritual development, the purpose of this analysis is to destroy our habitual tendency to cling to things by showing that they do not exist in the way we conventionally imagine them to exist, which is what fuels our grasping tendencies. According to basic Buddhist teaching, such grasping always leads to suffering.

believes in revelation and finds metaphysics attractive, Buddhist insistence on the primacy of analytical explorations of direct experience would not be sufficient, convincing, or conclusive because such beliefs, including belief in personal immortality, do not stem from or depend on direct experience. Nor, in my view, do such metaphysical beliefs usually deeply affect ordinary, everyday, on-the-ground choices and experiences, and that is what I am talking about in my discussions of identity.

Instead I suggest that even if one wishes to believe in personal immortality, the recognition that in terms of everyday, on-the-ground experience, there are many facets to one's sense of who one is has tremendous implications for issues of religious diversity. One may be a member of any given religion, and that identity may be very strong, but it is never one's sole identity. It would be self-deceptive to claim otherwise. One may have a religious identity, but one also has family roles, an occupation, political views, a sexual orientation, a cultural identity, a racial identity, national citizenship, an educational level, membership in an age cohort, sexual identity, gender identity, membership in a denomination within one's larger religion, a relationship with the arts and/or sports . . . and other identities depending on the specifics of one's experience. Even for people for whom their religion is very important, these other identities—especially family roles and occupational identities, as well as political identities—are also important and may well absorb more time, money, and energy than religious activities. For some people, it is hard to believe that their religious identity is more important to them than their identity as a fan of their favorite sports team. Furthermore, one's identity is never confined to a single element in this list of possible identities; who one is is always a combination of various possible identities. One is never only a Christian or a Buddhist and nothing else, a father or a child and nothing else, a political conservative or liberal and nothing else. It is an illusion to imagine that one identity ever trumps all others. Even if one is not biracial, bicultural, or a multiple religious belonger, one always has a hyphenated identity.

Furthermore, throughout one's life, these various identities shift and change. Some become more dominant, and others decline in importance or drop away altogether. Family roles certainly change; at some stages of life being a child is more important, and at other stages being a parent (or a nonparent) becomes more important. At one point in life being a spouse may be central to one's identity, but then the partner may die. Or one may be abandoned or divorced. After enough such experiences, people often decide to live alone rather than to seek to be partnered. So what happened to one's identity as a spouse? Occupational roles also change significantly. One may change citizenship. Many people take on a different identity when they move from the city to the country, from the country to the city, or state to state. People may have a best friend or a set of friends, and one's identity may be bound up with being part of this circle of friends. But then things change. Conflicts develop. People move away. People get married. One may find new friends or become a loner. One's political affiliations may change—sometimes drastically. One may be part of a close-knit community focused around an interest or a common concern, but the community may splinter, or one's interests may change, along with one's identity. Many people discover a whole new self relatively late in life. Where was that self previously?

If there was a permanent, enduring self, then none of these things should happen. Indeed, a classic Buddhist proof that a permanent, enduring, real self cannot be found is such persistent, never-ending change in one's sense of who one is. This more open-ended sense of who we are is obvious if we rely on everyday, ordinary experience rather than on dogmas, metaphysics or beliefs that are superimposed onto experience. It is as if one has actually lived many lives, been many people throughout the life of one's body. I often feel that way when I reflect on my life (so to speak), the life lived in this body. It is as if rebirth is not merely a matter of rebirth into another body but also of changing identities experienced in *this* life, *this* body. Beyond the singularity of the body, which is also always changing, and our memories of what has happened to this body and what we have done with it, where is the permanent, abiding, singular identity or self? Buddhist analysis also has complex and subtle teachings on how we come to believe in the illusion of a permanently enduring self. Teachings on the twelve *nidanas* discuss, among other things, the development of our belief in a singular, enduring self. The fourth step in the teachings on interdependence or the twelve *nidanas* is called *nama-rupa*: name and form.[5] Prior to this step in the developmental process, there is little sense of individuality. However, the experience of being a form and giving it a name fosters the belief that a permanent, singular, enduring self is somehow also intertwined into that name-and-form. However, the vitality of our experience is in no way diminished by recognizing the fleeting impermanence of every experience. The alternative to positing a single, unhyphenated, rigidly held enduring self is not chaos or lack of identity but flexibility and confidence.

5. Teachings on interdependence or the twelve *nidanas* are central to all Buddhist schools. They are also complex and difficult to understand accurately, though many introductory books on Buddhism do include some materials about the twelve nidanas, and the popular wheel-of-life diagram depicting the twelve nidanas as a circle is almost omnipresent, including online. For a simple textbook presentation of the twelve nidanas, see Robinson et al., *Buddhist Religions*, 16–17. For a thorough scholarly account see Thanissaro, *The Shape of Suffering*. Find a free pdf download online: http://www.dhammatalks.org/Archive/Writings/DependentCo-arising.pdf/.

Furthermore, regarding religious identity, no matter how much conviction people may feel about their religious views, those views inevitably change, develop, and mature throughout one's life span, especially if one is thoughtful and continues to investigate and contemplate religious and spiritual issues. Though one may imagine at one stage of life that one could never take on a different identity spiritually or religiously, nevertheless some years later one may find that either one has changed significantly or that the denomination to which one belonged has changed significantly. Then one moves on and takes on a new religious label. That has happened to me several times—and I have always been quite serious about religion and spirituality. Religious identities that I never expected to shift or diminish did; others have taken their place. And that's just *religious* identity. Other identities, as a scholar or a feminist, for example, which are also important to me, are not taken into account when I discuss religious identity. And what those other identities actually consist of has also changed significantly throughout my life. So where is the enduring self, the dominant religious identity that trumps all other identities, the *singular* self that is not hyphenated? What happened to the religious identity we were so sure was correct and enduring that we were willing to make exclusive truth claims on its behalf?

One person narrates his conversion from militant white supremacy, an ideology that can rival fervent religious exclusivism in its ardor, to postracism through a single dramatic experience of recognizing that black parents feel the same love for their children that he felt for his.

> There was one particular afternoon that drove the epiphany home.
> I arrived early to pick up my daughter from daycare. No one had noticed me so I took in the moment, watching with teared eyes as my little girl played with the other kids.
> It struck me that the first thing I noticed was that they were all children; not black children and white children but the sons and daughters of mothers and fathers.
> A young black man about my age walked in to pick up his daughter who leaped into his arms and hugged him the same way my little girl hugged me. The smile on his face as he listened to her relate her day in a gleeful excited stream was the same smile my daughter gave me on a daily basis.[6]

Some people who do not take the inevitability of hyphenated identities seriously have a favorite trick question. They want to know which element of a hyphenated identity is actually more important, as if that were a valid question. This question resides in a worldview that assumes singularity is

6. Michaels, *My Life after Hate*, 99.

always preferable to multiplicity, that internal difference and diversity, like external diversity and difference, are a problem and must be resolved in favor of unity by picking a favorite, a winner, some one alternative that is declared superior to all other options. Dualistic, either/or thinking, which is the default mode of much conventional Western thinking, frequently makes this mistake. So we see from a different angle how important it is to rethink our habitual allegiance to duality and the resultant competitive ranking of coexisting aspects of a pluralistic reality, in this case hyphenated identities. (Chapter 8 discussed this issue with regard to external diversity.)

Sometimes hyphenated identities are used against folks politically when these people fall into the trap of ranking their multiple identities vis-à-vis one another. Muslim Americans are sometimes asked whether they are Muslims first or Americans first. If they fall into the trap of answering the question, they often rank their Muslim identities ahead of their American identities, as do many Christians when asked the same question. But regarding Muslims, some commentators then use this information to suggest that Muslim Americans are not sufficiently reliable as United States citizens because of this divided loyalty. Notice that lurking behind such questions and conclusions are the assumptions that *real* or trustworthy Americans are Christians, and that the loyalty of Christians need not be questioned or evaluated. And, of course, lurking behind those assumptions is the supposition that the United States really is a Christian nation rather than a religious diverse nation that guarantees both freedom of religion and freedom from religion to all, a topic to be taken up in chapter 12.

This trick question about hyphenated identities has often been put to me, especially regarding Buddhism and feminism. The questioner assumes a conflict between Buddhism and feminism because traditional Buddhism has usually been male dominated, and then tries to postulate some situation in which I would have to choose between Buddhism and feminism. But why can't I have equal loyalties to both Buddhism and feminism even if they do conflict on some points? In the days when I was still more under the sway of Western dualistic logic, I was sometimes tempted to try to answer the question by ranking my loyalties. But now the question itself seems like complete nonsense, and I refuse to entertain it at all. Even if two identities do conflict on some points, one does not have to choose between them. One can affirm both and work in both camps.

Another dual identity that is very important to me is that of the scholar-practitioner, an identity I often use for myself. However, many people, both scholars and Buddhists, think this dual identity is made up of two incompatible elements, despite multiple examples of people who are honored as both. Earlier in my life, insisting on this dual identity cost me more in scholarly circles. There was a pronounced bias against religion among many scholars of religion when I began my career. Though that bias is still found, it has diminished recently. Among Western Buddhists, a pronounced antiacademic, antischolarly bias is common, but it also is less extreme than in prior years. Nevertheless, especially in Buddhist publications, I consistently find myself labeled as "scholar Rita Gross," despite the fact that I always identify myself as a scholar-practitioner. This is problematic because the practitioner dimension of my identity is crucial to the work I do as a Buddhist critical-constructive thinker and that I often publish in Buddhist publications. Because my work as a Buddhist critical-constructive thinker is often unconventional, radical, and innovative, I cannot help but wonder if the practitioner part of my identity is dropped as a subtle way of discounting my Buddhist credentials, thus minimizing the impact of my work.

The point of all these examples of hyphenated and shifting identities is that as Buddhist analyses of the self suggest, identity is a myriad, ever-shifting, ever-changing constellation, not something fixed, rigid, stabile, and enduring. Buddhist categories of analysis, such as the five *skandhas*, or consciousness divided twelve or eighteen ways, may seem curious, even irrelevant to most non-Buddhists. But the basic point—that what feels to unreflective awareness like a single self is always a composite of myriad elements—is hard to refute if we take everyday, on-the-ground experience seriously instead of dwelling only in belief systems and metaphysical speculation.

Yet the profound implications of this reality for issues of religious diversity have almost never been explored. Instead, most commentators isolate religious identity, elevate its importance, and then assume that different religious identities coexisting in a single society or world must present problems. With a more nuanced and realistic naming of one's identities, one recognizes how much, or how little, of one's identity is actually bound up in religious identity and how many other identities also define us and are important to us. One would recognize that there are many other aspects to one's kaleidoscopic identity, and that some of them are equally, perhaps more important, in some contexts than is one's religious identity. Therefore, I suggest that if the reality that everyone has a hyphenated, composite identity, in which religious identity is sometimes but not always dominant, were taken seriously, the "problem" of religious diversity would be diminished significantly. It would diminish significantly because, when one recognizes the complexity and multiplicity of one's identities at any given point in time, making exclusive or inclusive truth claims on behalf of one's religious identity is much less cogent and urgent.

For example, in times of national crisis, one's national or cultural identity may well be more dominant than one's religious identity. One will join with those of other religions within one's own nation to support one's own nation, even if that means standing against one's coreligionists on the other side of an international conflict. Such a scenario has happened many times as Christians on both sides of a conflict prayed for victory to the "same" God while asking for and accepting the support of members of other religions whose members lived within the borders of either nation in the conflict.

One would also recognize that, when it comes to some aspects of one's kaleidoscopic identity, religious identity might make little difference. When those aspects of one's identity come to the fore, one may share a great deal with people whose religious affiliations are vastly different. Do Muslim parents really have different hopes for their children than Buddhist parents do? Vis-à-vis their hopes for their children, which identity matters more? Identity as a Muslim or a Buddhist, or identity as a parent? Religious identity might separate them as people who belong to a specific religious tradition, but as parents, they could easily understand and empathize with one another. Their beliefs about deity, revelation, and soul are very different, but is their love for their children really any different as a result of those differing religious beliefs? Can they not join hands and forces across religious lines because other important identities are held in common? The same thing could be said about people as citizens of a nation, as members of a profession, as members of an interest group, or about any number of other shared concerns.

Unfortunately, it is common for members of religious groups to be encouraged to emphasize their religious identities above all other identities, to feel competitive with other religions, and to denigrate them. Such moves do nothing to defuse interreligious hostilities, and intensify oppositional *us/them* identities, which poison our communities and even our families. It is not at all unknown for family members to become extremely hostile toward other family members who change their religious labels. But, having sprung from the same matrix and environment, these family member still share so many aspects of an identity that is always hyphenated and changing in any case.

The Failure of Single-Identity Movements: The Case of Feminism

To many, it seems that no identity is more obvious, clear-cut, and nonnegotiable than sexual identity. Though some people are born as intersexuals and others develop transgender identities, most people do not question which sex they are, and many do not question the social roles and stereotypes attached to their sex by the society in which they live. Instead, many conflate nature and nurture regarding sexual identities. As a result, the most common argument against any movement to change gender roles is that men and women are very different from each other and that their conventional roles are predetermined in nature. If that position were correct, cultural definitions of masculinity would be completely grounded in nature and, thus, unchangeable, as would cultural definitions of femininity.

Thus, it would seem that a movement that coalesces around sexual identity and has powerful and cogent agendas and issues would have a built-in propensity for success. Groups may splinter over many other identities, but if sexual identities are so unquestioned, shouldn't a cause that depends on sexual identity easily be able to create a unified, powerful movement? Especially if one sex has moral outrage and justice overwhelmingly on its side? Thus it seemed to feminists, especially feminist theologians, in the 1970s. That very vibrant movement began in the late 1960s and gained great momentum in the 1970s. Women from a number of religious affiliations found themselves largely on the same page, so to speak, about many issues. We all found male dominance in religions unacceptable and wanted to do something about it. We also concluded that male dominance in religions was universal. We agreed on many of the things we wanted to change. We wanted women in roles of religious leadership; we wanted women to be constructing theology; we wanted women to be studied as religious subjects and actors in the same ways that men had always been studied. Though we were different in many ways, we were unified, and we could not imagine, given the universality of male dominance, that we were not speaking for and with women everywhere. Furthermore, from the beginning, the movement claimed to value diversity. In the 1979 landmark anthology *Womanspirit Rising: A Feminist Reader in Religion*, Carol P. Christ and Judith Plaskow wrote, "the diversity within feminist theology and spirituality is its strength."[7]

Nevertheless, by the mid-1980s, the movement had fractured. Many women complained that the phrase "women's experience" did not really include them. It was claimed that the movement reflected only white, middle-class, heterosexual women's concerns. Black women, poor women, lesbians, women of other cultures, and many others did not find themselves included in the rhetoric of the feminist-theology movement. Some women argued that men of their social group were also oppressed, and they could not in good conscious join a movement that seemed to divide women and men. (That such a division was *not* part of the agenda of feminist theology made no difference in these perceptions.) Other women felt that while they were

7. Christ and Plaskow, *Womanspirit Rising*, 15.

sympathetic to many of the movement's goals, their own cultures and religions were not sufficiently represented. Their loyalties to their own cultures and religions were also centrally important to them, which meant that they could not and did not identify with a movement that was then dominated by women quite different from them. Because so many early feminist leaders came from North America, many Asians and Africans even claimed that the feminist movement was another colonial project. One of the most successful arguments against feminist reforms in Asian and African contexts, made by both women and men, is that such reforms are Western impositions that are inappropriate for their own cultures.

In other words, even an identity as seemingly monolithic and non-negotiable as sexual identity proved to be a partial identity, part of a much more complex, kaleidoscopic identity. Hyphenated identities, such as black woman, lesbian woman, Muslim woman, Buddhist woman, African woman, and many, many others, proved to be so strong that a unified, global women's movement remains a dream. The feminist movement, which had perhaps more cogent claims to be universally relevant than any of the world's major religions, could not overcome the allure of other, more specific identities. The resulting hyphenated identities often overwhelmed the call to bond and take action as women across other dividing lines.[8]

The implications for any religion claiming exclusive and universal relevance should be obvious on two counts. First, nearly universally, people already have a clear sexual identity, but that is not enough to overcome other identities in favor of a universal women's movement with universally agreed-upon agendas. So how realistic could it possibly be to imagine that people, already having very diverse religious identities, are going to agree on a common, universal religious identity in the future? Second, given that identity is always hyphenated, why should religious identity be foregrounded and highlighted the way it is when people make exclusive truth claims on behalf of any religion? The religions are always competing with other loyalties and are never the only identity marker a person values.

However, out of this failure of early second-wave feminism, a new feminist understanding has developed and been used to construct "a feminist approach to religious pluralism," to quote the subtitle of Jeannine Hill Fletcher's book.[9] In my view, the greatest failure of earlier second-wave feminist thought was its complete lack of any real interest in non-Western cultures and religions, or in true cross-cultural understanding. (This will be discussed more fully in chapter 11.) There are very few feminist approaches

---

8. For a fuller discussion of this history, see Gross, *Feminism and Religion*, 39–64.
9. Fletcher, *Monopoly on Salvation?*

to religious pluralism and also very few books on religious diversity that take the reality of hyphenated identities into account. It is interesting that Fletcher links the two in her book. An important part of her way of approaching issues of religious diversity is to plead that we recognize that "we are all hybrids," the title of her fourth chapter. This, more than any other aspect of her work is what she identifies as a "feminist approach." She writes:

> From a feminist perspective, identity is not something we inherit or are born into; it is not pregiven with the analytical or religious categories identified in our discourses. Rather, identity and the emergence of self occurs relationally. "Self" is contingent and negotiated.[10]

The implications for religious identity and religious diversity follow. "Identity—even religious identity—is not given once and for all with a collective label of our 'religions.'"[11] "Identity—even Christian identity—is formed in contact and conversation with religious others."[12]

She continues:

> In recognizing our own multiple selves and shifting identities, we are given the freedom to reinvent religious identities that create solidarity. Far from a core and unchanging "Christian" identity, even Christian identity is one which can be informed by contact with different religious forms.
>
> The recognition of multi-faceted identities that arises from feminist thought provides the framework for a theology of religious difference where encounter is encouraged and communicative exchange possible.[13]

It is remarkable how similar these conclusions are to those derived from Buddhist analysis of identity, self, or ego as a changing composite, not as an enduring monolith.

The Fallacy of Linking "Strong Faith" with Exclusive Truth Claims: The Psychology of Conviction

As we have seen several times when discussing religious others, the default position for most people is a dualistic, *us/them* attitude towards others,

10. Ibid., 96.

11. Ibid.

12. Ibid.

13. Ibid., 101.

especially religious others, in the case of those who make exclusive or inclusive truth claims. In this chapter, I am more concerned with the subjective side of this experience, with the variety of ways one can experience conviction about one's own stance in the midst of diversity. Subjectively, *us/them* attitudes probably begin with feelings of comfort and love for what is familiar, for one's own culture or religion. The ease with which such feelings spring up can be demonstrated by a comment my Buddhist teacher, Jetsun Khandro Rinpoche, made as we were discussing religious diversity. She said, "But it's hard not to feel that your own is the best!"

But this same teacher has also taught me one of the most valuable lessons about diversity and compassion that I have ever learned. It was also one of the hardest to assimilate. She regularly teaches that the greatest act of compassion is to stop interfering so much with other people, to stop trying to change them. If we reflect at all on this statement, we cannot help but recognize that when we try to change people, we are actually trying to convince them to be more like us. We must also recognize that when we try to convince people to be more like us, we like to think we are doing so out of concern and compassion, but if we reflect honestly, we cannot help but see how aggressive and self-centered such attitudes actually are.

So how do we put together her two statements: that on the one hand, it's hard not to feel that one's own religion is the best, but on the other hand, if we were more compassionate, we would stop interfering so much with other people? We have already discussed one solution in chapter 5; religious diversity reflects human diversity. But that solution does not deal with all the subjective, psychological reactions that can come up in the face of diversity, especially if we have inherited cultural habits of preferring oneness to manyness. "Yes, diversity if fine, but not in my family or community; we all need to be on the same page" is a common reaction. Another solution is for communities to live side by side with relatively little interaction, including no interference with one another's cultural or religious habits and convictions. Nonproselytizing religions can easily adopt this solution and often do. It is relatively common in some parts of Asia. But in the Western world, people have deeply ingrained habits of trying to influence one another, to convert them to our side. (I write this days after the 2012 presidential campaign in the United States ended.) Furthermore, our workplaces and neighborhoods frequently bring us into contact with people from other religions and cultures.

Thus, I contend that we have to look more deeply into the reaction, so common in many Western contexts, that if one has great conviction about one's own religion (or politics or anything else), it is normal and natural to want other people to share it. When I argue against inclusive or exclusive truth claims and against missionary activities, many people respond to me that if one deeply believes in one's religion, one cannot help but want to spread it to others because one thinks that it is the best. It would be selfish and uncompassionate to keep it to oneself, I am told. But this assumption hides two other very problematic habits. It very easily hides an *us/them* mentality and fosters hostility towards the others if they do not come over to our side. Thus, the valued strong identity is actually an oppositional identity: I know who I am because I'm not them. Many groups, religious and otherwise, use this tactic to stir up in-group loyalty and enthusiasm, often in support of very questionable goals. Another insidious claims is hidden in this frequent reaction. If one is not trying to convince others to be more like oneself (in other words, if one is not trying to interfere with other people), it is because one has no real convictions oneself. One is wishy-washy, spineless, and stands for nothing. One has no principles. One will go along with anything.

I can vouch that these suppositions are 100-percent incorrect. I make this strong claim because of my own experience. I am deeply committed to Buddhist teachings and practices, and I experience them as life giving and life transformative. But I have no investment whatsoever in whether or not others join me as Buddhist meditators. Nor do I make any effort to encourage them to do so. If they decide for themselves and by themselves that they would like to explore Buddhism, I am available as a teacher. But their journey remains their own. If they choose to discontinue their journey into Buddhism at some point, I do not grieve or fear for them. Nor do I try to convince them to come back to Buddhist practice. Nevertheless, personal relationships can continue without change or interruption.

I suspect that such a stance comes more easily to one who belongs to a religion that does not have a heritage of making exclusive truth claims and sponsoring vigorous, often aggressive missionary movements. I agree with Christian writers such as Brian McLaren who warn that solving the problem of an oppositional identity based on *us/them* hostility by downplaying or weakening one's Christian identity, one's convictions about the relevance of Christianity for oneself, will not work. He contrasts a strong Christian identity that is basically hostile to other religions with an identity that is friendly towards other religions, but also not strongly Christian. He concludes, correctly, I think, that if these are the only two alternatives, those with a weaker Christian identity will give the playing field to groups relying on ever more strident oppositional identities. It is difficult to avoid the conclusion that this is happening today.

McLaren, however, devotes his book to articulating a third option, a Christian identity that is both strong and kind. He defines such an identity in the following manner:

> By strong I mean vigorous, vital, durable, motivating, faithful and defining—an authentic Christian identity that matters. By kind I mean something far more robust than mere tolerance, political correctness or co-existence. I mean benevolent, hospitable, accepting, interested and loving, so that the stronger our Christian faith, the more goodwill we will feel and show to those of other faiths, seeking to understand and appreciate their religion from their point of view.[14]

Is such a Christianity possible? Of course it is. There are already many such Christians who claim such an identity. The only question is why they are not in the majority. I will attempt to provide some answers to that question in chapter 16.

But I think there are actually much more interesting questions than overcoming oppositional identities thriving on hostility to others in the psychology of religious conviction. What of the intense feelings of conviction and love? Liturgical language, not only Christian and theistic, but also Buddhist nontheism, at least in some contexts, turns on phrases like "one and only," or "the best." I frequently use such liturgical language in the context of Vajrayana Buddhist practice. But I take it emotionally and symbolically, not literally and logically. Herein lies the solution to this supposed contradiction between the insider's love language about her religious tradition and the ethical obligation not to interfere with other people so much.

As was the case with much exclusivist and inclusivist thinking about religious others, much of the immense confusion caused to Christians (and others) by insiders' love language about the object of their faith results from failure to develop nuanced and subtle understandings of religious language—of both its limits and its uses.[15] Relying on the work of Lutheran bishop Christer Stendahl among others, Paul Knitter devotes a short section of his book *No Other Name?* to this issue. The issue is simple. Language functions in multiple modes and serves many purposes. The poetic love language of intimate encounters cannot and should not be taken out of its proper context to be used as logical, discursive, descriptive language in a public context. Doing so truly perverts a wonderful, uplifting experi-

---

14. McLaren, *Why Did Jesus, Moses, the Buddha, and Mohammed Cross the Road?*, 11.

15. For a still-unsurpassed account of the problems created by phrases such as "no other name," see Knitter, *No Other Name?*

ence into something degraded and aggressive. The words may be the same words, but they do not carry the same meanings in the two contexts. What is affectionate, appreciative language in a private, personal setting or among religious insiders becomes aggressive, competitive language when the same words are used in a public context involving members of multiple faith communities. It is a terrible thing when one's love of and appreciation for one's own religious community becomes a weapon used against religious others. But that is what happens whenever members of one religious community use their insiders' language to talk about other religions. Unfortunately, it happens very frequently, not just among religions but between different denominations within the same religions. Nothing makes me sadder than the ease and frequency with which Buddhists use such language about other Buddhists.

Stendahl uses an apt analogy. He compares insiders' religious language about how the object of their faith is the "one and only" to marital language. A spouse might well feel, and say in conversation with their partner that their spouse is the most wonderful person in the world. But in a court of law giving sworn testimony, the same person should be reluctant to make a similar statement. The context is vastly different. In Knitter's commentary, to do so "would be transforming love language into scientific or philosophical language." Knitter goes on to suggest that dogmatic language about exclusive truth claims may well have done the same thing to "the love language of the early church. The language of the heart and the head are not necessarily contradictory, but they are different. And their differences must be respected."[16]

I cannot understand why this elegant and eminently sensible method of dealing with inherited religious language that fosters exclusive truth claims when taken literally is not more widely used and taught. In terms of the subjective experience of a religious insider, it answers so many questions. It honors the intense gratitude and joy one can feel about one's own religious identity while also protecting one from becoming overbearing with others. It protects one from thinking that one needs to interfere in others' lives to save them from themselves, and also protects one from spreading hostility and defensiveness in the outside world.

An additional nuance is also required to take into account the shifting and varied components of identity that this chapter has so emphasized. The intense feelings of the love relationship, whether with one's object of faith or another being, are experiences *in the present moment*. Those feelings are not necessarily enduring or constant. People regularly fall out of love, not just in love. It is also easily possible to have one singular love object in one

16. Ibid., 185.

moment and another in another moment, without rejecting the first love object. These are important principles in the psychology of religious experience and help defuse the reactivity involved in assuming that what works for me is also best for everyone else—the basis of exclusive truth claims. I will illustrate this with a few seemingly trivial examples.

In the nineteenth century, when Europeans first began to study Indian, and especially Vedic, religions, they were extremely confused by the way Vedic poets related to the multiple deities of the early Indian pantheon. Whichever deity was spoken to in a hymn was addressed as "Supreme," "All-powerful," "Most wonderful," and so forth. Habituated to monotheism, early Indologists could not imagine how the poets could say exactly the same things about different deities. But the hymns were not abstract, discursive philosophical statements; they were expressions of discrete and deeply felt religious moments. There is no reason at all why one cannot deeply and exclusively appreciate one symbolic expression in one moment and another in a subsequent moment. The experiences and language about them are the same; that which generates the experience is not. In a perhaps even more trivial example, three cats are now sitting in my lap with my laptop. Each one of them is simultaneously the greatest kitty in the world. Each one is quite different from the others, and each one is also my favorite. It is actually quite easy to have multiple favorites at the same time. Most people do it without thinking. If it were not possible, parents should be prohibited on ethical grounds from having more than one child.

What makes it different for religions? People do not usually have multiple religious identities at the same time, largely for the practical reason of time limitations rather than because only one religion is worthy. (The same could perhaps be said of the inadvisability of having multiple spouses at the same time.) However, it is easy to have a relationship of friendliness, curiosity, admiration, and respect with a religious tradition with which one does not identify. Such a relationship with other religions deeply enriches one's own life and makes for a more peaceful and harmonious world. One may even disagree with some aspects of those religions without feeling a need to fix them or interfere with their members. And as more people become multiple religious belongers, we will learn more about how it is possible to have feelings of intense love for and commitment to religions that are very different from one another—such as Buddhism and Christianity.

Beyond Identity

Someone committed to a rigid, inflexible, monolithic identity, contrary to some popular ideas, has neither a strong nor a viable ego. It is in fact very brittle and fragile, easily threatened by change and diversity, timid and often overcome by fear. By contrast, those who recognize that identity is always hyphenated and changing are cheerful, flexible, and easily accommodate new information and situations. Their minds are flexible and malleable, not stuck, clinging to outmoded familiarities. In the long run, identity is not something to reinforce or to hang on to, but something more like a cane or a stepping-stone. We use it as long as we need it to steady ourselves, but eventually it becomes a prison rather than an aide. Then we let go. We become so confident, so much simply ourselves, that we are no longer attached to stories or labels in communicating to others who we are. We are simply comfortable with things as they are, whatever they may be. We also do not need certainty or answers to every question to feel safe and serene. We have some ability to be comfortable with uncertainty, which feels much better than always needing to protect and defend certainties and identities.

Relaxing and taming our fear and rigidity about identity is most important in regard to those identities most likely to cause harm both to self and others when held too tightly. Those potentially harmful identities certainly can derive from religion, gender, race, nation, culture, class, sexual orientation, and political affiliations. It is easy to develop hostile, oppositional *us/them* styles of identity around such issues, And it is easy to see simply by following the daily news how much suffering such identities can inflict on others, when held too tightly, with too much attachment. How do such identities cause suffering to self? The word *uptight* communicates well the painful ego style, the internal suffering, caused when people are uncomfortable about or with those with different identities, especially with different religious, racial, or cultural identities, or with a different sexual orientation.

If one is not uptight about those identities or uncomfortable with diversity, it does not mean that one becomes nobody, an amorphous blob. As I have contended many times about gender identity, I know perfectly well that biologically I am a woman, not a man. But what that determines about me as a human being is quite minor, and others can be very misguided as to what I am about if they rely very much on labeling me a woman. Regarding religion, I am quite definite that I am a Buddhist, but it causes me not one iota of discomfort that most other people in the world are not Buddhists. And so on. It is very sad when identities, whether those of oneself or of others, cause suffering. It does not have to be that way.

Being comfortable, rather than uptight, with one's own identities easily allows one to go beyond them without abandoning them. An example of such spiritual and ethical excellence is provided by the Dalai Lama in his recent book *Beyond Religion: Ethics for a Whole World*. Obviously, the Dalai Lama has not and is not going to stop being a Buddhist and a specific kind of Buddhist. He is and will remain a Tibetan Buddhist who personally practices Vajrayana Buddhism. But he does not propose universal adoption of his own religion as the solution to global problems, as those who adhere to exclusivist or inclusivist positions about religious diversity do. Instead, he sets aside his own religion, his personal inspiration and fallback, to seek a framework for ethics applicable to people of any religion as well as of no religion. Would that other prominent religious leaders could be so unselfish, compassionate, and nonegotistical!

This project requires finding a viable basis for ethics separate from religion while not denigrating religion. The Dalai Lama claims that we can live without religion but not without ethics. In a clever analogy, he compares ethics to water and religion to tea. For people with certain tastes, tea may improve water, but tea is nevertheless mostly water. We can live without tea but not without water.[17] Building on the fact that we need water but not tea to live, he points out that "we are born free of religion, but we are not born free of the need for compassion."[18] He continues: "More fundamental than religion then, is our basic human spirituality. We have an underlying human disposition toward love, kindness and affection, irrespective of whether we have a religious framework or not."[19]

Clearly, this innate disposition toward love, kindness, and compassion needs to be nurtured and can be suppressed. Otherwise crime, greed, and warfare would not exist. But whether or not that innate tendency is nurtured or suppressed has little to do with any specific religion or with religion in general. Despite very strong religious identities, members of all the world's religions have committed horrible crimes. Each religion has produced exemplary saints. And many ethically upright and admirable are not outwardly especially religious. There is no danger in transcending any particular religious identity, and much to recommend it, even if one continues to practice a specific spiritual discipline.

But what kind of spiritual disciplines nurture our innate disposition to love, kindness, and compassion? What kind of spiritual discipline helps us become comfortable with diversity, especially religious diversity? We turn our attention to that topic in chapter 10.

17. His Holiness, the His Holiness, the Dalai Lama XIV, *Beyond Religion*, 17.
18. Ibid.
19. Ibid.

Chapter 10

Training the Mind

*The Role of Contemplative Practices and Spiritual Disciplines
in Becoming Comfortable with Religious Diversity*

M OST OF THE PROBLEMS that people encounter with religious diversity, extensively detailed in previous chapters, stem from a constricted, fear-based state of mind.[1] Thus, it follows that mind training or
spiritual disciplines will be crucial in giving one the mental and emotional
skills necessary for being at ease with religious diversity. One's own state of
mind determines so much about one's well-being and ease or lack thereof.
One's well-being and ease are only minimally dependent on others and the
external environment because, as we saw in chapter 7, self and other arise
interdependently. One's own subjectivity largely determines the world one
perceives. An untrained mind, however, does not realize this. It is not aware
of its own freedom but lets itself be pushed and pulled, manipulated by

1. For a recent discussion of such issues, see Nussbaum *The New Religious Intolerance*. Writers on Buddhist spiritual discipline frequently take up the topics of fear and
genuine fearlessness. Nhat Hanh has recently published a book on fear—*Fear: Essential
Wisdom for Getting through the Storm*. The popular author Pema Chödrön has also
written on the topic: *The Places That Scare You*. Finally, fear and fearless are major
topic in the Shambhala Training program, developed by Chogyan Trungpa, Rinpoche.
For more information, see http://www.shambhala.org/shambhala-training.php/. The
highly recommended book presenting this material is Trungpa, *Shambhala*, which has
been republished many times.

174

outside forces and willy-nilly compelled into affection or hatred by seeming others. Even worse, an untrained mind does not even realize that it is allowing itself to be compelled into these often painful, or sometimes momentarily pleasureful, reactions. Instead, it thinks, either that it is actually in charge of its own reactivity, or else that it is powerless about how it reacts to others and their provocations. Very often in situations of confrontation, perpetrators of violence or those with hostile feelings do not own their own attitudes but blame their attitudes and reactions on others. For example, women (but not only women) are very familiar with this scenario. Men often blame us for their own sexual arousal when we have had nothing to do with that arousal. Negative attitudes towards women and restrictions on our participation in religions usually follow. What stems from an untrained and undisciplined mind is mistaken for an objectively accurate assessment of the situation. Texts stemming from monastic contexts, both Buddhist and Christian, are filled with such projections.

In the same way, desire for a religious monoculture in which everyone belongs to the same religion and discomfort with or fear of religious diversity is never a necessary reaction to diversity but is always chosen over other alternatives, at least to some extent. It really is time for those who make exclusive and inclusive truth claims about their own religion to stop blaming God for their attitudes, to stop claiming that their own discomfort with religious diversity is not of their own choosing but that they are only obeying God's commands. If exclusive or inclusive truth claims were an inevitable part of any specific religion, then every believer in that religions would share those claims. But many loyal and committed religious practitioners come to other, more generous and ethically palatable conclusions.

The different other as someone whom we need to convert, who is frightening, pitiable, or misguided is not objectively given but is largely constructed out of our own subjectivity, prejudices, assumptions, and values. Whether we are neutral, friendly, or hostile to different others is largely our own doing and cannot be blamed on the others, whatever they may do or think. In other words, rather than being given a world by others, we largely construct the world we inhabit, though sometimes that subjective world is more socially than individually constructed. However, if that subjective world is socially constructed by religious or political authorities, responsible individuals are morally obligated to evaluate what they have been taught, to test it for its ethical uprightness.

Meditation and Contemplation: The Basics

Many of the previous chapters of this book have dealt with subtleties of attitudes toward religious diversity, giving many recommendations for developing spiritual outlooks that are not so troubled by religious diversity. Thus, I have suggested that religious diversity is normal and natural, not a mistake or a problem. I have suggested that words and concepts are provisional and do not extend all the way to ultimate reality. I have suggested that self and other do not exist independently but are cocreated interdependently. I have suggested that uniqueness and diversity are more foundational than unity and universalism. I have suggested that identity is an ever-shifting, hyphenated composite, constructed out of many available materials, rather than a given monolith. I have suggested that true compassion often involves not interfering with others so much, being with them rather than trying to fix them. These may all be good suggestions. Obviously, I would argue that they are. But to effectively defuse dis-ease with religious diversity, they must become more than ideas or beliefs. It is not enough to agree with such ideas. Mere beliefs fly out the window when one encounters stress or difficulties. These ideas must be internalized to the extent that one no longer has to make an effort to feel and act in accord with such principles. They must become spontaneous values rather than rehearsed beliefs. My own experience suggests that it is very difficult to experience this level of transformation without deep and consistent practice of a relevant spiritual discipline.

It is not possible or appropriate for me to try to list, describe, or evaluate all possible or relevant spiritual disciplines in this context. I do not have firsthand knowledge of some important spiritual disciplines and techniques, including yoga, tai chi, and contemplative prayer. Therefore, I could not comment on them adequately. However, I do have forty years of experience as a practitioner of mindfulness practices of calming meditation and many years as a teacher of such disciplines. Based on the experience, I can offer some relevant testimonials as well as considered judgments about what makes spiritual disciplines reliable and trustworthy for healing a mind that is uncomfortable with religious diversity, or that regards it as a theological or spiritual problem.

The most important criterion for spiritual disciplines that can effect the spiritual transformation I am seeking is their neutrality, their lack of metaphysical, philosophical, or theological content. Spiritual discipline is *not* about inculcating a set of beliefs and concepts. Perhaps the most important point about what I have been calling spiritual disciplines or meditation practices is that they are neutral *techniques* independent of belief systems. They could as easily be called by a more neutral name—mind training—and seen as analogous to physical regimens for training the body. Just as physical exercises train and condition the body and are thus seen as necessary for good physical health, so mindfulness practices tame and train the mind. It could be argued that such disciplines are helpful, if not necessary, for mental health. Therefore, they are not inherently connected with any metaphysical, theological, or religious point of view and are frequently pursued in conjunction with any or no religious, theological, or metaphysical point of view. It is not at all uncommon for practicing Christians or secular atheists to be involved in mindfulness disciplines and other forms of mental training.[2]

It is important to clarify that while many people associate mindfulness training with Buddhism, Buddhists have always carefully distinguished between two different types of spiritual discipline. These are calm abiding—*samatha*—and special insight or clear seeing—*vipashyana*. Only *vipashyana* or clear seeing is considered to be specifically Buddhist. It deals with the analytical meditations that demonstrate the cogency of specifically Buddhist teachings, such as nontheism, egolessness, and emptiness. *Samatha*, which can be and is practiced independently from *vipashyana*, is considered to be generic mind training not specific to Buddhism and predating the historical Buddha. Therefore in the modern world, especially in the West, various mindfulness disciplines are freely offered without expectation or coercion that those who practice them will eventually take on a Buddhist worldview and become card-carrying Buddhists. Some do, but most don't. This is the way I have always presented spiritual disciplines of mindfulness when teaching in contexts that are not specifically Buddhist.

As is somewhat well known, mindfulness practices often involve focusing on one's breathing as a technique to quiet the wandering, distracted mind and remain in the immediate present, in one's life as it is actually happening while it is happening. When mindfulness practices are discussed more theoretically, it is generally agreed that the chosen focal point is actually irrelevant. It could be anything that is neutral in content. But breath is usually chosen because it is always with us (until we die) and is completely religiously and culturally neutral. When teaching beginning meditation in secular contexts, I often challenge those present to find some difference between how an Easterner or a Westerner breathes, how a Christian or a Buddhist breathes. No one has yet come up any differences at all, which definitely proves the religious and cultural neutrality of basic mindfulness practices.

---

2. For two among many examples, see Habito, *Healing Breath*; and Stabile, *Growing in Love and Wisdom*. Major Christian advocates for such neutral meditation practices include Thomas Merton, David Stendl-Rast, and Thomas Keating.

Just as this is not an appropriate context to list and evaluate the various methods of mind training associated with various cultural and religious contexts, this is not an appropriate context in which to give full instruction in mindfulness practice. These days, instruction in many formats is easily available in both secular and religious institutions. However, because there are charlatans in the business of spirituality, I will give a few guidelines on what to avoid. Though books and tapes can be accurate and very useful as a supplement, it is always better to receive instruction in person from a living teacher who is trained in and authorized to teach whatever technique she is teaching.[3] In most locations it is now possible to find such instruction. Any teacher who claims to be a great enlightened master (of whatever gender) is probably not one. Anyone who insists on too much loyalty to their brand, especially early in the process of learning a spiritual discipline, should be regarded with suspicion. Any center that charges truly exorbitant prices is to be avoided, though it must also be understood that, one way or another, meditation instruction has to be paid for. Many Westerners are under the misimpression that such instruction is free in Asia and so should be in the West as well. They simply do not understand how Asian patronage systems support teachers and meditation centers financially. Whether in Asia or the West, landlords and power companies do not supply free space or electrical power to institutions simply because they are involved in providing spiritual instruction. Finally, it is crucial to avoid a teacher who promises too much too fast. Developing stabile mindfulness is usually quite slow and frustrating, even though the results are often impressive eventually.

If mindfulness is not about inculcating specific intellectual, theological, or religious content, what is its purpose? It is about advancing mental health by allowing a relaxed, stabile, and flexible state of mind to emerge. That mind has no particular intellectual content, but it is clear and knowing, to use the specific terminology of one school of mental training. Its clarity has to do, among other things, with no longer being easily distracted and diverted, so that it can apply itself to the task at hand. The knowing quality has

3. Meditation teachers of all stripes, even those who produce books and tapes about the technique they teach, agree with this claim. There is something irreplaceable about direct verbal instruction, which could include interactive online instruction. Mind-training instructions are subtle and can be misheard, which happens frequently. Continuing verbal interactions provide clarification and corrections. My own favorite story I tell on myself to make this point concerns my attempts many years ago to learn word processing from a manual. I failed for months and eventually gave in, signing up for a beginning course in word processing at the local technical college. After a small amount of individualized, in-person instruction that showed me where I was getting lost, I was happily and successfully using my first computer. But now, when I run into problems, I do not hesitate to call someone who knows more that I do about word processing and the programs I use regularly.

to do with the ability of a mind that is both stabile and flexible to know what it is observing and experiencing with less distortion and self-referencing. Such a mind is also kind, gentle, and strong. It is capable of overcoming what Buddhists have always seen as the major defilements a confused mind falls prey to—aggression, grasping, and ignorance.

Aggression is any kind of anger or aversion, such as one often encounters in political, cultural, or religious conflicts, and which is endemic in much self-righteous political activity. It is also a key emotion in exclusive or inclusive truth claims. Grasping is neediness for anything external or internal. Religious or political ideological dogmatism is a form of grasping. Ignorance is the bewilderment of not knowing how to proceed, and also of wrong or misguided beliefs about reality. However, in spiritual discipline, these three poisons, as they are called, are not fought with directly. Instead, with increasing mindfulness, they are noted but not heeded, and eventually wear out. Awareness that they are counterproductive and unnecessary, never fulfilling the promises with which they seduce the naïve and unreflective, grows exponentially.

In this context, I will not say much about my own experiences with meditation. But two incidents stand out. During my career I have received many compliments for being a clear, good writer, but it was not always that way. Several years after I began serious meditation practice, colleagues starting asking me what had changed with me that could explain why my writing was suddenly so much clearer. I had always had good ideas, they said, but my writing had been rather difficult to follow. In my own perspective, the more notable and very surprising change was the cooling of my feminist rage, something I had not sought and would never have predicted. I spent my teenage years hating being a girl because of the limitations placed on women in the 1950s, which were plainly evident to a bright fifteen-year-old, even in the poverty and cultural deprivation of my youth. Those feelings only increased due to what I experienced as one of the few women in an elite graduate program. The system had failed me, I reasoned, and I had every reason to be extremely angry. Of course, expressing that level of aggression did not make me a very successful communicator, much as I wanted people to understand what was so painful about sexism and patriarchy. Inexplicably, against all my expectations and logic, after a few years of serious meditation practice, I simply could not crank up that rage any longer. At the same time, I noticed that suddenly people could hear me when I talked about gender issues. All of this was unexpected but really a tremendous relief, perhaps the single greatest development of my life. I have often written about this surprising, fortunate transformation.[4]

4. Gross, *A Garland of Feminist Reflections,* 235–44. Like fear, anger is an emotion

How Spiritual Disciplines Work

How could such change happen? A mind that is constricted and fear-based must be transformed into a well-trained mind. A mind that is comfortable and relaxed does not react with fear or dislike to what is unfamiliar or different from one's own customs and beliefs. Contemplative practices and spiritual disciplines can transform one's state of mind from being constricted, narrow, and tight to being expansive and relaxed, stabile and flexible. Such a mind is much less reactive and much more able to simply take in information and stimuli without knee-jerk, stereotypical responses. A well-trained mind can register each new stimulus thoroughly, in an even-minded fashion, without shock or surprise, no matter what comes along. Information can then be processed in an even-handed manner, without relying on prejudice or previously formed opinions.

One of my spiritual mentors taught about this stabile and flexible state of mind in an amusing way. He suggested that if a pterodactyl suddenly landed in the lap of a well-trained, experienced contemplative, that person would simply notice it, without shock, fear, or any other reaction, but with completely awake attentiveness. The contemplative would be unfazed by this development because her mind is completely alert, in the present space and time, not lost in thoughts of past or future, not fantasizing, not speculating, but simply resting calmly, peacefully, and pleasantly in the immediacy of the present situation. The stability of the meditating, contemplative mind is its continuing focus on the immediate present as things change and morph. Because of this stability, the mind is flexible enough to take in whatever comes along without either rejecting it out of hand or grasping it. Out of this relaxed, flexible stability, one can then make reasoned and reasonable decisions about what, if anything, one should do with or about pterodactyls. One is not driven by a received ideology about pterodactyls, nor does one react with an irrational fear of pterodactyls.

Perhaps I can also illustrate the same thing on a much more mundane level. Frequently I teach introductory workshops on meditation in which I introduce a simple mindfulness technique that uses the breath as the focal point. Focus on the breath brings the mind back to the present when it wanders off on its own devices, as frequently happens with beginning meditators. Beginners easily lose their ability to stay in the present, instead becoming absorbed in memories, fantasies, daydreams, or discursive thought. As I sit facing the new meditators, it is often very easy for

---

often encountered when one explores one's experience more deeply through mind training. As a result, Buddhists have also commented frequently on how to work more skillfully with anger. See Nhat Hanh, *Anger*; and Chodron, *Working with Anger*.

me to see that some of them have drifted from the immediate present. At a workshop I taught in the fall of 2012, I had no gong, so I clapped my hands once, sharply, to indicate that the meditation period was over. A woman whom I had been watching jumped, indicating that mentally she had been somewhere else, not in the present, not in the room. I pointed this out to the group to give them a clear understanding of the difference between mindfulness and lack of mindfulness. When one is fully present, a ringing telephone does not cause one to jolt and one does not stumble on cracks in the sidewalk. Nor is one the victim of one's own aggression or grasping, one's ideologies and opinionatedness.

One may wonder about the beginner whose mind wandered from the present, from the focus on breathing, into daydreaming or some other form of obsessive thinking. In many years of teaching meditation, I have encountered many people who became discouraged, sometimes to the point of giving up their practice, because what contemplative practices usually reveal initially is how wild and undisciplined our minds actually are, how completely out of control and random are our untrained thought processes. This is the case even for people who are adept at abstract disciplines such as law, medicine, or theology. Told to hold a simple, nondiscursive reference point, such as the breath, the untrained mind quickly veers off on its own whims. This is nothing to be alarmed about. It happens to everyone, but it is often hard for beginning meditators to hear this or trust their teachers. With practice, we do learn to stay in the present more and more, with the result that our minds, being both more stabile and more flexible, become more open, receptive, curious, nonjudgmental, and capable of great discernment.

Along the way, however, and at all times to some extent, one must be able to cope with repetitiveness and boredom in practice. For beginners, that boredom can also be quite discouraging. How interesting can one's own breathing be, hour after hour, day after day, year after year? A story circulates among meditation teachers about a student who complained to the teacher that the technique of noting or being with the breath was becoming very boring. The student asked for a more interesting technique. The teacher thought for a while, then said, "I've got it. Instead of focusing on your breathing, do the opposite! Just don't breathe!" Switching to a different focus would bring only very temporary relief.

Why must it be this way? Because, as human beings with the karmic patterns endemic to an untrained human mind, we have been indulging in restlessness and distraction for a long time. We are totally unused to being with our naked awareness, free of entertainment, drama, and glamour. Overcoming habits is always difficult and takes time. Meditation is often hyped as something that produces great pleasure, even bliss, as well as contentment, and, in its own way, it does. However, this is a very low-key bliss and contentment, without many fireworks or much elation. The contentment and bliss, if they occur, are unconditional, needing nothing specific, and thus a very different proposition from mundane or conventional bliss and contentment, which are completely conditional and disappear unless certain terms are met. Such trustworthy contentment and joy are not instantaneous because many impediments to them have to be worn out first.

A key point in the development of greater mindfulness occurs when one becomes aware of one's thoughts as they occur rather than being seduced by them, which means that one no longer buys into them completely. One realizes that just because one has a thought, one doesn't have to believe in it, nor is that thought necessarily true or even an accurate description of reality. Rather, thoughts are quite arbitrary and contingent, dependent on many contextual factors. Thoughts are just thoughts; they come and go and are quite ephemeral and impermanent. One doesn't need to take any specific thought so seriously. One moment they seem very real, impressing themselves insistently on our consciousness but the next moment they are gone, replaced by another thought. Often one cannot even remember what seemed so real and important a few moments ago. Now something else is equally insistent, seems equally real and important. Realizing this ephemeral quality of thoughts and discovering the clear, knowing, open and spacious awareness beneath them are wondrously freeing. Discovering a realm of awareness beyond conceptuality, which then allows us to use conceptuality as a tool rather than letting it become a straightjacket, is a monumental, life-altering discovery.

Meditators with somewhat trained and tamed minds often describe this experience as thoughts dissolving. One can literally experience a thought, an opinion, or a prejudice that threatens to completely take over one's consciousness lose its power as one becomes aware of both the thought and its contingency at the same time. Sometimes one realizes on the spot that there is no reason even to finish that stream of thought. This experience is very difficult to imagine without experiencing it oneself. Recently, when we were discussing meditation experiences in the small group I lead in Eau Claire, a long-term meditator reported how uncomprehending she had once been when more experienced meditators would talk about thoughts dissolving. "It's because no thought I had ever had was transparent to me. Every one of them insisted on being thought, dominating my consciousness entirely, and seeming to be completely true," she said.

The Fruits of Mind Training

Before this point in mind training is reached, one can reason logically, even doing so quite well. But one will have great difficulty with contemplation because the open-ended tentativeness and nondogmatic quality of contemplation will be foreign and uncomfortable. In Buddhist disciplines of mind training, contemplation is the second step in the process of gaining confidence in one's outlook. It follows the first step, called hearing, which involves gathering accurate information. This stage mainly involves working with words and concepts. One listens to teachers and reads books to find out what conclusions have been reached by others whom one trusts. One needs to understand the words correctly. For example, one needs to understand what Buddhists mean when they say that they do not assert individual immortality of a monolithic self but posit a composite identity that is always changing. But this first step is very preliminary because this information is still *external*. It has not penetrated one's system, become part of one's bones and being, and, therefore, cannot effect deep or lasting transformation.

Such transformation only comes with deep contemplation. I often tell my students that contemplation is the process that transforms spiritual teachings from being words in a book to being life-giving insights that have been internalized into one's system. Contemplation is concerned not so much with *words* but primarily with *meaning*, to return to the distinction introduced in chapter 6. In contemplation, one mainly works with *questions* rather than grasping for answers. What do these words mean? Do these teachings accord with experience? It is crucial at this stage to *rest comfortably in the question* without grasping for answers. Insights certainly arise, but they are not grasped at as the final, definitive answer; rather they are allowed to float, followed by a question mark. Whatever insights or conclusions one reaches are always subject to revision. Therefore, and *only* therefore, deeper insights easily arise, whereas if one grasps whatever answers may have arisen, the process of deepening insight is blocked.

Until one becomes more adept at and comfortable with contemplation, one seeks a level of verbal, conceptual, propositional, discursive certainty that is unrealistic to hope for and impossible to attain. The impossibility of fulfilling this dream then makes one rigid and dogmatic, which means that spiritual well-being, *faith* in the true sense, is difficult, if not impossible. Faith, which has a lot more to do with confidence than with certainty, cannot develop in the absence of keen self-awareness and deep introspection of the kind that result from contemplation. Such contemplation is what makes us able to bear, to be okay, with the limitation that only provisional truth is available doctrinally, conceptually, or verbally. Contemplation also frees us to rejoice in the limits of language to express Things As They Are, rather than to feel impoverished or uncertain because of that fact.

The more fully one contemplates what one has heard and studied, the more one realizes that definitive, satisfying conceptual answers to many questions simply are not available. But the more one practices mindfulness, to the point of seeing the transparency, contingency, and ephemeral nature of our conceptual thought, the less bothersome uncertainty is. We can entertain many possible answers to our quandaries without needing to grasp one among the many hypotheses. Remembering the advice of many teachers who have told us that cherishing views and opinions is very detrimental to spiritual well-being, we become comfortable with uncertainty and unanswered questions. Important is that the sequence is developing comfort with unanswered and unanswerable questions, whereupon mental, spiritual ease may follow, not the other way around, despite what many religious seekers desire and what some so-called experts teach.

Perhaps the greatest failing of religions has been to provide easy, but essentially unsatisfying answers to questions that simply cannot be answered, at least not conceptually. Two questions are perhaps most urgent. The first is, what does happen after the death of one's physical body? Every religion provides detailed answers, but they are very, very different from one another, which makes it less likely that any one of them is correct. We have to learn to live well in spite of this uncertainty because we really have no other choice. An even more urgent question, in my view, because it deeply affects our lives in the here and now before death, surrounds the inscrutability, inevitability, and intractability of injustice. No form of suffering is more impenetrable than that caused by seeming injustice. Why are seemingly innocent people swept away in natural disasters? Why do they find themselves in the path of aggressors? Why are they born into situations of impossible poverty, disease, and mental deprivation?

Religions provide many conceptual answers. Both Buddhists and Christians attribute a great deal of such suffering to human mistakes. It is unwise to settle in floodplains or to build nuclear reactors in locations subject to natural disasters. Poverty and warfare are never inevitable, completely beyond human control. Nevertheless, those answers often do not satisfy existential questions about my suffering, the suffering of those I love. Then Buddhists, Christians, and others supply theoretical answers: it's the will of God, or it's due to people's karma. But do those answers really say anything? I am always tempted to ask Buddhist teachers who provide such facile, though logically consistent answers, what's wrong with admitting that we simply don't have a good answer?

If there is ever a time when Buddhist advice to seek "only don't know" mind is relevant, this would seem to be it.[5] This admission of not knowing has nothing to do with the ignorance or willful ignoring that Buddhists so decry. It is the wisdom of admitting the limits of human ability to know. It is the wisdom of recognizing that crossing that line and claiming to know when we don't brings more harm than good. It may be difficult to learn how to live well with uncertainty, but it is possible and much more freeing and satisfying than trying to believe in answers that, though traditional, really don't make much sense. The fruition of mind training, a relaxed "mind at ease,"[6] and uncertainty are not at all incompatible, though the opposite is usually not true: a mind that is too certain of its rightness is often defensive and fearful, rigid and brittle.

Regarding injustice, Buddhist teachings do have one cogent but difficult suggestion. Being angry about injustice is not recommended and is considered to be quite dangerous. This is because, according to Buddhist teachings, anger is such an unpleasant and counterproductive emotion, producing negative results both for self and others. This is the case no matter how attractive and reasonable, even justifiable, anger may appear to be, and how difficult or impossible resisting anger might seem to be. Anger is simply unworkable and has no redeeming social value.

For many Westerners, these teachings are very hard to hear, mainly because we live in an extremely aggressive culture that validates aggression at every turn. "Nice guys finish last," we are told, which means that niceness, compassion, and altruism should be avoided most of the time. So it's okay to be aggressive, so long as one's aggression is directed toward the right causes: eliminating racism, sexism, poverty, homophobia; or even overcoming religious intolerance based on exclusive truth claims, we are told. But for those with opposite values, their anger against liberals and those who value diversity seems just as justified. We even have a category—self-righteous anger—that many well-meaning people approve of.

As I've already narrated, I have considerable personal experience with anger about injustice (in my case, gender injustice) and have not agreed for many years with popular beliefs about the usefulness and justifiability of appropriately directed anger. No matter what it is directed against, anger is a corrosive, poisonous emotion that actually makes one miserable. It is very

---

5. Though this emphasis is found throughout Buddhist teachings from the very earliest texts to contemporary masters, this particularly shocking phrasing is associated with Korean Zen Buddhism and is often attributed to the twentieth-century Korean Zen master Seung Sahn. See Schrobe, *Don't-Know Mind*.

6. For one example, see Kyabgon, *Mind at Ease*. Other similar books include Chödrön *Comfortable with Uncertainty*; and Chödrön, *Living Beautifully*.

easy to demonstrate this fact by watching both conservative and liberal politicians and ideological religious practitioners. Being on the so-called right side does not make anger and ideology more persuasive or appropriate. Not only does anger destroy oneself internally; it rarely is effective in convincing those against whom it is directed to change. Instead, it often increases polarization. When it becomes too uncontrollable, it results in violence against those with whom one is angry, which is always more harmful than helpful. So where is its redeeming social value?

People unfamiliar with the effects of mindfulness training and with awareness beyond conceptuality and ideology often suppose that the only alternative to anger and ideology is passivity and acquiescence to an unjust status quo. It is supposed that one would simply become a spineless wet noodle. Such suppositions result from dualistic thinking, from thinking that there is no middle path between opposites. That middle path is well illustrated by a story I often tell. Someone asked my teacher about anger, and she replied quickly and sharply that anger was always a waste of time. The shocked questioner then asked, "But what about things you should be angry about, like abuse?" Without a second of hesitation, the teacher shot back, "I didn't tell you to give up your critical intelligence. I told you anger is always a waste of time."

These days it is very clear to me what my values and opinions are, but they do not possess me. I am not obsessed by them or with them, and therefore they don't make me miserable. Nor do I make myself obnoxious to others because of my own views—or at least I try not to do so! This more relaxed state of mind has everything to recommend it over so-called self-righteous, justifiable anger. Critical intelligence knows what to accept and what to reject. In addition, it is more likely to come up with effective strategies for promoting what should be accepted and resisting what should be rejected. Therefore, transforming and transcending anger does not imply that nothing needs to be changed or destroyed. Those familiar with Buddhist art, especially Tibetan Buddhist art, know that many figures are portrayed expressing seeming wrath. Most schools of Buddhism include teachings not only about overcoming anger but also about "destroying what needs to be destroyed."[7] However, these teachings state even more clearly that such actions must be based on wisdom, without even a trace or a whisper of anger or self-interest in one's motivation. This is a very high bar, and self-righteous individuals are directed to apply it to themselves first.

Is there anything more self-righteous and therefore pain inducing than exclusive or inclusive truth claims about religion (or politics, for that

---

7. This is a quotation from an unpublished Tibetan Buddhist liturgy.

matter)? Such claims are inherently dualistic, turning on the proposition that there is an absolute, clear difference between right and wrong, truth and falsity, regarding conceptual statements about ultimate matters. We have already disputed the cogency of such claims on many grounds—the inevitability of religious diversity given human diversity, the limits of words and concepts, and so forth. However, the psychological and spiritual poverty of a mind state consumed by exclusive truth claims has not yet been discussed. In most instances, such a mind state is very different from the spacious, relaxed mind at ease that results from the pursuit of appropriate and healing spiritual disciplines. The mind state that craves exclusive truth claims also includes a good deal of anger and aggression, something not often noted by those who discuss theologies of religion. But because such claims are inherently dualistic, they encompass not only enthusiasm for one's own perspective but also negative attitudes towards other perspectives. Furthermore, these negative attitudes are almost always untempered by awareness that one does not have to believe every thought one generates.

What always comes to mind for me when I think of people who are obsessed with exclusive truth claims is the minister who excommunicated me (see the preface), shaking with rage that a college student would not shut up and meekly try to believe his version of the One True Faith. How could such behavior and such a mind state model deep spiritual insight? Unfortunately, such conduct seems to be very common among those who make exclusive truth claims. Dogmatic people with too much certainty about religion do not seem to be cheerful, relaxed, comfortable, and happy or to have much of a sense of humor. Their tightness and aggression does little to recommend their belief system. By way of contrast, it is very difficult, if not impossible, to be dogmatic with a spacious flexible mind.

Perhaps it is necessary to state the obvious once more: When I criticize exclusive (or inclusive) truth claims in religion, I am not suggesting that people need to change, not *what* they believe, but *how* they believe it. Their enthusiasm for the examples set by Jesus or Mohammed and for what they taught is not at issue. I rejoice that those with great enthusiasm for their religions have a deep, meaningful spiritual life. I am sure that they find the same life-giving relevance in their religions that I find in mine. The difference is that I do not work towards and pray for their conversion to my religion. That is the difference in how these diverse beliefs are held, and that difference makes all the difference in the world. It is completely unnecessary for deep appreciation of one's own religion to be so strongly linked with a belief that it is also the only truth for all people for all time. It is also extremely unfortunate when such linkages are made.

Mindfulness Training in Contemporary Society

Though a topic that could be a whole book unto itself can be no more than a mere footnote in this chapter, it is important to note that in the past thirty years, various mind-training programs have had a great impact outside of religion and religious studies. The fields of medicine, therapy, and education are all exploring how mind training could help those who use their services. One of the most successful has been Mindfulness Based Stress Reduction, initiated by Jon Kabat-Zinn, which is widely used with cardiac patients.[8] Many therapists and other mental-health professionals routinely recommend yoga and meditation to their patients. A whole field of contemplative education is gaining currency, as many educators realize that simply imparting impartial information does not truly educate a person.[9]

In addition, the field of cognitive studies is now very interested in investigating scientifically the effects of calming mindfulness practices. One of the best-known and well-funded programs is Richard Davidson's Center for Investigating Healthy Minds at the University of Wisconsin in Madison. The University of California–Davis has a similar center headed by Clifford Saron.[10] This center recently received a major grant from the Templeton Foundation to investigate raw data collected by measuring brain activity of meditators during a three-month meditation retreat (the *samatha* project).[11] This work, which is still in its early stages, owes much to the inspiration of the Dalai Lama and his keen interest in Western science, which led him and others to initiate the Mind and Life Institutes in 1983. Many conferences and dialogues have been held by the Mind and Life Institute since 1987.[12]

Living in the age in which we do, many long-term meditators have begun to speak of the effects of meditation using the analogy of rewiring. Habitual patterns are gradually replaced by other circuits that are less dualistic and self-centered, and also much more relaxed and contented. It is possible that in the near future, such conclusions will be not only subjective testimonials but also the results of precise measurements demonstrable to skeptics and critics of meditation.

Not all Buddhists are happy with such ventures. Buddhist transformation and transcendence are ultimately about something much more profound than mundane happiness, reduced blood pressure, and more engaged

---

8. Kabat-Zinn, *Full Catastrophe Living*.

9. Simmer-Brown and Grace, *Meditation and the Classroom*.

10. Online: http://mindbrain.ucdavis.edu/people/jeremy/shamatha-project.

11. For an account of the kind of meditation done while brain activity was being measured, see Wallace, *The Attention Revolution*.

12. For their extremely informative website, see http://www.mindandlife.org/.

students, they claim. As a Buddhist, I agree with that assessment. But I would also suggest that in the meanwhile and in the short run, if meditation produces demonstrable results in terms of health and mental well-being, surely that is not a problem. No one is claiming that these are the *only* fruitions of mind training or the *only* reason people should practice contemplative disciplines. It also seems quite clear that these fruitions of mind training equip people with the skills and attitudes conducive to flourishing with religious diversity rather than regarding it as a problem and a flaw. Such disciplines may be extremely helpful in the transition from regarding religious diversity as a problem to regarding *discomfort* with religious diversity, not religious diversity itself, as the real problem.

Chapter 11

Women, Feminism, and Religious Diversity

A T LEAST HALF THE members of all religions are women. Many claim that women are more religious than men because in many situations women attend traditional religious services and uphold traditional religious values and practice much more frequently than men.[1] All major religions have had a great deal to say about gender and about relationships between men and women, most of it favoring men over women, probably because the vast majority of such statements are male authored. This fact about religions is so pronounced that I sometimes joke that religious male dominance and misogyny may be the long sought lowest common denominator shared by all religions that some pluralist theologians of religion are searching for. But, of course, that would be a very embarrassing and unsatisfactory place to ground our quest for cooperation and understanding among religions, though some religious conservatives do just that. Conservatives do unite across religious lines to restrict women's access to reproductive choices and health care, as well as other dimensions of equal rights.

There are also some indications that when women are protected in expressing their own opinions, they do not always agree with men on many debated issues. The so-called gender gap in politics in the United States, very evident in recent elections, demonstrates that while women are divided

1. Trzebiatowska and Bruce, *Why Are Women More Religious Than Men?*

190

among themselves and there does not seem to be an essential women's position on any major issues, there are significant differences between men as a group and women as a group. Thus, no particular woman's position on any issue is predetermined by the fact that she is a woman, but relevant generalizations about women can be made. This distinction between essences and averages is crucial because much muddled thinking about gender does not honor the difference between an essence and an average. When that distinction is not recognized and respected, all women or all men are pressured to act and think in conformity with the averages for their sex, an extremely imprisoning position in which to be placed.

Despite women's overwhelming participation in religions, the enormous impact religions have on women's lives, and tendencies for women to have their own views about many issues, nevertheless women have been singularly invisible in movements to defuse tension between religions through inter-religious dialogue and in discussions about theologies of religions. This is the case not only for more traditional women, but also for women who self-identify as feminists. The contributions of feminists to discussions of religious diversity and to theologies of religions are, thus far, extremely negligible. Why, given how deeply religions affect women and how dominant feminist movements in religions have been?

Religious Feminism in the West and Issues of Religious Diversity

Although at this point, I have been seriously engaged in issues pertaining to religious diversity and interreligious dialogue for more than thirty years, only two of my nearly two hundred published articles and essays concern women or feminism and interfaith dialogue.[2] Why so little writing revealing a direct connection between feminist theology and interreligious dialogue, especially given how important both have been to me? In my case, the answer is quite simple. For most of my career, my colleagues in feminist theology were simply not interested in dialogue or in so-called non-Western religions. For me, trying to bridge my intensive concerns with interreligious dialogue and with feminism in the same group of colleagues has proved very frustrating, and ultimately unsuccessful. I would have to contend that although their concerns about gender and Western religions were radical and innovative, about religious diversity the outlook and values of my colleagues in feminist theology were quite Eurocentric—in fact, quite Christian-centered.

2. Gross, "Feminist Theology," 73–78; Gross, *A Garland of Feminist Reflections*, 211–28.

My first direct experience of this lack of interest occurred at the 1975 America Academy of Religion annual meeting. I was the newly appointed section chair of the newly minted section on Women and Religion, a heady and scary responsibility for a thirty-two-year-old who had been at the All-But-Dissertation stage of a doctorate when taking on this responsibility.[3] I wanted our first set of sessions as a section to be exemplary and, in my view, that meant including a session that went beyond Christian and Euro-centric materials, so I solicited the papers for such a session to occur. I was shocked and disappointed when none of my close colleagues in the fledging feminist-theology movement came to that session. When I asked why, they said that materials on women or female imagery in "non-Western" religious traditions were not relevant or interesting to them. Other times, I would be told that, as feminists, they didn't want to concern themselves with patri-archal religious traditions (even though the Christianity with which they were so concerned is at least as patriarchal), or that reading and listening to papers on "non-Western" religions involved "too many foreign words and unfamiliar terms."

This stance on the part of my feminist colleagues mystified and frustrated me for several reasons. First, it was clear to me, and had been for a long time, that the familiar religions of the West did not have any monopoly on religious concepts and practices that might be helpful to women. Many other such concepts and practices were found around the world. Additionally, even if one did not wish to study such materials because of a personal interest in them, I had found Max Müller's famous motto "to know one religion is to know none" more than accurate. If one thinks about this motto, one sees that even if one's only aim is understanding one's own religion better, it is helpful, perhaps even necessary, to study other religions seriously, in an empathetic and nonjudgmental manner. (This point was discussed in chapter 8 and will be discussed again in chapter 14 to make a different point.) Thus, it was and is hard for me to understand such singular Euro-centric attachment to the religions of one's culture of origin. Furthermore, in the United States at least, as our society becomes more diverse religiously, many Christian institutions are becoming less skilled in dealing with that diversity. So how could my largely Christian feminist colleagues ignore such pressing concerns so consistently?

In a previous article on "Feminist Theology as Theology of Religions," I presented what I still see as the natural affinity between (on the one hand) feminist theology as critique and reformulation of one's own tradition and (on the other hand) interest in and concern for diverse religions other than

3. Gross, *Beyond Androcentrism*, my first book, came out of that meeting.

one's own. I suggested that a key feminist value has always been including what had previously been excluded by mainstream theologies. This moral value stems from our own experience of having been excluded from theological discourse and leadership roles in our own traditions simply and only because we are women. Knowing firsthand the inappropriateness of excluding others for arbitrary reasons because it had been done to us as women, how could we then exclude others who happened to belong to other religions? I quote myself:

> A major value of feminist theology is to include the voices that have not been heard, to widen the circle, to learn how to welcome diversity. It makes no sense for those values to stop when they hit the boundary of one's own religion and for another set of values to take over at that point.[4]

The moral incentive to include previously excluded voices from other religious traditions could lead to "widening the canon," which had become a slogan in feminist theology. Feminists generally agreed that neglected and forgotten stories and source materials were important because the received canon contained so little material that was truly empowering for women. At the same time, mainstream theologians were beginning to realize that in a world characterized by religious diversity, one could no longer do reputable theology if one only knew one's own tradition. In the felicitous phrase of one commentator, in the process of seriously studying other religions, we "become a phenomenon to ourselves."[5] To quote myself again,

> For theological reflection, feminist or otherwise, nothing is so useful as becoming a phenomenon to oneself because in that process, we see and understand ourselves much more clearly. Part of that seeing includes seeing the strengths and weaknesses of the perspectives we take for granted. As we begin to experience that there really are religious *alternatives*, our own perspective must also become an *alternative*, not merely the only viable theological position or something with which we are stuck.[6]

In the 1990s, when diversity had finally become a hot topic generally, interest in and concern for non-Western Christianity emerged among my colleagues in feminist theology. Nevertheless, their concern was *only* with Christian cultural diversity, not with *religious* diversity. I found it incomprehensible that when concern with diversity finally began to emerge in feminist

4. Gross, *A Garland of Feminist Reflections*, 216–17.

5. Paden, *Religious Worlds*, 165.

6. Gross, *A Garland of Reflections*, 219.

theology, there was still no concern with *religious diversity*. In fact, these feminist theologians routinely used the word *religion* when what they meant was Christianity. At a number of meetings with them about diversity, I consistently called them on such usage. They found that irritating and just couldn't train themselves to distinguish between religion and Christianity.

Unfortunately, in this bias, the rhetoric of feminist theology mirrors North American discourse on diversity in general. Every other kind of diversity is highlighted, but religious diversity is not even regarded as a kind of diversity that deserves recognition, protection, and encouragement. As the United States grows significantly more diverse religiously, that fact fails to register. Or, for many, if that fact does register, it registers as a negative, not a positive. According to many, this is, after all, a Christian nation.

I remember with great sadness meetings of the editorial board of the *Journal of Feminist Studies in Religion* in which certain board members would complain about lack of diversity among those present or those who presented papers on women and religion at the American Academy of Religion annual meetings. Let me quote myself as I wrote about those events shortly after they happened in the late 1990s, probably 1998.

> Not too long ago, I sat in a gathering of feminist theologians. The topic was "diversity;" numerous complaints about lack of diversity were being voiced, but it was clear that lack of diversity *among* the Christians, not the absence of *religious* diversity was being protested. I pointed out that the diversity among *Christians* represented was far greater than the diversity among *religions*, and that the discussion presumed a Christian context which I, a non-Christian, found problematic. The conversation paused momentarily to allow me to make my comment, then returned to its previous direction as if I had never spoken. I felt as if I had momentarily surfaced from underwater in some giant ocean, only to have the waters submerge me again immediately. I also noted that I had felt this way before. In earlier days, it had not been uncommon for men to treat women's observations about religious studies or theology in the same way. One of the few other non-Christian feminists locked eyes with me and whispered, "The just don't get it, do they?" How many times had we said the same thing about men when trying to explain to them what feminism is and why it matters?[7]

Thus, despite their willingness to be radical on so many other issues, my Christian feminist colleagues were unwilling to stand against the

---

7. Ibid., 211.

theological mainstream on this issue. It has been suggested that Christian feminists, feeling vulnerable because of their feminism, needed to prove their Christian orthodoxy to skeptical colleagues and issues of religious diversity seemed like an easy place to take their more conventionally Christian stand.[8] But when one thinks about how important interreligious dialogue and issues of religious diversity are, it is clear that this is not the place to cut corners to prove one's Christian orthodoxy.

I have finally come to the conclusion that I was trying too hard to understand my feminist colleagues' uninterest in religious diversity. Their unwillingness to take these issues seriously reflects more their immersion in the North American Christian theological milieu of the day than any deeply reflective, conscious choice. After all, almost all of my feminist colleagues had been trained in (Christian) theology at a time when most (Christian) theologians saw no need to know anything about any religion other than their own. They simply did not yet understand the importance of using the comparative mirror in their theologizing. Though Christian feminists thought creatively and radically about many issues *within* Christianity, they unreflectively bought into Christianity's blind spot about religious diversity. At the same time, feminists more oriented to cross-cultural studies of religion were severely discouraged from any normative, critical, or constructive engagement with the materials they studied. Thus, almost no one brought together issues of feminism and of religious diversity.

I have always been reluctant to give credence to Asian and African criticisms that Western feminisms are largely irrelevant to the rest of the world, but feminist theology's distinct lack of engagement with issues of religious diversity makes their case much more compelling. To be sure, Western feminists who lack any cross-cultural training, awareness, or sensitivity have often been extremely dense in their pronouncements about women and gender in other cultural contexts and extremely arrogant in regard to feelings of superiority about Western values and customs. As we saw in chapter 9, despite the universality and near intractability of female identity, building a global, united feminist movement proved to be impossible, in large part because of insufficient attention to various forms of diversity among women and their different needs and preferences.

As it became clear to me that I needed to look beyond my feminist colleagues for scholarly interchange on issues pertaining to religious diversity, beginning in 1980, I started to immerse myself in venues devoted specifically to interreligious dialogue, especially Buddhist-Christian dialogue. Interestingly, these venues, while not concerned with feminism or

---

8. Christ, "Response," 79–84.

with gender issues, were not antifeminist either. In fact, I found those primarily oriented to interreligious exchange far more receptive to feminist concerns than feminists were to interreligious issues. When feminism was appropriate to the topic at hand, it easily received slots in the program at these gatherings devoted to dialogue and interreligious exchange. In these venues, especially in the world of Buddhist-Christian dialogue, I also enjoyed many years of supportive, friendly, noncompetitive collegiality. I cannot explain this difference between the two sets of colleagues and will not attempt to do so, though I continue to regard this blind spot as feminist theology's greatest failing.

Ironically, I encountered the colleague in feminist theology with whom I have worked most closely over the last twenty-five years, Rosemary Reuther, in the interreligious exchange world, not the feminist theology world. Rosemary agreed to join the prestigious and formerly all-male Cobb-Abe International Buddhist-Christian Theological Encounter after protests from the floor of the larger conference with which it was meeting concurrently, resulted, in 1983, in its gender integration. For many years after that, we met annually for meetings of that group and were often asked to do a Buddhist-Christian-feminist dialogue as a public program. Eventually, we led such a dialogue together as a weekend-long program at the Grailville Retreat Center in Loveland, Ohio. This program resulted in a book we coauthored, *Religious Feminism and the Future of the Planet: A Buddhist-Christian-Feminist Dialogue*. It is a good example of what sustained feminist interreligious dialogue between various traditions could be. But, to my knowledge this book has had very little, if any, impact on the world of feminist theology. Nor has that workshop, which would be an ideal way for seminaries to educate their students about feminism and interreligious dialogue, ever been repeated.

Who Keeps Women Out of the Dialogues?

From this narrative, I think it is clear that women and feminists cannot simply blame their lack of involvement in interreligious dialogue on being excluded by male-dominant religions. Women have also excluded themselves, which does not mean that there are not real obstacles to women's full participation in interreligious dialogue. A major disincentive for feminists is the male monopoly on religious institutions and positions of religious leadership in them. As a result of this monopoly, almost all, if not all, the participants in the flashy meetings of world religious leaders are men. Because religious institutions in all cases are so male dominated, women do not have leadership roles at the highest levels and have virtually no chance to participate in these forums. Casual observers of this situation can be forgiven for concluding that women are out of the picture in the world of interreligious exchange.

However, I would urge another conclusion. These flashy meetings may produce good news copy and interesting photographs, as well as a few pious resolutions. But that is not where the serious interreligious work is going on, and so it doesn't matter too much that women are locked out of these venues. Instead, I suggest that for serious interreligious dialogue, we rely less on official religious leaders and more on thoughtful, well-educated scholar-practitioners, many of whom are women, and more of whom are now interested in dialogue and religious diversity.[9]

We also need to remember, when we despair over the fact that all the most newsworthy interreligious venues look very male dominated, not receptive to women at all, that things can change, sometimes very rapidly. In 1971, when feminists packed the business meeting of the American Academy of Religion to elect the first woman president of that organization, the American Academy of Religion also looked very male dominated and not receptive to women at all. That tactic would not have been successful and could not have worked if there had not been women already in the organization, well trained, and prepared to step into waiting leadership positions. Probably for some time into the future, organizers of flashy interreligious meetings will think that they should invite the Dalai Lama and the pope to be chief speakers at such meetings. But those invitations will be turned down in most cases. Women are not going to be the ones next on the list of invitees if we have not already distinguished ourselves in less prestigious interfaith meetings.

Superficially, it might look as if women have been kept out of the interfaith arena, as historically they have been kept out of so many others, by the male dominance of religions and by the near monopoly men have on most leadership roles in religious institutions. However, in the last forty-five years, women have broken through many, many gender barriers in religion, have gained ordination in many denominations, have become bishops and other religious leaders, have become seminary and university professors of religion and religious studies. Why, then, such a limited advance into arenas concerned with religious diversity and interreligious dialogue on the part of feminist theologians?

Things have changed a great deal from thirty years ago when, in 1983, I was the lone female participant in the Cobb-Abe International

9. For example, see Fletcher, *Monopoly on Salvation?*; and Cornille, *The Im-Possibility of Interreligious Dialogue*.

Buddhist- Christian Theological Encounter and was there by demand from the floor of the larger concurrently running conference, not because I had been invited by the male leadership. By the time of its last meeting twenty years later, the group was almost half female. The same pertains for meetings of the Society for Buddhist-Christian Studies and the other interreligious forums in which I have participated over the years. In so far as I can tell, women come to these discussions because we are interested in and care about religious diversity and interreligious dialogue, not because we are women, though some of us also do feminist and gender-related scholarly studies in other contexts. It is telling that recent movements of women into the world of interreligious dialogue are occurring in venues devoted to dialogue, not to feminism.

What Do Women Bring to the Dialogue Table?

Sometimes one hears messages urging that women be more visible at inter-religious dialogues and in discussions of religious diversity. These messages have two primary justifications, one of which I agree with heartily and the other of which I find much less convincing. Some people want women at dialogue tables because they suppose that women will bring a unique message or style of interacting in dialogue that will supply a "missing ingredient" that would make such meetings more successful.[10] Some of the same commentators advocate for dialogues among women only, for much the same reason. Other commentators, myself included, advocate for women's presence and participation in such formats simply because it is ludicrous to suppose that meetings about important topics from which women are excluded could possibly represent *human* rather than *male* concerns and conclusions. Even if women do not bring unique perspectives or methods to such meetings, how could they have any credibility if women are absent, given that women represent about half of every religion, and given how much about women's lives is determined by religions?

I resist justifications for including women in dialogue groups when they turn on gender essentialism because, as I have argued many times, I regard such conclusions as both highly inaccurate and extremely imprisoning for both women and men. Though gender essentialist theories were once popular in feminist circles, I always claimed that they were more dangerous than helpful. Gender essentialisms are fundamentally dualistic. In this book, we have already found dualistic constructs to be seriously lacking on multiple occasions. The same is true regarding gender. Dualistic evaluations

10. O'Neill, *Mending a Torn World*, 3–7.

usually also involve hierarchical claims about superiority and inferiority. Often they simply reverse patriarchal versions of gender essentialism. A common patriarchal gender essentialism claims that women are unfit for leadership because they are more passive and less willing to be confrontational when confrontation is needed. But feminist essentialism often simply reversed that hierarchical dualism by using more positive words to label the "female traits," which then promoted the conclusion that women are more morally fit than men. Men were evaluated as more inherently aggressive, women as more innately peaceful. It is hard to see how such gender-essentialist dualities could foster human well-being and flourishing. For me, feminism is about freedom from the prison of gender roles, and that has been my understanding for many, many years. Nothing is more imprisoning than expectations based on gender, especially when one imposes them on oneself. Rather than finding a better, improved, more equal set of gender roles, why not junk the whole idea of putting so much freight on gender identity?[11] That is the much more liberating alternative.

While culturally constructed gender norms are omnipresent and deeply influence individuals, they do not add up to gender essences. Clearly, when one scores many individuals for certain traits or achievements, average differences between men and women often show up, but those are averages, not gender essences. The averages may discourage or encourage certain individuals, but they do not predetermine what any specific individual could achieve. Instead they give rise to a lot of stereotypes that contribute to the cultural gender norms that then limit the individuals who internalize them—but that do not limit those who do not buy into them to the same extent. If girls were inherently less capable of achievement in math or science, for example, no woman would ever accomplish anything in those realms, which is not the case. But if it were the case, then efforts to alter cultural messages that discourage girls from thinking they could be competent at math or science would be useless.

Thus, arguing to include women in discussions of religious diversity for gender-essentialist reasons is a bad idea, I would argue, because gender essentialisms are so flawed. As for suggestions to sponsor dialogues for women only, I see no harm in such programs, so long as they are regarded as simply another venue for interaction on interreligious issues rather than as the only format in which women should participate. Many women do find a single-sex group much more satisfying and rewarding, especially in earlier

11. I have written a great deal on this point. Two articles that I especially recommend are in Gross, *A Garland of Feminist Reflections*, 250–62; and Gross, "How Clinging to Gender Subverts Enlightenment," 18–19, 32. This article is also available on my website: http://ritamgross.com/.

stages of their participation in interfaith venues. Trying to interact with self-confident, often verbally aggressive men who have not been taught to allow women to speak can be difficult. One of the most infuriating inter-faith interactions I have ever experienced took place in a usually very satisfying small interfaith group sponsored by the World Council of Churches. But on one occasion, for whatever reasons, Asian men—Christian, Hindu, and Buddhist—all refused to yield to the moderator when he recognized me, and repeatedly interrupted me or cut me off. Especially for younger, less experienced women, trying to participate in such groups can be frustrating and discouraging. Additionally, if women learn to understand and appreciate each other across lines of religious difference, they may well be able to help defuse interreligious hostility in their home communities. Especially in religious and cultural contexts in which sexual segregation is the norm, single-sex groups may be much more effective at promoting such inter-religious understanding simply because they are much more comfortable for participants than are mixed groups. For all these reasons, dialogue among women can be useful and helpful.

But if we are not making a case for women and feminists to be involved in discussions of religious diversity on essentialist grounds, why does it matter whether or not women are present at such gatherings? Indeed, I have long thought that while it is important for women and feminists to be involved in discussions of religious diversity, because religious diversity is such an overridingly important issue, I have not felt that, regarding religious diversity itself, there is a position or a point of view that would appeal more to women than to men, or that only women would be likely to contribute. The phrase "feminist position about religious diversity" is truly mystifying to me. This is because the central issues for religious diversity (e.g., how to think about the inevitability and existence of religious diversity itself, and how to work within a tradition's theological and textual resources to come to the point of valuing rather than fearing religious diversity) are not gendered. This does not mean that no issues that might be discussed in interreligious gatherings are gendered. Many of them are, including religious views of gender and of men's and women's roles in religions and societies. To discuss such issues, which affect both women and men very significantly, in the absence of women is ludicrous, even though it often happens. On these topics that pertain to gender, of course feminist positions are likely.

Sometimes I suspect that women and feminists have not participated significantly in discussions of religious diversity and in interreligious dialogue because those enterprises did not seem gender-urgent enough to them. According to this view, women are unlikely to penetrate the glass ceiling of prestigious and high-powered dialogue venues soon, and very few of the topics generally discussed at such meetings pertain directly to gender issues. It may well have seemed to many such feminists that there was little for them to gain, *qua* women or feminists, at such meetings. So why bother to put up with the annoying male dominance of the venue—especially, if, as I contend, when it comes to the most critical and important questions about religious diversity, women will not offer different insights than men could? If women are not going to significantly alter the theological discourse, and if the dialogue table looks inhospitable to women, why should women participate in significant numbers? The most cogent answer is that the questions are too important for women not to lend their learning and wisdom to life-giving ways of coping with religious diversity and defusing discomfort with it. Women should be involved in such discussions because otherwise religions are once again demonstrating their historical patriarchy rather than their universal human relevance. In other words, questions about selection and self-selection for who sits at the dialogue table are questions about gender, and there is a clear feminist perspective on these questions, even if there is no clear feminist perspective on how to think about religious diversity.

When asked what difference it makes if women are included in discussions of religious diversity, I have begun to say that the most important thing we bring to these discussion is our sheer presence. By this, I do not mean that all women need to do is sit around the table, being visible as women and radiating some mysterious feminine presence. I mean the presence of verbally active women who contribute significantly to the discussion. I also would argue that women must be present in significant numbers to make any real difference. A few token women are powerless to shift the dynamics of the conversation and may well have difficulty even getting a word in edgewise.

What difference could the presence of women make? Unless participating women are totally male identified and are only going to rubber-stamp positions and views that men have already decided upon, our presence gives some credibility to the proceedings and their possible results. But because religions have been such boys-only clubs, the *presence* of women at the interfaith table loudly proclaims a critical message that can be proclaimed no other way. Religions are no longer going to be male sanctuaries, closed off to women except in the supportive roles we have traditionally played. Religions claim to have messages relevant to all human beings. But that claim is hollow when the only people who proclaim the messages are men. How can all-male gatherings pretend to represent all humans or have messages relevant for all? The messages that emanate from conferences of major religious leaders would have more credibility if half the people at those conference tables were women. The most important thing women bring to the interfaith table is our sheer presence. There is no other way for religions to live up to claims they make about their universal relevance.

A Buddhist Analogue

In many ways the arguments and conclusions I have reached about women and issues of religious diversity are similar to conclusions I have reached on a Buddhist issue about which I care passionately. I have long argued that because of the supreme importance of the role of *dharma* teacher in Buddhism, the acid test for whether Buddhism has overcome its patriarchal ways is whether or not women become *dharma* teachers in significant numbers.[12] But others have argued against me, claiming that authentic *dharma* does not depend on any accidental traits characterizing the *dharma* teacher, including his or her gender. "If women were gurus, would their *dharma* be different from that of male gurus?" I have been asked. When I answer in the negative, I have faced a "Gotcha!" reaction. Some claim that given *dharma's* liberative potential, it is overridingly important that *dharma* be taught by competent teachers and irrelevant whether any of those teachers happen to women. Given that "enlightened mind is beyond gender, neither male nor female,"[13] women and men do teach essentially the same *dharma*. Note that the argument is the same: if the discourse itself is not radically changed by women's presence, it does not matter if they are absent. In this case, however, the argument is made by men (and some women) wanting to justify a status quo that excludes women from the discourse; when it comes to participating in conversations about religious diversity and interreligious dialogue, we have more examples of women excusing their own absence and disinclination to participate.

In the Buddhist case, my rejoinder is multifaceted but mainly revolves around two points. First, the presence or absence of female role models is crucially important to Buddhist students, both female and male. Again, our sheer *presence* or *absence* speaks as loudly as the words being said, perhaps more loudly. Is Buddhism really welcoming to women? Or is it essentially a religions created by men and for men? Furthermore, in the case of Buddhism,

12. This case was made recently in an article in Gross, *A Garland of Feminist Reflections*, 281–90.

13. This, Buddhism's most frequently recited cliché about Buddhism and gender, is often used to dismiss feminist critiques of Buddhism as irrelevant and to subtly pressure critics to ignore and overlook extreme male dominance in Buddhist institutions, as if the truth of this slogan at the absolute level renders patriarchy at the relative level nonexistent or irrelevant. Exposing this erroneous use of Buddhist ideas of the two truths has been important in my feminist critique of Buddhism.

when gendered subjects of Buddhist institutions who happen to be women speak, they tell us a great deal from their experiences on the ground (so to speak) that cannot be expressed by men. Their abstract *dharma* teachings may not be different from those of men, but how they express their teachings and how those teachings are received will be subtly different. At least we must concede that because each teacher expresses the universal *dharma* in idiosyncratic ways, the uniquely relevant message of a great teacher may go unheard if women's voices are not part of the conversation. The same is certainly true for issues of religious diversity and interreligious dialogue.

Gender Issues and Religious Diversity

At the beginning of this chapter, I pointed out that women participate in religions in great numbers, that religions deeply affect the quality of women's lives, and that all religions have been male dominated and have restricted women in many ways, though the ways they restrict women differ among the various religions. For every religion we now have considerably more knowledge about women's roles and how they fare within any religious community. In every major religion, gender and the treatment of women are now contested issues and male dominance is no longer unquestioningly accepted in any of them. There are feminist movements promoting greater equity and equality for women in every religion, and it is relatively easy to find out about them.

But should we promote interreligious symposia on these matters as part of fostering acceptance of religious diversity? Venues devoted mainly to informing across religious lines could be very helpful, but those in which outsiders reprimand or council members of other religions and communities about internal gender issues usually backfire. I am mindful of the way Western feminism has often been very ineffective because of its cultural chauvinism. Criticisms of indigenous treatment of women has a long, deeply troubling history in colonial enterprises. Well-meaning reformers from the outside often end up causing entrenchment rather than reform, as local people, including women, resist what they perceive as Westernization. It seems more judicious to support those inside a religious community advocating feminist reforms with quiet financial and moral support than it does to preach at the community from the outside. When I think of this issue as a Buddhist, I find that outsiders' views about the position of women in Buddhism are usually ill informed and not very helpful. Therefore, I extend this insight to Muslims, Hindus, and others, and usually listen to what they have to say about their own situations and how they are working with their own gender issues.

However, there is another subtlety to this issue. I am both a Westerner and a Buddhist. As a Buddhist, I have participated significantly in Buddhist discussions of Buddhism and gender. And I insist that my contributions be taken seriously as *Buddhist* contributions, not dismissed as tainted by my Western origins. When I have done prepublication reviews of articles submitted for publication, especially articles about nuns' ordination in Buddhism, I have frequently encountered social scientists who claim that the many Western Buddhist nuns who advocate for women's full ordination do so because they are Westerners. These social scientists then conclude that the nuns' advocacy is inappropriate because they are Westerners. I always insist that publication be dependent on revising the article to acknowledge that these Buddhist nuns, who are fully ordained themselves, advocate for nuns' ordination on *Buddhist* grounds. That they are Westerners is quite incidental to the case they are making. As religions originating in Asia and the Middle East are more widely practiced in Western countries, whether through immigration or conversion, we should expect internal changes to gender practices and women's participation in them. Such internal evolution, in part due to immersion of these religions into a more egalitarian culture, is entirely different from colonial imposition. Nor should Asian or Middle Eastern religious authorities expect that they will be able to control their members who live in other parts of the world. That is part of the price of being a religion with global constituency.

Chapter 12

Religious Diversity
and National Identity

Pluralistic Society or Christian Nation?

IN 2003, WITH A group of Western coreligionists, I visited Bhutan, a small Himalayan country and the only independent nation-state in the world in which the religion I practice, Vajrayana Buddhism, is the majority religion. Almost the first thing we noticed was that familiar religious symbols were everywhere in public spaces and also on the local currency. At first, it seemed exhilarating and astonishing! Imagine! A place where everyone understood and used the symbols with which we were familiar, a place in which even the money proclaimed Buddhism! It seemed ideal! It also initiated a train of thought about contested church-state relations in the United States, about crèches in public parks and about the pledge of allegiance and its offensive "under God" clause. It was a valuable moment, for it gave me some insight into the feelings of the Christian majority in the United States—both why it feels good to them to have Christian symbols be displayed so publicly and how they could be so uncomprehending of and insensitive to the sensibilities of the non-Christian minority.

Bhutan is famous for its declaration that "gross national happiness" matters more than "gross national product," and for its very careful, slow introduction of modern and Western ways into its traditional society. It is also a singularly beautiful country. It often presents itself as a "Shangri-la," the British mispronunciation of *Shambhala*, the word for the Tibetan Buddhist mythical enlightened society somewhere north of Tibet, where everyone is happy and good because they practice spiritual discipline. One of my major gurus, Chogyam Trungpa, made creative use of this legend in his own teaching. He introduced a meditation program independent of Buddhism, "Shambhala Training," based on his teachings about what an enlightened society would be like and would require.[1] In his contemporary redoing of the legend, it was clearly stated that in Shambhala, all religions would be practiced openly and would flourish because they would all be based on spiritual disciplines that fostered people's basic goodness, their innate preference for kindness and compassion over aggression and competition. I myself have taught many, many weekend programs in this nonsectarian program of spiritual discipline. So my trip to Bhutan had a certain fairy-tale quality about it.

However, reality checks are always in order. The idyllic nature of life in Bhutan has been contested by some. There is a significant population of Nepali "guest workers" who are not Buddhists and also a significant Hindu population in southern border regions near India. Vajrayana Buddhism may be the majority religion in Bhutan, but it is not the only religion. Members of other religions and ethnic groups do not always feel that they receive fair treatment, and some outside observers concur with this assessment.

The Multireligious State

Issues about the relationship between religious identity and national identity have been discussed in earlier chapters, especially in chapter 3, which is a precursor to this chapter. The main thesis of that chapter was so show how badly things can go in an attempt to make religious and political boundaries correspond so that all citizens of a state would share the same religion. I also tried to show, using Buddhist examples, how badly things can go when religions become too invested in trying to intervene in, control, or support state policies. Clearly, religious institutions and political institutions have always vied against each other for power. Trying to solve the problem of a balance of power between them is not my main concern, nor is this chapter about Buddhist theories of the state, if there even are such things.

Instead, this chapter is primarily concerned with what is required from both the state and religious institutions to promote flourishing with religious diversity within a *multireligious state*, a state *characterized* by religious diversity rather than a religious monopoly. We have been reimagining

1. Trungpa, *Shambhala.*

theology and religion from a perspective that takes it for granted that religious diversity is not a mistake or a problem, but is normal and here to stay. In the same way, we need to ask what law and politics would be like if it were taken for granted that religious diversity is the unproblematic norm in a multireligious state. In such a state, no religion could expect or ask for any measure of special privilege, as if it were more worthy than any other religion. What is required from religious institutions to accommodate themselves to such a legal situation? What does the state owe the various religions in a situation in which they are all on a level playing field?

These days most states in the world are multireligious states, in the sense that people with many different religious identities live within the same state boundaries, and most nation-states, including the United States, are rapidly becoming even more religiously diverse. Additionally, all the so-called major world religions are now practiced globally in many different states outside those with which they are traditionally associated. A religion's global distribution requires significant adjustments on its part, especially if it is the kind of religion, commonplace in premodern situations, that sought to be a comprehensive package, governing not only belief systems but also minute details of lifestyle. If religious and political authority are collapsed within the state, religions have recourse to law to enforce their lifestyle regulations. Such a situation was once commonplace and is, I believe, in the background of many church-state controversies in the United States and around the world. But a situation in which religious and political boundaries correspond is becoming less and less common. In fact, it never was an absolute standard. Instead, religious minorities within states were sometimes tolerated but usually subjected to discrimination. At one time, Jews in Christian Europe were limited in where they could settle. Non-Muslims in Muslim states were required to pay additional taxes for the privilege of being non-Muslims. Catholics in Protestant England were subjected to certain restrictions until 1832. And so on. All such legal discriminations stem from theological exclusive truth claims and from oppositional, dualistic identities. They proclaim, We will put up with your being different, but we don't like it. Diversity makes us uncomfortable, and because we are in the majority, we will penalize you for being different.

Perhaps the most succinct way of summarizing this situation is to return to our claims about hyphenated identity—that identity is always multifaceted, consisting of many discrete parts, rather than monolithic and singular. It is truly helpful to distinguish between national identity and religious identity rather than to assume that they are the same or that they should be the same. This is one arena in which routinely separating identities that some people may not be used to separating would help defuse many tensions.

For one thing, if it is clearly realized that national identity and religious identity are two different things, questions such as whether the United States is or should be a Christian nation would not even occur. Instead, American exceptionalism would include the recognition that the flourishing of religious diversity is one of the greatest demonstrations of American excptionalism. Everyone would understand that people of many different religious identities hold citizenship in the United States and that their specific religious differences and needs must be accommodated. It would also be understood that because many different religions are being practiced within one state, no specific religion can or should expect that its preferences and practices will be required of all, especially of those who hold different religious views. When religious identity and national identity are clearly recognized to be two identities, not one, and are separated from each other, then two basic principles will have to be honored: First, the state must be truly neutral religiously, not favoring any specific religion or the non-religious in any way. Second, each religion, and *especially the majority* religion, must be sensitive to the fact that it is only one religion among others, and therefore must do what it takes to be considerate of the needs of members of other religions, especially minority religions, thereby promoting flourishing with religious diversity.

State Neutrality and the Disestablishment of Religion

As is well known, the Bill of Rights appended to the United States Constitution promotes both freedom of religion and freedom from religion. Generally, the phrase "freedom of religion" is better known and more popular than the phrase "freedom from religion," another way of talking about the Non-Establishment Clause of the First Amendment. The third phrase that completes the basic vocabulary about the neutrality of the state is Thomas Jefferson's "wall of separation between church and state," which is in neither the Constitution nor the Bill of Rights but is found in one of his letters detailing his understanding of the implications of what had been accomplished in those documents.[2] However, it is not the case that the disestablishment of religion and clear separation of church and state were accomplished completely at the nation's founding, or even today.[3] An important extension of these principles did not occur until the 1940s with Supreme Court decisions

2. Harris and Kidd, *The Founding Fathers and the Debate over Religion*, 20–21, 149–52.

3. For a detailed consideration of the development of separation of church and state see Gunn and Witte, *No Establishment of Religion*.

that ruled that states must also abide by the First Amendment, which had not been the case earlier.[4] Prayer and Bible reading in public schools were not abolished until the 1960s.

All three phrases are equally important, especially for members of minority religions, who need not only freedom to practice their chosen religion but freedom from being coerced into observing aspects of the dominant religion. When the "wall of separation" works to full effect, both freedoms are assured. The former freedom is easier to secure than the latter, which is often compromised even in the United States in my experience as a member of a minority religion. I have never felt limited in my ability to freely practice Buddhism, but I certainly am constrained and confined by many customs that are Christian and have nothing to do with Buddhism. Furthermore, though members of the dominant religion never argue against freedom of *religion* because it is never dis-advantageous to them, they often argue that they should be able to impose aspects of their religion on all citizens, which amounts to an argument against the Non-Establishment Clause. Unfortunately, they are sometimes successful.

The title, and especially the subtitle, of a recent book on the First Amendment says it all: *No Establishment of Religion: America's Original Contribution to Religious Liberty.*[5] In recent years, there has been significant debate over what the founders actually meant by freedom of and from religion.[6] However contested and difficult church-state interactions in the United States have been, it cannot be contested that the founding documents of the United States took up the issues of religion and state that resulted from the Reformation and the endless wars over religion that ensued in Europe (see chapter 3). The early history of the American colonies and the founding documents of the United States are definitely a continuation of that story. Therefore they continue all the ambiguities found in the earlier stories. In elementary- and secondary-school classes on American history, it is commonly taught that colonists came to the so-called New World in search of "freedom of religion." So far, so good; but it is usually not taught that early in their histories, the various colonies, all seeking freedom of religion, sometimes established their own religion while prohibiting or disadvantaging all others. Without disestablishment, "freedom of religion" only means *freedom of religion for me, but not for you.* Religious majorities especially have to be on guard to avoid this perversion of the meaning of freedom of religion.

---

4. Sullivan, *The Impossibility of Religious Freedom.* 25. Other scholars attribute this extension to a 1947 case. See Gunn and Witte, *No Establishment of Religion.* 309–12.

5. See fn. 3, above.

6. Harris and Kidd, *The Founding Fathers and the Debate over Religion*, 3–23.

They often fail. But with the Non-Establishment Clause and the resulting "wall of separation," the founding documents of the United States solved, at least theoretically, the problems that had plagued Europe for centuries and that still plague many parts of the world.

The religious neutrality of the state in a multireligious state is absolutely necessary if freedom of religion is to be possible. Even those who sometimes resist valuing freedom from religion rarely argue against the desirability of freedom of religion. Nevertheless, it seems to me that the neutrality of the state is often seriously misconceived. Neutrality is often taken to be not favoring one side of a dualistic battle: the secular Left vs. the religious Right. However, the neutrality of the state *is not one position among others* but the *basis, ground, or matrix* that allows and accommodates many positions, both antireligious and proreligious. Called "America's Sacred Ground" by Barbara McGraw in her recent book *Rediscovering America's Sacred Ground: Public Religion and the Good in a Pluralistic America*,[7] this neutrality of the state vis-à-vis religion and nonreligion is in no way an antireligious position, as some who want state endorsement of their various religious or non-religious projects often contend. Like others have, McGraw traces the history of this idea of state neutrality in matters of religion back to the post-Reformation religious wars in Europe and to the development of the European Enlightenment in response. In her reconstruction of this history, the thought of John Locke and his influence on the founders of the American constitutional system loom large. Utterly basic to this "sacred ground" is individual freedom of conscience, which overrides religious authority and can lead both to a variety of religious views and to antireligious or nonreligious views. All expressions of individual conscience are welcome in the public sphere so long as they do not involve attempts to destroy that sacred ground or to limit other noncoercive expressions. McGraw makes a fine distinction: the *expression* of intolerance is allowed, but not to the point where the rights and liberties of those of whom one is intolerant are harmed.[8] Thus, in some recent highly publicized cases, it was decided that pharmacists who disapprove of the so-called morning-after pill are free to express their moral misgivings about it, but they should not be free to refuse to fill a prescription for it, as has happened recently in a city near the city in which I live. In such a case, individual freedom of conscience would be allowed to infringe on the rights and freedoms of others. Or we could deduce

7. For a groundbreaking book making and exploring this point using different terminology, see McGraw, *Rediscovering America's Sacred Ground*. McGraw's phrase "sacred ground," which has come into the literature about church and state in the United States, is very close to, if it is not identical with, what I am calling state neutrality.

8. McGraw, *Rediscovering America's Sacred Ground*, 88–95.

that one could express disapproval of homosexuality, but legal discrimination against homosexuals violates the neutral sacred ground.

The most important point in this discussion is the recognition that to be neutral towards something is not to be against it, or to be for it, for that matter. The logic of "if you're not for something, then you're against it" simply doesn't hold. To suppose that state neutrality is an antireligious position or to expect that the state should support certain religious projects is to be mired in the kind of dualistic, either/or thinking that is so superficial and so unhelpful for promoting flourishing with religious diversity. Nonduality is always more profound than duality. State neutrality—nonduality—gives space for both proreligious and antireligious factions to make their arguments and to flourish. It is not an antireligious stance because it equally protects both the religious and the nonreligious, equally protects members of both majority religions and minority religions. I can think of no point that, when understood, contributes more to flourishing with religious diversity in a multireligious state.

In a previous publication, I explored at length the similarity between McGraw's concept of "America's sacred ground" and what Buddhists call emptiness.[9] It is not necessary to repeat that discussion in this context, but it is helpful to know that Buddhist thought is very familiar and comfortable with that "sacred ground." If we were to explicate that empty sacred ground more fully, using Buddhist terminology, we would be more likely to use analogies of space and sound. Both are a background out of which multiple, disparate phenomena arise, just as a state that is religiously neutral allows many different points of view about religion—both pro and con—to flourish. Space and silence are not negative and do not denote absence. Rather they are the matrix that accommodates and allows for diverse forms to arise and coexist. These Buddhist analogies of space and silence may well prove helpful in discussions of specific issues that arise when implementing a policy of neutrality vis-à-vis religions.

Buddhist familiarity with this "sacred ground" may well explain why Buddhists usually cope well in situations of religious diversity. In Asia, Buddhists never had the kind of religious monopoly that Catholic Christians held for so long in Europe, and that Muslims still have in some parts of the world. Even in parts of Asia where Buddhism is the dominant religion, it always coexisted with pre-Buddhist, indigenous traditions, which it accommodated rather than exterminated. In East Asia, it is usually no more than an equal partner in a multireligious state.

9. Gross, "Buddhism and Rediscovering America's Sacred Ground" 213–33.

Whether it is at all helpful to call this neutral "sacred ground" the realm of the secular, as is quite common, is another issue. McGraw argues against using such terminology, and I agree completely, given the two major current meanings of the term *secular*, both of which refer to something different from that neutral "sacred ground." On the one hand, the term *secular*, both in its history and its contemporary usage, is a dualistic term, often used as the opposite of *religious*. Therefore secularity also becomes an ideological position in its own right, a quasi-religious stance, if by the word *religion* we mean someone's life orientation and set of values. I am insisting that the neutral state must strive to be beyond duality by providing a "sacred ground" in which diverse religions and value systems, including secularity, can flourish.

Originally, the term *secular* meant "having to do with this time and this world, as opposed to the ultimate and eternal." From these origins, it has come to mean, at least in popular usage, something that is the opposite of what people usually mean by *religious* or *religion*. Thus, a secular Jew identifies as Jewish culturally but does not follow Jewish religious observances such as the dietary laws or the Sabbath observance. The term *secular Jew* is widely used, and now the term *secular Buddhist* is also coming into currency. Usually it means someone who meditates and accepts some Buddhist principles but is agnostic towards or rejects doctrines often associated with Buddhism, such as rebirth. In both cases, secularity is an oppositional term, used to contrast the secular Jew or Buddhist with the more conventionally religious Jew or Buddhist. Therefore, especially in Buddhist contexts, the word *secular* has been used as a positive term, intending to attract people who have been deeply wounded by traditional religions to the neutrality of some Buddhist spiritual disciplines. From these usages, we can see that *secular* often connotes something different from a traditional religious position rather than an antireligious posture.

Secularity now means many different things in many different social and political contexts.[10] But because it is so important to understand that the neutral state is not antireligious just because it is not proreligious, and because in most people's minds, the secular and the religious seem to be opposed, I will not use the term *secular* to refer to the neutral state. I argue that to regard neutrality as secularity is a serious conceptual mistake, and I reject language of the secular-Left-versus-religious-Right as a false dichotomy.

10. There is a large body of contemporary literature discussing the true meaning of the term *secular*. For a recent collection of such comments, see Calhoun et al., *Rethinking Secularism*.

The Moral Obligations of Powerful Religious Majorities

No topic is more neglected in discussions of religious diversity in the multi-religious state than the moral obligations of the majority religion, which by definition is more powerful than any of the minority religions. Throughout history, majorities and the more powerful have a horrible history of lack of self-awareness and awareness of how much suffering they cause to minorities by assumptions about their own entitlement and privilege. Simply think of Jews and Christians throughout most of European history, women and men in most cultures, Native Americans and European settlers, homosexuals and heterosexuals, blacks and whites in the United States, and so forth.

Likewise in situations of religious diversity, it is much easier for the dominant religion to impose its ways on the religious minorities than vice versa. Therefore members of dominant religions always need to be careful to question how they would feel if they suddenly became the religious minority and were asked to accommodate to some of the things they expect religious minorities to accept without reservation or objection. For these purposes it is important to remember that the nonreligious are also a religious minority. Essentially, members of majority religions are only being asked to observe the so-called silver rule: if you would dislike having x done to you, don't do that same thing to others. Such reversibility should be the acid test for whether any religious practice that affects all citizens is appropriate in a religiously diverse state. If the majority religion wouldn't care to be on the receiving end of such treatment, how can its members justify doing these same things to others simply because those others happen to belong to a minority religion?

Nevertheless, many Christians in the United States still expect the state to favor Christianity in many ways, including using Christian symbols, and thus far they have been successful in their campaigns. That is why American money displays the slogan "In God we trust" rather than Buddhist symbols, as it does in Bhutan. But is the expectation that the state should endorse specific religious symbols but not others reasonable or fair? Why should money in the United States include the Christian slogan "In God we trust" but not portraits of the Buddha? Does the fact that there are many more Christians than Buddhists in the United States make it fair or reasonable? Probably most Christians don't even realize how specifically Christian or monotheistic the slogan "In God we trust" actually is, which is part of the problem.

Because majorities are so often so blind to the ways in which they ignore or dominate minorities, it is often helpful for them to hear directly from minorities about how majority practices affect them. What is it like to be a non-Christian in a state with a mildly established religion—generic Christianity or generic monotheism? I often used to tell my students that it is difficult to see how established as the state religion Christianity actually is unless you are a non-Christian. Time is measured in Christian terms—with the initials BC (Before Christ) and AD (in the Year of Our Lord), which are only slightly improved when BCE (Before the Common Era) and CE (Common Era) or ACE (After the Common Era) are substituted. The calendar is thoroughly Christian, with some holidays from American civil religion thrown in. We all have to deal with Jesus's birthday every year but no one even knows when Buddha's birthday, which is celebrated at different times of the year in different parts of the Buddhist world, is. Sunday, not Friday or Saturday is the so-called day of rest for everyone, not just for Christians, though now that blue laws are not as common, life on Sundays is not as onerous for non-Christians as it once was. What would happen if politicians did not always end their speeches with the phrase "God bless America"?

Given how many such privileges the Christian majority already has, I am always incredulous when conservative Christians claim that they are being victimized because they cannot have prayers read out loud in the public schools, display the Ten Commandments in courthouses, teach creationism in science classes, or put up crèches in public parks. They are simply being asked to play by the same rules as we non-Christians, whose religions are not played out in public spaces or supported by protective legislation. Generally, we neither want nor seek government support for comparable religious practice, though in some cases, such as for memorials in military cemeteries or chaplaincy in prisons or the army, it is important that our religions be recognized. When religious services are provided in such contexts, part of government neutrality requires the government to recognize the diversity of religions. But in such cases, conservative Christians sometimes argue that some religions of which they disapprove, such as Paganism or Wicca, are not authentic religions. These Christians then argue that members of these religions should not receive religious services, even though conservative Christians want religious services for themselves.

Most of the examples of mildly established Christianity are not really problematic and are pointed out more for heuristic purposes than to register an objection. Some forms of Christian establishment, however, are truly onerous to non-Christians because their Christianness makes it difficult for non-Christians to fully function as citizens of the United States. In other words, these practices collapse Christian identity and identity as an American citizen as if they were a singular identity. But we have seen how important it is to recognize that identity is always hyphenated. Dealing with the phrase "In God we trust" on money, which we nontheists have to use almost every day is problematic enough, especially when we know that the phrase was not used on all coins and paper bills until 1957. The Pledge of allegiance with its "under God" phrase is even worse. The phrase, which did not become part of the Pledge of Allegiance until 1954, requires those of us who are not theists to lie publicly whenever we recite the Pledge of Allegiance. That is a very steep requirement, which I would think the theistic majority should be loath to impose on the rest of us if they understood what they are doing.

Some, such as retired Supreme Court Justice Sandra Day O'Connor, claim that the phrase "under God" is merely "ceremonial deism" and therefore "carries no religious currency."[11] I find that position strange—strange in that I seem to be taking monotheistic language more seriously than monotheists themselves. I would think that those for whom the existence of God is a serious matter would find O'Connor's solution problematic and would prefer my suggested solution of silence for all—both theists and nontheists—to dismissing the phrase "under God" as essentially meaningless.

Others who want the "under God" phrase in the Pledge of Allegiance suggest that we should just shut our ears or not listen to the phrase, but that is hardly an adequate solution. They also claim that it is important for them to be able to express their beliefs verbally and publicly. But at what cost? It is crucial for all believers to understand that their own freedom of religious expression does not include the freedom to impose their beliefs on other people. What would they lose that even begins to compare with the cost of having to choose between lying and not saying the Pledge of Allegiance? The existence of God is not being denied if the phrase is not in the pledge. For theists, a truly comparable instance of what nontheists experience when confronted with "under God" would happen if theists found themselves in a situation in which they longed to participate, but where participating would require them to deny the existence of God. That is the recommended acid test of reversal in this case. Without the phrase "under God," only silence—not disbelief in the existence of God—is required. That silence can accommodate both sets of beliefs without causing stress to either set of believers.

The solution of silence, of not verbalizing either or any of the possible alternatives, would also work well in many other situations. For example, "school silence" would be much more appropriate than "school prayer." That mind training should be part of education is a reasonable request. But verbal prayers could never express all the appropriate alternative options and would inevitably elicit objections from some group or other. Genuine, complete inclusivity is very difficult, and the more religiously diverse a society becomes, the more difficult genuine inclusivity becomes. But in silence,

11. Murray, *Religious Liberty in America*, 50.

each participant can hear their own verbal forms in the voice of their own mind—and if they object to silence as an inadequate religious expression, they can think about whatever they want to.

This acid test of reversibility should be applied to all hot-button social issues for an effective test of the appropriateness of proposed ways of dealing with those issues. In almost all cases, applying this reversibility test will require much more critical and honest thinking about such issues than they usually receive.

Religion in the Public Square: Finding a Safe Space for Discussing Religion and Politics

The wall of separation between church and state does not and cannot translate into a wall of separation between religion and politics. It is important to recognize that issues of church and state are not the same as issues of whether people can or should bring their religious values into political discussion and debate. The requirement to have a truly neutral state does not translate into a ban on public discussions of religion and its impact on relevant social issues. In fact, if we can trust that the state will be truly neutral in the face of competing ethical positions, public discussions of difficult issues could be much more forthright. Many thoughtful people would welcome expression of religious views among the many ideas put forth by those who seek ways to work with the myriad dissatisfactions of our lives. There is an inevitable and natural mixing of religion and politics. I am not claiming that there should be no religious reflection on political issues. Of course people for whom religion is important cannot and do not abandon their religious orientations when they make political decisions. Thus, people who are pacifists by religious conviction would be more likely to work for and support an antiwar candidate than a prowar candidate in an election. One venture of this book is to make it safe to admit religious and spiritual voices into political debates about the fate of our society. These voices can be admitted legitimately and without fear after we find and internalize spiritually profound and satisfying alternatives to exclusive truth claims—alternatives that are genuinely nonharming both to others and to our own being and identity.

Those who claim that religion is not merely a private belief system about the transcendent but also something that encompasses all of life, including politics, economics, and social norms, are surely correct. Around the globe, religions usually do concern themselves with such matters. Therefore, claims that religion is a completely private affair having to do with only theological beliefs that can be divorced from politics are incorrect.

When all members of a community belong to the same religion, religious discussions of such issues are unproblematic. But in a religiously diverse society, resolution of such discussions is much more problematic and difficult. In such a situation, both religious and nonreligious people have to tolerate that fact that, just as there is diversity of religious beliefs, so there is diversity of ethical norms regarding lifestyle, behavior, and the like. Unless ethical choices are restricted by a government that is not truly religiously neutral, not everyone will adopt or live by exactly the same ethical stance. Catholic bishops will have to deal with the fact that many people, Catholics included, do practice birth control and have abortions. Religious conservatives who are uncomfortable with homosexuality will have to learn how to cope with marriage equality. And so on.

Unfortunately, many people and groups are unwilling to develop the flexibility to willingly let others abide by their own ethical norms, which is the real problem surrounding most of the so-called hot-button issues. Many people still insist that they should be able to determine not only their own ethics but other people's ethics as well: that in the playing field of the public square, they should have the whole playing field for themselves because they have a monopoly on the One True Faith regarding ethical norms and issues. Or to use another analogy, any religious or political group that wants a voice in political and social debates (including religious conservatives) must recognize that its voice is part of a chorus, not a solo. Giving up the demand to sing a solo is nonnegotiable in the attempt to bring religion into the public square. Instead of joining the chorus or leveling the playing field, some people are becoming more strident in their demands for conformity, more willing to impose their standards on people who do not agree with them, more willing to interfere with other people's lives, thus defying one understanding of what compassionate behavior entails. Such a stance is simply intolerable in a multireligious society. Thus, the true problem for discussions of religion and politics is the presence of so many participants in that discussion who still make exclusive truth claims for their religious points of view. When this is done, such discussions become both unsafe and unpalatable for the rest of us.

Sometimes folks who make exclusive truth claims for their religions clamor that their views are resisted because they are expressing *religious* views, that only *secular* views (whatever that might mean) are tolerated in the public square. But it is not the religiousness of their views that is resisted. Their views are resisted because the view holders are seeking to control important aspects of other people's lives, not merely recommending certain behaviors as more appropriate than others. Thus, their ethical claims are similar to exclusive truth claims in theology. Ironically, such people do not seem to realize that their religious views would be much less resisted, much more welcomed in the public square, if only they left at home their claims of exclusive relevance for their views; or better yet, if they outgrew them as they reached spiritual maturity. As we have seen so often in previous chapters, the problem is rarely the beliefs people hold, but *how* they hold those beliefs. It is incorrect to claim that religious arguments are resisted in public debate because of their religious nature. This distinction between voicing a religious position regarding public issues and claiming exclusive relevance for any specific position is crucial and must always be remembered. Any religious position whatsoever could be admitted into public debate. But any religious position whatsoever, when exclusive truth is claimed for it, becomes dangerous and unacceptable in public debate. The price for having a voice in society is recognizing that everyone else also has the same right to have their voice taken seriously. But it is impossible to take others' voices seriously while claiming exclusive relevance for one's own. As we discovered with theology, so with ethics. *Religious diversity and exclusive truth claims are incompatible and do not mutually survive or thrive.* On every imaginable moral, intellectual, and spiritual basis, diversity is more valuable than any claim to exclusive truth because those who make exclusive truth claims would do away with diversity if they could. That is what makes claims to exclusive truth so dangerous.

When the Church Tries to Legislate in the Public Sphere

By no means do all attempts to breach the wall of separation between church and state come from the side of the state. Various religious groups also still try to gain state support to enforce their ethics and morality, not only on their own adherents but also on all citizens. They often do this especially concerning hot-button issues surrounding sexuality. By discussing some examples of how religious leaders try, not only to influence people in the public square but also to gain government support for their positions, we can refine the distinction between issues of church and state on the one hand, and religion and politics on the other hand. As we look at these examples, we can also apply two principles that help untangle appropriate from inappropriate recommendations regarding these issues. Whenever anyone claims that their own freedom of religion is at stake, it must also be asked if, in granting that person what they ask for, someone else's freedom of religion is being compromised. We should avoid becoming like early settlers in America who sought religious freedom for themselves but denied it to others. In a religiously diverse society, such situations can be difficult to resolve, as is demonstrated by the very interesting book *The Impossibility of Religious Freedom.*[12] A second, relevant question is always whether the lives of others would be harmed or made more difficult by insisting that they adopt, whether voluntarily or because of legislation, the morality favored by any group.

One of the most distressing examples of meddling in what should be for the state a neutral matter and for individuals a private choice concerns attempts by the Roman Catholic Church to control the sexual and reproductive behavior of all citizens of the United States (as well as people all over the world) through legislation. In less formal ways, they are often joined in those efforts by conservative non-Catholic Christians. The most often targeted behaviors include birth control, abortion, and homosexuality. It is important to remember that there is no ethical consensus on these matters. Many religious people oppose them, but many others support them. The lack of any consensus about their acceptability makes it even more improper for those who already hold great institutional power as religious leaders to also seek to control what laws are made by the state. To do so violates the separation of church and state.

It is perfectly understandable that religious people who oppose birth control or abortion, such as Roman Catholic bishops, would not themselves have abortions or practice birth control. It is also understandable that they would encourage other Catholics to follow the same ethic. It is even unproblematic when they encourage people in general to voluntarily adopt Catholic ethics on birth control, abortion, or sexual behavior in general. However, these leaders are quite ineffective at persuading their own coreligionists to adopt their norms. It is estimated the 98 percent of all Catholic women in the United States have practiced birth control at some time in their lives. Perhaps that is why such religious authorities are so unwilling to observe the wall of separation between church and state or to respect the neutrality of the state. They routinely seek to have their views on sexuality and abortion made the law of the land, thus forcing everyone to abide by Catholic norms, whether or not they are Catholic, and whether or not they agree with those norms. They do this when they seek to influence elections by telling their parishioners how to vote or by publicly criticizing Catholic politicians whose views on those issues are different from those of the Catholic hierarchy. Church officials attempt not only to influence elections but also to affect what legislation is drafted and accepted. Why should Roman Catholic bishops be able to determine practices surrounding sexuality, birth control, and abortion for all people belonging to all the various religions and nonreligions practiced in the United States? Isn't their influence over

12. See fn. 4, above, for publication information.

their Catholic laity enough? If they are unsuccessful in persuading their own laity to abide by their rules, how can it be fair or reasonable for them to call upon the state to force that ethic on everyone?

Even more difficult to understand is how Catholics and others could appeal to the sacrosanct principle of freedom of religion, as they did in 2012, in their attempt to exempt Catholic employers from being required to provide the same health insurance for their employees as is required of all other employers. This is a glaring example of claiming freedom of religion for me but not for you, of demanding what I define as my freedom even though it restricts your freedom. But to buy my freedom at the expense of your freedom is unworthy of morally upright people. It can never be reasonable to claim that for me to be free, you must be restricted, but that is precisely what happens when reproductive choice is legally restricted. The solutions for those who disapprove of birth control or abortion seem so simple and straightforward. Don't practice birth control! Don't have abortions! But also, don't attempt to restrict the freedom of those who have no moral qualms about those practices.

Regarding homosexuality, most of the same observations and arguments apply. This is a case in which recognizing that what the majority of more conservative people want—varying degrees of discrimination against homosexuals—causes such people great harm. Apply the reversibility test: Would heterosexuals put up either with financial and legal liabilities stemming from their choice of partners or with prohibitions disallowing them from marrying the person they love? Does being in the majority give heterosexuals permission to make life so difficult for homosexuals? Additionally, one has to ask what those who seek to ban homosexuality gain from its banishment, or how its open practice would harm or even inconvenience them. People with whom I have discussed this topic seem to have little to say beyond the fact that because they personally dislike homosexuality, they should not have to encounter it. The trade-off between that small level of discomfort for them and the grave harm caused to homosexuals is rather unbalanced. Why be so invested in someone else's lifestyle?

These issues present good examples of the difference between mutual influence and interaction between religion and politics (something that does not violate separation of church and state), and an improper collapsing together of church and state. It is not always easy to discern the line separating these two concerns, but it is crucial that attempts to influence people politically do not turn into attempts to constrain them legally from exercising choices about which legal constraint is inappropriate. If Catholic bishops were to be successful in their attempts to control legislation on reproductive policy for all Americans, rather than simply advising their own church members about reproduction, an acceptable mingling of religion and politics would become an unacceptable merger of church and state. Religious reflection on political issues is a vastly different matter from religious authorities also wielding political or legal power, whether they wield that power over followers of their own religion or of another religion.

Assessing the Threat to Religious Freedom from Religious Conservatives

But how dangerous are these more conservative religious voices? Several recent studies have suggested that conservative Christians are not nearly as united and monolithic as they are perceived to be. It is well known that many Catholics do not follow the commands of the Catholic hierarchy. This scholarship suggests that in the same way, non-Catholic conservative Christians also do not follow their vociferous and flamboyant leaders lockstep. This scholarship also demonstrates that the political opinions of conservative Christians are much more varied than they are usually given credit for.[13] Such scholarship represents a truly important perspective in the contemporary conversation. Why wouldn't theologically conservative Christians actually have diverse political positions? To find that they do is very reassuring and helps assuage some of the anxiety induced in me by letters to the editor in my local newspaper.

These letters, which I used to collect as evidence for this chapter, indicate that many people in my community and in the United States would eagerly abolish both freedom of religion and the separation of church and state if they could. In fact, many such letters claim that neither principle is actually part of our constitutional framework but is an interpretation foisted upon our country by secularists and liberals. They continually declare that the United States is a "Christian nation." They demand total control over other people's conduct of marriage and reproduction, not just their own marriages and reproduction. No one contests that they should be able to control their own sexuality and reproduction, but on what grounds could they possibly think they also deserve to control everyone else's? They insist on the "under God" phrase in the Pledge of Allegiance and demand to put religious articles, such as the Ten Commandments, in public spaces. Clearly, if the authors of these letters to the editor had their way, Christianity would be the state religion, and there would be little freedom of religion for the rest

13 Greeley and Hout, *The Truth about Conservative Christians*; Smith, *Christian America?*

of us. It is troubling that there are any such letters, even if scholarship based on widespread interviews can disprove that they represent the norm.

How does evidence in these scholarly books stack up against my pile of local letters to the editor? The books contain a great deal of statistical information and transcribed interviews. They do present a convincing case that conservative Christians are not monolithically determined to force the agenda of the religious Right onto the country no matter what it would take. Nevertheless, it is troubling that about half of all conservative and fundamentalist Christians do think that Christian morality should be the law of the land even though they know full well that not all Americans are Christian.[14]

Several additional observations do stand out for me and are quite relevant to this discussion. Greeley and Hout state that conservative Christians do feel like outsiders, embattled against a status quo. But they also feel, very strongly, that they really should be in control of the nation. They also project an "unmistakable entitlement." They feel they are

> outsiders by mistake. They are certain of their place at the heart of America . . . From the point of view of Conservative Protestant leadership their movement differs from what is going on with outsider groups because the others are neither as American nor as close to God. To evangelical leaders, Conservative Protestants deserve more say, and the others can wait to speak.[15]

But demographics are changing such that white Protestants are never again going to control the United States in the way they feel entitled to. Their proportion of the populations continues to decline. Recent Pew Research Forum reports indicate that all Protestants, including not only conservative white Protestants but also black and mainline Protestants, are just half the population.[16] Their sense of entitlement grows ever more unrealistic and inappropriate, and as it grows more inappropriate, it also becomes more irritating both to members of other religions and to the nonreligious.

One of the most interesting findings in Smith's account of "What Evangelicals Want" is that even though half the conservative Christians think that national laws should support Christian ideas about morality, consistently they do not want to "shove Christianity down the throats" of the general public. That phrase occurred time after time in the book's

---

14. Smith, *Christian America?*, 200–201.

15. Greeley and Hout, *The Truth about Conservative Christians*, 67.

16. See, online, http://religions.pewforum.org/reports/.

transcribed interviews and led Smith to conclude that one of eight main evangelical strategies is "never force Christian beliefs on others."[17]

That does not mean, however, that these conservative Christians have given up on trying to convert others to Christianity. The bulk of the interviews recorded in Smith's book are quite mild mannered. But it is also very clear that these Christians regard their non-Christian counterparts as mistaken and misguided, in need of prayers for their conversion, and in need of conversion.[18] "American evangelicals are clearly not liberal universalists who affirm all people in their belief and lifestyles."[19] Most of them believe that non-Christians will go to hell, but also that such people should be allowed to make their own decisions about "coming to Jesus." Conservative Christians' recognition that it is not a good idea to "shove Christianity down the throats" of others comes more from recognizing that such tactics don't work than from any genuine recognition that other religions could be just as valid and just as satisfying for others. These interviews revealed a deep-seated feeling on the part of conservative Christians that if only they could find the right words, or the right examples, everyone would "come to Jesus," that there is no viable alternative. As I noted in chapter 8, this feeling that everyone really does need to appreciate Jesus extends even to notable Christian theologians who are deeply sympathetic to non-Christians. But Jesus isn't like gravity—irresistible—or like oxygen—literally necessary for life. This lingering sense of Christian superiority over and disdain for non-Christians makes the interreligious environment very difficult for others. The subtle obsession with converting the whole world to Christianity is still very evident and very unwelcome.

Some Concluding Observations

Cultural life in the United States includes many, many opportunities for voluntary public religious expression, usually of a generic interdenominational nature. But though they are generic, they are also usually vaguely Christian or at least monotheistic. Most of them are also very well meaning. It seems mean spirited to object to them on grounds that they involve insufficient recognition of religious diversity. What is one to do?

I will conclude by offering several observations. I live in a small city with little religious diversity. In the spring of 2012, I received an e-mail from local people involved with a freedom-from-religion organization, asking

17. Smith, *Christian America?*, 37.
18. Ibid., 91.
19. Ibid., 87.

me to make a statement about the fact that the city council usually began its meetings with a specifically Christian prayer. I agreed to speak and appeared at the appointed time. Three of us came to make statements: I to make a Buddhist statement, one of the local Jewish leaders who had also been a colleague of mine, and a young woman who was obviously Christian. She was surprised that any one would object to beginning public meetings "in the name of Jesus Christ." The Jew made a statement pleading for prayers that included no specifically Christian content. I made a statement suggesting silence as the best alternative. I also suggested that if a verbal statement were to be made, it should avoid any content that could be identified with any specific religion (which would also include references to God). The council members seemed surprised. They obviously had never thought about the fact that the Christian prayers with which they were familiar did not suit all their constituents. They did change their protocols for beginning meetings as a result of our interventions.

Is is clear to me that my uneasiness about public expressions of religion stems from two facts. The vast majority of public expressions of religion in the United States will be Christian oriented. The problem with that is that I also know that many Christians still believe that their religion is superior to mine, that I would be better off if I were Christian, not Buddhist. In other words, the mischief caused by lingering exclusive truth claims spoils the promise of public expressions of religiosity. I often wince when Christian clergy are asked to offer prayers at public events. I note with interest that when a Native American elder is asked to offer such an invocation, I do not react in a similar fashion. I also know that the reason for my different reaction is that Native Americans have never made exclusive truth claims for their religions. Nor are they currently engaged in extensive and expensive, often quite aggressive, missionary efforts to convert the whole world to their version of the truth. Therefore, their invocations are not dangerous to flourishing with religious diversity but actually contribute to it.

I really would prefer a situation in which we could have genuine and safe interfaith religious observances. Those would have be defined as interfaith observances in which all participants were truly on a level playing field, equally respected by all and equally regarded by all as bearers of meaningful and relevant religious expressions. I do believe, quite firmly, that if Christianity did not have such a history of making exclusive truth claims, and if such claims were not still so prevalent, I would not find crèches in public parks so problematic. I might find the slogan "In God we trust" on the money less problematic, and I might even be less troubled by the "under God" phrase in the Pledge of Allegiance!

On the other hand, to return to Bhutan with its Buddhist symbols on the money, it is also clear to me that such public, state recognition and promotion of my religion is not necessary at all for my own spiritual well-being. In fact, if one thinks carefully about the matter, one could easily conclude that such state recognition may actually be detrimental to one's own spiritual well-being. When Christians try to reason with me that it is important to their spiritual well-being that they be able to express their specifically Christian faith rather than some generic mumbo-jumbo in public expressions of religion, I reply that no such opportunity for public expression of Buddhism is available to me. It has not harmed my confidence in Buddhism one iota. In silence and space, any specific form can flourish and, because it is invisible to others, it is also unproblematic for them. Such solutions to problems that may arise in a religiously diverse community or state may well deserve more attention than they usually receive.

Chapter 13

Changing Religious Identity

Conversion versus Missions

D ELIBERATELY CHANGING ONE'S RELIGIOUS identity can bring many
emotional reactions. The person who converts usually feels happy
about the choice, but members of the person's family and community
could well be devastated by that same choice. Is this a reasonable reaction
to someone's conversion? But what if that conversion comes as a result of
pressure and inducements, subtle or otherwise? Can we ever be sure about
the purity of a conversion that is the result of missionary activity? On
the one hand, most members of democratic societies would take the right
to make a personal choice about religious membership (or nonmember-
ship) for granted and would support that right even if they disapproved
vociferously of a family member's conversion to an unfamiliar religion.
But what about deliberate missionary activities, the carefully thought out,
well-financed attempt to get other people to change their religious identities? Can people who believe in human dignity and who value freedom
of religion really be sanguine about such an agenda? Thus the topics of
changing one's religious identity through conversion and the appropriateness of missionary activity are intimately connected, though from another
point of view they are at opposite ends of a spectrum.

An implication of both freedoms regarding religion—the freedom
of religion as well as freedom from religion—is that one has the freedom

to change one's religious identity but also the freedom *not* to change one's religion. That second freedom, which is usually not spelled out in lists of freedoms, might seem to be logically obvious. But what about the freedom not *to be asked* to change religions?[1] Is the freedom not to change one's religion meaningful if one is also subjected to constant pressure to change one's religion, which will be one's fate in situations of active, persistent missionary activity? Are there contexts in which freedom from religion translates into freedom simply to be left alone and not pestered about one's religious choices? If so, who should lead in promoting and protecting that freedom? Can the religions themselves rise to the occasion? Or do governments need to restrain some religions to protect other religions as part of governmental neutrality vis-à-vis competing religious claims?

Conversion and missions are both intimately linked and at opposite ends of a spectrum. The purpose of missionary work is obviously to promote conversions, to the point of eliminating religious diversity, according to some missionary agendas. So if one values religious diversity, missionary activity may not be high on the list of religious activities one promotes. But one would nevertheless regard the possibility of religious conversion as a right to be protected. Certainly someone like myself, like most Western Buddhists a convert to my religion, and someone who routinely works with Buddhist converts as their teacher, would be hard pressed to oppose conversion. But the activities of contemporary Buddhists that may lead to conversion are vastly different from missionary campaigns engaged in by the Church of Latter Day Saints or by both Protestant and Roman Catholic Christians.

Conversion and Missions: Some Guidelines

Because missionary work and conversion are both controversial and disapproved of, though for different reasons, the exercise of reversibility is quite revealing. As was the case with issues of religion and politics, so it is with issues of conversion and missions: it is always a good idea to imaginatively apply to oneself what one thinks would be good for others. If I find something problematic and distasteful if it were to be applied to me or to our group, how can it be appropriate for our group to do something similar to others?

Most religious people are at least unhappy, if not adamantly opposed, when someone close to them abandons their common natal religion. Sometimes they are so opposed to conversion by a family or community member that they completely ostracize that person, fight with them, and

---

1. For an excellent presentation of this right, which is often not recognized, and the need for it, see Sharma, *Problematizing Religious Freedom*.

expel or banish them. In traditional Judaism, the person who converts out is mourned as if they had died and is considered dead thereafter. The reaction of conservative Christians may not be as severe, but I personally know many Buddhist ex-Christians who have been given a lot of grief by their natal families. The Muslim reaction can include permission to kill an apostate. These reactions, especially on the part of Christians and Muslims, who also seek converts, seem very one sided. If we don't want *our* people abandoning *our* natal religion and converting to another religion, how can we justify intense efforts to get others to do exactly that—to abandon their natal religion, which they would have to do to convert to our religion? If it's so bad for our people to convert out to another religion, how can it be good or necessary for members of other religions to convert out of their natal religions and into ours? Additionally, if we accept, even seek, converts into our religion, how can we be hostile to people who convert out of our religion, to the point of killing them? If converting is good, then why is it so bad when it involves conversion out of our religion rather than into it? This is the test of reversibility that should be applied to concerted missionary activity. Both tests reveal an incredible double standard. But I doubt that many missionary societies ever notice or think about that double standard, which applies different expectations to members of our religion than to members of other religions regarding exactly the same phenomenon—conversion from one religion to another.

If we want to carry the logic of reversibility even a bit further, one can easily claim that the convert, who chooses a religious identity, is one who truly understands and is committed to the chosen religion, perhaps much more so than someone born into a religious identity. Those born into a religion are often relatively unknowledgeable about that religion, even though they often are also very dogmatic and opinionated about that religion. Part of my comfort with and confidence in Buddhism is precisely based on the fact that I know a lot about all the available options and have found my true home. Perhaps everyone should convert! This mistrust of inherited religious identity is what fuels anxiety, and a lot of resulting pain, about whether one has truly been "born again" in some segments of Christianity.

Converts can also be mistrusted by certain segments of the tradition into which they convert. One the one hand, it is feared that they bring too much of their home culture into their practice and understanding of their new religious community. On the other hand, converts are also notorious for being too zealous in their promotion of their new religion. (Certainly in contemporary Buddhist circles, there is a great deal of concern about too much Westernization of Buddhism.) One of the most resented features of Christian missionary activity in some parts of the world is the way missionaries demanded converts to Christianity to renounce treasured aspects of their native culture as paganism. For those who do not convert, it is as if their family members are not only renouncing their traditional religious practices but also their whole culture—everything familiar and comforting. One could equally make the argument that it simply makes more sense for people to flourish where they are planted, in their home religions, and to transform them if need be. This is often the first alternative suggested by very famous Buddhist teachers to star-struck admirers who ask to convert to Buddhism.

If one wants to preserve and protect people's ability to change religious identity and also finds large-scale missionary activity unpalatable, then so-called silver rule is again appropriate and applicable. Buddhists usually begin the application of this rule by asking us to notice that each being's most fundamental longing is to not suffer and to be happy. Given that we know this about ourselves in an unalterably basic way, it becomes the first principle of ethics in our activity towards others. Do not cause suffering! If you wouldn't want something done to you, don't do it to others! I think most people like to be able to explore their options but don't want to be pestered to change who or how they are. I suspect that most groups who sponsor large-scale missionary programs would be anything but willing and eager to welcome such missionary delegations of another religion into their own communities, or even to allow them to operate. I suspect that most people who support missionary activities to convert "the heathen" would not themselves think it appropriate for others to engage in similar activities aimed at converting them away from their religion. So the obvious solution is not to engage in those activities oneself.

Some Generalizations about Conversion and Missions

Chapter 2, on different methods of religious belonging in the world's religions, is an important prelude to this chapter. It is critically important for members of the two monotheistic religions that make exclusive truth claims and that regard themselves as followers of God's favored religion to realize how aberrant their position is. Most of my students in world-religions classes took it for granted that all members of all religions regarded their own religion as the best for everyone and that therefore followers of all religions want to convert everyone else to their religion. (I have even heard as esteemed a person as Madeleine Albright, former U.S. secretary of state, voice that opinion. One would think that secretaries of state should be better informed about religions!) But as we have seen, seeking to convert all is only one example of how religious membership works. Other options include not seeking or even accepting new members from outside one's own community, multiple religious belonging, and approved coexistence of many equal options within one religious context. It seems to me that if people truly internalize that information, it will have deep implications for how they think about missionary work and religious conversion.

Not only are there major differences about how various religions think about religious belonging. There are also significant differences between two types of religions, identified in chapter 2 as universalizing religions, which are relatively less embedded in specific cultural contexts, and ethnoreligions, which are relatively more embedded in specific cultural contexts. These are ideal types, and there is a sliding scale between them, with many religions sharing characteristics of each type. Nevertheless, the typology is very useful when thinking about religious diversity, and especially when thinking about conversion and missions.

It is easy to understand that only so-called universalizing religions would also become missionary religions, spreading with relative ease from one culture to another. It should also be easy to understand that members of ethnoreligions would have very different attitudes toward conversion and missionary activities than members of universalizing religions. That difference is brought into sharper relief if we call these two religious types by alternative names: proselytizing and nonproselytizing religions. Conversion—in either direction (either into or out of one's home base)—simply makes no sense to members of nonproselytizing religions, nor do claims that there is or could be a universally and exclusively relevant religion to which everyone on the face of the earth should belong. This is because to followers of ethnoreligions, religion is much more than a portable intellectual and spiritual belief system. It is also thoroughly bound up with a totalizing lifestyle involving language, culture, diet, dress, and many other mundane aspects of life as well. In fact, to most insiders of such religions, social and cultural aspects of religion are usually far more important than theological beliefs, about which they may be relatively untutored. As was pointed out in chapter 2, one could perhaps, under certain circumstances, be adopted into such a system, but converting into it makes little sense to insiders, and converting out is often seen as virtual suicide. It should also be easy to see that most framers of discourse on freedom of religion, more so than framers of discourse on freedom from religion, have almost no familiarity with the lived ethos of a nonproselytizing religion and little sympathy for such a perspective. The same can be said of those who make exclusive or inclusive truth claims about religions. Even more liberal pluralist theologians of religion, used to thinking of religions mainly as theological systems, are quite uninformed about ethnoreligious sensibilities.

But, when they are forced into the same arena of interaction, can the playing field possibly be level between a proselytizing and a nonproselytizing religion? The well-financed proselytizer travels from afar for one purpose only, with a clear-cut agenda and many arguments for their own perspective and against the perspectives of those whom they have come to convert. Furthermore, if the proselytizer also belongs to a religion that makes exclusive truth claims, he or she has no interest in the survival of the indigenous nonproselytizing religion. In fact, the missionary agenda usually calls for the elimination of the nonproselytizing religion. Adherents of the nonproselytizing perspective are totally unprepared for such an onslaught. They have never been trained in counterarguments to theological propositions of which they have never heard. Furthermore, advocates of the proselytizing religion usually represent a technologically more advanced society and often are from a society that has political hegemony or near hegemony over the society with the indigenous, nonproselytizing religion. No wonder proselytizing religions are often successful! No wonder representatives of non-proselytizing religions sometimes cry foul and want some protection from what they consider to be unethical conversions.

In his provocative book *Problematizing Religious Freedom*, Arvind Sharma makes the suggestion that such a match is like asking heavyweight and featherweight boxers to fight against each other in the same ring.[2] It's just not done because the outcome is a foregone conclusion! The result of such unequal contests between small-scale nonproselytizing, indigenous traditions and large, well-financed religions with an ideology that promotes and justifies proselytization is that the field is littered with the corpses of once-vibrant indigenous traditions that were no more equipped to withstand Christian missionaries than they were equipped to withstand European domination and colonization. This process has been going on for a long time, and in most parts of the world where Christianity or Islam have become dominant, there is not a great deal of religious diversity because missionaries of these religions were not interested in coexistence and mutual equality among diverse religious perspectives. They were happy to eliminate the older, indigenous perspectives. As a result, many religious options and spiritual perspectives have become extinct as we move ever closer to religious monopolies.

To some, that may not seem like much of a problem. But if we value religious diversity, it is. If we regard religious diversity as the normal human condition and religious monocultures as abnormal and unhealthy,

---

2. Sharma, *Problematizing Religious Freedom*, 10.

it is a great loss. We understand that biological diversity is necessary for environmental well-being, that biological monocultures are unnatural and cannot be sustained without great artificial intervention into the environment. Sustaining such monocultures often involves very negative effects for overall health and well-being. As a result, we often go to great lengths to protect endangered species. We know that their decline may well signal the loss of environmental sustainability in the future, that if we destroy the common environment to the point that some species become extinct, we may well have the same fate in store for us further down the line. To a lesser extent, we even value preserving languages that are in danger of becoming extinct. Why is there no similar concern about the unnaturalness and dangers of spiritual or religious monocultures, no similar attempt to preserve small, endangered spiritual perspectives? I have never heard anyone suggest that it would be a great loss to humanity if the last person to understand and be able to transmit a spiritual perspective were to die without an heir. Why not? Are we so arrogant as to think that we already know everything worth knowing spiritually and that there is nothing we could possibly learn from others, whether they are representatives of small or of large traditions? Could one religion ever have everything that everyone needs? That question has already been dealt with in chapter 5.

Sharma's analogy about boxers indicates that it could be fair and appropriate for proselytizing religions to compete with each other—to proselytize against each other—if they limited their proselytizing efforts to such ventures. If that rule were followed, Christianity and Islam would take each other on. These two traditions, however, usually do not compete with each other for religious converts. In Africa they may compete for the same converts from smaller indigenous traditions, but that is not the same as proselytizing each other. Tension between Christians and Muslims in Europe and North America is about cultural differences and mutual fear. It is not about attempts to proselytize each other, which are not undertaken at all except perhaps in American prisons. Many Muslim-majority nation-states, such as Saudi Arabia, do not even allow public practice of Christianity within their borders, so Christians don't have much of a chance to spread their message there. Such Muslims would justify their restrictions because of the ubiquity of Christian missionaries in the absence of such restrictions. Such Muslims also could claim that, though a great deal of Muslim money is spent to promote stricter adherence to Muslim orthodoxy among Muslims who do not live traditionally Muslim areas, Muslims do not usually target solidly Christian audiences for conversion to Islam. These Muslims are probably correct in their assessment that the favor would not be returned by at least some Christians.

What about Hinduism or Buddhism? Both are quite different from either Christianity or Islam. Hinduism has many resemblances to an ethno-religion even though it is an old, widespread tradition with a strong literary dimensions and is the majority religion in India. It is a strongly nonprosel-ytizing religion with incredible internal diversity, such that it is called a single religion mainly because of Western needs to find parallels to the three Abrahamic religions in the rest of the world.[3] Even the term *Hinduism* is a modern creation. It is something of an umbrella label that covers all the diverse religious options that have always been available in the traditional Hindu context. Today there are many Hindus in North America, but they are mainly Indian immigrants and their descendents, and they do not target non-Indian populations for conversion to Hinduism.

Another fact about Hinduism should be pointed out in passing. It is the only religion more on the ethnoreligion side of the scale than on the universalizing side to successfully withstand proselytizing campaigns. It is also the only so-called polytheistic religion (that is, a religion offering many different personifications of divine transcendence) to withstand proselytiz-ing by monotheistic religions. Therefore it is a rarity among major world re-ligions, thus providing an invaluable religious example for further reflection and research. Furthermore, Hinduism has withstood these efforts over cen-turies. Muslims have been in India for a long time, and Christian mission-ary efforts have been quite intense for some centuries. This alone suggests there must be something special about Hinduism. It also means that Hindu perspectives on conversion and proselytization should be taken much more seriously in discussions of religious diversity. They certainly have not been listened to much by Christian theologians who write theology of religion.[4]

Hinduism is so much a nonproselytizing religion that people not born into Hindu families who are attracted to its more philosophical schools have difficulty being accepted as Hindus. As nonproselytizers, Hindu teachers often tell those who ask to convert to Hinduism that all religions are equal and equally true. Therefore, they should and could find what they seek in their own religions. Because Hinduism is so internally diverse, such a claim is surely true for Hindus. They do not have to convert

3. The issue of the validity of the category *religion* and its origins in Western schol-arship is too complex to be dealt with in this context or this book. Nevertheless, it is generally conceded that the term fits Western religions much more adequately than their counterparts in other parts of the world, and that the term has no exact coun-terpart in many of the world's other languages. See Sharma, *Problemizing Religious Freedom*, 17–33.

4. For presentation and discussion of both the Christian and the Hindu arguments, see Kim, *In Search of Identity*, 132–200.

out to find virtually any kind of religious practice or belief, which is not really the case for any other major religion. Nor, for the most part, would Hindus be troubled by a Hindu who wanted to add devotion to Jesus to his or her personal religious practice. The problem with Christian or Muslim proselytizers is that they demand total, exclusive loyalty to Christian or Muslim forms and total repudiation of and separation from traditional Hindu forms. In other words, Christian proselytization in India is, ultimately but covertly, a project to eliminate Hinduism, as it has eliminated so many smaller indigenous traditions. This demand, more than anything, fuels antiproselytization feelings among Hindus. Hindus do not have a problem with Christianity, which they can easily regard as equally true and worthy with Hinduism. The reason Hindus oppose Christian missionaries is not so much because of theological disagreement with Christianity, which they are perfectly content to live with, but because of Christian exclusivism, which wants to obliterate Hinduism. That is what is really so dangerous for Hinduism. Can such a religion actually compete with either Christianity or Islam when both have an agenda to convert Hindus to either religion? Many, many more Hindus have converted out to both religions over the years than have converted into Hinduism from either.

As for Buddhism, it is a universalizing religion that has spread around the world without a self-conscious agenda to do so, without especially proselytizing. As such, it presents the only viable alternative thus far to proselytizing religions making exclusive truth claims. Its methods can be seen as a middle path between, on the one hand, the tactics of proselytizing and, on the other hand, nonproselytizing religions. A much fuller discussion of how it has spread around the world will follow.

These considerations about different types of religions, however, mean that the question raised especially sharply by Sharma in his book remains. To put the question most sharply, perhaps even more sharply than he does: does freedom of religion translate into an unequivocal right to proselytize under any and all circumstances? To those who are excessively concerned with being able to proselytize about Christianity, freedom of religion often means primarily freedom to proselytize anywhere and everywhere, under all circumstances, no matter the consequences. Western discourse is quite addicted to *rights* language, which other civilizations correctly point out, has its limits, especially when such language is not balanced by equal concern with responsibilities. That balance is often sorely lacking in Western discourse. As we saw in the previous chapter, language about the sacrosanct right to freedom of religion is sometimes perverted by those who equate their own freedom of religion with being able to restrict the rights and freedoms of others.

I am skeptical that freedom of religion includes the right to proselytize under any and all circumstances, though it certainly does include a right to offer one's own religion as an option to those who seek it out. I would contend that making one's religion available to others is *very different* from proselytizing on behalf of one's religion. Making one's religion available to others takes into account whether or not others wish to hear about what one has to offer. It's somewhat like the distinction between receiving robocalls from political candidates and asking to be on their e-mail or phone contact lists. One could argue that politicians' freedom of speech gives them rights to place robocalls to those who really don't want to receive them, but one could also argue that simple human dignity and decency would prohibit them from engaging in such unwanted conduct that interferes so much with other people's peace and quiet. Intelligent reflection motivated by their own self-interest would also indicate they would probably be more impressive and successful if they engaged in less obnoxious and pushy behavior.

Considering the difference between conversion and proselytizing, making a finely drawn distinction, Sharma asks us to consider the difference between my right to change my religion and someone else's right to *ask me* to change my religion. The two rights are not symmetrical, he claims, because another person's right to ask me to change my religion violates my right to noninterference in the practice of my own religion. This point needs to be taken very seriously in all discussions of conversion and missions. As we have seen above, members of small and nonproselytizing traditions are far more vulnerable to conversion than members of large, proselytizing traditions. From these facts, Sharma deduces that nonproselytizing religions may well need to restrict proselytizing to protect their own members' freedom of religion.[5] Sharma is also clear about the fact that restricting proselytizing cannot and should not restrict the availability of any religious option to anyone who wishes to explore it and adopt it. In other words, personal freedom of religion and freedom to convert are not affected by restrictions on proselytizing.

But could responsible religious people themselves observe the distinction between proselytizing for one's religion and making it available to those who want to know more about it? Unless religious people and institutions themselves make this distinction and are very careful to delink the possibility of conversion from missionary activities aimed at conversion, the relationship between the two becomes adversarial, as in the subtitle of this chapter ("Conversion versus Mission"). Separating conversion from missionary work would be far superior to inviting governments to involve

5. Sharma, *Problematizing Religious Freedom*, 255–56.

themselves in religious affairs. In India, where the confrontation between the Hindu majority and Christian proselytizing has become intense, such legal interventions are often suggested seriously. I do not want to enter into that discussion with my suggestion that people have a right not be the victims of proselytizing. Why invite a situation in which governments may need to do what sensitive, ethical considerations about the religious needs of others would suggest religious people should do themselves? How to find this delicate balance is precisely what I think the example of Buddhism as a missionary religion can provide.

Comparative Missionary Projects

In the Vinaya (monastic discipline) section of the Pali Tripitika, one of the oldest Buddhist texts, the Buddha is represented as having given the following discourse to his monastics:

> Freed am I, bhikshus, from all snares, divine and human! You too bhikshus, are freed from all snares, divine and human. Go forth, O bhikshus, on a mission for the good of the many, for the happiness of the many, out of compassion for the world, for the good and happiness of the gods and humans. Let not two of you go the same way. Teach the Dharma, bhikshus, good in the beginning, good in the middle, good in the end, both in the spirit and in the letter. Declare the holy life in its whole and complete purity. There are beings with little dust in their eyes who, not listening, would be ruined. They will grow if they understand the Dharma.[6]

Given the nature of early Buddhist texts, we cannot say with certainty that the historical Buddha actually uttered these words or when in his teaching career he might have said them. Nevertheless, they represent a charge that Buddhists take seriously. Buddhism is one of the three major religions that has spread widely beyond its point of origin. However, I would suggest the Buddhism has spread so far and wide, not so much because of these words of the Buddha, but because it is the type of religion that can spread relatively easily. Its basic messages are not culture bound, and it sees human fulfillment as something different from cultural and social success and from economic and familial roles. On the sliding scale

---

6. From the *Mahavagga* section of the Vinaya Pitaka, among other places, this text is available in a number of print and web sources. For one translation, see Tan, *Mahāvagga* 1.7–11. Online: http://dharmafarer.org/wordpress/wp-content/uploads/2009/12/11.2-Great-Commission-v1.6–11-piya.pdf/.

between ethnoreligions and universalizing religions, it is much further toward the universalizing end of the scale.

In spite of its current global reach, Buddhist missionary work and goals are quite different from evangelical and much Roman Catholic Christian missionary work. Historically, Buddhism spread almost accidentally. There has never been a movement in Buddhism parallel to the Christian missionary movement that accompanied European colonialism and that is still fully operational in many parts of the world. Buddhism had spread throughout Asia and was important in all parts of Asia, including to many that are now dominated by Muslims, by the seventh century CE. But neither Indians nor Buddhists ever conquered or dominated militarily, economically, or politically the areas outside India to which Buddhism spread. Buddhism did not spread around Asia in the wake of colonialism. Nor are there records of organized missions apart from those sent out by Emperor Ashoka. So what explains Buddhism's success at spreading? In most cases, there was more of a reverse missionary movement. Ashoka's missionaries did begin the process of conversion to Buddhism in Sri Lanka, but apart from that single exception, in other cases for the most part, the receiving population initiated and sustained the exchange. The case of Chinese Buddhism is especially instructive because Chinese civilization was certainly equivalent to Indian civilization in sophistication, and yet Chinese people themselves imported Buddhism into their culture. Clearly, Buddhism must have offered something very appealing to be so widely adopted in China against all these odds and without strong initiative from the Indian side. If a religion has this kind of appeal, it does not have to proselytize, which strikes me as a vastly superior way for a religion to spread around the world.

In the modern world, as Buddhism spreads to the West, the story is much the same. One example is instructive. Today the San Francisco Zen Center and its satellite institutions is one of the largest and most admired Western Buddhist groups. Its Japanese founder was the well-known teacher Shunryu Suzuki, Roshi. But he did not come to North America to proselytize non-Buddhist and non-Japanese North America. He was sent to minister to a Japanese American Buddhist congregation. When some young non-Japanese seekers went to him to ask about learning Zen meditation, they were invited to meditate with him every morning at 5:00 a.m. when he meditated by himself, because Japanese Americans were not interested in such practices. From these beginnings came the famous institution with thousands of members (most of them converts) and many satellite centers all over the country and even outside North America. The institution provides regular programs and opens its doors but does little, if anything, more to lure people in. They are attracted, and they come.

My own case may also be instructive. As I've narrated a number of times, I lead a small meditation group in Eau Claire and also teach, when invited, in other places. The Eau Claire group is very small, and we do no advertising or outreach at all. If one Googles "Buddhism in Eau Claire, WI," one can find listings for me as a Buddhist teacher and for our group, among the listings for head shops, yoga centers, and other miscellaneous offerings. That's how people find out about us. Nothing more. Nevertheless, over the years many people have found their way to us to learn to meditate and to learn about Buddhist teachings. Some become Buddhists; others do not. While I work with an Asian teacher, as do many other Western Buddhists, Asian teachers are in the West at the initiative of Westerners themselves. The Asian teachers simply do not have the economic base to set up un-invited mission stations in the West. Nor are there large numbers of such Asian teachers in the West, and many of those that are here work with Asian American Buddhists rather than with converts.

Compare this situation with that of Christianity. Writing in 1993, Lewis R. Rambo informed us:

> More than thirty-seven thousand missionaries of the Church of Jesus Christ of Latter-Day Saints are criss-crossing the streets and roads of cities, villages, and rural areas throughout the world . . . At least thirty-nine thousand Protestant missionaries from Canada and the United States are seeking converts in inner city of Singapore, the jungles of Brazil, the villages of Tanzania and elsewhere. Another nine thousand Roman Catholic missionaries from North America are in diverse places serving and preaching to people.[7]

Many evangelical Christians, with their obligations to proselytize and a great deal of much more obvious activity, would probably be happy with as much success as I and other Buddhist teachers in the West have had. Perhaps our success indicates that our methods have something to recommend them. Attraction works better than promotion because it is more in accord with basic human psychology and much more respectful of people to know what they need and want spiritually. De-linking conversion from missionary outreach ensures the honesty and integrity of conversions.

The world's most famous Buddhist, the Dalai Lama, frequently suggests that people who are interested in conversion—to Buddhism or to any other religion—should first try to find ways to work within their religion of origin. In an older speech, dating from November 21, 2005, in Edinburgh, Scotland, the Dalai Lama urged Western Christians and Muslims not to

---

7. Rambo, *Understanding Religious Conversion*, 66.

convert to Buddhism but instead to "embrace the teachings of compassion and peace that can be found in their own religious traditions. 'All major religions carry the same messages. Messages of love, compassion, forgiveness, tolerance, contentment and self-discipline.'"[8] He has also said unequivocally: "I cannot advise everyone to practice Buddhism. That I cannot do. Certainly for some people the Buddhist religion or ideology is most suitable, most effective. But that does not mean it is suitable for *all*."[9] Such a statement clearly delinks the possibility of conversion, which remains an option, from needing to proselytize.

Googling "Dalai Lama and religious conversion" brings up scores of newspaper stories about the Dalai Lama delivering yet another speech in which he states that he disfavors active proselytizing. As of this writing, the most recent was delivered less than a month before this writing. In a speech on November 27, 2012, given in Bangalore, India, it is reported that the Dalai Lama said that religions should restrict themselves to service-oriented interventions such as imparting education and providing healthcare systems, and should not indulge in conversions.

> Citing examples of the work done by the Christian missionaries in the fields of education and health, the Dalai Lama said that the religious community was, however, imparting these services with a rider—'conversions.' "Christians have made the greatest contribution to education. But they also indulge in conversions, sometimes causing problems. It is much better if we kept our own religious faith. Else, it will lead to confusions," he said.[10]

Another speech, instead of focusing on would-be Western converts to Buddhism, addresses itself to Christian missionaries in Asia and other parts of the world. Not too surprisingly, this message regarding Christian (and Muslim) missionary efforts in other parts of the world was not as well received by leaders of such movements as was his advice to starry-eyed, naïve Western would-be converts to Buddhism.[11]

The Dalai Lama makes an additional crucial point to those who wish to work in foreign lands for the betterment of humanity, a truly laudable vocation if done with ethically proper motivations: They would do better to focus on human services rather than religious conversions. It is not that religious conversions are off limits, either into Buddhism or into Christianity,

8. Race, "Dalai Lama Urges Christians Not to Convert to Buddhism."

9. His Holiness, the Dalai Lama XIV, "'Religious Harmony' and Extracts from *The Bodhgaya Interviews*," 170.

10. Nandalike, *Daijiworld Media Pvt Ltd Mangalore*.

11. Khan, "Dalai Lama Condemns Islamic and Christian Practice of Conversions."

depending on the circumstances, but that there are human needs that transcend and make irrelevant whether either oneself or the recipient is a Buddhist, a Christian, or a member of any other religious or nonreligious group. Faithful people have enough work to do to meet those more basic and transcendent needs. Recruiting members to one's own religious affiliation should be totally irrelevant while one is performing any life-saving service. And afterwards, having truly helped someone, one should not be attached to any results of those actions, including appreciation from those one has helped. If one expects that those whom one has helped will now become more like oneself and convert to one's own religion as a result, one is truly misguided. One should seriously question one's motivation for being on the front lines, wherever they may be, in the first place.

In addition to questioning the unseemly large numbers of Westerners involved in missionary work in other parts of the world, one must question their motivation. Are they truly simply trying to serve, or are they attempting to convert, sometimes linking aid and conversion? Given Western wealth, it is appropriate for Westerners to help out in most parts of the world. It is not appropriate for them to link their help with an agenda of conversion. While initially it might seem that serious investigation of such linkages could be uncomfortable, clearly confronting such links between helping people and expecting conversion could be extremely liberating for all. Christian missions around the world have done a great deal of good in education (especially for girls) and in medicine. Nevertheless, many questions remain about ulterior motives for this humanitarian work. If the ulterior motive is conversion to one's own religion, whatever it might be, is not the whole enterprise completely tainted and unworthy? The Buddhist answer is an overwhelming yes. It is more than time for Christian ethical leaders to confront this situation.

On June 6, 2011, the World Council of Churches, the Vatican, and the World Evangelical Alliance jointly issued a document on "Christian Witness in Multi-Religious World," which had been in preparation for many years.[12] This document provides guidelines on many topics pertaining to inter-religious interactions, including the necessity for interreligious dialogue and mutual respect. These recommendations, if fully accepted, would set a high bar protecting from unethical conversions. The document specifically states that "Christians should denounce and refrain from all forms of allurements, including financial incentives and rewards, in their acts of service." Nevertheless, on the same day that I read this document about appropriate "Christian witness," the local newspaper ran a column by the

---

12. World Council of Churches, "Christian Witness in a Multi-Religious World."

very conservative columnist Cal Thomas praising Christian missionaries in Bangkok who worked to rescue girl prostitutes, certainly laudable work. Thomas discusses how these missionaries offer such girls a new life "if only they will trust God."[13] It seems there is still much work to be done to delink humanitarian service from religious conversion.

Buddhists also have standards and guidelines on generosity, a very highly praised virtue for Buddhists. In fact, Buddhist folklore, which is taken very seriously, states that if one wishes to retain one's good fortune, it is necessary to be generous with one's means. The wealthier one is, the more that guideline applies. In addition to such high praise for generosity, Buddhist regard for compassion is virtually unlimited. One could not exaggerate how important it is in the Buddhist ethos and for Buddhist sensibilities.

In this context, it is especially important to explore the subjective side of generosity and compassion, the ideal motivations and mind state of the person who is generous and compassionate. Giving with the proper attitude and motivation is, if anything, more important than the mechanics of what is given and to whom. Refining and perfecting that attitude is an important part of mind training. If one understands basic Buddhist approaches to life, one will not be surprised that an attitude of detachment and lack of self-interest is paramount for the giver. One strives eventually to be able to engage in generosity and compassion with the "threefold purity," with complete comprehension of the nondual interdependence/emptiness of gift, giver, and recipient. On the path of training, one strives to avoid serving others with an eye to "what's in it for me." Instead, one should ask carefully, "for whom am I doing these things"? If, even at the most subtle level, one is expecting something in return, true generosity and compassion have not yet been achieved. One of the trickiest forms of self-deception that can accompany giving is taking pride in one's own supposed compassion—something that is by no means rare. At a more crude level, it is not unusual for supposed generosity to be accompanied by an agenda of expecting the recipient to become more like oneself. Needless to say, in all such cases, one's generosity is tainted and still tinged with egotism. This does not mean that one should not attempt to be generous, but introspection is required. It also means that could be no linking whatsoever of humanitarian aid with religious conversion. In fact, I would say that such a linkage seems monstrous to Buddhist sensibilities.

Buddhists do discuss when and how one should offer *dharma*, religious teachings, to people. One well-known Tibetan Buddhist manual, translated as *The Jewel Ornament of Liberation* or as *Gems of Dharma, Jewels*

---

13. Thomas, "Accepting Help Offered," 3F.

of Freedom discusses both what one should give and with what attitudes one should give in its presentation of the *paramita* of generosity, the foundation of Mahayana Buddhist practice.[14] Three things are to be given, namely, material goods, fearlessness or psychological comfort, and the *dharma*, Buddhist teachings. Though it is not explicitly stated, the implication drawn by most who teach this text is that without a basis of freedom from want and from fear, it is pointless to try to educate people about *dharma*. Regarding the gift of *dharma*, the text very carefully states that one should make this gift to "those who wish to hear it, [and] have respect for both it and the one who expounds it."[15] The text goes on to state that, when *asked* to explain the *dharma*, one should defer at first to examine the suitability of one asking for instruction and also to set up a proper environment for teaching.[16] When I was training to become a *dharma* teacher, such guidelines were taken with utmost seriousness. We are encouraged to avoid proselytizing about *dharma*, not to proclaim *dharma*'s superiority to those who were not interested in it, and especially, not to cause offense to family and friends by arguing with them about religion. Certainly we are never instructed to try to bring our families into the Buddhist orbit, unlike what is often expected of new converts to Christianity. Another guideline is also recommended: "the student chases the teacher; the teacher does not chase the student." This slogan is often repeated to assemblies of Buddhist students, telling them that, while teachers are more than available, it is up to the student to take the initiative to discuss their spiritual paths.

But how can Buddhists be so casual about whether or not others adopt the *dharma*? To those seriously involved in missionary work aimed at converting others to their own religion, it must seem strange that Buddhists can be so convinced of Buddhism's appropriateness for themselves and yet not engage in deliberate, large-scale missionary movements. Several aspects of Buddhist thought and Buddhist sensibilities can help explain this seeming paradox. I would suggest that these ideas could also be quite helpful in promoting flourishing with religious diversity rather than being troubled by it and wanting to eliminate it through missionary work.

The first part of solving this puzzle lies in recognizing the difference between *universal* truth claims and *exclusive* truth claims. Buddhists do make universal truth claims, in that we would claim that interdependence and impermanence apply to all people, whether or not they are Buddhists.

---

14. Gampopa, *The Jewel Ornament of Liberation*; and Gampopa, *Gems of Dharma, Jewels of Liberation*.

15. Gampopa, *The Jewel Ornament of Liberation*, 173.

16. Ibid., 174; Gampopa, *Gems of Dharma, Jewels of Liberation*, 158.

But we do not claim that unless one becomes a Buddhist, one cannot learn to live well with impermanence and interdependence. In other words, we do not claim that we alone exclusively have the solutions to living with Things As They Are—with interdependence and impermanence. The religious or nonreligious label one applies to oneself is irrelevant. To a Buddhist, it seems incredible that anyone could possibly believe that spiritual well-being is a matter of repeating the correct words and concepts, of confessing something conceptual. What matters is a heart and mind that is not frightened by the reality of impermanence and interdependence, that can be kind and compassionate despite these realities. Formally becoming a Buddhist is not going to guarantee that! We do claim that we have methods that really help one cope with impermanence and interdependence. But we do not say one has to become a Buddhist to be able to use and benefit from those methods. Anyone can learn to meditate and freely make use of Buddhist teachings which are widely available. Such an attitude is so much more conducive to living and flourishing in a religiously diverse world than is claiming an exclusive monopoly on the right words with which to speak about reality.

Also, I would suggest that an interesting kind of individualism, not frequently noted, is important in Buddhism. Many commentators praise Western thought as the inventor of notions about the dignity of the individual, and some claim that currently individualism and lack of concern for the social fabric have become dangerous. By contrast, Asian societies are often thought to lack any respect for the individual. But, especially when it is difficult to comprehend why others do what they do or are unresponsive to seeming common sense, it is suggested that we should realize that each being has its own unique *karma*, to use traditional language. Different individuals each have their own agendas and issues and must become enlightened in their own time and on their own terms. There is only so much anyone can do about what is ultimately someone else's situation. We need to respect that, which usually means much less interference with them and much, much more patience on our part. It means that we must recognize that we don't have the answers for everyone, that often we simply cannot fix things, and—most important—that a great deal of human suffering has been caused by well-meaning people aggressively pushing their solutions to vexing problems onto people who do not find them palatable. This kind of individualism, which calls on us to pull back, can be very challenging. But it can also be very comforting, especially when we have tried our best to change a situation for the better but it remains intractable. Remembering that others have their own issues and agendas is also comforting when one feels frustrated by a situation that makes it impossible to help as much as one thinks one could. Certainly remembering such realities very effectively cuts any frustration that people don't change the way we think they should. It also explains Buddhists' lack of obsessiveness about whether or not other people become Buddhists. Such patience and noninterference would be most welcome from those who do obsess about everyone confessing the correct creeds and joining the One True Faith.

All this advice about not interfering with and not obsessing about others' spiritual choices involves an aspect of Buddhism that has not been discussed heretofore: right speech, the third element of the Buddhist Eightfold Path. In addition to recognizing that religion cannot be a one-size-fits-all phenomenon but one which calls for Skillful Means and the difficult but necessary discipline of not interfering with others so much, Buddhists can offer the discipline of Right Speech as a suggestion about how to flourish with religious diversity. Right speech is taken very seriously in Buddhism and it involves much more than not lying. There are four kinds of wrong or unvirtuous speech, according to many manuals on the topic. In addition to lying, they are speech that creates disharmony, frivolous speech, and speech that is harsh and offensive. Buddhists recognize that speech is very powerful and can easily cause great harm and suffering. Except in truly weighty cases, Buddhist sensibilities about speech give greater importance to the impact one's speech would have on others than to its bald truth. It is really important to avoid offending others or causing them pain with one's speech. Much of the time it is unnecessary to tell others what we really think of them or of something they value. Aggressive speech, even in behalf of an important cause, is always to be avoided, for many reasons. Making a pest of oneself, badgering people with the truth that they don't want to hear right now only makes them more resistant to ever listening.

If missionary enterprises would discipline themselves to observe such Right Speech rather than exploiting notions of freedom of religion and freedom of speech to the extent that they invite expulsion from their theaters of activity, much would be gained by all. In India and some other parts of the world, missionaries intent on religious conversions are disliked so much that there is great support for declaring them illegal. As was noted earlier in this chapter, Arvind Sharma has written an elegant and persuasive argument that human rights and freedom of religion include the right not to be asked to change one's religion. He has also argued that legal protection of that right may sometimes be necessary, especially in cases of religions that are ill prepared to ward off aggressive, well-financed missionaries intent on converting them. Certainly it seems reasonable that one should not be asked repeatedly to change one's religion when one has made it clear that such advice is unwelcome. And it seems quite clear that in many parts of the world, people simply don't want to be subjected to pressure to change their religion anymore. In such situations, listening to feedback from host countries and people and taking it seriously would be far wiser than insisting that freedom of religion is the same thing as the freedom to proselytize aggressively. Such a solution would be far preferable to states' needing to enact legislation to protect their citizens from being repeatedly badgered to change their religion.

As assurance that such mild presentations of one's religion can be very effective, look at the Buddhist case. Clearly, a religion can spread around the world without making exclusive truth claims and without engaging in heavy-handed foreign missionary activity. It can also coexist with other religions, as Buddhism has done throughout its history in most of the places it has flourished. Attraction is truly more persuasive than promotion. If one has a life-giving message, that message can and will be heard. A heavy hand is more likely to stifle the message than to promote it.

A Final Word on Christian Missions

How normative is deliberate and extensive missionary work for Christianity? I am often told that we must let Christians freely and forcefully evangelize wherever and whenever they want because such activity is essential to their practice of their religion. But I am quite skeptical of that claim.

For one thing, not all Christians evangelize, which proves that it is not *essential* to Christianity. If it were, all Christians would be compelled by the inner logic of their religion to proselytize, but they are not. To proselytize is a choice made by some but not all about which passages of Scripture to emphasize, and whether such a practice makes sense or is appropriate in today's world. As I have said in other contexts, I think it is time for religious people who do proselytize to own their choices as *their* choices and stop blaming God for them. They prefer, for whatever reasons, a more mission-oriented interpretation of Christianity, with all of its disadvantages, to a more pluralistic, humane, and compassionate interpretation. But God does not compel their choices about scriptural interpretations. It is really important that people recognize such basic facts about religious life.

Many varieties of Christianity, especially in the Eastern Christian orbit, do not engage in significant missionary activity, nor do mainline Protestants. For example, Rambo tells us that a Syrian Orthodox bishop in Jerusalem told him that "his church has no interest is converting 'outsiders' because 'they would have to learn the language and become a part of the culture. Why would anyone want to do that?'"[17] Yet all these Christians read

17. Rambo, *Understanding Religious Conversion.* 78.

the same scriptures, which strengthens my argument that differing interpretations of scripture, rather than anything inherent to Christianity, fuels much of the missionary frenzy.

It makes more sense to see the intense Christian missionary activity of recent centuries as part of a specific historical situation—European colonialism—rather than as something inherent to Christianity. Some, but not all, churches in areas most successful in their colonialism are also the most prone to strident and aggressive missionary activity. In political terms, in terms of national sovereignty, the colonial enterprise has largely folded by now. But it does not seem to have receded culturally, nor, especially, religiously and spiritually. Western forms of religion and spirituality are still overtaking many local and indigenous forms of religion and spirituality. This state of affairs saddens me greatly, for I take endangered forms of spirituality as seriously as I take endangered forms of biological life. It is incomprehensible to me that religious people are so indifferent to this particular holocaust. I am especially concerned about those who have been victims of Western political and economic hegemony. Why should they so willingly accede to spiritual hegemony as well? If one resists colonialism and Westernization, why would one think that the religion on the colonialists is so great? That has always puzzled me.

Mass Conversions of Dalits to Buddhism in India

The major motivation for many, if not most, conversions out of Hinduism is the caste system so closely associated with that religion. While it is easy to criticize that system from afar, it is important to recognize that many of those very willing to criticize Hindu caste themselves participate in and even promote segregation, racism, sexism, and other forms of inequality and oppression in their own societies—societies over which they have some control. It is also important, not just to recognize how problematic caste is, but to recognize how many movements against caste have occurred in India, the first of which was Buddhism itself. Attempts to eliminate caste were central to the Indian independence movement, and caste is officially banned in the Indian constitution. But, as similar legal reforms in the United States did not end segregation or really enfranchise African American citizens, so caste discriminations have not been ended in India. Regarding entrenched social inequality Christian America and Hindu India are actually more similar than different.

Over time, the vast majority of these conversions out of Hinduism have been to Islam or Christianity, not to Buddhism. But there is one significant exception to this generalization: a movement led by the great Untouchable leader B. R. Ambedkar, who was very active in the Indian independence movement, and who was the main author of the Indian constitution. Early in the independence movement, he and Gandhi seriously disagreed about the possibility of reform from within Hinduism about caste. Gandhi fought hard to get Hindus to renounce caste discriminations, but, after several bitter failures in attempts to actually bring Untouchables to water tanks and temples normally closed to them, Ambedkar came to the conclusion that this would never happen. In 1936, he declared that though he had been born a Hindu, he would not die a Hindu.[18] Because by then, Ambedkar was the well-known leader of a large community, this declaration had implications: many followers would come with him, so it would be very advantageous to whichever religion he chose. Representatives of all the major options— Muslims, Christians, Sikhs, and Buddhists—contacted him, offering conversion. The Buddhist responses were, however, the most muted. One of them suggested that caste would soon be eliminated by thoughtful Hindus, but if Ambedkar wanted to carry through with his plans, Buddhists did not observe caste, so Buddhism would be appropriate.[19] At that time, Ambedkar gave no indication of which religion he favored. Over time it became clear that he intended to convert to Buddhism, despite the fact that there were very few Buddhists in India, and that Buddhism itself was not well known, having been almost extinct in India for about eight hundred years. Finally, only seven weeks before his death, in October of 1956, Ambedkar finally received the Triple Refuge and the Five Precepts from the most senior monk living in India in a conventional conversion ceremony much like one any new convert to Buddhism would go through. Then, in departure from any established Buddhist practice, he himself immediately gave the Three Refuges and the Five Precepts to 400,000 white-clad followers who had come to witness the ceremony and convert to Buddhism themselves. He also administered twenty-two additional vows, not given by any other Buddhist school, to his followers. These twenty-two additional vows are an essential part of converting to Navayana Buddhism, as Ambedkar called his movement. More mass conversions followed, and despite very little contact with the rest of the Buddhist world and a very low state of Buddhist learning among Navayana Buddhists, the movement has survived.

This event is interesting to analyze in terms of the major concerns of the chapter. First of all, it seems that Ambedkar's choice of Buddhism was entirely a matter of attraction rather than promotion. Christianity and Islam

18. Tartakov, "B. K. Ambedkar and the Navayana Diksha," 193.
19. Sanghrakshita, *Ambedkar and Buddhism* 42.

were readily available, and Christians were proselytizing vigorously. By contrast, Ambedkar received no real instruction from Buddhist teachers and had only very limited experience in a Buddhist environment—a few short trips to Sri Lanka and Burma toward the end of this life. He sought out knowledge about Buddhism mainly from books and thought very carefully about the available choices for many years.

In part because he is a self-taught Buddhist, in part because of how much he thought through what he wanted from religion, and in part because of the extent to which issues of caste and untouchability dominated his experience and thinking, the form of Buddhism he eventually proposed is quite idiosyncratic. Most of the twenty-two vows specific to Navanayan Buddhism are meant to curb reversion to Hindu practices by the new converts. For many reasons, including poverty and cultural differences, Navayana Buddhists have little contact with the rest of the Buddhist world, which really inhibits their becoming more informed about what Buddhism involves. However, in Buddhist terms, the idiosyncrasies of Navayana Buddhism are not problematic. Buddhism is very internally diverse, and many forms of Buddhism have developed in many local cultures to meet local needs.

A final comment on caste in India is important, however. It is very difficult to escape the liabilities of caste simply by converting to a different religion. For one thing, converts to both Christianity and Islam continue to observe some caste distinctions among themselves. Even more problematic is that religious conversion does not change one's caste status in the eyes of Hindus. Religious movements that reject caste are simply regarded as another caste by Hindus. This reality is borne out by the experience of an English Buddhist, Sangharakshita, who worked extensively with Navayana Buddhists in India. When he was included in the 1951 census, despite his protest, he was listed as "Hindu by religion and Buddhist by caste."[20] Caste cannot not be eliminated only by changing religion externally; it is also important to recognize and support the many Hindus who long for Hinduism without caste and deeply believe that it is possible, just as citizens of the United State believe that we can eventually transcend racism and homophobia, maybe even sexism!

20. Sangarakshita, *Ambedkar and Buddhism*, 114–15.

Section 5

Integrity
Relating with Religious Others

Chapter 14

Learning about Religious Others

The Virtues and Joys of the Comparative Mirror

IN THE FINAL SECTION of this book, we turn to issues of how people who differ religiously can relate to each other with integrity. Having realized how interdependent self and other are by clarifying who religious others actually are and by thinking more carefully about how our own identities form and change, we come to a point of wanting interpersonal, interreligious relationships to be filled with integrity and uprightness. We are no longer satisfied with claims of superiority and attempts to convert the whole world to our religion. Having made that intrapsychic conversion, we want something more ethically upright and intellectually satisfying than the chauvinism of exclusive or inclusive truth claims. The first step in that journey is education—education about religious others that is accurate, neutral, and nonsectarian. Many advocate for interreligious dialogue immediately at this point, but, for many reasons I argue that dialogue can be very difficult and is best preceded by more neutral study.

At a January 2013 conference in India on women and Buddhism, I was very moved as I listened to a Bhutanese woman who had earned a PhD in the United States passionately proclaim that "education is freedom." She added that the kind of education that is freedom promotes critical thinking rather than merely reproducing received traditional knowledge. She narrated how her education had begun in Bhutan at a school that was a day's walk from her natal village, how she went there with no shoes, and how the neighbors criticized her parents for "not keeping that girl home." Her passionate characterization of the chance to engage in education that promotes critical thinking as "freedom" rang so true to me.

Nowhere is critical thinking more important than regarding religion, which has so much power for good or ill, depending on whether or not critical thinking about religions is possible and encouraged. Traditional religions often do not encourage critical thinking about religions, but today all the tools for such critical thinking about religion are readily available to everyone. This is because of the most significant advance in religious thinking in many centuries, which is the recognition that one can study *about* religions as an academic subject matter without taking any confessional position about those religions. This ability to gain accurate, neutral, unbiased, nonconfessional information about religions is tremendously freeing. It frees one from the constraints of received tradition and authoritarian dogmatism. It allows one to test whether the derogatory comments often made about other religions by religious insiders have any validity. This is a far more freeing and more ethical option than being forced to accept such comments simply because one has no other source of information. Truly the emergence of the discipline of the academic study of religion is a great gift and a great resource for flourishing with religious diversity. It undercuts completely the ignorance and misinformation that so often fuels interreligious hostility.

One must wonder why this approach to religion does not figure much more largely in discussions of theologies of religion. Perhaps because most theologians themselves are not well trained in the academic study of religion? But such education would be freedom for them too. More important, such education is freedom for every person who lives in a religiously diverse world—which is to say, virtually everyone. Used well, education about the religions of the world easily frees one from the burden of the prejudice involved in exclusive or inclusive truth claims, from inability to take delight in the fascinating display of viable symbol systems human beings have created, and from the stifling effects of religious dogmatism.

What are our ethical responsibilities in this situation we have inherited? We live in an inevitably religiously plural world. Unfortunately, the dominant inherited positions about religious diversity are not sympathetic to that diversity. For citizens of the United States, though not necessarily for citizens of Europe or Canada, we also live with a strange combination of religious enthusiasm and ignorance about religions. As Stephen Prothero writes, "Americans are both deeply religious and profoundly ignorant about religion. They are Protestants who can't name the four Gospels, Catholics who can't name the seven sacraments, and Jews who can't name the five books of Moses."[1] Anyone who has taught religious studies to American undergraduates can attest to this frustrating combination of strong opinions about religion and basic religious ignorance. But we have also inherited a situation that brings a radically new way of studying and evaluating religions—the neutral, nonsectarian, nonconfessional approach presented by the academic study of religion. In that situation, I would argue that each person, whether religious or not, has an ethical responsibility to learn about at least one other religion with which they are currently unfamiliar, to the point at which they know almost as much about an unfamiliar approach to religion as about the one with which they are familiar.

Whereas it was once difficult to learn about other religions in a neutral and unbiased manner, the academic study of religion has made it easy and pleasant to do so. There are many, many accessible and accurate books and other media. Reliable documentaries are readily available, and, for the more affluent, travel seminars. Courses are offered in many venues and could be offered in many more if the urgency of the task were more clearly recognized. I have taught such courses not only at the university but at a local senior center and at local churches.

The Academic Course on Religions of the World

When great human discoveries are listed, all the information about forgotten, buried religions, as well as about living religions culturally unknown to Europeans and European Americans, that became available in the nineteenth and twentieth centuries is seldom listed. Yet I believe that discovery is as momentous as any of the more technologically oriented discoveries we have made throughout the centuries. That discovery is so important because of the perspective that the comparative mirror gives us on our own religious convictions and commitments, and our consequent ability to experience religious diversity as a boon rather than a problem, perhaps for the first time. It is also important for the sheer joy afforded by being able to study and contemplate so many meaningful and interesting religious symbol systems.

When I taught my course called Introduction to the Religions of the World, I often marveled that almost all the information contained in that freshman course, taught at a regional state university to students who are not especially religious seekers, was unavailable one hundred fifty years ago. How much was unavailable in the 1950s, when departments of religious studies were first launched at some public universities! Most of it! How

---

1. Prothero, *Religious Literacy* 1.

much was unavailable even fifty years ago when I was a graduate student! Then there were only a few introductory books on Buddhism; now one cannot begin to be familiar with all of them. Then history was thought to begin at Sumer and other ancient civilizations of the Fertile Crescent; now one routinely teaches about Catal Huyuk and Old Europe, with their matrifocal, peaceful cultures. Then androcentric methods were the norm; now only someone who is distinctly out of date would ignore the results of feminist scholarship and theology. This is indeed an unheralded information explosion, both in terms of sheer information and in terms of methods of interpreting and understanding that information. How incredibly fortunate we are! For these reasons, I would place the discovery of the information we need for looking into the comparative mirror close to the top of the list of major human discoveries.

I would also argue that acquiring accurate information about the diverse religions found worldwide and in multireligious nation-states is absolutely critical for everyone today. Learning about the world's various religions in a neutral, accurate, nonsectarian way may well be the most necessary and helpful tool we have for flourishing with the inevitable religious diversity that we must live with. What is distinctive about the approach of the academic study of religion? First, the discipline of religious studies defuses the potential explosiveness of competing truth claims. External theological judgments about any religion are off limits in the academic study of religion. Instead, we engage in the dispassionate quest for accurate information about each religion, followed by the effort to understand each particular religious symbol system in its own terms, in an empathetic manner. Then, well equipped with both accurate information about other religions and an empathetic understanding of them, we can begin to look into the comparative mirror to gain insight into both our own perspectives and those of others. Second, religious studies understands religions to be historical phenomena, at least partially dependent on the unique particularities of the time and place in which any specific religion is found. Though the religions themselves often deny this historical conditioning or are ignorant of it, knowledge about the results of historical scholarship is very helpful in our learning to flourish with religious diversity. Finally, the discipline of religious studies is inherently cross-cultural. Clearly, if we are trying to understand something about the nature of religion, we will not do very well if we have a sample of one; or as Max Müller, the founder of comparative studies of religion said famously, "To know one religion is to know none."[2]

---

2. This famous statement by Max Müller was published in his 1870 book *Lectures on the Science of Religion*. See Stone, *The Essential Max Müller*, 112–13.

Based on this distinctive approach to religion, the tripartite agenda of religious studies is, first, to gather *accurate* information about the various religious options. This is followed by, second, divining an *empathetic* understanding of each religion, by learning how to glimpse momentarily each religious position *as if* it were one's own, thus enabling one to understand to some extent why religious others love their own religious positions. Well equipped with both accurate information and empathetic understanding of each religion, or at least one other religion, we can then, third, gaze into the *comparative mirror*, seeing both ourselves and others in the same lens. In the comparative mirror we see, not only others, but also ourselves, as *phenomena*. Then, what used to seem to be the only perspective one could take begins to be simply *a* perspective on the world, but no longer *the* only possible perspective that we imagine we could have. This tripartite agenda is set in the matrix of historical and cross-cultural approaches to the study of religion.

This threefold agenda must first be preceded by willingness to engage neutrally and openly in the study of religions. On the first day of my class, called Introduction to the Study of World Religions, I asked students to come into the classroom without presuppositions, as much as possible. I used the analogy of leaving one's shoes outside the door of an Asian sanctuary of any denomination, noting that the shoes of presuppositions would be waiting for them outside the classroom door if they wanted to take them up again. But for a little while, could we please suspend judgments, listen, and try to understand? On the other side of the desk, there are also important basic guidelines. The teachers who guide us through this journey should not be missionaries, and there can be no agenda of conversion, of persuading someone that *x* religion is (so to speak) better than *y* religion, or that religions altogether are something to be valued or something to be rejected. Teachers themselves must be well trained in the cross-cultural comparative study of religion and should present the various options regarding religion in an even-handed, neutral manner. Though the ground rules may be different in educational venues such as seminaries, which I will discuss in chapter 16, for the basic, neutral academic survey course on the world's religious options, the teacher must be absolutely even-handed about the various options and betray no sense at all of personal preferences. If he or she does display such preferences, the students' opportunity to truly experience the virtues and joys of the comparative mirror will be thwarted. If these ground rules are not observed, we can get nowhere because the entire purpose of looking into the comparative mirror will be subverted before it even begins.

For teachers and students operating with as few presuppositions as possible, listening and learning with open ears and minds, the first task for those looking into the comparative mirror is gathering accurate information about the various religions. There is so much we need to know and should know about the religious others who inhabit our world. To have any kind of in-depth look, it will be necessary to learn a lot of new terms and facts, and it will be necessary to take the amount of time required to gain some real understanding of another religion, not just the superficial knowledge that comes with reading a book or two.

It is important to stress that at this point all we are seeking is *accurate* information about the various religions—*data* as that term would be used by scientists, and *facts* as journalists might use that term. Regarding this information, there is no need at all for any emotional investment or reactions whatsoever. In fact, emotional reactions to basic information about religions are inappropriate. Someone should not be troubled to learn that Muslims do not believe that Jesus is divine, part of Godhead. It is simply a fact that Muslim theology is different on this point from Christian theology. Both Muslims and Christians as well members of other religions and people who are nonreligious need to be able to take in such materials as merely information—nothing more, nothing that causes any emotional reaction or makes one upset, and certainly nothing upon which to base judgments about the adequacy of Islam. Nevertheless, even at this basic level, problems often arise as students do react emotionally to basic information about religions. interestingly, I have also discovered that if one teaches the same information in a class labeled *anthropology* rather than *religious studies*, students are much less likely to become defensive about and emotionally upset by what they are learning. These reactions are probably part of the combination of religious opinionatedness and ignorance so characteristic of Americans.

There are many other flash points that come up in learning basic information about religions: Hinduism has polytheistic dimensions; Buddhism is nontheistic; Jews do not regard Jesus as the long-awaited Messiah; many religions do not posit personal immortality, and so forth. Even regarding subjects about which there could be eventual disagreement or discomfort, such as the Hindu caste system or the treatment of women in various religions, the initial task must be simply finding out more information about them. How exactly does the Hindu caste system affect different individuals? What, exactly, are women's lives like in any specific situation? It is amazing how much of the content of a basic course in the world's religions turns out to be mere information rather than anything that should elicit immediate reactions. Nevertheless, this information is often lacking when people form opinions and judgments about other religions. In a religiously diverse society, such uninformed judgments are a luxury we can ill afford.

The next step in learning about religious others is perhaps more difficult. On the foundation of accurate, nonsectarian information about the various religions, we need to develop empathy for the other, which is not becoming the other we are studying—an impossible task—but using our imagination to mentally enter into the spirit of what we are studying. That exercise gives us a fleeting glimpse into the worlds of others, a temporary sense of *as if*. There is a glimpse of seeing how and why others' worldviews make so much sense to them—almost as if that were my worldview. I present this practice as a two-step process. First, we must temporarily set aside our own preconceptions, judgments, opinions, and beliefs. That is necessary preparation for the second step: becoming able to imagine ourselves as Christians, Buddhists, Hindus, or what have you, and beginning to see how the world looks from those vantage points. This kind of learning is often greatly aided by films, field trips, and well-managed visits from religious insiders to the perspective we are studying. A successful practice of empathy would result in being able to understand and explain religious ideas and practices that are not our own. One example that I like to use is that if we succeed with empathy, we would be able to understand and explain the polytheistic strand of Hinduism with the same cogency that we can understand and explain monotheism, or vice versa. These two are seen as viable alternative theologies rather than as black-and-white opposites. It makes sense to practice polytheism if we look at it with empathy, from the viewpoint of its own logic, rather than of our culturally familiar logic.

It is absolutely essential to add empathy to information if the study of religious others is to bear fruit. Someone who merely learns that Hindus may worship many deities, or that Muslims do not believe that Jesus is part of the Godhead may be worse off than they were without the information. They may use that information only to solidify their own smug sense of superiority because they have not looked into *why* Hindus or Muslims believe as they do, how their beliefs make sense in the own frames of reference.

If we work hard enough at this task, we will become rather proficient at it and reap all the benefits of looking into the comparative mirror. When I teach, whatever religion I am teaching, I teach with as much empathy as possible, always presenting the logic and point of view of the religion we are studying. I also refused to disclose my own religious inclinations to students, telling them when they asked, "That's for me to know and you to guess." They often reported that each time we began to study another religion, they would think that must be my religion of choice because I presented it so enthusiastically and so much from the inside. This practice also earned me my all-time favorite student evaluation. I was often accused of being anti-Christian at my provincial university, which was the result of the fact that I did not privilege Christianity but put it on a level playing field as one religion among others. One of my most conservative students finally thought he had figured it out. He proclaimed in class, "Rita isn't really anti-Christian. She doesn't say negative things about Christianity. What's *wrong* with the way she teaches is that she makes all those other religions sound as if they could be true!" Need I say more about the possibility of cultivating empathy for many diverse points of view while knowing who we are? In that process, we see not only others, but also ourselves, more clearly. Such seeing is absolutely essential to flourishing with religious diversity, rather than being troubled by it or regarding it as a problem.

The Virtues and Joys of the Comparative Mirror

Clearly, the term *comparative mirror* points to something more complex than taking a course in world religions and then forgetting what one learned. It also involves more than simply gathering and learning data about world religions. Building on the foundation of accurate information about the various religions and the superstructure of empathetic understanding of those religions, the culmination of such study—experiencing the virtues and joys of the comparative mirror—can occur. Through gaining accurate information about Buddhism, or any other religious perspective that is not our own, and then delving into an empathetic experience of that tradition, we would actually learn, to some extent, to see the world through Buddhist eyes, Christian eyes, or the eyes of whatever religion we are studying. Such learning involves much more that simply assimilating some facts and figures about Buddhism or Christianity, for example.

The information gathered by the comparative study of religion is the necessary basis for looking into the comparative mirror but is not quite the comparative mirror itself. A mirror is something in which we see ourselves, whereas simple comparative studies do not necessarily involve the reflexive quality of the comparative mirror. In the comparative mirror, we see ourselves in the context and from the perspective of many other religious phenomena; such seeing invites, even necessitates, self-reflection about our own cultural and religious systems. This is the virtue and joy of the comparative mirror. When we look into the comparative mirror, as William Paden has written, "Our own world, instead of being taken for granted, becomes exposed *as* a world, its contents held up to the comparative mirror and we become a phenomenon to ourselves."[3]

In that process, we see and understand *ourselves* much more clearly. As people often discover, when they travel or live abroad, they learn as

---

3. Paden, *Religious Worlds*, 165.

much, if not more, about themselves, about being North American in our case, as they learn about the cultures they are visiting. It is the same with the comparative study of religion. In seeing the world through Buddhist eyes, for example, we also become "a phenomenon to ourselves," to quote Paden again.[4] In that experience, our world is exposed as *a* world instead of seeming to be the only world. Important is that when we see our world as *a* world rather than *the* world, we can then see our own uniqueness and distinctiveness much more clearly. Nothing so powerfully demonstrates the specificity and uniqueness of Christianity, or any other religion, as a long look into the comparative mirror. That is part of what it means to reach a level of understanding in which our world is no longer taken for granted, no longer seems obvious and normal, but is clearly seen as *a* religious world, one among many. It is difficult to understand the specificity and peculiarity of monotheism, for example, until we know something about the alternatives. That reflexive quality of the comparative mirror is its first virtue and joy.

However important the reflexive quality of the comparative mirror may be, that is not the only outcome of looking into the comparative mirror. When we have really practiced empathy, we genuinely understand alternative religions as *alternatives*, not as deluded opinions. We can recapture the wisdom of some children, born to parents belonging to a minority religion, who tell their parents that if they had happened to be born instead to the parents living next door, they would belong to a different religion. This insight can occur because, at least for thoroughly acculturated adults, it is easier initially to see the contingent cultural, historical, and social forces that determine why other religions have taken the forms they have than to see the same thing about our own culture or religion. It is easy to see that their rituals and ideologies, while compelling in their own context, are not unmediated but contingent, and thus, not absolutely true for all time and all contexts. We easily understand how the rituals and belief systems of others can be compelling and coherent in their own context but not especially compelling or relevant universally.

But how could our religion be different? Especially, we see that the same kinds of historical forces and processes that determine why other religions are as they are have also formed our religion. That is the most profound result of becoming a phenomenon to ourselves. The lowest common denominator shared by all religions, long sought by many theologians of religions, is that all ideologies and belief systems are the contingent products of specific historical situations, a conclusion that is unavoidable

4. Ibid.

when we look into the comparative mirror, but difficult to ascertain by any other method. To say that in Buddhist language is to say that all cultures and belief systems are the results of interdependent causes and conditions. Like any other interdependently arisen phenomena, they therefore lack inherent, independent, lasting reality. In Buddhist language, they are empty of inherent existence, no matter how meaningful and compelling they may be to their adherents and in their own cultural contexts. There is no logical reason to exempt one religion among the many religions from being such a contingent, historical product. That would be tantamount to claiming that everyone else participates in a *culture*, which mediates and conditions their view of the world, while we are not immersed in culture but have direct access to reality beyond culture. Without study and reflection, many people may fall prey to such conceit, which makes immersion in the comparative mirror even more urgent. Because this is a difficult step for most people psychologically, it is critically important.

Thus, when we look deeply into the comparative mirror, our own religious worldview is decentered and de-absolutized, a necessary prerequisite for living comfortably in the religiously diverse world we now inhabit and always will inhabit. Religious diversity then is no longer a problem. We are no longer threatened and made uneasy by differences. Looking into the comparative mirror thus brings a welcome double appreciation: We come to appreciate our own tradition and its uniqueness in a way not possible if we don't know the alternatives. We also come to appreciate other religious systems as completely sensible and viable when we take the time and effort to look at the world through them, no longer looking at these systems only through our own familiar presuppositions.[5]

Finally, we come to appreciate diversity itself, regarding it as a boon rather than a problem. We do not have to blur religious differences by claiming that at some level all religions teach the same thing. I regard this conclusion as evidence of lingering fears of diversity. Religions *may* be the same or similar at a nonverbal, deep level of mystical experience, but that claim cannot be verified. When I look into the comparative mirror, I do not see religions that are basically the same; I see tremendous differences of theology and religious practice, and I delight in those differences. On the other hand, the *sameness* of all religions is that they are all interdependently arisen, contingent systems of belief and ritual. Their contingency does not

5. For detailed demonstrations of this double effect seen from the Christian point of view, see Berling, *A Pilgrim in Chinese Culture*; and Eck, *Encountering God*. These spiritual autobiographies narrate how two Christian women scholars of Asian religions looked into the comparative mirror, took what they saw to heart, and grew in their Christian spiritual lives.

mar their specific, contextual relevance in any way. Only when adherents of any specific system attempt to elevate a dependently arisen, contingent system to ultimacy do problems arise. Interesting is that on this point, Buddhism and the academic study of religion are largely in agreement, as was demonstrated in chapter 6, on the limits of religious language.

In this frightening world of impending ecological disaster and under the constant threat of violence, the existence of religious diversity and the ease with which we can now look into the comparative mirror is one of the few positive experiences readily available to us. I marvel at the fascinating variations we see. Humans have responded to the same human biology, the same experience of life and death, in so many diverse ways, with so many diverse religious symbol systems. What a joy-filled opportunity to be able to encounter them firsthand, to explore their depths, test their logic, and taste their beauty: this is the fruition of gazing into the comparative mirror.

With that fascination and joy comes the virtue of seeing our own perspective as one among many, on a level playing field, decentered from seeming to be the only normal or possible way to put the world together. The virtues and joys of the comparative mirror make exclusive or inclusive truth claims impossible. And the virtues and joys of the comparative mirror make abundantly clear that religious diversity is a boon rather than a problem. The perspective we gain on ourselves is available in no other way. In addition, so many religious ideas, symbols, and practices that we could never think up on our own are now available for contemplation. This explains why looking into the comparative mirror is such a good antidote to exclusive truth claims. If one uses the comparative mirror honestly, one will find (for example) that non-Christian religions make sense and are cogent, thus freeing those who adhere to religions that make exclusive or inclusive truth claims to reconstitute their religions on some other basis than such truth claims. We come around again to the founding motto of the discipline of comparative studies in religion: "to know one religion is to know none." One's self-understanding and understanding of others are so profoundly limited by not understanding and not being familiar with any of the options.

A final virtue promoted by looking into the comparative mirror is the ability to be less judgmental, to withhold judgment and rest in the open, curious, flexible state of mind discussed at length in chapter 10 on spiritual discipline. Simply knowing the alternatives to one's own religious worldview more accurately, even without moving on to empathetic understanding and looking into the comparative mirror, promotes nonjudgment about the various options. This is because one realizes how subtle the choices are, and how complex the issues are. Recognizing this subtlety and complexity, one realizes how irresponsible it is to make superficial, uninformed judgments. Being too quick to demand yes-or-no answers and to engage in black-and- white judgments about complex, ambiguous situations is one of the great faults of many overly zealous religious people (and others, of course), even though that vice is sometimes promoted as if it were a virtue. Ability to rest in nonjudgment certainly promotes ease and flourishing with religious diversity, whereas being overly quick to make judgments results in the discomfort of bias and opinionatedness. And it is much easier to rest in nonjudgment and to be comfortable with ambiguity when one has actually experienced the alternatives to one's own worldview with a flash of empathy—as if one momentarily stands in the shoes of the other.

But What about Truth?

Whenever I present this proposal for empathetic understanding of religious others in the light of the comparative mirror, someone always asks whether I am proposing sheer relativism with no concern at all for truth or values. The response is multifaceted, but most of the relevant points have already been addressed in chapters 5 and 6. Religious diversity is inevitable. Religion never has been and never can be a one-size-fits-all phenomenon. Given the history of schism and sectarianism even within each and every religion, it should be obvious that agreement about theological truth will never occur. If an agreed-upon truth is not findable even within one religion, how could it possibly be found among the various religions? Our only choice is to learn how to live together in peace despite our theological disagreements, and living peacefully with those disagreements is greatly enhanced if we actually understand those with whom we disagree more empathetically.

There are many theological viewpoints because theological disagreements cannot easily be resolved either rationally or empirically. It is hard to disagree with sound reason or tangible evidence available to all, but those are not available concerning theological positions and conclusions. What people are disagreeing about has no tangible, common referent. Essentially (as discussed in chapter 6) people are disagreeing about what can never be fully brought into language or conceptuality. So it not surprising that many proposals about what is often called ultimate reality have been put forth by many religions throughout history. Nor is it surprising that many of them are cogent, if we only take the time to understand them accurately and empathetically. When we do so, we cannot fail to realize that diverse, varying ways of conceptualizing or symbolizing ultimate reality have a great deal to do with on-the-ground cultural factors. We also cannot fail to realize that many idiosyncratic, personal psychological needs and styles influence personal choices about symbol systems that make sense. In the light of the comparative mirror, it seems impossible to avoid the conclusion that theologies and religious symbol systems are more akin to literature and the arts than to science and history. These are disciplines in which public verifiability is somewhat possible and truth claims can have some cogency. But even in those disciplines, we must recognize that conclusions about what is the truth change regularly. The science that most of us learned in high school is now outmoded, new data enter textbooks regularly, and understandings of broad historical trends regularly change. It seems that verbal, conceptual understanding that will stand for all time is impossible to attain, even in these more empirical, fact-based disciplines. Why should we expect theology and religious symbols systems to be different? The only position among all the various possibilities that doesn't make sense is to claim that one symbol system or one small group of religious followers along among all the options could be right, correct for all time and all cultures, while everyone else is wrong.

However, it is also crucial to realize that understanding does not equal either approval or acceptance. It is entirely possible to understand other religious ideas at least reasonably well but find them neither cogent nor appealing nor relevant. What then? All parties to such impasses desperately need the self-discipline to be able to disagree agreeably, to disagree with someone without becoming disagreeable, argumentative, intolerant, and condescending. These skills do not have to do with theologies or religious symbol systems per se; they have to do with identity issues and with the presence or absence of adequate spiritual discipline. Fundamentally, people fail to handle disagreements without conflict, not because of failures in symbol systems but because of their own personal inclinations and preferences—often because of an inability to comfortably and compassionately allow others to be different, to be who they are. So often one hears of families driven to estrangement or friendships ending because people insist that others must think like they do or must agree with them for amicable relationships to continue. What an unreasonable position!

It is especially problematic when people justify their drive toward estrangement from or hostility toward others by claiming that they are only obeying the dictates of their religion. Instead, they are only listening to one especially narrow version of their own religion. Others are available. As has been argued several times previously, it is time for people to own their own preferences and choices, especially those that promote harshness over gentleness. It is unconscionable for folks to blame their scorn for and discomfort with others on anything other than themselves, and especially for them to blame the deity whom they claim to honor and obey for their discomfort with religious others and their inability to exercise the compassion of noninterference toward those religious others.

With self-discipline in place, people can disagree with each other about important matters but fruitfully debate and discuss the pros and cons of the various positions. Each might actually learn and grow in such interchanges. Such conversations, however, shade more into the exercise of dialogue rather than learning about religious others accurately and empathetically. This material will be more fully discussed in the next chapter.

But what if people are being hurt or oppressed? Is judgment still inappropriate? Answers to this question have also been largely dealt with in chapter 7. There is no correlation between oppressive or unethical behaviors and any specific religion. Members of any and all religions are equally culpable of oppressing women and minorities of various kinds, of engaging in or promoting warfare and violence, of permitting economic injustice to flourish, and of being indifferent to environmental degradation. People who self-identify with each of the world's major religious labels do regularly engage in unethical and inappropriate behaviors, often while vociferously proclaiming their religious allegiances and loyalties. Sometimes, they even claim that their oppressive behaviors are justifiable according to their own specific religion. This fallibility is another dimension of religions' lowest common denominator: their interdependently arisen contingency and lack of ultimacy. As John Hick and many other have noted frequently, if one of the world's religions is in fact superior to all others and uniquely true while all other religions are false, there should be some tangible evidence for its superiority. Ethical superiority on the part of those who believe in any specific religion would be the most convincing evidence that the given belief system is somehow uniquely true, superior to all others. Why else should anyone take seriously its claims that it possesses a unique truth? However, no such evidence is available.

When one is troubled by the unethical and oppressive behaviors of religious believers, it is much more appropriate to judge individuals and groups rather than whatever religion they may proclaim and promote, even if they justify their behavior by appeal to their chosen religion. Judging the entire religion instead would only be appropriate if every adherent of that religion engaged in such conduct, which is never the case. Even in the most stereotypical cases, ethical norms that trouble many people are always rejected by some insiders to whichever religion permits such behaviors. Perhaps the most cogent case concerns treatment of women. Every current religion, including Buddhism, has a very strong and stubborn streak of misogyny and male dominance. Yet many religious insiders criticize and combat these practices, usually citing ethical norms of their religions largely ignored by those who favor male dominance. A religious system cannot be blamed for the failure of so many of its adherents to live up to its normative ideals. If that were the test for the worthiness of any religion's theology and symbol system, all would fail miserably.

However, there are many pitfalls in the worthy enterprise of critiquing ethical lapses and oppressions endorsed and promoted by religious people. First of all, it is important to be modest and humble about one's own insights, or at least completely willing to modify them in the light of further information about and deeper understanding of those whom one is faulting. Perhaps one's objections have more to do with cultural chauvinism than with truly existing problems? This possibility is especially prevalent in the case of cross-cultural assessments. For example, Western feminists have often made matters worse by uninformed and strident criticisms of how other cultures and religions deal with gender.[6] Even if one is right, so to speak, in one's criticisms, will negative comments from outsiders be effective? Often, especially if such criticisms come from those whose culture or political system is dominant, the effect is entrenchment rather than reform. Great skill is required in cross-cultural evaluations of what is an ethical lapse or oppression. Thus, in my own case, as a vigorous feminist critic of both Buddhism and religious studies in general, I mainly confine my comments to enterprises in which I am a stakeholder (the academic study of religions, the dominant religious culture of my own milieu—Western culture in general and the United States in particular—and Buddhism). Thus, I severely limit my comments on the situation of Muslim women, for example, even though many feminists feel quite free to criticize Islam. My opinions are much less relevant than those of Muslim women. Unless my opinions could be helpful to Muslim women, they are best kept to myself.

The Comparative Mirror and Personal Change

The comparative mirror is neutral about the truth and value of the world's major religions and also about the smaller traditions that are less often

6. As someone who has been concerned about the ethics and methodology of cross-cultural studies my whole career and has taught about women in cross-cultural perspective many times, I have often dealt with the issue of how to present gender practices that initially seem "wrong" or oppressive to most Western women, whether feminist or not. I have always stressed that some of these practices may not be as negative for women as we initially suppose. Modest dress codes, arranged marriage, and polygyny are some of the most ambiguous and thought provoking if we take indigenous perspectives into account, not simply our own prejudices and presuppositions. See my *Garland of Feminist Reflections*, 69–73 and 220–25, for discussions of these issues.

noted. However, its emphasis on the importance of neutral and accurate information and on developing an empathetic appreciation of the globe's various religions options does not mean that the pursuit of the academic study of religion is value free. This distinction between being neutral regarding differing and competing religious systems and being value free is critically important and must be understood. Not all values are equally conducive to human survival and well-being. Values that result in prejudice, hostility, and oppression cannot be promoted as just another value system (perhaps different) from those that promote tolerance, mutual acceptance, and understanding. An ethically upright person could never claim that neutrality vis-à-vis competing religious truth claims translates into neutrality about racism, sexism, homophobia, classism, or any other value system that condones, or even promotes, discrimination against and hostility to specific groups or individuals. In fact, central to my case against exclusive and inclusive truth claims is that such solutions to the so-called problem of religious diversity promote prejudice, hostility, and scorn rather than friendliness and goodwill toward those who are different.

Sometimes critics have claimed that because I do not condone exclusive truth claims, I am just as intolerant as those I criticize. But I can see no grounds whatsoever for a claim that an ethic seeking to eliminate religious diversity and an ethic valuing religious diversity are equivalent and should be regarded as simply different ideologies about which one can or should be neutral. That would be to confuse being neutral vis-à-vis competing religious symbol systems with being value free or completely relativistic. Looking into the comparative mirror promotes being neutral about the relative value and truth of the world's various religions, but it does not promote being value free regarding the worth or survival of any one of them.

Thus, one must be prepared that some things might change in one's outlook when one looks deeply into the comparative mirror. The study of religion can never be value free because the very existence of the discipline depends on the development of a worldview that prizes an ability to be neutral vis-à-vis the various religions as well as an ability to see the internal coherence and logic that empowers each of them. These values are emphatically rejected by at least some segments of all major religions. Information about unfamiliar perspectives on religion is *meant* to challenge monolithic or universalistic presuppositions about the world. One *should* feel that sexist, racist, ethnocentric, and religious chauvinisms, if present, are being threatened by the academic study of religion. Being value free about such oppressive values is definitely not recommended. One result of the successful pursuit of the neutral and empathetic study of religion is that such values become much less attractive and tenable.

But Are These Suggestions Practical?

Proposals for widespread or universal education about the variety and diversity of religions are sometimes met with skepticism or dismissed as impractical. Years ago, whenever I would urge my colleagues at the university to require more study of the world's religions, either to complete a program in religious studies or as general-education requirements, they would argue that it is far more important for students to know more about their own culture and religion first. Seminary professors have also made similar arguments to me about why seminary students can't study non-Christian religions, despite the fact that they will be ministering in a religiously diverse country. There is so much to know about one's own religion and so little time, it is argued. Their arguments, however, overlook the way studying something different and unfamiliar illuminates the familiar in a way that simply is not possible only with more courses on what is already familiar.

Nowadays at liberal-arts colleges and universities, both private and public, survey courses on world religions are numerous and popular. Many such schools now require coursework in cultural diversity for graduation, and courses on world religions usually meet these requirements. However, many other constituencies, both older and younger than college students, also need similar courses. Seminary students in particular need to be much better educated about religious diversity. How to do this will be discussed in chapter 16. For postcollegiate constituencies, given that many reliable materials are now available, many venues would be possible, if the will to make such study available were there. Churches and other religious institutions could take the lead in educating their memberships. Adult-education programs and senior centers could offer courses for those who would not attend courses sponsored by religious institutions.

However, the most effective way to close this knowledge gap is to add information-based courses about the world's religions to humanities and social-sciences curricula for the upper grades and for high school students. Such courses would reach most of the population, including those who do not pursue higher education. Religion is simply too important a part of cultures and of people's lives to be ignored; yet this so often happens in social-science and humanities curricula in precollege education. At the age when students begin to study history, geography, and literature, they could also be begin to learn information about the various religions, including information about where religious followers are located geographically, and how they have affected history. Students could also read excerpts from the literatures produced by the various religions. Such studies would have been totally inappropriate before the development of the academic study of religion, but its emphasis on accurate information about each religion and its nonadvocacy for or against religion in general, or for or against any specific religion, make religion an appropriate object of study at all levels of education. But the academic study of religions has made it safe to teach about religions more widely by distinguishing teaching about religions in a detached, neutral manner from teaching religion confessionally in a sectarian fashion. This development makes it not only possible but also necessary to teach much more widely about religions and their massive impact on history, culture, and society.

Ironically, many more conservative people call for religion or the Ten Commandments, or what have you to be taught in public schools. Others want the biblical creation story to be taught in such schools. Strangely, or perhaps not so strangely, these folks are correct that such materials should be taught. They are too important to be ignored. But the proper venue for such teaching is through information-based, religiously neutral courses that include all religions without favoring any. (For example, the biblical story of creation could be taught in a unit on religious literature that brings together many creation stories from around the world. The Ten Commandments could be part of a unit on ethical norms of the various religions.) Whether or not they come from religions homes, for students to learn such information early in their lives would be very practical and beneficial for promoting flourishing with religious diversity.

In conclusion, given the inevitably religiously diverse world we all now inhabit and will inhabit for the foreseeable future, I would argue strongly that everyone has a new ethical obligation. To be a responsible citizen of this world, everyone needs to learn something about the world's religions in a neutral and empathetic fashion and to know at least one other viewpoint, whether traditionally religious or secular, relatively well. Fortunately, the academic study of religion, with its methods for looking deeply into the comparative mirror, makes it easy and pleasant to fulfill this ethical obligation.

Chapter 15

Talking with Religious Others

Dialogue and Interreligious Interchange

I N HIS BOOK *TOWARD a True Kinship of Faiths: How the World's Religions Can Come Together,* the Dalai Lama movingly writes of the impact meeting people of faiths different from his own had on him when he was a young man. Even before his long-term exile from Tibet, which began in 1959, the Dalai Lama visited India in 1956 when he was nineteen. He came to India well educated, but educated only in his own tradition. He had not met or interacted with people of other faiths. In India he interacted with "many people from all walks of life as well as from all kinds of religious backgrounds."[1] He writes movingly of the impact those meetings had on him.

> When I returned to Tibet in 1957, after more than three months in what was a most amazing country for a young Tibetan monk, I was a changed man. I could no longer live in the comfort of an exclusivist standpoint that takes Buddhism to be the only true religion.[2]

One of those meetings was with a senior Jain master. The young Dalai Lama wrote how, for the first time, he met with a real Jain practitioner "whose articulation of his own faith tradition had little resemblance to the

---

1. His Holiness, the Dalai Lama XIV, *Toward a True Kinship of Faiths*, 3.
2. Ibid., 6.

characterization of Jain views in the scholastic texts and refutations I had studied in my youth."[3]

In this comment, the Dalai Lama presents one of the major justifications for interreligious dialogue and interaction. Especially if we have gained our knowledge of other religions from texts of our own traditions that try to refute the validity of those traditions and to demonstrate the superiority of our own religion, we are very likely to have distorted and inaccurate views of other traditions. The polemical treatises of one tradition rarely contain accurate information about the traditions against which they are arguing. When we actually meet and interact honestly and openly with members of those religions, we are very likely to discover that their adherents do not bear much resemblance to the stereotypes about them found in our texts. One need only think of the negative portraits of Judaism in the New Testament, or of the descriptions of early Buddhism in Mahayana Buddhist texts, to perceive that it can be quite dangerous and misleading to rely on polemical texts of our own tradition for information about religious others. It might well be more accurate and upright to meet with actual practitioners of those traditions so that they can represent themselves.

Especially for clergy and other religious leaders, even the kind of empathetic study discussed in the previous chapter would be enhanced if people actually met with living representatives of various religious traditions. Books and classes are very effective tools for greater learning, but it is easier to ignore the information they contain about religious others than to ignore the evidence of lives well lived presented by living representatives of other religious traditions. It is relevant to remember once again that the great pluralist John Hick was first convinced that his exclusivist views about other religions were inadequate because of his interactions with members of other religions.

There is no question that dialogue and other forms of interreligious interaction are a good idea and an important tool in our arsenal of methods for learning how to flourish with religious diversity. For those seriously committed to gaining and promoting interreligious respect and understanding, at a certain point, nothing can substitute for face-to-face meetings with one's counterparts in other traditions.

Nevertheless, unlike many other advocates for interreligious interchange, I do not regard dialogue as the main panacea for interreligious hostility or foil against exclusive truth claims. I have heard many people complain that "those who really need to engage in dialogue don't," and then these people ask what to do about that reality. My answer to them is

---

3. Ibid., 2.

that genuine dialogue is quite difficult and can be very stressful. I have a good bit of sympathy for those unprepared for dialogue or other forms of interreligious interaction trying to sit through interfaith services or visit other religious institutions simply because they are trying to fulfill someone else's expectations. If one is not already predisposed to give up one's ingrained presuppositions about the superiority of one's own faith and the inferiority of all others, such exercises can actually be counterproductive. If people enter interreligious interactions with the wrong motivations, those interactions can be ineffective or even destructive. In the multifaith world we now inhabit, everyone needs to acquire some empathetic understanding of the world's religious options, but except for religious leaders, only those especially drawn to interreligious dialogue need to participate in them. For those, whether they are religious leaders or more ordinary dialogers, certain guidelines about what dialogue is and isn't are crucial. If dialogue is to lead to greater flourishing with religious diversity rather than mutual entrenchment, it is helpful if people enter into dialogue with these guidelines well in place rather than encountering them in the process of dialoguing.

A recent book about dialogue, Catherine Cornille's *The Im-Possibility of Interreligious Dialogue*, provides one such set of guidelines for qualities people need to cultivate if they are to engage in successful dialogue. The first of these qualities is doctrinal humility, by which she means that the dialoger must realize that their own religion teaches them that no matter how much they may know, their knowledge is limited. Cornille's second guideline is commitment to one's own tradition. Third, it is helpful for people engaged in dialogue to believe that it is possible for religious believers to understand each other and work together across religious boundaries. Beyond that, it is necessary to develop empathy for religious points of view that are quite different from one's own. Finally, Cornille talks about hospitality as the virtue of being willing to listen to and learn from one's dialogue partners.[4] In one way or another, most dialogers would affirm and live by those guidelines, though other questions nevertheless emerge. Based on my own experience of dialogue, I offer the following recommendations and comments.

What Dialogue Is Not

I am often asked whether or not I would dialogue with fundamentalists or exclusivists. My answer is positive, with the ground rule that dialogue must

---

4. Cornille, *The Im-Possibility of Interreligious Dialogue*. For a succinct summary of these points, see Knitter, "Inter-Religious Dialogue and Social Action."

be carried out on a level playing field with mutual respect among dialogue partners who all regard each other as equals. There seems to be little point to a dialogue if one of the partners is mainly concerned with winning a debate or gaining converts to their point of view. Anyone who sees missionary activity aimed at the possible conversion of dialogue partners to one's own religion as a legitimate part of interreligious dialogue does great disservice to the activity. Because the main fruition of dialogue is greater understanding and goodwill among practitioners of the various religions, it is crucial that people not enter into dialogue hoping to convert their dialogue partners to their own tradition. Given that most practitioners of interreligious dialogue are deeply immersed in and quite knowledgeable about their own traditions, such a hope is rather unrealistic in any case. But one does not want to have to be on guard against covert missionary activities when one enters into dialogue with a sincere wish to understand members of other religions more accurately and empathetically. Missionary activity in the midst of a dialogue is simply inappropriate, and it is hard to understand how anyone could claim otherwise.

Nevertheless, when we read commentators on interreligious dialogue, we find that not all of them rule out activities aimed at conversion as illegitimate in the dialogue arena. I remember listening to one discussion, whose participants I do not currently remember, in which one contributor eagerly proclaimed that he would not hesitate to "proclaim Christ" to the Dalai Lama in the context of interreligious dialogue. One wonders what kind of hubris he was infected with! The Dalai Lama is quite familiar with Christianity and has engaged in many meetings with much more learned and impressive Christian spokespersons. If he were going to convert to Christianity, he would have done so long ago. Furthermore, anyone who reads any of the Dalai Lama's writings cannot help but notice that he loves Buddhism as much as Christians love Christianity. But he does not encourage Christians to convert to Buddhism!

Nor are such attitudes as this one Christian displayed confined to single individuals who may not represent large groups. More recent (post–Vatican II) documents from the Roman Catholic Church recommend "proclamation" as part of the agenda for Christians in dialogue with members of other religions. In fact, in these documents, the Church declares that "true interreligious dialogue on the part of the Christian supposes the desire to make Jesus Christ better known, recognized and loved; proclaiming Jesus Christ is to be carried out in the Gospel spirit of dialogue."[5] These documents

5. These words are from paragraph 77 of an official 1984 document of the Roman Catholic Church called *Dialogue and Proclamation*. The document is quoted in a helpful online discussion of the Church's major statements on dialogue and mission, beginning with Vatican II documents from 1965. Bevans, "Church Teaching on Mission," 12.

also declare that dialogue should not replace proclamation, but rather that dialogue "remains oriented towards proclamation insofar as the dynamic process of the Church's evangelizing mission reaches in it, its climax and fullness."[6] In other words, I should not relax and cannot enjoy a collegial interchange between mutually respectful practitioners of different religions. My (Roman Catholic) dialogue partner still regards me as someone in need of theological correction, and I would be naïve if I did not remain on guard against attempts to convince me of the superiority of (Catholic) Christianity over Buddhism (or whatever religion to which I might belong)! Fortunately, many dialogers would not regard me as so in need of a spiritual intervention!

Others sometimes expect that interreligious dialogue would mainly consist of debates between adherents of different religions. After all, the religions disagree with one another, and debate is a time-honored mode of interaction between intellectual opponents. Indeed, in one teaching situation that two teachers expected to be a dialogue with educational and informational goals, one of the participants arrived expecting to spend the week "arguing about religion." He had not done any of the assigned reading and assumed he already knew enough about Buddhism to debate its validity with anyone and everyone, even though he was relatively uninformed about Buddhism. Needless to say, he did not benefit from the experience and became very frustrated with being expected to do more than argue.

If the purpose of interreligious dialogue is the development of deeper mutual appreciation and understanding among people of diverse religions, the medium of debate is not well suited to accomplishing that purpose, even though it can be entertaining and serves well in situations in which people need to decide between two or more alternatives, rather than to understand each of them more fully. Thus, debates are much more appropriate in the context of election campaigns than in the context of interreligions relations. Debate is, by definition, an adversarial, combative activity. In a debate, one is trying to collect points for one's side or team, not to understand the other. Participants are scored, and winners and losers are declared. As with settling intellectual or spiritual disputes by physical combat, so winning a debate does not necessarily prove that the winner's position is superior. It only proves that he or she is a better debater. Next time, a flashier debater from the other side may well be declared the winner. What has been proved by this—especially if the task at hand is developing mutual respect and understanding, leading to greater peace and harmony among the various religions?

---

6. *Dialogue and Proclamation*, 82, quoted in Cornille, *The Im-possibility of Interreligious Dialogue*, 70.

Those familiar with Indian and Tibetan contexts may be surprised at this dismissal of debate as a relevant interfaith practice, given how prominent debate was in Indian traditions, both Hindu and Buddhist. If the texts are to be taken literally, debates were taken very seriously and were intensely competitive, with the losing side being required to convert to the winning school in some cases. According to some traditions, early in the history of Tibetan Buddhism, both Chinese and Indian masters, representing two very different schools of Buddhism, were prevalent. Because they were so different, it was decided that Tibetans needed a unified Buddhist path, and that a debate would decide which school would be followed. The Indian scholars were declared the winners of the debate, and the Chinese masters were sent home—at least according to widely circulated legends that many Tibetans take as fact, whether or not the debate ever occurred. To the present day, debate is widely practiced by Tibetan Buddhists. However, everyone knows which arguments and schools are ranked higher and more definitive. Those conclusions were established long ago. Winning the debate depends completely on verbal skills and memorization of many texts. The debater who can remember the appropriate text with which to respond to an opponent's argument wins the debate. Though debating is considered to be good training and people enjoy debates, nothing has been settled by them for centuries, in part because there has been little innovation in Tibetan Buddhism for a long time.

In one case, debate could be an exciting, mutually enriching learning experience, but probably not as a public exercise to be viewed by observers, as debates often are. Suppose colleagues or friends, all highly trained and experienced in their own traditions, who really trust each other's integrity, were to debate really key issues, such as theism versus nontheism or personal immortality versus nonself or rebirth versus nonrebirth? Such a conversation could be truly valuable and helpful for all concerned. But it would work only because all participants have already definitively established that no one claims superiority over their dialogue partners, and so no one is trying to convert anyone to anything. Only differences, which are honored and respected by all participants, are being acknowledged—not deficiency because of difference,. In such an environment, we could openly ask all the questions we've always had about a religious position we just can't fathom but which makes so much sense to people we respect and trust. Such a debate or learning situation would take empathy far beyond anything we can discern with our imagination and with books. But the conditions must be right for such encounters.

Just as dialogue cannot involve debate, fruitful dialogue must not involve mutual fault finding. I remember well one incident in which a very well-known Christian theologian was invited to join an established Buddhist-Christian dialogue group. At that time, we were exploring issues of mutual and general social concern, not theological points of controversy. Our explorations frequently took the form of the Buddhists and the Christians informing each other about what we thought would be a general Buddhist or Christian position on any particular issue, while the other team mainly listened and tried to understand what was being said. There was also a lot of questioning for mutual clarification. But every time a Buddhist tried to explain a likely Buddhist response to an specific issue or problem, the new participant, who knew almost nothing about Buddhism, proclaimed what was wrong with the Buddhist position. (Knowledge about the other tradition was not a prerequisite for participation in this group.) Finally one of the Buddhists gently tried to explain that in dialogue, one needed to take in and understand the other position first, and only much later offer suggestions about similarities, differences, and common concerns, as well as criticisms of positions put forth by one's dialogue partners. The Christian theologian never returned to the group. Perhaps her observations had some validity, but because she simply would not engage as an equal, interested in learning more about her dialogue partners' positions, the situation became unworkable. None of the Buddhists tried to tutor her about what might be wrong with Christian positions on these problems—only about her inadequate dialogue skills.

Finally, though comparative scholarship and discussions of similarities across lines of religious difference often emerge during dialogue, these are not the main purpose of dialogue. Comparisons across religious lines are often helpful for pointing out both similarities and differences among religions and their basic teachings. These similarities and differences can be very difficult to discover on one's own through empathetic study alone. But friendly and exploratory discussions spark mutual discoveries about one another, often followed by the excited comment, "I could never have figured that out on my own!" Not infrequently, we discover that there may be more consonance among people of similar theological and spiritual inclinations across religious lines than with people who are technically one's coreligionists. Those who appreciate dialogue and are sympathetic to modern scholarship about religion usually feel as if they are on common ground, no matter which of the world's differing religions the dialogers may belong to. But it can be difficult to feel much camaraderie with coreligionists who are hostile or indifferent to religious others, or who do not find dialogue interesting or challenging. Nevertheless, such discoveries are more the spontaneous by-product of open-ended discussion and exploration than the deliberate agenda of dialogue. To declare that the agenda of a dialogue is to find similarities or differences across religious boundaries would be too limiting. Even more so, searching for common ground or for a lowest common denominator among the various religions would be far too limiting an agenda for dialogue. It would prejudice the conclusions by favoring the conclusion that there is a lowest common denominator among religions, rather than the conclusion that there are deep differences among the world's major religions. The attempt to find common ground would also play into the lingering fear of diversity and difference that has been criticized so often throughout this book. Better is to have a much more open-ended agenda. Bring together curious, flexible-minded scholar-practitioners of many orientations to simply explore without presuppositions. See what can be discovered together.

What Dialogue Involves

If my suggestion that study of unfamiliar religions rather than dialogue be the first exercise in relating with religious others were followed, those who come to dialogue would be relatively knowledgeable and open minded. Thus, genuine dialogue should be relatively easy for such people, and few guidelines would be necessary. Nevertheless, a few suggestions may be helpful.

The first is that dialogue requires an ability to listen to others attentively, to let them have their say, and to take what they say seriously. One must also be able to listen to things with which one may disagree or that may disturb and upset one without becoming defensive and without having to argue about that point. To be a participant in dialogue also requires polite conversational skills—not interrupting others, not monopolizing speaking time or jumping into the conversation ahead of speakers who have been recognized by the moderator. These comments may seem trivial, but such guidelines are sometimes not so easy for highly educated, opinionated people who are used to talking a lot themselves to follow. I have been in dialogue groups in which there was so much interruption and so many refusals to let those recognized by the moderator speak that finally I refused to participate any further in the session. These issues are especially prevalent when the group is composed mainly of men, with only a few women present. Very recently, even though my presentation was being discussed, I had to demand that I be allowed to enter the discussion. The men in the group simply would not respect or respond to clear signals that after a long silence on my part, it was my turn to speak, and I had something to say. The need for listening skills may seem obvious, but sometimes it is a skill that must be taught and emphasized.

After listening skills, the next most important qualification for successful dialogue is that one be well versed in one's own tradition. Because one will be educating dialogue partners from other religions about one's own tradition, it would be inappropriate for those who participate in dialogue not to be able to represent their own tradition accurately and adequately. Once again, dialogue is serious business, not amateur hour! It is not the most appropriate medium for those who are not knowledgeable at least about their own tradition, even if they sincerely wish to promote interreligious understanding and cooperation. Adult education in one's own tradition and study involving the comparative mirror would be more appropriate first steps. In some dialogue groups significant knowledge about other traditions is not presupposed, especially for participants who are already well established in their own tradition and their own field. Such people will usually know how to learn unfamiliar material quickly. But at least they must be genuinely interested in other, unfamiliar traditions and be committed to furthering interreligious respect and understanding. Given that good dialogue takes considerable amounts of time and some preparation for dialogue meetings, one can also presume that those who become involved in dialogue groups will be committed to the process and its purpose. If one genuinely dislikes or is bored by some of the traditions in the dialogue group, the dialogue will probably not yield favorable results, at least not for that person.

The main requirement for successful dialogue is actually a double requirement. We must be willing to be changed ourselves, if need be, at the same time as we are utterly willing to let others be who they are, without asking them to change. The more one enters into dialogue without significant knowledge about the other traditions in the dialogue, the more this guideline applies. These guidelines apply whether the dialogue is primarily interreligious or intrareligious. Conversations with coreligionists from a different denomination can be more challenging than conversations with members of very different traditions. Clearly, this double guideline is the opposite of entering a dialogue stubbornly convinced that our own understanding is impeccable while thinking that our dialogue partners are deficient in their understanding—which is often the default position from which many people begin difficult conversations.

John Cobb, one of the most important theoreticians of dialogue, put it well. He wrote that "authentic dialogue changes its participants in such a way that new developments beyond dialogue must follow." He calls that the "risk" of dialogue, the risk that "in the process of listening, one will be forced to change in more than a superficial way."[7] He is adamant that in

---

7. Cobb, *Beyond Dialogue*, 47–48.

dialogue, when change is the issue, one must attend to how the dialogue might change oneself, not to how one might want it to change the other. In a potent example, that of Jewish-Christian dialogue, Cobb writes that however much Christians might long for Jews to integrate the story of Jesus into their history, it is not appropriate for Christians to urge Jews in that direction. Instead, "the Christian purpose in the dialogue with Jews must be to change Christianity."[8] After dialogue with Jews, for Christians, the phase "beyond dialogue" would entail Christian transformation away from anti-Jewish teachings and practices. Whether Jews might ever want to incorporate the story of Jesus into Jewish history must be left entirely to them.

This understanding accords well with my own dictum that responsible dialogue demands that we be willing to let our dialogue partners remain who they are. However, the same is expected of them, that they not have an agenda of changing us to be more like them. This is the only possible basis on which I can envision what may well be the most difficult dialogue of all and the dialogue about which I am most often asked: the dialogue between those who make exclusive truth claims or other religious conservatives and those who decry such stances. Even if change or mutual transformation is unlikely to result from such a dialogue, deeper mutual understanding and respect might be possible. That, in itself, would be a worthwhile achievement.

By "mutual transformation," John Cobb does not mean syncretism, nor is he advocating that religions merge their distinct identities so that Buddhism and Christianity, for example, become a single tradition. Rather, each tradition would be transformed by learning something vital from the other that it takes into itself. For Cobb, "Buddhists have a depth of insight into the nature of reality which we [Christians] lack."[9] He claims that it is necessary for Christians to incorporate that understanding into their own theologies before it would be relevant or appropriate to suggest to Buddhists that they might want to convert to Christianity. Before that, they would lose too much in the process of giving up Buddhism and becoming Christians. In the meanwhile, Cobb suggests that Buddhists would become "better Buddhists" if they would incorporate "Jesus Christ into their Buddhism."[10]

The suggestion that religions be open to "mutual transformation through dialogue" has been quite influential in the dialogue movement. After all, the reasoning goes, it is unlikely that any current tradition is perfect,

8. Ibid., 49.

9. Ibid., 51.

10. Ibid., 52.

and it is clear that different religions have different strengths and specialties. It is also quite possible that each religion lacks or is weak in insights that are abundant in another tradition. So, instead of conversion or syncretism, why doesn't each tradition learn from its dialogue partners, incorporating insights from other traditions into itself? Haven't religions always grown and changed by this very process?

In the Buddhist-Christian case, which has been one of the most fruitful, Christians have become enamored of Buddhist discussions of emptiness or the nonsubstantial nature of reality. Because this topic is difficult even for Buddhists to understand and articulate, many Christian discussions of emptiness leave a lot to be desired, but such discussions significantly advance more sophisticated, less personal God-talk among Christians. Christians, especially more contemplative and monastic movements within Christianity, have also been deeply transformed by their participation in Buddhist meditation disciplines. Many Christians, Jews, secularists, and others now practice meditation disciplines derived from Buddhism, regarding them as essential to how their practice of their home tradition. Activists especially, both Christian and from other perspectives, have come to regard such spiritual disciplines as an essential counterbalance to their activism, helping them maintain equanimity in the face of difficult situations and protecting them from burnout

On the Buddhist side, the usual suggestion is that Buddhists should adopt specific allegiance to Jesus Christ is not very workable for Buddhists. We have no problem regarding Jesus as an exemplary, heroic person,[11] but to regard him as uniquely relevant simply goes against the grain of too many Buddhist sensibilities. Easily he can be relevant, but not uniquely relevant in the way that Christians hold so dear. Not even the historical Buddha, Siddartha Gautama, is regarded as unique. Instead, we talk about the "Buddhas of the three times," which clearly indicates that Siddhartha Gautama is not unique but one in a series of similar or identical teachers. Furthermore, eventual Buddhahood is the goal of practitioners of Mahayana Buddhism according to most understandings of that tradition. Given that understanding of the Buddha and Buddhahood, it simply would not be possible for Buddhists to adopt Christian theological understandings of the unique role of Jesus in human history or to regard him as necessary to human well-being.

What is generally much more compelling to Buddhists is the example of effective this-worldly social engagement at which Christians, with their concern for justice, have excelled. The contemporary movement of socially

11. His Holiness, the Dalai Lama XIV, *The Good Heart*; Nhat Hanh, *Living Buddha, Living Christ*; and Nhat Hanh, *Going Home*.

engaged Buddhism, a major movement in contemporary Buddhism, perhaps owes something to Christian inspiration. Buddhists have well developed concepts and practices of compassion, but the term *justice* is not easily
found in Buddhist discourse. Furthermore, many of these practices regarding compassion are contemplative rather than active and focus on becoming
a more skilled and wise person in the future—one who will be much better
equipped to actually help people than one is at present. By contrast, much of
the Engaged Buddhist movement concerns righting things right here, right
now, in this world, rather than waiting for karma and rebirth to eventually
result in payback for unjust dealings in the present situation. In fact, the
Dalai Lama says that the "active model of compassion in Christianity is one
that I urge on my fellow Buddhist monks and nuns."[12] Unfortunately, more
conservative elements of the monastic *sangha* do not believe such activity is proper for those who have renounced the world as monks and nuns.
Despite their protests, however, the Engaged Buddhist movement is quite
alive and well. Thus, this movement could be seen as the Buddhist parallel
to Christian liberation theology, which likewise is impatient with the claim
that the next world and the next life will make up for injustice in this world.

One very famous example of Christian influence on a Buddhist concerns *Dharma* master Cheng Yen, the founder of the largest Buddhist relief
organization in the world, Tzu Chi. Two events in her life were deeply trans-
formational. In 1966, already a Buddhist nun, she saw a pool of blood on
the floor of a local clinic and learned that an Aboriginal woman suffering a
miscarriage had been denied treatment because her relatives did not have
the money to pay the clinic's fees. The woman died as a result. Not long afterwards, some Christian nuns came to visit Cheng Yen and they conversed
about the precepts and teachings of their respective religions. When Cheng
Yen explained that Buddhism teaches love and compassion for all living beings, which is certainly correct, the Christian nuns asked, "Why have we
not seen Buddhists doing good works for the society, such as setting up
nursing homes, orphanages, and hospitals?" This question, combined with
the recent incident regarding the Aboriginal woman, had a deep impact on
Cheng Yen and was the impetus for her to found her very successful relief
movement.[13] She did not convert to Christianity, nor does she regard Jesus
Christ as her mentor in founding Tzu Chi after her conversation with the
Christian nuns, but I suspect that John Cobb might regard this as a valid
example of "transformation through dialogue" nevertheless!

---

12. His Holiness, the Dalai Lama XIV, *Toward a True Kinship of Faiths*, 63.

13. Tzu Chi Foundation, "Biography of Dharma Master ChengYen." This story is
found in many sources and is frequently retold.

Tzu Chi is only one example of socially engaged Buddhism, which is now quite prevalent in Asian Buddhism. It is impossible to determine exactly how much of the Engaged Buddhist movement is due specifically to the Christian example and how much is due to modernity in general, which has shifted most religions from an emphasis on the afterlife to an emphasis on the here and now. What is often called humanistic Buddhism and sometimes called secular Buddhism is now widely practiced. Direct Christian influence, so obvious in the case of Master Cheng Yen, is not always so easy to demonstrate, and some Engaged Buddhists would resist the claim that examples of Christian charity are their main inspiration for more social engagement than was characteristic of most Buddhisms some centuries ago. However, other theoreticians of Engaged Buddhism, such as John Makransky, argue that Buddhists could learn a great deal from those concerns—especially of Christian liberation theology with its claim that religious people should be specifically oriented to those most marginalized in society. He claims that Buddhism does not currently include such concern, to Buddhism's detriment.[14]

However, in the end, I would not regard the main purpose of dialogue as changing either one's self or one's partners. Such changes may happen, especially for dialogue participants who know less about the religions of their dialogue partners when they begin the dialogue. But the main point of dialogue is simply to learn about and understand others better, because face-to-face contact goes beyond what other forms of learning can provide. More accurate and empathetic understanding of our coinhabitants on the small planet Earth is change enough. It results in a level of understanding and appreciation that we could never come up with by ourselves. Could there be any deeper motivation for dialogue?

Kinds of Dialogue and Subjects for Dialogue

It is common in dialogue circles to talk of four main arenas for dialogue: the dialogue of life, which pertains mainly to coexistence and mutual tolerance among religions; the dialogue of social action, which involves different religions working together on common issues; the dialogue of discourse, which involves discussion of theological similarities and differences; and the dialogue of religious experience, which involves participating together in religious practices, especially meditation and liturgy. There is, of course, no sharp division among these four arenas. A single dialogue group could

14. Makransky, "A Buddhist Critique of and Learning from Christian Liberation Theology."

discuss all four arenas, though there tends to be some difference between groups that focus on theology and those that focus on religious experience. Understandably, theologians and scholars are drawn to the dialogue of discourse while monastics and contemplatives are drawn to the dialogue of religious experience. However, both types of group tend to also focus on the dialogue of social action from time to time because it is both easier and more practical to focus on common problems. To many, these common problems facing all religions, such as poverty, injustice, and environmental degradation, also have more urgency than theological agreements and disagreements or the compatibility of various spiritual disciplines. It is also much easier to find areas of agreement about these social issues than to find other such agreement, especially on metaphysical and theological issues.

In his proposals of how the world's religions can come together, the Dalai Lama also suggests four major arenas in which religions could cooperate, learn from each other, and work together. Two of them, dialogues among academic spokespersons from the various traditions and dialogues among accomplished contemplatives from the various traditions, duplicate those found in the more general list presented above. His other two proposals, meetings among high-level religious leaders, and joint pilgrimages to places sacred to the various religions, are different.[15]

As chapter 11 discussed, I am somewhat skeptical about highly publicized meetings of major religious authorities from the various religions. Probably they do no harm, but whether they actually make any difference is questionable because the proclamations that come out of these meetings are often vague and platitudinous. Whether they have yet led to real changes in the internal policies of the various religions is open to question. Furthermore, they are not very representative, given that few, if any, women will be included in those meetings. How relevant can dialogues that exclude more than half of humanity be? Joint pilgrimage to sacred places, which would probably be illuminating, could be an seen as extension of the dialogue of religious practice.

Other, more practical questions are also important if successful dialogues are to occur. Is dialogue more effective between two partners or among a larger group representing many religions? In my experience in dialogue, there is no definitive answer to this question. In a dialogue between representatives of two traditions, discussion can be more focused, comparisons and contrasts are easier to highlight, and joint proposals are easier to come by. Furthermore, some issues pertain only to two or a small number of the world's traditions. For example, Jews and Christians, Jews and

15. His Holiness, the Dalai Lama XIV, *Toward a True Kinship of Faiths*, 133.

Muslims, and Protestants and Catholics have specific issues between them. Sometimes, as in the case of Jews and Christians, a difficult history between the two traditions makes dialogue essential to healing and ability to work together in the future. Another such case, much less well-known in most of the world, would involve Buddhists and Muslims, who have had a difficult history with each other and also have difficult relations with each other in some parts of the world today. Another case sorely needing, but not yet receiving, specific attention involves the four so-called *dharma* traditions: Buddhism, Hinduism, Jainism, and Sikhism. It is often assumed that because these four traditions have a common origin in India and share aspects of the same worldview, relationships among them are smooth, and that adherents largely agree with each other. But this is not an accurate perception, and dialogue among these traditions is sorely needed, even though finding sponsorship for such dialogues is quite difficult. In all these cases, members of other traditions would probably have little they could contribute to these discussions. Their presence might even inhibit open, frank discussions or the development of deep trust between the dialogers. Definitely in some cases restricting dialogue to specific dialogue partners is warranted.

However, there are more than two or three major religions in the world, which means that dialogues limited to specific religions are not always adequate. Many problems that religions need to deal with are global issues from which no religion is exempt. Certainly key among them is the question of how to cope, and then to flourish, with religious diversity itself. Surely this is an issue concerning which the various religions could inspire and advise each other. Perhaps no other issue is so central to the well-being of the religions themselves. Yet very few interreligious meetings are devoted specifically to developing strategies and theologies that promote flourishing with religious diversity. Instead of simply issuing their own proclamations about religious diversity, based only on internal theological and spiritual resources and often rather unimaginative, why don't religious people and their organizations come to appreciate each other's humanity, theological acumen, and spiritual depth through dialogue?

Another topic very low on the radar for interreligious discussion but deeply problematic for all religions is their sexism and male dominance. In chapter 11 I jokingly suggested that the long-sought lowest common denominator among religions might be their sexism, but that is hardly a common feature to be celebrated. Instead, it should be overcome. But, except for small meetings of women who have little institutional power, I know of no major international interreligious meetings specifically devoted to the topic of how religions could cooperate and learn from each other to overcome sexism. There is usually much more willingness to meet to discuss topics such as poverty, racism, violence, or environmental degradation, which are also urgent, of course. But willingness to discuss such topics cannot excuse overlooking topics like how to cooperate and inspire each other to overcome discomfort with religious diversity, sexism and male dominance, homophobia, or disenfranchisement of minority groups. I know of no dialogue group or format specifically designed to discuss any of those above-mentioned, equally urgent issues. But such dialogue groups and topics would be more than timely.

One of the major problems with larger, more inclusive forums for inter-religious exchange is that, somehow, the notion has developed that there are five major traditions—Hinduism, Buddhism, Christianity, Judaism, and Islam. This is a highly inaccurate characterization of the world's religions because it entirely omits East Asian traditions (except for East Asian Buddhisms), the indigenous traditions found around the world, and many smaller religions. It would be helpful if those responsible for organizing such meetings could take this major oversight into account and make corrections.

Another question about what kinds of dialogues are most successful and productive concerns size and continuity. Very large meetings, such as the Parliament of the World's Religions, can be exciting, and certainly many people can benefit and learn from such meetings. On the other hand, they are not very effective for intensive, sustained discussions of major topics and may well not produce lasting or significant results. In my own experience, I have found smaller groups to be much more effective in the long run. However, even more important, at least in my experience, is continuity. Being in a dialogue group involves and invites a certain kind of vulnerability. If we are going to discuss difficult, sensitive issues together across religious lines, it is important for dialogers to come to know each other well and to develop trust in each other. That takes time. Thus, the most successful dialogue groups are smaller groups that gather for a series of meetings over a number of years. Otherwise, such meetings can be interesting but may not result in much real transformation, either for individuals or for religious groups.

When such relationships of trust have developed, one of the most interesting and effective techniques, which works better with two partners (groups or individuals) rather than in more inclusive groups, is for members of one partnering religious group to comment on a topic important to the *other* partnering religious group, rather than to present materials about their own religion. Then members of the religion being commented on reply to initial comments on their religion made by their dialogue partners. In two examples of such dialogues, Buddhists offered their reflections on Jesus, and Christians did the same about the Buddha. Then Christians commented on what the Buddhists had said about Jesus and vice versa. The same exercise was undertaken on the subjects Christian prayer and Buddhist meditation.[16] When enough trust has developed to proceed with this kind of dialogue, some truly interesting reflections can occur. In many case, they result in the reaction, "How interesting! I could never have thought that up by myself!" In such examples, we see how far actual dialogue with religious others, rather than simply studying them and reading about them can take us—if we are willing to abide by the disciplines and guidelines required for safe and effective dialogue.

Thus, interreligious dialogue and exchange is one important tool in the project of developing integrity in our dealings with religious others and beginning to flourish with religious diversity. But it is by no means a panacea or an overarching solution because dialogue is too difficult and presents so many challenges. As has repeatedly been emphasized, internal preparation and readiness for dialogue on the part of each participant in a dialogue is crucial. Without it, dialogue would be largely ineffective, perhaps even counterproductive. Much of that preparation is the work of individuals and religious institutions. Individuals need to take on the responsibility of learning enough about unfamiliar religions to be able to live comfortably and responsibly in a religiously diverse world. And religious institutions need to learn how better to minister to their members who live in a religiously diverse world, which begins with more responsible training of those who minister to those who live in that religiously diverse world.

16. Gross and Muck, *Buddhists Talk about Jesus, Christians Talk about the Buddha*; and Gross and Muck, *Christians Talk about Buddhist Meditation, Buddhists Talk about Christian Prayer*.

Chapter 16

Ministry in a Multifaith World

Training and Responsibilities of Leaders of (Majority) Religions

NEAR THE END OF his large sociological account of religious diversity in America, Robert Wuthnow reports:

> Although it is common to give lip service to the value of diversity, many Americans regard religions other than their own as fanatical, conducive to violence, closed-minded, backward and strange. A large minority (at least a third) say they would not welcome these religions becoming a stronger presence in our society. A large minority would not be happy about mosques and temples being built in their neighborhoods, they would not want a child of theirs to marry a Muslim or Hindu, and some would even make it illegal for those religious groups to meet.[1]

He also reports that though many people think they should learn more about other religions, "few of those who belong to churches have experienced opportunities to learn more about the teachings and practices of other religions in those contexts."[2] That may be because, as Diana Eck reports, "few theological schools are able to equip Christian or Jewish clergy for their changing educational roles in this new ministerial context."[3] As

1. Wuthnow, *America and the Challenges of Religious Diversity,* 228.

2. Ibid., 229.

3. Eck, *A New Religious America,* 23.

a result, these clergy, for various reasons, avoid educating their members about religious diversity and avoid meeting with their counterparts in other religions, even in neighborhoods characterized by religious diversity. In fact, they pretend that their neighborhoods, cities, and nation are as monolithic as they were a generation or two ago. But changes in immigration laws in the 1960s drastically altered that situation. Now most of their parishioners will encounter members of other religions at work or school. Many of them will have neighbors of other faiths, and some of them will even have family members who belong to no variety of Christianity. Nevertheless, their religious leaders know no more about these other religions than the generally negative views summarized above.

Most people are not natural leaders but follow patterns that are already well laid out in their religion or society. Original thought is very difficult, which is why it is so rare. So whatever patterns are exhibited by large numbers of people in any society probably result from what a few leaders are teaching and presenting. I would also argue, both because of Buddhist teachings, and through and my own experiences and observations, that most people are kind and well meaning by disposition, that in most situations folks are more inclined to help others than to harm them. Nevertheless, students frequently came to my classes in world religions with rather negative attitudes about other (usually non-Christian) religions, attitudes not too different from those described above by Wuthnow. This seems like a contradiction. People are generally more inclined to kindness than to hostility, except regarding abstractions called other religions. If such students were to meet living human beings, adherents of these religions, they might well strike up friendships with them. But they also know, ahead of time and without much information about them, that these other religions are something to be avoided and feared, something that could be quite dangerous.

Where do these attitudes come from? Only two sources are likely—their parents, and the religious institutions that indoctrinated them as children. These two sources are really only one source, for their parents were also formed by the same or very similar religious institutions. Most people do follow their leaders. And many leaders of majority religions, Christianity for most North Americans, lead their followers into *us/them* oppositional dualism regarding unfamiliar religions. In many cases, they teach their followers that other religions are a problem. They build up enthusiasm for their own religion among their followers by negative contrasts with other religions. They often discourage even such nontheological, content-free practices as basic mindfulness meditation or yoga. Much of their leadership appears to be fear based rather than confidence based, as if they do not think that their followers will love their own tradition simply on its own merits, without recourse to whipped-up enthusiasm depending on negative comments about other religions and *us/them* oppositional dualisms. As one commentator put it, "Our root problem is the *hostility* that we often employ to make and keep our identities strong."[4] Being so dependent on hostility and fear is odd, even inexplicable for the leaders of an old, well-established, strong, majority tradition. Why do they lead in such counterintuitive and counterproductive ways?

Very likely it is because that's where these leaders themselves were led, especially when they were students at seminaries and other institutions for training pastors and other religious leaders. If flourishing with religious diversity is to become a reality, these institutions are the bottleneck that must change. They hold one of the major keys to such change. As interfaith leader Eboo Patel put it, seminaries "will play an outsize role in America's interfaith future. They train religious leaders, they advance new theological understandings, and they send signals that point the way for denominations and congregations."[5] If they graduate new ministers and other religious leaders who are well educated about religious diversity, who appreciate rather than fear religious diversity, then the local congregations to which they are sent will begin to educate their own members differently. But if seminaries and other such institutions do not teach accurate information about other religions and instead build strong religion-specific identities by fostering oppositional *us/them* identities in their students, professors of comparative studies in religion will continue to encounter university students who are uncomfortable when asked to develop empathy for different, unfamiliar religions. These students will be uncomfortable because they will have been trained in such attitudes at their churches and other religious institutions. The leaders of those local congregations, in turn, have trained their congregants as they have because of how they themselves were trained in their own student days as seminarians. Their training involved a combination of ignoring other religions and building up a strong identity dependent on *us/them* contrasts with other religions—ours is unquestionably better, truer, or the like. It is difficult to avoid the conclusion that the weak link in the project of learning how to flourish with religious diversity is seminary training; or that if the training improved, seminaries could become the lynchpin fostering congregations and citizens that delight in religious diversity.

---

4. McLaren, *Why Did Jesus, Moses, the Buddha, and Mohammed Cross the Road?*, 63.

5. Patel, *Sacred Ground*, 128.

Problems with Identity Formation
in Religious Majorities and Other Groups

All over the world and throughout history, majorities and dominant groups have misused their status to enforce conformity and to exercise privileges over minorities and less dominant groups. Even more problematic, however, is the negativity and hostility majority groups have often fostered towards minority groups and those who are different. As we have seen many times, when religion is at stake, that hostility often includes a view that the others—those who differ religiously—shouldn't even exist. If we have been taught by religious authorities whom we respect that religious others are wrong and inferior, it becomes easy to think that "the long-term existence and well-being of *them* . . . [is] unacceptable, perhaps . . . an offense or threat to us and our religion, and perhaps even . . . an offense to God." It also becomes easy to think that "the world would be a better place without *them* in it." They become acceptable only if they convert to become *us*, and are no longer *them*. "After all, if *they* were good, they would ask to be admitted under *our* sacred canopy and they would join us in circling around *our* sacred center."[6]

It is shocking enough when racial or ethnic groups or the dominant gender or sexual orientation think about themselves with such attitudes of superiority and scorn, never even stopping to reflect that in those cases, the *others* cannot even become *us*, cannot join the in-group. But it is even more shocking when religious groups think in such manner. After all, religions are supposed to foster love and compassion, not hostility and scorn. How can religions go so far astray, becoming such purveyors of negative attitudes toward those who are different religiously?

With Christian author Brian D. McLaren, I would argue that such outcomes result when the process of identity formation goes awry, as well as when it is not understood that identity is always a work in progress and never a finished entity (see chapter 9). Such mistakes about identity formation are a special problem when engaged in by majorities because of the power majorities have. But minorities also indulge in the same mistakes in identity formation, making it very easy for them to nurture a perpetual sense of victimhood, which makes large scale reconciliation and healing more difficult. McLaren differentiates between a religious identity that is "strong/benevolent" and one that is "strong/hostile" rather than between religious identities that are "weak/benign" versus "strong/hostile" (the more usual dichotomy drawn between types of religious identity). Many fundamentalists

6. McLaren, *Why Did Jesus, Moses, the Buddha, and Mohammed Cross the Road?*, 63.

and other religious conservatives value having a strong religious identity, being definite about being Christian or of whatever other religious group they identify with; these find a weak or wishy-washy religious stance unattractive, even repellent. If their only choices are between a "weak/benign" identity or a "strong/hostile" identity, they will choose the "strong/hostile" identity. McLaren clarifies that for many, including himself at one time, a strong religious identity includes hostility towards or at least disapproval of those with other religious persuasions or no religious persuasion. To such people, those who have benign attitudes towards other religions also seem to have a weak Christian (or other) religious identity.[7] But why the correlation between a strong religious identity and hostility towards or discomfort with other religions?

McLaren clarifies that the *intention* on the part of the person with the "strong/hostile" religious identity is not hostility at all. Instead, in their own minds, they are acting on their love of and enthusiasm for their own tradition. As he puts it, religion inspires not hate but "love so powerful that [it] can be expressed without conscious intention through hateful action."[8] Religious hostility "'comes from a kind of love or desire for love for one's own group and a willingness to do whatever it takes to obtain it.'"[9] What to those on the receiving end of such actions feels hostile is only an expression of faithfulness to the perpetrators. That is why many with a "strong/hostile" identity hear a plea for them to be more knowledgeable about and friendly towards those who are different religiously as "a temptation to love God, their religion, their community, their ancestors, their history, and their future less."[10] Using duality to create, reinforce or maintain a specific identity is quite common, perhaps even unavoidable at a certain, somewhat early stage of development. Nevertheless, reifying such duality and regarding it as supremely important is deeply, sadly mistaken. The flourishing of differences is not a zero-sum game in which if my group is no longer disapproved of, that results in your group being less favored or loved. There is room for both of us to experience love and approval.

Nevertheless, especially when the epitome of love is expressed as the desire to convert me, or even when it takes the milder form of disliking my religion, it is hostility. When you want to interfere with my very being, what is most important to me, what makes me *me*, how can you mistake that interference for love? It is hostility, pure and simple—hostility towards me,

---

7. Ibid., 40–43.

8. Ibid., 43.

9. Ariel Glucklick, quoted in ibid., 43–44.

10. Ibid., 44.

towards what and who I am. What makes you think you know what I need or what is best for me? Why does difference make you uncomfortable? What makes you so insecure that you want the whole world to be more like you? At points such as these, it is crucial to remember that *compassion has nothing to do with interfering with others.* Compassion is letting them/us be as they/we are and fostering well-being both for them and for us. In so doing, we are much more in touch with our deepest inclinations, which are toward friendliness rather than hostility. We have let ourselves be betrayed when we give in to dualistic leanings toward hostility. And if we have been led down that path by religious teachers and authorities, that is really a problem, especially in the case of a large, dominant, well-established religion, which Christianity is in North America. But why do those leaders lead us in such misguided directions? We are back to the question of how they themselves were taught and led.

Leadership Responsibilities of Liberal and Moderate Christians or Other Religious Majorities

Because diversity is a reality within religions as well as between religions, there is always a variety of attitudes towards other religions within any religion, whether it is a majority, dominant religion or a smaller tradition. Though exclusive truth claims have been the official doctrine of many Christian denominations for most of their history and many still adhere to these claims rather aggressively, there have always been dissenters. Their numbers have increased dramatically in the past half century, as people everywhere become more knowledgeable about other religions and as local religious diversity increases everywhere in the world. As we know. Christian pluralists now proclaim that Christianity is *not* the only true religion, that other religions also contain truth and relevance, and that their members are not at any spiritual disadvantage to Christians. However, at this time, pluralism is probably not the dominant theology of religions among Christians.

In this situation, pluralist and even inclusivist members of religions that characteristically make exclusive truth claims have certain responsibilities to articulate their positions forcefully, especially if they are pastors, theologians, professors at seminaries, or other religious leaders. Given that, according to Wuthnow, approximately a third of their fellow citizens still have negative attitudes towards other religions, it is crucial for this more moderate contingent to speak up forcefully rather than to be timid about proclaiming the inappropriateness of exclusive truth claims in a religiously diverse society (or in any other society, for that matter).

Such people usually also have progressive views on matters such as racism, sexism, poverty, homophobia, and other such issues. They usually criticize ethnocentrism of any kind. (Given the link between religion and culture and the fact that their religious affiliation is a matter of birth for most people, exclusive truth claims could and should be considered a species of ethnocentrism, in my view.) Typically, these people declare their stands on such issues quite publicly, writing and speaking on these issues if they are in positions to do so. I advocate that they should be equally vociferous about their pluralist stance vis-à-vis other religions.

Nevertheless, I sometimes detect less fervor in their proclamations about their pluralist theologies than in their proclamations about racism, sexism, poverty, or ethnocentrism. They denounce those positions without excusing those who hold them for being sincere but misguided. Regarding racism, sexism, or the pursuit of policies that lead to huge economic ineq-uities, there simply is no latitude for mistaken sincerity. Generally, we take sincerity to be an admirable quality, but we do not exempt positions from criticism because those who hold the positions are sincere. The *position* is ruthlessly and thoroughly critiqued. But when cataloguing and discussing positions in the theology of religions, pluralists and other liberals often simply list the exclusivist position as one of the possible options within the theology of religions. They may mention that they do not agree with it, but often the exclusivist position is not severely critiqued, nor are its inadequacies made apparent.

When I have discussed this problem with certain pluralist theologians, they have replied that I am not sufficiently cognizant of how painful it is for exclusivists to give up their position, so it is appropriate to go easier on them. But they would never make the same case for racists, sexists, so-called class enemies, and, increasingly, homophobes—all positions that were once as acceptable, even for religious people, as exclusive truth claims have been and still are for many. Instead, most liberal and pluralist spokespersons for religions now find it exceedingly embarrassing to be reminded that their re-ligions once supported not just racism but slavery, not just sexism but total lack of self-determination for women, not just the acceptability of economic inequity but the necessity of social Darwinism. It is to be hoped that in the future, they will be equally embarrassed that their religions once sup-ported exclusive truth claims, sought to become the sole surviving religion on planet Earth, and fostered beliefs that those who did not agree with them religiously would suffer eternal woe.

Often the latitude given to those who still make exclusive truth claims derives from long-standing interpretations of certain familiar Bible verses, especially the one (Acts 4:12) that led Paul Knitter to title his first book on the theology of religions *No Other Name?*[11] This is not much of an excuse, however, for biblical interpretation is enormously plastic. As a child, I was taught biblical interpretations used to justify regarding people of color as inferior to white people, to say nothing of interpretations that justified sexism, homophobia, anti-Catholicism, anti-Judaism, antiscience, and a whole host of other *antis* As an outsider to the game of biblical interpretation who is, nevertheless, quite familiar with it, I find it difficult to avoid the somewhat cynical conclusion that many have made about this enterprise: one can prove anything you want to from the Bible. Biblical interpretation often follows, rather than leads, prevailing social opinions. The fact that Christians have long believed in exclusive truth claims is no excuse for maintaining such beliefs in vastly changed circumstances.

What has changed? I appeal again to John Hick's notion of a "Copernican revolution" regarding both our knowledge of religion and our thinking about religion. Though our world has always been characterized by religious diversity, we are now much more aware of it than in previous centuries. This is the case especially for the Christian West, which was very isolated intellectually and spiritually during its most formative periods and after it became almost the only religion in its known world—Europe. Furthermore, religions are no longer geographically isolated in regions of the world that are relatively homogeneous religiously. Almost everywhere, people of different religious persuasions live in close proximity with one another. Even for adherents in regions that suffer the misfortune of being relatively monolithic religiously, accurate, in-depth knowledge about other religions is readily available. People who live in such places also have an ethical responsibility to avoid antagonistic attitudes about people of other faiths and to learn more about them.

Furthermore, it is important to be clear about the specifics of what parts of exclusive truth claims are inappropriate now, and perhaps always were inappropriate. First of all, as discussed above, building up and protecting a strong identity by means of negative contrast with others, which essentially demonizes others, is inappropriate. Such a move is always tempting, and great diligence is required to avoid it. Nevertheless, it seems to me that finding one's own strength by denigrating others violates Christian ethics about loving neighbors and enemies. It also seems to me that such ethics take precedence over proclamations about the exclusive relevance of certain names. Such ethics become even more relevant when we remember the guideline that compassion and love includes not interfering so much with others. Religiously, the supreme interference with others is obsessive

11. Knitter, *No Other Name?*

concern with converting them to one's own religion. As was demonstrated in my close analysis of religious exclusivity in chapter 4, it is entirely possible to experience a strong love for Jesus, even regarding him as a *universal* savior without needing to think that everyone else also *must* come to hold that belief "for their own good," the phrase that so commonly comes to our lips when we feel driven to interfere with others. Only these two strategies commonly employed by those who hold exclusive truth claims—building up one's own identity by means of negative contrast with others, and trying so hard to interfere with others' religious affiliations and orientations—need to be given up. Nothing else.

These comments are relevant in many religious contexts, of course. However, currently in the North American context, it would be most helpful for comments such as these to emanate especially from the liberal and progressive Christians most likely to hold pluralist theologies of religion. I really do think it is important for such people not to be timid or hesitant in arguing against exclusive truth claims. Because such claims are as problematic as sexism, racism, or homophobia, they should be countered with equal vigor. It is crucial that coreligionists of those most likely to hold and voice exclusively truth claims and negative attitudes towards other religions speak up forcefully and often. That responsibility should not be left to Muslims, Hindus, and Buddhists—those most likely to be on the receiving end of Christian discomfort with other religions. Certainly more folks are likely to take seriously the comments and advice of a co-religionist than the advice of an outsider from another religion, such as myself.

The Responsibilities of (Christian) Seminaries in a Religiously Diverse World

As Eboo Patel points out, "seminaries will play an outsize role in America's interfaith future" because they train the next generation of local religious leaders, and are where emerging religious issues are most extensively discussed.[12] So, given that Christianity is the majority religion in North America, what goes on in Christian seminaries and schools of theology will determine whether or not North Americans become more adept at flourishing with religious diversity. Paying attention to religious diversity and ascertaining what promotes or diminishes ability to be comfortable with religious diversity must become major agendas for seminaries and schools of theology if this vision is to be fulfilled.

12. See note 4.

The agenda of such institutions must change from producing graduates educated only in their own denominational tradition, devoted to it as the One True Faith, and dedicated only to reproducing those views in their congregants to graduating ministers and pastors who are religiously literate in broad and comprehensive ways. Their graduates must be competent and fit to serve in a religiously diverse world, to serve congregants who will have many different interactions with people of many religious persuasions. To be able to function well in a multifaith world, seminarians, like everyone else, need to become well educated in the comparative mirror. (See chapter 14.) For many seminaries and schools of religion to be able to fulfill these new agendas, curricula and faculty will need to be augmented and supplemented because, at present, they do not and cannot provide adequate instruction in the diverse religions.

However, given that seminaries are educating students to fill different roles in society than the colleges and other educational institutions discussed in chapter 14, somewhat different solutions are required. In universities, high schools, community colleges, and other such institutions, the emphasis must be on neutrality, both among religions and between religious versus nonreligious options. The purpose of such forums is to produce not adherents of any religious position but people who are well informed about the various options. Therefore, I have always advocated that those who teach in such forums keep their religious affiliations to themselves as much as possible. Even more, their job is to present all options as empathetically as possible. They teach *about* religion, but they do not provide religious instruction. The distinction between teaching *about* religion and teaching religion is always crucial. By contrast, seminaries are producing religious leaders with specific religious loyalties, who will function in religion-specific institutions. They have always done that. What is new is that such leaders now have much more responsibility to lead cognizant of the fact that religious diversity is an inevitable, enduring fact of human existence. That means that seminarians must be much better educated, both in terms of accuracy and of empathy, about the world's religions. The major question is how to do that.

Seminaries are places where people with specific religious orientations and affiliations gather for educational purposes. In such institutions, professors not only teach *about* religion; they also teach religion. That is to say, a legitimate part of their teaching mission is to influence students' views about religions. But currently the educational mission of seminaries must expand to include teaching the world's diverse religions. In an institution in which religious instruction is appropriate, those who teach those diverse religions should teach them with the same forthrightness and conviction with which the mainstream religion of the seminary is taught. This can be done most authentically and enthusiastically by scholar-practitioners of those traditions, not by Christians or unaffiliated scholars. Religions other than Christianity need to be presented unmediated by a Christian lens. Seminary students, tomorrow's religious leaders and pastors of local congregations, need and deserve that level of engaged, realistic contact with other religions. Anything less would result in a tepid, unconvincing representation of those traditions, not the real thing. The various religions would not be on a level playing field, and the comparative mirror would not be truly available. The home religion of the institution would be presented authentically, but the others much less so.

Two points are essential here: First, seminary students preparing to be religious leaders and ministers in a multifaith world need adequate training about the other religions. That claim would be difficult to deny or ignore under current conditions. Second, the adequate training is best delivered by scholar-practitioners of those other religions. As when one studies a foreign language, one benefits greatly from talking with native speakers of the language, so in the study of religion, insiders have something to offer that is difficult for outsiders to duplicate. Scholar-practitioner speakers of Buddhism and other religions would be much more able to engender empathy in students than outsiders. If the justification for this innovation is still unclear, remember the Dalai Lama's comment that meeting living practitioners of other religions gave him a vastly different impression of those religions from what he had learned about them from his Buddhist "seminary" professors.

Nevertheless, despite these strong arguments that non-Christian scholar-practitioners should have a role in seminary education, I know firsthand that many Christians object to non-Christians teaching anything, even their own religions, at seminaries. Because of my commitment to multifaith work, at one point I tried very hard to be hired to teach world religions at a seminary. I could deliver the scholar-practitioner's insider perspective on Buddhism and was well equipped to offer empathic portraits of other religions. But sometimes job listings for positions to teach interreligious dialogue and world religions would specify that the applicant had to be an actively practicing Christian. On other occasions, I would be told that the seminary's donors and board of directors simply would not allow the seminary to hire any non-Christian, no matter how qualified or interested in multifaith education. The same would sometimes happen at church-affiliated colleges. Apparently, in such cases, it is legal to discriminate on the basis of religion, even though it is commonly thought that such discrimination is illegal. I have always been shocked by such outright prejudice, especially given the need for authentic, adequate teaching of other religions in today's religiously diverse world.

Instead of pursuing the solution of employing religious insiders to teach their own traditions, thus improving seminary education in myriad ways, many other solutions, none of them very courageous or adequate, are offered instead. In some schools of theology, courses in non-Christian religions may be required, but they are taught by part-time adjuncts who may not have the training that would be desirable for teaching these courses. This strikes me as feeble, as not taking religious diversity seriously, but as trying to look good on paper, as if training in diversity is being provided. But serious teaching of non-Christian religions would require appointments of the same caliber as the appointments in Christian topics. If adjuncts must be used for financial reasons, which is relatively common, it would be less damaging to the overall curriculum to have a few of the many courses on Christianity taught by adjuncts than to hire adjuncts for the few courses on non-Christian religion.

Sometimes a local religious leader from one of the non-Christian religions is invited to teach a course or two. But that solution also does not take the non-Christian religions very seriously. All other courses are taught by academically trained professionals who have ongoing seminary positions, not by local Christian clergy who may have little or no academic training in religious studies. Again, a commitment to taking education in religious diversity seriously would require that faculty appointments for teaching Christian and non-Christian religions be of the same caliber.

Another solution is hiring a committed Christian to teach about Buddhism or other religions to other committed Christians. This solution also strikes me as trying to have it both ways, as a solution that provides some exposure to non-Christian religions but in a very safe, unchallenging environment. Because most Christian seminary professors will espouse either exclusive or inclusive truth claims regarding Christianity, they are ill prepared to present non-Christian religions in an authentic way, making this perhaps the least adequate solution of all. Under these conditions, students would be able to study *about* Buddhism, but they will not be able to study Buddhism. Because a level playing field is not set up, it will be difficult for the comparative mirror to work. Students are unlikely to become "a phenomenon to themselves" and to see their world as *a* world, rather than *the* normal, obvious world of Christianity when both the students and their professor know ahead of time that Christianity is *the* privileged position for both. (A Christian pluralist well trained in non-Western religions might be the sole exception to this generalization.)

Finally, in the context of a seminary, the adequate solution would not involve hiring a supposedly neutral specialist to teach about the various non-Christian religions. However valuable such scholars can be in departments of religious studies, their approach and strategy are much less useful in the context of a seminary. Such religiously neutral area specialists only teach *about* Buddhism; they do not have the requirements for teaching Buddhism from the inside, as would a scholar-practitioner. Nor would this solution put the various religions on a level playing field either. Christianity would be taught as a living, vibrant tradition by Christian scholar-practitioners, whereas Buddhism or other religions would be taught as a set of facts and figures, again *othering* them and keeping them at a distance.

All these pseudosolutions for addressing a real need at seminaries leave me asking a real question. What is the agenda of seminaries? Is it true education, or is it only indoctrination? If the goal is genuine education appropriate for addressing the real situation that will be faced by seminary graduates, such institutions should be eager to provide their students with ways to study more authentically and accurately with and about their partners and colleagues in the religiously diverse world. That is to say, they would be eager to have their students study directly *with* scholar-practitioners of those traditions. Indoctrination, on the other hand, involves isolating students from members of other traditions and teaching about other traditions only by means of apologetic literature from their own tradition. Such literature is deliberately one-sided, designed to convince students that their religion is vastly superior to any other tradition. (Remember the Dalai Lama's assessment of such literature from his own tradition.) This is indoctrination, not education.

As was the case with individuals, so it is with institutions and denominations. "Our root problem is the *hostility* that we often employ to make and keep our identities strong."[13] One should not have to promote one's own religion by inaccurate representations of other religions. If that is the only way that seminaries and other religious institutions can produce loyal, enthusiastic leaders for their congregations, something is drastically wrong. A strong identity in one's own tradition should not be the result of isolation from and negative comparisons with other traditions but of simple joy in one's own being. People are inclined to friendliness, not hostility, all other things being equal. But if seminaries do not see their way to educating and then graduating students who are *both* deeply appreciative of their own traditions and respectful of and informed about other traditions, the conditions described by Wuthnow at the beginning of this chapter will continue to

13. See note 3 above.

prevail. As Eboo Patel said, seminaries "will play an outsize role in America's interfaith future. They train religious leaders, they advance new theological understandings, and they send signals that point the way for denominations and congregations."[14] Which will it be? Weak link or lynchpin?

The Fear Factor

Much of the entrenchment of current seminary teaching about religious diversity is, I believe, based in fear. As I said at the beginning of this chapter, much conventional religious leadership seems more fear based than confidence based. Leaders act and speak as if they do not think people will continue to be loyal to their tradition on its merits alone but need some extra boosting in the form of negative comparisons with other religions. It is as if our tradition becomes more worthy only by deeming other traditions to be less worthy. But if the worth of one's own tradition is dualistically based, if that worth depends on the inferiority of other traditions, what happens if it becomes impossible to definitively demonstrate that other traditions are, in fact, inferior? As Wilfred Cantwell Smith noticed long ago, in such dualistic systems of evaluating religions, "one's chances of getting to Heaven . . . are dependent on other people not getting there." In the same essay, he also commented:

> From the notion that if Christianity is true, then other religions must be false . . . it is possible to go on to the converse proposition: if anyone else's faith turns out to be valid or adequate, then it would turn out that Christianity must be false.[15]

If one holds that logic, consciously or unconsciously, it would be a frightening prospect indeed if other religions turn out to be sensible and attractive when taught by insider scholar-practitioners. Remember the student from chapter 14 who claimed both that I never taught anything anti-Christian or made negative comments about Christianity but that my teaching was nevertheless defective because "she makes all those other religions sound as if they could be true." Perhaps the explanation for policies of not hiring non-Christian scholar-practitioners is fear that if non-Christian religions are taught genuinely and authentically from the inside, students may not leave the classroom with the desired attitude that these religions are obviously inferior to Christianity. Goddess thealogian Carol Christ tells of a time when she taught a course on feminist theology at a Christian seminary

14. See note 4 above.
15. Smith, *Religious Diversity*, 14.

in northern California. She mainly taught Christian feminists, but she also critiqued their positions for not going far enough. She was not rehired and later found out through a friend that the decision not to rehire her was based on the fact that a student had complained that "because I [Carol Christ] was not a Christian, she [the student] had begun to question her own faith." The friend argued with the seminary's administration that it did not make sense to deprive students of interaction with a leading feminist theologian. The seminary then offered to rehire Christ, but only if her friend cotaught the course with her "to represent the Christian position."[16] Yet maintaining such a subtly hostile attitude toward those who are different is painful because it contradicts our more fundamental inclination to kindness and friendliness. It is also counterproductive and unnecessary.

Another dimension of the fear driving resistance to appreciating religious diversity as a fact and an interesting blessing rather than as a defect waiting to be repaired is reluctance to change. For those who have historically made exclusive truth claims, significant psychological and ideological change is required to move into comfort with religious diversity. But change is the one fact of life that we can always count on, even though religions sometimes make the mistake of promising people safety from change. Resisting change is futile; the only question is, which changes are actually beneficial? But even the slightest acquaintance with the history of any religious tradition makes it abundantly clear that the tradition has changed in many ways. Indeed, when Paul Knitter lists his reasons for, as a faithful Christian, insisting that Christianity is *not* the only true religion, he begins with historical reasons. "If we look at the history of our churches, we cannot deny that although at one time just about all the churches held firmly that Christianity is the only true religion, today many churches do not."[17] They have severed the link between appreciating how life giving one's own religion is and thinking that everyone else needs to believe the same things and belong to the same religion.

Those who have changed their beliefs about Christianity's exclusive truth have done so for many reasons, not the least of them ethical. Religious exclusivism may not be dangerous in religiously monolithic settings, but most people no longer live in monolithically religious situations. The subtle hostility implicit in religious exclusivism is not very neighborly. Change may be scary, but not as scary as the results of interreligious ignorance and hostility. It is simply incredible that people could think that the same attitudes about religious diversity that prevailed centuries ago, when accurate,

---

16. Christ, "Response," 79–80.

17. Steward, *Can Only One Religion Be True?*, 28.

insider knowledge about other religions was almost impossible to obtain, would still be relevant in the twenty-first century. Accurate, empathetic knowledge about other religions is now easily available. Some institutions in our society, especially colleges and universities, have taken up the challenge of teaching about the world's diverse religions in responsible ways. Most seminaries lag far behind.

Fear is something of which Buddhists are very aware and about which we have a lot to say. Some fears result from mistaken perceptions. One of the most famous analogies in Buddhism is that of mistaking a rope for a snake and acting as if one were being threatened by a snake. But all that fear is totally unnecessary. A snake never was present, even though we were positive about the snake. Buddhists suggest constant vigilance and introspection to overcome mistaken perceptions. Buddhists also suggest that mistaken perceptions are very common—much more common than we usually realize. A great deal of the fear generated by unfamiliar religions is easily defused by knowledge. Many people have discovered through study and acquaintance with people of other religions that those religions are nothing like the stereotypes about them that are so common.

Other types of fear are deeper and more subtle. Frequently they are more deeply buried and may not often surface into awareness. The conventional reaction is to suppress such fear as soon as it surfaces. Fear of change in one of these deep-seated fears; one is barely aware that one even is afraid of change because, even though everything is changing all the time, one maintains strong denial of that fact. When one realizes that one is changing, that experience can be very frightening.

One of the primary purposes of Buddhist meditation disciplines is to become aware of those deep-seated fears and learn how to live with them rather than suppressing them, which only allows them to continue to cripple us. Buddhists are absolutely clear that the only way to tame fear is to bring fear into awareness, to be aware of it rather than to run away from it, deny it, or try to hide from it. This does not mean that one does not feel fear, but that one is willing to look straight into it. According to the great meditation master Chogyam Trungpa, to be fearless is not to be without fear but to have the courage to examine our fear, to let it come into consciousness rather than shying away from it.[18] Thich Nhat Hanh has described this process in more detail.

> Only by looking deeply into the nature of your fear can you find your way out.

18. Trungpa, *Shambhala*, 48.

. . . The seed of fear is there in us, and if we don't practice embracing it with mindfulness, then every time these truths show themselves, we will feel very uncomfortable. Like ostriches that see a lion, we stick our heads into the sand. Using diversions like television, computer games, alcohol, and drugs, we try to ignore the realities of aging, illness, death, and the impermanence of things we cherish.

If we allow ourselves to be overwhelmed by our fears, we will suffer and the seed of fear in us will grow stronger. But when we are mindful, we use the energy of mindfulness to embrace our fear. Every time fear is embraced by mindfulness, the energy of fear decreases.[19]

I would suggest that another of those diversions is holding onto worn-out methods of dealing with religious diversity. A strong specific identity as a Christian or a Buddhist does not require oppositional *us/them* dualism. No one needs to embody and teach this truth more than our religious leaders. But how can they when they are not properly taught about the world's diverse religions? Are seminaries the weak link or lynchpin promoting the world's interreligious future?

Coda

In order to end this chapter on a more positive note, I would like to cite instances of which I am aware in which Christian seminaries have moved to address religious diversity more adequately in their educational programs. There may be others of which I am not aware, and if so, I welcome that news. Union Theological Seminary, which recently hired a Muslim to teach Islamic studies there, now lists interfaith learning as a newly added field of concentration and boasts that many of its faculty are already qualified to teach in that area. For some years now, two of its faculty members have been dual-belongers, confessing both Buddhism and Christianity and Buddhist meditation has been taught there for years.

Even more promising, Claremont Graduate School of Theology has announced a program to add clerical training for Muslim imams and Jewish rabbis to its study program, so that they, as well as clerics from other religions, will be educated side by side with future Christian clerics. The newly formed Claremont Lincoln University, which is also part of the Claremont cluster of colleges and graduate schools, will also be affiliated with a Buddhist university, a Sikh center, a Jain center, and a Hindu studies program.

19. Nhat Hanh, *Fear*, 38.

This means that students, including future clergy in most of the world's major religions, will be able to study side by side in each other's institutions. These institutions will both maintain the specificity of each tradition and educate future clergy to be fully conversant with the diverse religions. Such institutions fulfill the daydream or fantasy I had many, many years ago when I was musing about the vigor with which Lutherans and Catholics went after each other. I though that maybe the solution would be for ministers and priests to be required to spend time at the other denominations' seminaries. Then they would have a much better chance of understanding each other adequately!

Chapter 17

Going Forward Together
and Separately

*Buddhist Proposals for Creating Enlightened Society
amid Religious Differences*

UNLIKE MANY (CHRISTIAN) PLURALISTS, I do not claim that there is
some lowest common denominator underlying all religions, about
which they agree, or *should* agree, even if some stubbornly refuse to do so.
At least not if that lowest common denominator is phrased in theological
or metaphysical terms, which has most often been the claim. Theologically
and metaphysically, the various religions are, in my view, quite distinct and
different from each other. But in my view, those theological differences are
also no excuse for not working with members of other religions on matters
of common concern and interest. The case for an ethical lowest common
denominator is considerably stronger than for a theological or ideological
common denominator. But even though wider common consensus is possible on ethical concerns, disagreements still emerge over which causes
take priority and which causes are completely off limits. In my view, the
cause of interreligious cooperation can never trump the distinctiveness
of each tradition. But also, the distinctiveness of each tradition is not a
valid excuse for refusing to engage in interreligious cooperation on many
issues. Nor are religious differences an excuse for refusing to engage in

dialogue and discussion as an equal partner with religious others, especially on the question of how to live together cordially despite strong religious differences in theology and even on ethical issues. In other words, religious differences are no barrier to mutual understanding, respect, and cooperation on many projects.

Perhaps one result of the turn to postmodernism and multiculturalism is the recognition that difference is *okay*, that difference does not mean deficiency or that one point of view is right and the other is wrong. Perhaps we can at last give up the impossible dream of achieving unity through uniformity and instead relax with differences and diversity, no longer regarding differences as necessitating disagreement and conflict. In a cultural or religious context as much given to dualism, and especially to *good/bad*, *right/wrong*, or *good/evil* dualisms as the West has typically been, such an intellectual and spiritual breakthrough is momentous. It may well usher in an era in which, to quote from the website of Claremont Lincoln University, a new graduate university dedicated to multireligious education, "what once seemed impossible—finding the common threads among religious and ethical traditions—while honoring the distinctiveness of each" can happen. This development undercuts one of the major arguments many more conservative thinkers make against pluralists—that they do not respect the distinctiveness of each religion sufficiently but want them to shave off what distinguishes them from other traditions to be more in conformity with a generic religion constructed by pluralists. But under guidelines that call for honoring distinctiveness, more conservative traditions could not object to interreligious cooperation on grounds that their specificity is not being properly recognized, honored, and taken into account. It remains to be seen if such people and groups are willing to join in multifaith enterprises as equals who do not claim to have the only valid point of view about what the issues are or what needs to be done. For if distinctiveness is recognized and honored, that leaves little room for any one to claim to have the One True Faith to which everyone else should give assent.

Common-sense Guidelines

One way to work together on common projects and also honor differences is simply to agree to disagree about certain things and not discuss them further, even while getting important tasks accomplished. I think this strategy is especially helpful when asking how religious conservatives and liberals can work together, which is something I am often asked, given that I have so little sympathy for exclusive truth claims. In fact, I was asked such a question by two people, including by Paul Knitter, at an American Academy of Religion session honoring my lifework. Paul specifically asked me "how to make space for and embrace those who make absolute, exclusive claims."[1] I replied that I do think that people who hold very different points of view and are very much convinced of the correctness of their viewpoint, can work together successfully if they can communicate civilly, with gentleness and respect, rather than stridently or aggressively. However, there is a bottom line that must be adhered to. People who know that I disagree with them theologically or politically *must* stop bugging me to change my point of view, and I, of course, must do likewise. Unfortunately, I have witnessed occasions when the more conservative person just cannot exercise enough discipline not to continue arguing, and friends also report such incidents to me. I'm sure it goes the other way too on some occasions. The only exception to this rule would be a mutual agreement to discuss some issue upon which there is disagreement for *mutual* edification—which is a two-way, not a one-way street.

I used as my example of how a more liberal and a more conservative religious person could work together well my ten-year-long collegial partnership with Terry Muck, coediting the *Buddhist-Christian Studies Journal*. Terry always claimed to be theologically conservative, with an emphasis on the *conservative* part, while for me the question of where I stand on the theological grid perhaps doesn't even make sense, given that I'm not a Christian. Still, I do have some idea what kind of Christian I probably would be if I were one, and it would not be conservative. But, frankly, from first-person experience, I couldn't say much about Terry's theology. We didn't talk theology very often. We did the work that needed to be done to get the journal out each year, and to coedit two books. Whenever we did talk about social issues, he usually seemed sensible to me, and we didn't disagree all that much, even though I consider myself liberal. I do remember one discussion about having Christian prayers at high school sporting events. I expressed my view that such practices were really an unwarranted imposition on non-Christians, to which Terry responded that he thought the religious majority should be able to express its faith publicly, and that those expressions were just something a religious minority would have to put up with. We didn't pursue the conversation. There was no good reason to do so. We disagreed, and it was unlikely that either of us would convince the other of our point of view. Besides, we had important work to do together, and on that there was no disagreement.

1. Knitter, "Rita Gross," 83.

Terry and I could get that work done together because our very different religious traditions had, despite their differences, made both of us disciplined, decent people. Theological agreement was, and is, irrelevant in the long run, I believe. Poverty and prejudice affect fundamentalists and liberals in exactly the same ways. It is more important to alleviate the poverty and prejudice than to talk theology all day trying to come to some theological agreement. Granted, some issues involving poverty and prejudice, such as homophobia, may also have theological dimensions, but there have to be many arenas in which it is possible to work together across the greatest ideological or theological divides. When disaster strikes, usually everyone tries to help, and everyone accepts the aid. Why wait for such extreme circumstances to work together on whatever we can?

There is no reason why this kind of cooperation on important projects could not be magnified for larger projects and very widely used. It is very easy to ascertain what we cannot agree on and what projects we can work on together. Only ideologically fixated people would insist that agreement on all points important to oneself must be in place before we can work together on anything. In most cases, such as coeditorship of *Buddhist-Christian Studies*, the final product is actually improved by having people of vastly different perspectives work together on it. All that is required are the politeness and discipline to know what topics and issues are not worth discussing—and the politeness and discipline to discuss them civilly when such discussions would improve outcomes for the project in question.

Buddhism and Enlightened Society

Many people who think of Buddhism as a somewhat socially disengaged religion may be surprised to learn that major Buddhist leaders, such as the Dalai Lama and Thich Nhat Hanh, are deeply concerned with what it would take to create and promote "enlightened society." One of Thich Nhat Hanh's most recent books is titled *Good Citizens: Creating Enlightened Society*. The phrase "enlightened society" was first used by Tibetan Buddhist teacher Chogyam Trungpa in the 1980s. The first chapter of his book *Shambhala: The Sacred Path of the Warrior* is titled "Creating an Enlightened Society." From the early 1980s onward, most of this teaching was about the topic of "enlightened society." He initiated the Shambhala Training Program, which provided meditation training outside a Buddhist context and taught extensively about enlightened society. The impression that Buddhism only promotes individual well-being but is not concerned with society at large is unfounded. Especially in Mahayana Buddhisms, the goal of universal awakening and well-being is well articulated and is understood by all practitioners of those traditions to be the point of their spiritual practices. So why the widely prevalent misimpression on the part of so many that Buddhists are passive individualists without serious social concerns?

This impression overlooks the way Buddhist institutions provided social services in many Asian societies. For example, monasteries and nunneries functioned, and still function, as orphanages in many parts of the Buddhist world. Parents who cannot care for their children give them up to monasteries where they are housed, fed, and educated. Beyond their role as orphanages, monasteries typically played a much larger role in educating children in many parts of the Buddhist world. Granted, this care was often less available for girls than for boys. In addition, Buddhists became the specialists for dealing with death in many parts of the world, especially in Japan. This emphasis has carried over into Western Buddhism. Buddhists have been at the forefront of the hospice movement and are taking up care for the terminally ill with great frequency.

Part of the mistaken impression about Buddhists also results from the fact that when Westerners first encountered Asian Buddhisms, most Buddhists were under colonial rule, fending off Western influences, or assimilating Western influences as best they could. Buddhists were often not in the position to interact with society at large as they would have, had they been more independent. It should also be remembered that the twentieth century was very difficult for Buddhism and Buddhists: Chinese and Tibetan Buddhists were severely restricted by Communism, Japanese Buddhists were recovering from the confusion and disillusionment of the Second World War, and Southeast Asian forms of Buddhism were riddled by civil wars and recovering from colonialism.

However, the most important reason for the misunderstanding about Buddhism probably stems from the fact that the methods promoted by Buddhists and by Western religions are quite different. Buddhists are very clear that an enlightened society results when, and only when, individuals are enlightened; or to put it less absolutely, when individuals have tamed their aggression, competitiveness, judgmentalism, and prejudice at least to some extent. To think that a society could be just and equitable while its individual citizens are self-centered and lack concern for general well-being strikes most Buddhists as extremely unrealistic. Hence the major emphasis is on individual training, especially meditation disciplines, which are tried-and-true methods that move people from self-centeredness to a more compassionate stance vis-à-vis society in general. It is also the conclusion of most deeply trained Buddhist meditators that at least since the Protestant Reformation, most Western religions have not focused much on internal individual spiritual development. The focus for individuals has mostly been outward, toward an external deity and a world thought to be wholly outside of and separate form the subject. Thus, well-trained Buddhist meditation masters, especially those from Asia, are not surprised at the level of conflict and competitiveness in modern (Western) societies, given that individual internal spiritual transformation is so little emphasized and pursued.

For many Westerners, by contrast, the first reaction to injustice is to struggle to pass new laws that would enforce more just and equitable relations between individuals and groups. Large groups of people gather to protest and demand changes. Sometimes they are successful and new laws are passed and sometimes even enforced. (Notice the repeated use of the term *force*, as in the word *enforce*. This is a system for social change that depends in large measure on forcing people to do what they don't spontaneously do and may not want to do.) To a Buddhist, this is a backwards approach. Many contemporary Western Buddhists experienced firsthand a conflict between their hopes and dreams (expressed in the large-scale social movements of the sixties and seventies) and what their Buddhist teachers asked of them. Many were very confused when their Buddhist teachers asked them to meditate more and demonstrate less. But many who had been extremely involved in the protest movements of the sixties and seventies also came to Buddhist meditation as a result of burnout, the inevitable result of activism that lacks an adequate spiritual base.

Like most dichotomies, this dichotomy between which should change—laws or individuals—is a false dichotomy. It is important that both change. Nevertheless, because most Westerners, especially those who are socially active as part of their religious commitments, are so oriented to changing laws and so dismissive of the power of changed individuals, the Buddhist perspective must be stated and its cogency recognized. I know how deep seated the push for forceful social change is in many Westerners, for I have had this discussion many times with Western feminists. They are dismissive, even scornful of a perspective that stresses individual change and liberation as the front line for creating an enlightened society. From the Buddhist side, nothing is more incredible than angry people ranting and raving, pumping their fists in the air, while proclaiming that they want peace and justice. Such mind—minds that are so unpeaceful themselves—could never collectively result in enlightened society! The Dalai Lama makes the case very well. He talks about efforts to change laws and then says:

> This is very good as far as it goes, but the fact is, we will never solve our problems simply by passing new laws and regulations. Ultimately, the source of our problems lies at the level of the

individual. If people lack moral values and integrity, no system of laws and regulations will be adequate. So long as people give priority to material values, then injustice, corruption, inequity, intolerance, and greed—all the outward manifestations of neglect of inner values—will persist.[2]

Buddhist Suggestions for Working Together across Religious Boundaries

Buddhist ethics have always have always been oriented to all sentient beings, not only human beings, and certainly not only other Buddhists. Some of our most important contemplations involve fostering unlimited friendliness and compassion, friendliness and compassion without boundaries, often based on the recognition that in a completely interdependent universe, all sentient beings have been our mothers. A sincere wish for universal well-being, without concern about labels, is the inevitable result of practicing these contemplations. Thus, it is not surprising that within fifty years of the time that Asian Buddhist teachers began to work actively in the West, becoming much more conversant with Western cultures, they would begin to discuss what Buddhism might offer to ease the sufferings so prevalent in those cultures. These suggestions for easing current sufferings in no way depend on people adopting a Buddhist affiliation. They are equally available to Buddhists and non-Buddhists, presuming that denominational lines and religious boundaries are rather irrelevant when it comes to easing suffering.

These recent Buddhist proposals for interreligious cooperation and creating enlightened society have several interlocking propositions. The first is that ideological agreement, including agreement on a religious point of view, is simply not the point. Nor are different or better ideologies the key to creating enlightened society. As part of this claim, all major Buddhist authors who write about enlightened society agree that current conventional religions are not adequate, that we have to go "beyond religion" to quote the title of the Dalai Lama's book. This judgment is made because it is abundantly clear to Buddhist observers that the world is not going to adopt a single religion, but Buddhists value religious diversity and want the individual religions to continue to flourish in their distinctive ways. Second, ethical concerns are far more general and far more easily shared across religious lines than ideological or theological concerns. This is also the arena in which suffering can really be addressed and alleviated, not in matters of

2. His Holiness, the Dalai Lama XIV, *Beyond Religion,* xii–xiii.

metaphysics and theology. Finally, individual spiritual discipline is absolutely essential to any resolution of the world's suffering and to creating enlightened society. If these three principles were put into practice, discomfort with religious diversity would decrease substantially. Then, interreligiously we (including those who are officially nonreligious) could actually make progress in resolving some of the world's problems.

For all these Buddhist authors, the claim that we need to go "beyond religion" is not an antireligious position. They are not suggesting that religions be abolished at all, but that each religion is too specific to be generally appealing. Therefore, none of them can provide solutions that people from all different religions and cultures can adopt and act upon. According to this suggestion, rather than trying to promote itself as the solution to the globe's problems, each religion should continue to flourish in its own enclave. There, its specific metaphysics and rituals, which could never be universally appealing, can manifest their idiosyncratic glory without any attention to pluralists' concerns with generic religion. Thus, as the Dalai Lama says, while he is most interested in ethical convergences among religions, he also wants a "model where differences between the religions can be genuinely appreciated."[3] At the same time, each Buddhist author proposes strategies that he believes can easily appeal to and be relevant to anyone of any or no religious persuasion. As Thich Nhat Hanh says about his specific program, the Five Mindfulness Trainings, they "are offered without dogma or religion. Everybody can use them as ethics for their life without becoming a Buddhist or becoming part of any tradition or faith."[4] He also writes that the program he offers "can be accepted by everyone, regardless of whether or not you believe in a god."[5] Thus, Buddhist solutions are not antireligions but do go "beyond religion."

Buddhists are perhaps uniquely equipped to come up with such a solution that both honors religion and goes beyond any specific religion. Our own verbal teachings, especially nontheism and the denial of personal immortality, are highly unusual positions among the world's religions, and we don't imagine widespread or universal acceptance of them anytime soon. Nevertheless, our training predisposes us to want to be helpful. So rather than trying to pull people into our camp, we offer what we have developed that is helpful to all but does not depend on accepting nontheism, denial of personal immortality, or any other more specifically Buddhist idea.

3. His Holiness, the Dalai Lama XIV. *Toward a True Kinship of Faith*, xii.
4. Nhat Hanh, *Good Citizens*, 104.
5. Ibid., 2.

One of the clearest statements about how unhelpful more dogma and more theories would be comes from Trungpa.

> While everyone has a responsibility to help the world, we can create additional chaos if we try to impose our ideas or our help upon others. Many people have theories about what the world needs. Some people think that the world needs communism; some people think that the world needs democracy; some people think that technology will save the world; some people think that technology will destroy the world. The Shambhala teachings are not based on converting the world to another theory.[6]

More than other Buddhist teachers in their proposals for enlightened society, Trungpa deliberately and forcefully taught that many societies, cultures, and religions throughout history and around the world, as well as many noteworthy individuals, provided examples of enlightened leadership and models for aspects of an enlightened society. Those of us who taught in his Shambhala Training Program were encouraged to use examples from many religions and cultures to illustrate the points we were making about human flourishing and creating enlightened society. Buddhist examples, of course, were also relevant materials for our talks, but we were definitely encouraged not to limit ourselves to Buddhist materials.

Thich Nhat Hanh is equally forceful in a different way. In his discussion of "Right View," the first element of the Buddhist Eightfold Path, he is adamant that in the long run, Right View is holding no view at all, or complete detachment from any view. This is not an aggressive ignorance but the mature detachment from holding absolutely to any propositional statement of what the view is. Nhat Hanh explains that because one cannot make spiritual progress while holding any proposition to be absolute, one should always be prepared to renounce any idea one has accepted in favor of a higher kind of truth.[7] He continues:

> Right view is the view that transcends all views. It is free from discrimination, free from dualistic thinking. As long as you're caught in one view, you can't have Right View. It is possible for us to consider all kinds of views and not to be caught by any of them.[8]

It is important to be clear that Nhat Hanh is not advocating being uninformed about the various options among views, nor even, in the everyday

---

6. Trungpa, *Shambhala*, 29.

7. Nhat Hanh, *Good Citizens*, 47.

8. Ibid., 7

sense of term, not thinking that some views are more *correct* and *adequate* than other views. He is talking about not being pathologically attached to or fixated on some propositional formulation of a view as something that is absolutely true and necessary for everyone to hold. In other words, he is advocating a mental virtue frequently praised by Buddhist meditators— flexibility of mind. It is also important to understand Nhat Hanh's teaching on the connection between being unattached to views and engaging in the most basic of ethical norms, such as not harming or killing: "A person who is free from all views, a person who is capable of seeing the interbeing nature of everything, will never have the desire to kill."[9] (These ideas should also be familiar from chapter 6.)

The Dalai Lama says essentially the same thing. He writes that "Although the world's religions may differ fundamentally from one another in their metaphysical views, when it comes to their teachings on the actual practice of ethics, there is great convergence."[10] However, the Dalai Lama's statement also involves a change in emphasis. Not attached to the specificity of our unique religious views, the focus can shift to ethics. On this point, the Dalai Lama makes the most direct case.

> My engagement with the world's religions has convinced me that, whatever the differences of doctrine, on the level of actually living a religious life or fulfilling a spiritual aspiration, there is a striking degree of shared understanding. In particular, all the great religions stress compassion as a fundamental spiritual value.[11]

The Dalai Lama then constructs an impressive list of common ethical teachings: all encourage refraining from harmful actions and interactions with others based on compassion. All advocate selfless service to others without regard for any return or benefit to oneself.[12]

But he goes even further, claiming that ethics do not need to be grounded in religion. He says, "I firmly believe that ethics can also emerge simply as a natural and rational response to our very humanity and our common human condition."[13] Again not denigrating religion, but also not claiming its necessity for ethics and spiritual well-being, he compares "our innate human nature as beings with a natural disposition toward compassion, kindness, and caring for others" to water, while ethics based on reli-

9. Ibid., 71.

10. Ibid., 109.

11. His Holiness, the Dalai Lama XIV, *Toward a True Kinship of the Faiths*, xiii.

12. Ibid., 109–11.

13. His Holiness, the Dalai Lama XIV, *Beyond Religion*, 13.

gion are compared to tea. He points out that, much as we might enjoy tea, tea is mostly water. "While we can live without tea, we can't live without water. Likewise, we are born free of religion, but we are not born free of the need for compassion."[14]

So is compassion a universal virtue, uniting all religions and non-religious people alike? No one is against compassion. In that sense, it is certainly more universal than any metaphysical construct, such as God or the common, more abstract replacement for God in pluralist theologies that attempt to be more universal: Ultimate Reality. It certainly is clear from comparative studies of religion that there is more consensus on ethical norms that on metaphysical constructs. In the abstract, the claim that compassion is a universal virtue, valued by all, seems to be verified.

But while some causes such as aid and relief work following natural disasters, do elicit almost universal responses of concern and compassion, people and religions often disagree about what compassion would consist of in more specific discussions. Especially when whole groups of people, such as genders, ethnic groups, or classes, are objectified, people and religions often disagree over what compassion toward those people would actually look like. As I myself commented in chapter 4, the word *compassion* can cover a multitude of sins. Aggressive, unethical missionaries also claim to be motivated by compassion, and I believe that, in their limited self-understanding, they are. No one ever taught them to take into account the sensibilities of the people whom they are seeking to convert. Additionally, as we saw in chapter 3, Japanese Buddhists who supported Japanese military aggression justified their acts as acts of compassion; Japanese were freeing Asia from European colonialists and, in so doing, were engaged in a compassionate holy war, it was argued.

While some caution is recommended in touting compassion as a universal unifying factor given that the specifics of what compassion might consist of can be controversial, nevertheless ethics and compassion are a far more workable basis for cooperation across religious lines than any metaphysical construct could be. They are also far more relevant for promoting human well-being. It would be a sorry state of things indeed if, before we would help those in need, we had to make sure their theologies were correct. It would be an equally sorry state of affairs if we felt it improper to join with those whose theologies we may disagree with in order to help those in need.

Thich Nhat Hanh's discussions of ethics, a global ethic, and compassion are more directly based on traditional Buddhism than the Dalai Lama's. Nhat Hanh's book on creating enlightened society follows the format of

14. Ibid., 17.

Buddhism's Four Truths and Eightfold Path, which he and most Buddhists consider not to be abstract, metaphysical, or dogmatic in any way, but to be the result of observing deeply what is going on in us and around us. These teachings and practices, he claims, are

> a path for everyone, not just for . . . Buddhists but for everyone living in the world. We have to live our daily lives in such a way that we live deeply in mindfulness, so that we can see the nature or interbeing in everything. Following the Eightfold Path brings us joy and ease and helps transform intolerance, dogmatism, attachment to views, discrimination, and violence.[15]

However, when it comes to specific recommendations and demands, some might find some of Nhat Hanh's requirements too specific and stringent, even moralistic. He makes a very strong case for vegetarianism on the grounds that meat eating adds significantly to global climate change and world poverty. He is equally forceful about abstention from alcohol and drugs, though, in a modern interpretation, he considers them to be part of a large class of toxins that are harmful to our bodies and minds, including much television, certain websites, and some magazines, books, and electronic games. Granted, these are traditional Buddhist prohibitions, but, given that even many card-carrying Buddhists do not observe these restrictions, it is unlikely that they would be widely acceptable as part of a global ethic.

In contrast to both the Dalai Lama and Nhat Hanh, Trungpa does not talk so much about large-scale social ethics but about uplifting individual lives, life by life. He strongly encouraged each person to uplift and dignify his or her individual life by appreciating the sharpness and vividness of perceptions, by doing everyday work oneself instead of hiring others to do it, and by basically cheering up, which he says does not depend on material wealth. He taught constantly about

> appreciating very simple experiences . . . When we see a bright color, we are witnessing our own inherent goodness. When we hear a beautiful sound, we are hearing out own basic goodness. When we step out of a shower, we feel fresh and clean, and when we walk out of a stuffy room, we appreciate the sudden whiff of fresh air . . . It is worthwhile to recognize and take advantage of these moments, because they are revealing basic non-aggression and freshness in our lives.[16]

15. Nhat Hanh, *Good Citizens*, 100.
16. Trungpa, *Shambhala*, 30.

Such comments may sound mundane and trivial, but closer inspection may reveal their profundity. Many of Trungpa's students, myself included, really experienced a subtle but significant improvement in our quality of life by paying attention to such details. This example demonstrates once again the cogency of the Buddhist point that improving society involves more than passing better laws. Without changed individuals, such laws will not improve individual quality of life significantly.

For all three contemporary Buddhists writing about enlightened society and global ethics, their optimism about the project rests on their conviction that every individual, without regard for whether they now or or later become Buddhists formally, carries the seed of enlightenment and a complete potential for decency and gentleness. When Trungpa first brings up this point in his book, he is heartbreakingly eloquent:

> If we are willing to take an unbiased look, we will find that in spite of all our problems and confusion, all our emotional and psychological ups and downs, there is something basically good about our existence as human beings. Unless we can discover that ground of goodness in our own lives, we cannot hope to improve the lives of others. If we are simply miserable and wretched beings, how can we possibly imagine, let alone realize, an enlightened society?
>
> . . .
>
> Every human being has a basic nature of goodness, which is undiluted and unconfused. That goodness contains tremendous gentleness and appreciation.[17]

"Basic goodness," a "goodness" beyond and more basic than the duality beyond good and evil, is Trungpa's translation of what is often called buddha-nature. That everyone has the potential to become awakened or enlightened is one of the most basic premises of Buddhism.

Thich Nhat Hanh says very simply, "Everyone has the seed of awakening and insight within his or her heart . . . We have the tools . . . We have the ability—with practice—to have the insight. All we need to do is to begin."[18] Quotations already cited from the Dalai Lama demonstrate his strong conviction that humans have an inborn propensity for compassion, that it not merely a learned response. That is why all religions as well as many people who do not identify with any religion, emphasize compassion, at least in the abstract, even if their specific recommendations about what is compassionate behavior are sometimes different.

17. Ibid.
18. Nhat Hanh, *Good Citizens*, 124–25.

Buddhists would insist, however, that across religious lines, all individuals have an obligation to develop gentle, nonaggressive ways of being in the world and of responding to provocation. That counteraggression can never be the solution to aggression is a well-established Buddhist bottom line, perhaps best summed up in the oft-quoted verse from the *Dhammapada*:

> Hatred never ends through hatred.
> By non-hate alone does it end.
> This is an ancient truth.[19]

This does not mean, as some outsiders often suppose, that Buddhists are indifferent to injustice or turn a blind eye to wrongdoing. It's just that the common, anger-filled and anger-motivated reactions to injustice don't work and don't solve the problem. If one wants to object that anger can motivate social change, the Dalai Lama would respond by making a distinction between anger and hatred. He says that anger can have some brief, momentary positive effects, but if it lingers beyond momentarily providing clarity about injustice and motivation to do something about it, most of the energy it generates is negative. It morphs easily into hatred, which is always destructive.[20] The Dalai Lama and Thich Nhat Hanh both express admiration for those who have resisted injustice nonviolently. Both give specific guidelines for working for justice without being motivated by desire for revenge. Thich Nhat Hanh has devoted considerable energy and attention to developing programs to help those who hate each other, such as Israelis and Palestinians, to be able to listen to each other and hear each other. His guidelines for deep listening and communication as ways of dealing with hostility and conflict are very challenging.[21] Both sides are expected to listen to each other and take responsibility for their own contributions to the conflict.

Almost universally, Buddhists would also suggest that becoming a peaceful individual who (or society that) can deal with injustice without resorting to hatred and violence is greatly aided by spiritual disciplines, especially mindfulness and other basic methods of meditation commonly associated with Buddhism. Though not all Buddhist meditation practices are religiously neutral or appropriate for non-Buddhists (for example, practices associated with Vajrayana Buddhism), some methods, especially mindfulness, are appropriate for all. Mindfulness practices have long been taught by Buddhists, but especially in modern times they are considered

19. Frosdal, *The Dhammapada*, 2.

20. His Holiness, the Dalai Lama XIV, *Beyond Religion*, 118–19.

21. Nhat Hanh, *Fear*, 91–99.

to be religiously and culturally neutral rather than specifically Buddhist. They in no way entail some views usually associated with Buddhism, such as nontheism or denial of personal immortality. These techniques are also eminently practical and effective for relevant personal transformation. Therefore, they have been freely offered to religious and nonreligious others by many Buddhist teachers, with no strings attached—with no need to become a Buddhist, or even pro-Buddhist.

For example, to return to Chogyam Trungpa and his specific teachings, he was among the earliest to offer a program of nonsectarian meditation training. His program, Shambhala Training, was launched in the early 1980s and had been offered nationally and internationally ever since. I taught in that program for many years, teaching about seventy-five weekend programs between the early 1990s and the middle 2000s. Though most of the teachers in this program were Buddhists, we were required to present our teachings in totally non-Buddhist vocabulary because it was presumed that our students were not interested in becoming Buddhists. We always presented Shambhala Training as something that was open to all and that could help members of other religions in their practice of that religion. Using more neutral and completely non-Buddhist vocabulary was quite challenging. But it was also very instructive. We had to learn how to present what we knew from our own experience of meditation without relying on any of the familiar jargon we had been taught and upon which we had previously relied.

Both the Dalai Lama and Thich Nhat Hanh take essentially the same perspective on basic Buddhist meditation techniques. The Dalai Lama's book *Beyond Religion* is very clear. In the first half of the book he discusses compassion as something towards which all humans are inclined. But, as he puts it, we need to learn how to act on that inclination. "How are we to become more compassionate, kinder, more forgiving, and more discerning in our behavior?"[22] His answer is mindfulness practice, which he says requires no religious belief or commitment. Instead, it provides "an approach to living ethically and in harmony with others, with a deeper sense of well-being, which can be practiced in a way that is independent of any specific religious or cultural perspective."[23] To quote Thich Nhat Hanh once more, he offers mindfulness "a practice that can be accepted by everyone, regardless of whether or not you believe in a god."[24]

22. His Holiness, the Dalai Lama XIV, *Beyond Religion*, 101.

23. Ibid.

24. Nhat Hanh, *Good Citizens*, 2.

But how and why is mindfulness meditation so effective? To return to a dominant theme of this chapter, real social change and creating enlightened society require transformed individuals. Though mindfulness practice is often done in groups, it works completely at the individual level. Even in a group, as one sits silently with others, not interacting with them, mindfulness practice is a solitary, private affair. No one knows what thoughts rise to consciousness in any other meditator, and there is no group debriefing or sharing of thoughts afterwards. But through silence, alertness, mindful breathing, and acknowledging to oneself whatever thoughts do come to the surface of one's consciousness, a very slow transformation towards peacefulness and self-acceptance occurs. It is impossible to describe in words how and why this process works, but it does.

Part of the way it works, however, is through a process of deep self-healing. As one sits silently with nothing to do except be mindful of one's breathing, many things come to the surface. They are neither accepted nor rejected, but just acknowledged. We say hello to whatever comes to the surface, and then we immediately say goodbye to it. Whatever it is, it may come back to visit many times, but eventually it does wear out, leaving more calmness and peacefulness, which leads to compassion for others in its wake. But it is completely essential and crucial to begin with oneself. As Thich Nhat Hanh says, "in order to have compassion to offer others, we have to offer it to ourselves first. We cultivate compassion by looking deeply to understand the suffering inside us and around us."[25] Why we must begins with ourselves is well explained by Nhat Hanh:

> We need to abolish poverty and social injustice, and to deal with the problems of global warming and economic recession. But we need to begin with the painful feelings we carry inside us. We have to deal with these things first. If they're not dealt with, we may inadvertently cause more suffering when we're trying to relieve it. The Buddha didn't begin his first teaching with the suffering of social injustice, poverty, and hunger, even though he cared very much about these things. He began with the lack of peace in our own bodies and minds. We want to deal with suffering realistically and at the roots.[26]

The alternative is angry, self-righteous people trying to save the world by yelling louder than those opposed to them. As is all too apparent in many cases, this brings, not peace and justice, but mutual entrenchment, each side proclaiming its own righteousness and the evils of the other side. People on

25. Ibid., 112.
26. Ibid., 20.

both sides suffer deeply from their own anger and frustration, for no one suffers more from anger than the person who is angry. There is no need for such feelings and such rhetoric in a nonviolent, peaceful movement or demonstration. But without deep self-healing, such movements easily turn violent.

But with deep self-healing, whatever its source, compassion and concern for others develops as naturally as day follows night. This is also a trustworthy compassion, not one based on ego, on a need to think of oneself as a compassionate person. It is also a compassion that does not burn out and run dry eventually, due to the fact that, no matter how hard one works to improve conditions in the world, there is always more to do.

Thich Nhat Hanh describes how the Engaged Buddhist movement began during the Vietnam War. Meditators, aware of the suffering all around them, wanted to do something to alleviate that suffering, and they also wanted to continue their meditation practice.

> We wanted to serve others and we wanted to practice sitting and walking meditation to give us the stability and peace we needed to go out of the temple and help relieve the suffering . . . If we hadn't practiced while we served, we would have lost ourselves, become burnt out, and we would not have been able to help anyone.[27]

Mindfulness practice has now become so well established, at least in the Western world, that some Buddhists are worried that it has become too watered down and is not always properly taught. Others worry that a practice that has always involved a relationship with a teacher and a community of fellow practitioners cannot really work in their absence, and in many contexts, there is no ongoing relationship with a teacher or a community. Nevertheless, many people have gone through programs such as Mindfulness-Based Stress Reduction and have certainly been helped. Many prisoners have learned mindfulness meditation, to their benefit. It is used in some schools and would be beneficial in many more.

The place where I take the most delight at the presence of mindfulness meditation, however, is at Union Theological Seminary in New York City. I have taught mindfulness there myself. And for years, an ongoing class is taught there, every morning at 7:00 a.m. No wonder Union Theological Seminary has now dedicated itself to multifaith education as one its specialties!

Buddhists value spiritual disciplines that change individuals so that they become more peaceful and compassionate, and we offer them as ways to go forward, together and separately, in a religiously diverse world. With

27. Ibid., 2–3.

discernment, we can easily determine what we need to agree to disagree about—mainly metaphysics, theology, and ritual. We can work on those issues separately, but we do need to respect others as equals rather than to regard them as misguided and in need of our correction. We can also discern when it might be helpful to discuss the things we disagree about, and when it is counterproductive. But comparative study of religions reveals that the Dalai Lama is correct: there is a great deal of convergence among the world's religions concerning ethics. Most of the world's major problems cry out for ethical action based on compassion, not metaphysical pronouncements. The world's religions could work together to solve those problems a great deal more than they currently do. One does have to wonder why some religious people have focused so exclusively on theological disagreements and ignored these ethical convergences, especially given how much suffering has been caused by that choice of focus.

Section 6

Conclusion
Flexibility and Comfort

Chapter 18

From Religious Chauvinism to Flourishing with Religious Diversity

A Developmental Model

THE DALAI LAMA DESCRIBES himself as a young man—a description most of us could probably identify with. We, too, felt that way at one point in our lives.

> When I was growing up in Tibet, and especially after my serious engagement in studies of classical Buddhist thought and practice from the age of fifteen, I used to feel that my own Buddhist religious tradition was the best. I thought that there simply could not be any other faith tradition that could rival the depth, sophistication, and inspirational power of Buddhism. Other religions must, at best, be "so-so." Looking back, I feel embarrassed by my naïveté, although it was the view of an adolescent boy immersed in his own inherited religious tradition.[1]

He narrates that he was vaguely aware that there was a religion called Christianity, which revolved around its savior, Jesus Christ. There were a few Muslims in Lhasa, one of whom repaired his beloved watch. As for Jains and Hindus, the two Indian sister religions, "I was convinced that the

1. His Holiness, the Dalai Lama XIV, *Toward a True Kinship of Faiths*, 1

philosophical arguments, found in the classical Buddhist critiques of their tenets, had effectively demonstrated the superiority of the Buddhist faith centuries ago."[2] Then comes the critical comment: "Needless to say, such naïveté could be maintained only so long as I remained isolated from any real contact with the world's other religions."[3]

Change the place-names and this account would be accurate for many people who have been traditionally educated about their religion and about religion in general.

First, there is cultural isolation and almost complete religious homogeneity. These conditions are not conducive to flourishing with religious diversity because under these conditions there is no real knowledge of the diverse religions. In addition to isolation and homogeneity, the religious education provided is very one sided, designed only to convince those being educated that theirs is the One True Faith. Any rival religions of which there is any knowledge are not allowed to represent themselves, but are presented only through the eyes of those who have rejected them and want everyone else to reject them as well. Actually, though the Dalai Lama omits that aspect of his education, he would have been taught equally negative versions of some other forms of Buddhism, especially the so-called *hinayana*, not merely of other Indian religions. Combining religious homogeneity, isolation, and a very sectarian education designed to produce true believers rather than people with accurate and empathetic knowledge about the religious options, is a formula for producing interreligious scorn and hostility. It may have been the best that could be done in previous centuries, but it is no longer appropriate for a world in which all the major religions are spread around the globe, in which followers of the religions live in close proximity to one another, and in which, even if they still live in largely monolithic religious communities, nevertheless, they are deeply affected by what goes on in religious communities halfway around the world.

As the history of every religion demonstrates, no matter how much the religions may claim that they are unchanging, that they proclaim only eternal verities, every living religion has changed significantly throughout its history. That is why it is still a living religion! Under current conditions, no change is more vital than changes that lead to accommodating comfortably, if not flourishing with, religious diversity. As the Dalai Lama said in the quotation above, the attitudes towards other religions in which he had been trained could last "only so long as I remained isolated from any real contact

2. Ibid., 1–2.
3. Ibid., 2.

with the world's other religions."[4] For all religious leaders and for many of their followers, that physical change has already occurred. Physical isolation from other religious traditions is very difficult to maintain at present, and intellectual isolation is even more difficult, though even in these conditions, it is possible to remain willfully ignorant of other religions—possible but not wise and certainly not liberating.

Especially in Tibetan Buddhism, analysis of how to deal with a situation frequently begins by describing the starting point of those in the situation. What can we assume they have to work with? What potentials are in the situation? What are the fundamental problems or issues they are dealing with? This is often called the working basis. With some clarity about what we have to work with, we can then make recommendations about how best to move forward, how we can work with the potentials and the pitfalls found in the working basis. Given what we have, what should we do? What are the best tactics, the most effective ways to move forward? This part of the analysis of the situation is often called simply the path, as in the way forward or the way out. Finally, there are results. Because certain actions are taken, certain results follow. Assuming that the initial analysis was correct and that the relevant antidotes were applied, the situation is rectified. How can that resultant condition be described?

A medical analogy is often applied to this threefold process. Discerning the working basis is like making a medical diagnosis. Then a prescription, a regimen, that best deals with the initial situation, is recommended. That is the path, the way out. If that path is followed, health, or at least a better way of working with the situation, should eventuate. This method of analysis is very effective for many topics. I will use it in this developmental model of moving from religious chauvinism to flourishing with religious diversity. Applying this model to this process also provides something of a summary and conclusion of this book.

The Starting Point: Duality by Default and Basic Goodness

As has been acknowledged many times throughout this book, duality, even oppositional duality, is extremely common, even unavoidable in ordinary psychology and in the usual processes of education and maturation. One could even say that duality is the default mode of human consciousness. Left to themselves, most people will define the world and others as completely separate from themselves. There seems to be a duality between self and other, and without further introspection and training that seeming duality

---

4. Ibid.

is taken to be the ways things really are. People assume that their impressions about that seeming outer world accurately represent that world. As a result, they often assume that people and things in that outer world cause them to act in react in the ways that they do. Buddhists agree that this is the way conventional psychology works. Simply by virtue of having a human birth, human senses, and a human mind, such duality will inevitably develop. That perceived duality then serves to reinforce an impression that self and other exist independently of each other. That impression is especially useful to the developing ego with its cherished illusion of separate, eternal, independent existence. It looks "outward" and, as Chogyam Trungpa put it so clearly, "by doing this, we reassure ourselves that we exist. 'If I can feel that out there, then I must be here.'"[5] It is not noticed that self and other actually co-arise. Instead, we leap to the metaphysical conclusion that each exists independently of the other. (This process was discussed in more depth in both chapters 7 and 9.)

By itself, that impression of seeming duality is not too problematic. But it is not the end of the story, and like any relatively accurate perception or idea that is taken to provide a deeper level of truth than is warranted (i.e., that is taken to be absolutely true), it then proves devastating. The problem is that many people never question that duality or look more deeply into it. Because we so easily enter into dualism as our default position, it is but a short step to develop hostility toward others when they trouble us, or to develop fear of whatever or whomever is different. Then we easily develop exclusive or inclusive truth claims: the world would be so much more workable if only everyone else were more like me. Most people are never genuinely curious about those others or ask why they think and act as they do. They never accord others what they so deeply value for themselves: the ability to be who they are. Instead they are eager to interfere with others "for their own good," imagining themselves to be motivated by compassion for those in error, for those who are different.

However, Buddhists also say that this inevitably developing default position of dualistic consciousness is not the entirety of our working basis. In fact, it is only a temporary obscuration (to use common Buddhist terminology), not anything we are condemned to be immersed in forever. Much more basic and fundamental to our being who we are is our potential to wake up by clearing away those temporary obscurations. Then we can much more readily tap into the wisdom and compassion that are our birthright. This potential, often called *Buddha-nature* or, more colloquially, basic goodness, is present as our bedrock nature, even while we are unaware of it and

5. Trungpa, *Cutting through Spiritual Materialism*, 126.

are acting contrary to its inclinations. Thus, it is always said by Buddhists that what is new as we come closer to our fundamental sanity and wisdom is that obscurations diminish, not that we gain something we previously did not know or have. For this process, the analogy of sun and clouds is often used. The sun is there, even on cloudy days, as we see clearly when we fly in an airplane. But while we are on the ground, we just can't see the sun or aren't aware of it. But even when we're on the ground, the clouds always dissipate eventually.

As became clearer in chapter 17, those Buddhist leaders who have taught extensively about creating enlightened society also express, very deeply, both faith and confidence that human beings are inherently *enlightenable,* to coin a word. This is the human quality, the *Buddha-nature* or potential for enlightenment, that Chogyam Trungpa called "basic goodness," a nonliteral translation that works well in the English language. This faith and confidence in human potential is deep seated in Buddhism, as is fitting for a nontheistic religion. Enlightenment or tapping into our basic goodness cannot be done vicariously. The true meaning of Buddhist nontheism is that there is no external savior or salvation. We have to go through that process ourselves, though we do have reliable teachers and teachings to inspire us in that journey.

This Buddhist faith and confidence in our own worthiness and workability presents a major contrast with some aspects of assumptions many Westerners have inherited about the depth of human flaws and failings. Though it may be impossible to prove either view definitively, it seems that the Buddhist view of human nature and human potential is at least as cogent as its Western alternative and opposite. And it may well be much more conducive to improving human flourishing and human society. As I mentioned in chapter 5, one of the religious ideas that may not serve us well in the long run is the teaching that human beings are inherently and inevitably more inclined to self-centeredness and negativity than to kindness and gentleness. As a result, many people suffer psychological wounding that many Asian Buddhist teachers find difficult to understand. The story is by now apocryphal among Buddhist meditation teachers of how the Dalai Lama, in early discussions with Westerners, just could not follow or understand what those Westerners meant by *low self-esteem,* a problem with which many of them struggled and about which they asked him for advice. It is said that the Dalai Lama repeatedly asked the translator for more clarification when the term *low self-esteem* would occur. The translator, because of cultural unfamiliarity with the phenomenon, also had difficulties with the term. I myself have heard my own Asian Buddhist teachers puzzle about what could possibly be the source of this problem, which they so frequently encounter among their Western students.

The Road Out: Spiritual Discipline and Real Encounter with Religious Others

The way out is to deal skillfully with our working basis. On the one hand, we definitely are equipped by default with a dualistic outlook, with a tendency to separate the world into *us* and *them* and to find *their* existence troubling. Returning to the widespread Buddhist analogy of the ever-present sun and the temporary clouds, how does the sun come out? How do the clouds dissipate? In this case, the sun is flourishing with religious diversity. The clouds preventing that flourishing are our own discomfort with religious diversity, our assessment that there is something *wrong* with religious diversity, and that in an ideal world, everyone would belong to the same religion. The "problem" of religious diversity is *not* caused by the existence of religious others, of religious diversity itself. It is caused by our attitudes toward religious diversity. Therefore, it is of our own making and, therefore, it can be solved only by us, individual by individual and group by group.

That is why I have suggested that theologies of religion should begin with topics pertaining to who we are and how we think; that is, with questions about our *identity*, not with the topic of *others*. They should be begin with our own minds and hearts, and *our* attitudes toward others, not with the *existence* of those different others. Thus, my foremost criticism of the leading current theologies of religion is that they all, including the pluralists, begin with religious others, with questions about how to think about *them*, rather than with introspection, curiosity, and self-discipline; with our own hearts, minds, curiosity, and discipline or lack thereof. This is a misplaced emphasis. My alternative is profoundly Buddhist, of course. Buddhists always insist that both our problems and their solutions are fundamentally of our own making. At root, our problems are not visited upon us by external forces, nor does their healing come from something outside us.

If, on the one hand we are equipped by default with a dualistic outlook, on the other hand, at least according to Buddhist teachings, we are not only prone to oppositional dualism. We also come deeply equipped with basic wakefulness and kind inclinations. How do they emerge? Sakyong Mipham, Chogyam Trungpa's *dharma* heir, puts it this way:

> If humanity is to survive—and not only that—to flourish, we
> must be brave enough to discover our wisdom and let it shine.
> We uncover it by beginning to examine our assumptions. We

may never before have considered human nature, but in order to move forward as a global community, it is vital that we do it now. Is it really our nature to be fearful and aggressive, or could it be that we are actually gentle and fearless at heart? Underneath the stress and anxiety, is it possible there is peace? If our self-reflection turns up an inkling of that, we can draw power from it, daring to shift our destiny. [In that process], confusion about human nature becomes confidence in human worthiness.[6]

Buddhist teachers who work with Western students acknowledge that the materialism, consumerism, and outward orientation of Western culture can make it more difficult for us to awaken our confidence in our inherent worth and workability as human beings: "Lulled to sleep by surface pleasure—and horror—most of us lack confidence in basic goodness."[7] In the Shambhala Training sequence of programs about generic, rather than specifically Buddhist, meditation, the topic of basic goodness was introduced immediately in the Friday evening talk, the first talk of the first weekend of a two-year-long sequence of trainings and talks. It was introduced so early because developing some confidence in our inherent enlightenability is considered to be so basic to creating enlightened society and because students in the program had a great deal of difficulty in taking the teaching seriously. I might also add that for us teachers in the program, that first talk on basic goodness was always one of the most difficult talks we gave, especially because we could not rely on familiar Buddhist jargon in our teaching.

To deal with this working basis of the somewhat disparate tendencies toward inherent basic goodness and the attractiveness of oppositional dualism, we have two basic tools: real contact with religious others and appropriate spiritual disciplines. We definitely need spiritual and contemplative disciplines that give us the ability to become more introspective, to deepen our basic sanity—our mental and spiritual flexibility—and to help us detach from fixed views. Spiritual disciplines that develop such states of mind are contemplative, not just discursive. They ground one in the nonconceptual and intuitive, and are deeply self-transformative as well as freeing. They free one from fixed beliefs and theories, especially about right and wrong. These attitudes must become a deep-seated part of our identity, of who are, and of how we respond to the world outside us. They must already be part of us, or at least part of our repertoire of self-discipline, when we begin to interact with religious others with integrity, when we begin to learn about and to dialogue with them, and to develop more adequate institutional responses to religious diversity.

6. Mipham, *The Shambhala Principle*, 21.
7. Ibid., 19.

However, available evidence suggests that by themselves, though necessary, such internal disciplines are not sufficient to develop flourishing with religious diversity. Sometimes, contact with something entirely new is the best antidote to deeply established obscurations. More training in what is already completely familiar can go only so far. When the young Dalai Lama was so convinced that his tradition was completely superior to any other tradition, he was already very well trained in his own tradition. That training included both intellectual and meditative knowledge about the superficiality of dualistic impressions and the underlying nonduality of self and other. He knew that self and other, or rather, our relative impressions about them, are interdependent and cocreated. Self and other do not exist independently of each other. Therefore, we can make no judgments about them that are independent of our own standpoint Yet, apparently, he, nevertheless, did not have the tools to modify, expand, or correct his views about the relative worth of Tibetan Buddhism vis-à-vis other traditions, religious and otherwise. He had only internal doctrinal refutations of some other religions, and those refutations did not depend on or allow for those traditions to represent themselves accurately or adequately. As he himself narrates, "real contact with the world's other religions"[8] was necessary for him to overcome his obscurations regarding non-Buddhist traditions. If such a well-educated and deeply spiritual person needed such contact, how much more so the rest of us!

As I have frequently argued in this book, such real contact needs to be added to whatever other repertoire of personal spiritual cultivation is already part of one's disciplines and already recommended by one's tradition. Though "loving one's neighbor," no matter how that command may be phrased, has always been part of all great traditions, nevertheless, this may be a new obligation, brought about by contemporary conditions. People now live much more intimately with religious diversity and are far more deeply affected by it. It is much more problematic to ignore religious diversity under such circumstances.

Fortunately for us, though one may search in vain for such training in many conventional religious institutions, it is now far easier to obtain information about religious others, our religious neighbors, than it was even fifty years ago, as was discussed in chapter 14. Whatever other difficulties and misfortunes may be part of economic and political situations today, we are truly fortunate to be living in a time that includes such a well-developed discipline of religious studies. We are at last free of situations in which religions are only taught confessionally. We are now able to study *about* religions as well, which adds greatly to our freedom and enables us more easily to be both wise and compassionate.

8. His Holiness, the Dalai Lama XIV, *Toward a True Kinship of Faiths*, 2.

There are many ways that this real contact with religious others may be initiated. One may be thrust unwittingly into a situation in which one cannot avoid contact with religious others, as was the young Dalai Lama, though such a scenario is not too likely. Or one may take a course on world religions, become involved in reading informative books on the topic, decide to visit the religious sanctuary of another faith, become friends with members of other religions, or even acquire a relative who belongs to another religion. No matter where we live, at least one of these options is now readily available to us.

So there is little excuse any more for the kind of ignorance about major world religions that I encountered recently. I was at a conference featuring dialogue between Christian liberation theologians and Engaged Buddhists at a prominent Christian seminary. An internationally known African Christian feminist became somewhat upset when several African American women talked about their very positive experiences with Buddhism. She asked why African American Christians were becoming so involved with the religion of the Chinese, whose economic inroads into Africa she thought were potentially very devastating for Africa. "Those Chinese are Buddhists!" she declared, implying that people of African descent should not be colluding with people whose economic activities could be so devastating for Africans. All the Buddhists gasped in disbelief and horror. How could someone think that the same Chinese who repress Buddhism (and other religions) in China and who have so cruelly destroyed Tibetan Buddhism for so many years were Buddhists themselves! Such lack of information may be excusable for someone with less influence, but it is difficult to overlook in someone with an international reputation as a theologian—a religious leader and an expert.

Once contact with religious others—neighbors—has been initiated, what is the usual developmental pattern? As I already narrated in chapter 4, one of the more common reactions among those who first start to think about, learn about, or encounter religious others is a relieved response that those others are not really so different from *us*. As chapter 4 also notes, Muslims and Hindus learning about each other's religions in my world-religions class frequently commented, with obvious relief, "They are just like us. They do the same things." While that reaction was somewhat common, I never had the opposite reaction: "Those Hindus or Muslims are really worse than they told us they were back home."

My own very early reactions to religious diversity and religious others were quite similar. In my late teens or early twenties, my argument to the pastor who was castigating me for being too positively disposed towards religious others, even Christian religious others, was, "Aren't they trying to do the same thing that we are, using different words?" I wasn't even claiming they were the same, just that they were trying to do the same things religiously. I'm not sure now what I meant by that, but probably that they were also trying to have a relationship with God, but using different prayers, maybe even a different scripture. To me, it seemed unlikely that they were actually willfully defying God by being different from us, which had always been implied in what I was taught. I was told in no uncertain terms that anyone who worshiped or prayed in a different way was an idolater who definitely was not worshiping the One True God.

Even more telling is my reaction the first time I attended a Friday evening synagogue service at the Reform Jewish Temple on the street across from the university where I went to college. I had not studied Judaism, and knew very little about it except for the anti-Jewish comments that were common fare in the church where I had been brought up. I was also nervous and scared, and had no idea what to expect. But by the end of the service, I was overwhelmingly impressed by the *familiarity* of the whole thing. Granted, this was a Reform synagogue. Most of the service was in English, there was an organ and choir, and a sermon. But many of the ritual gestures were also completely familiar. In fact they were the same as would be done in my local church, especially the rabbi raising of his arms to give the benediction. This is a rather remarkable reaction for someone as inexperienced as I then was, who had always been trained to think of Judaism as perhaps the most God-defying of all religions—because (as I was taught) Judaism was supposed to be the inheritor of God's promises to Israel, but Jews stubbornly and pridefully refused to recognize the fulfillment of those promises.

Thus, at least for some people, a kind of natural inclusivism seems to prevail as a first reaction to what one hears when one begins to learn about other religions and to think about religious diversity. Perhaps it was inevitable that Christian theologies of religion, given their dualistic starting point, would have first developed inclusivist and then pluralist theologies of religion. This suggests that Christian theologians of religions may be at a very fruitful stage of development. When we actually encounter those who are different and actually learn about them accurately, we often conclude that they are more similar than different. I take this as an indication that many people are predisposed to think kindly of others even though they may be quite different. It can also be taken as an indication that Buddhist teachings about Buddha-nature and basic goodness have some real cogency. I also take it as an indication that fear of and hostility towards those who are different, if these feelings are to be sustained, must be reinforced. In many situations, there are plenty of cultural messages reinforcing that *us/them* mentality.

My criticisms of the inclusive and pluralist positions in chapter 4 have more to do with the fact that if we continue our explorations of diverse religions, inevitably we will come up against intractable differences among them. Religions don't all teach the same thing despite many popular opinions to that effect. We may even find things that deeply trouble us. Then we need tools for living and flourishing with religious diversity, including some clarity about which differences matter and which do not. We also need to know the most skillful methods for working with religious practices with which we cannot agree. As a lifelong feminist, I certainly have had a lot of experience doing just that.

However, in some cases, that initial reaction to unfamiliar religious phenomena can also include dismay, even horror. Then it is important to be suspicious of that first reaction, to take the time and the discipline to find out more about the insider's point of view on that belief or practice. Thus, the practice of empathy must precede whatever judgments we may eventually make. Usually, only in more extreme cases involving ethics, not theology, will our initial reservations be sustainable once we understand the situation more fully, from the inside.

Finally, regarding the way out of default dualism, as we make real contact with religious others, it is crucial for us to realize that no one is ever compelled to believe anything, no matter how frequently they have been taught a certain point of view. My university students used to claim, for example, that because they were biblical literalists, they were not interpreting the Bible at all, unlike those who took certain statements as symbolic. They resisted my observation that they were also interpreting the Bible. I suggested to them that they were simply choosing a literalist *interpretation* over a nonliteralist, symbolic interpretation. I would then ask them to justify their hermeneutical stance, which they were very rarely able to do. They would simply repeat their assertion that they were faithful and loyal to scripture, unlike those other people who interpreted it "any way they wanted to." But they obviously *wanted* to take scriptures more rather than less literally. This kind of claim always reminds me of a cartoon of a preacher who has scribbled a note in the margin of his sermon. "Shout louder. Point weak."

There are always multiple positions about any controversial issue, such as religious diversity (or gender and religion, to name another area in which religious conservatives often argue that they are simply "following scripture" rather than making a choice). If those differing positions were not real possibilities, they would not exist, and no one would ever have constructed them. So out of many positions regarding complex topics like religious diversity, everyone *chooses* one among those positions. It is disingenuous to claim that one's position is dictated by scripture, tradition, or God; that one would *prefer* to regard all religions as worthy but is compelled not to by something or some-one else. The question I always insistently place before people is the question of *why* they prefer exclusive or inclusive truth claims to a position that regards religious diversity as inevitable, normal, natural, and therefore not troubling or disturbing. That question puts responsibility where it belongs—on the re-ligious practitioner, not on God, scripture, or dead religious authorities from the past. As I have said before, it is especially important that believers stop blaming God for their fear, hostility, or discomfort regarding religious oth-ers, or for their unwillingness to make real contact with them. Instead, they need to look within, to question *why* they hold the attitudes that they do. It is important to explore whether those attitudes actually bring one restfulness or agitation, and whether they are conducive to peace within oneself and with the world. Curiosity and deep introspection are often the missing links when people fail to flourish with religious diversity.

Eventually, Flexible Mind—Not Opinionated, and Comfortable with Diversity

Real contact with the world's religions, combined with consistent practice of a relevant spiritual discipline, will result in an ability to flourish with re-ligious diversity. Flourishing with religious diversity is actually a matter of internal transformation, of developing a flexible state of mind, a mind that is not opinionated or fixated on dogmas and views. With such a state of mind, one is profoundly *comfortable* and at ease with oneself and the world. One is also alert, and committed to working compassionately with the whole world. Because one is no longer consumed with dualism and judgmental-ism, one does not need to maintain suspicions about the others or a fearful state of mind. Thus, in the end, we bring everything back to the subject and the subject's dispositions. Flourishing with religious diversity has little to do with so-called objectivity and external truths, in no small part because, regarding much of what religion is about, there is no objective place from which to determine timeless or external truths.

We can only move forward with as much kindness and wisdom as we can muster, using the tools we have. Because the world's religious are so very diverse, when we interact widely with them, we are very likely to come upon things that are deeply problematic, such as persistent sexism, oppression, and exploitation—to name only the most common and evident flaws that damage all religions. But with plenty of information and appropriate spiritual disci-plines well in place, we are able to address these problems with intelligence, not with the anger and condemnation that are so often the major response of those without well established spiritual disciplines. With fewer opinions and less self-righteousness, we can actually work with the world with energy and deep caring. Intelligence and deep caring feel completely different from anger, condemnation, and self-righteousness and are much more effective.

Coda

To learn how to flourish with religious diversity is a goal that would benefit every religious tradition. Each tradition has its own tools that would promote that goal, no matter what its traditional position about religious diversity may have been in the past. While I could make suggestions about how different traditions could use their own theologies and scriptures to encourage their adherents to become proactive regarding religious diversity, I do not feel that is my job. Such teachings would be more effective coming from the leaders of those traditions. What I have offered here are the tools that Buddhism, especially Buddhist meditation practices, and the comparative study of religions can offer. Most or all of them, I believe, are widely applicable for people of any religious tradition or with no religious tradition.

The Dalai Lama makes a similar plea at the end of his major book about religious diversity: *Toward a True Kinship of Faiths*. He writes, "If you believe in God, see others as God's children. If you are a nontheist, see all beings as your mother. When you do this, there will be no room for prejudice, intolerance, or exclusivity . . . Make the vow today that you may become an instrument of peace, living according to the ethical teachings of compassion in your own religion."[9]

As we can see from what the Dalai Lama said, flourishing *with* religious diversity also promotes flourishing *of* religious diversity. Both, however, presuppose acceptance of the fact that religious diversity is normal, natural, here to stay, not a mistake. Like many other diversities, religious diversity really does not need to elicit a lot of discussion. Nevertheless, religious diversity has elicited a great deal of discussion and controversy. Resistance to religious diversity has also engendered a great deal of suffering, both for those who try to get others to conform to their demands and needs for religious unity, and for those who are on the receiving end of this unwanted and unwarranted solicitousness. However one justifies and explains religious diversity to oneself, it is crucial that everyone engage in the internal conversation with oneself and one's own religious understandings and spiritual disciplines.

9. Ibid., 181.

Bibliography

Abe, Masao. *Buddhism and Interfaith Dialogue*. Edited by Steven Heine. Honolulu: University of Hawaii Press, 1995.

———. *Zen and Comparative Studies*. Honolulu: University of Hawaii Press, 1997.

Anderson, Gerald H., and Thomas F. Stransky, eds. *Christ's Lordship and Religious Pluralism*. Maryknoll, NY: Orbis, 1981.

Assmann, Jan. *The Price of Monotheism*. Translated by Robert Savage. Stanford: Stanford University Press, 2010.

Ayoub, Mahmoud. "Religious Pluralism and the Qu'ran." On the website of the International Institute of Islamic Thought. Online: http://iiit.org/Research/ScholarsSummerInstitute/TableofContents/ReligiousPluralismAndTheQuran/tabid/244/Default.aspx/.

Bartholomeusz, Tessa J. *In Defense of Dharma: Just-War Ideology in Buddhist Sri Lanka*. Routledge Curzon Critical Studies in Buddhism. London: Routledge Curzon, 2002.

Bartholomeusz, Tessa J., and Chandra R. de Silva, eds. *Buddhist Fundamentalism and Minority Identities in Sri Lanka*. Albany: State University of New York Press, 1998.

Bauman, Gerd. *The Multicultural Riddle: Rethinking National, Ethnic, and Religious Identities*. Zones of Religion. New York: Routledge, 1999.

Beauvoir, Simone de. *The Second Sex*. Translated by H. M. Parshley. New York: Knopf, 1953.

Becker, Karl J., and Ilaria Morali, eds. *Catholic Engagement with World Religions: A Comprehensive Study*. Faith Meets Faith Series. Maryknoll, NY: Orbis, 2010.

Berger. Peter, editor. *The Desecularization of the World: Resurgent Religion and World Politics*. Washington DC: Ethics and Public Policy Center, 1999.

Berling, Judith. *A Pilgrim in Chinese Culture: Negotiating Religious Diversity*. Faith Meets Faith Series. Maryknoll, NY: Orbis, 1997.

Berreby, David. *Us and Them: The Science of Identity*. Chicago: University of Chicago Press, 2005.

Bevans, Stephen. "Church Teaching on Mission: *Ad Gentes, Evangelii Nuntiandi, Redemptoris Missio*, and *Dialogue and Proclamation*." Online: http://www.maryknollvocations.com/mission.pdf/.

Bivins, Jason C. *Religion of Fear: The Politics of Horror in Conservative Evangelism*. Oxford: Oxford University Press, 2008.

Bloom, Irene et al. *Religious Diversity and Human Rights*. New York: Columbia University Press, 1996.

Bodhi, Bhikkhu, ed. and intro. *In the Buddha's Words: An Anthology of Discourses from the Pali Canon*. Teachings of the Buddha. Boston: Wisdom Publications, 2005.

Brown, Lesley, editor-in-chief. *Shorter Oxford English Dictionary on Historical Principles*. 2 vols. 6th ed. Oxford: Oxford University Press, 2007.

Calhoun, Craig et al. *Rethinking Secularism*. Oxford: Oxford University Press, 2011.

Christ, Carol P. "Response: Roundtable—Feminist Theology and Religious Diversity." *Journal of Feminist Studies* 16/2 (2000) 79–84

Christ, Carol P., and Judith Plaskow, eds. *Womanspirit Rising: A Feminist Reader in Religion*. Harper Forum Books. San Francisco: Harper & Row, 1979.

Chödrön, Pema. *Comfortable with Uncertainty: 108 Teachings on Cultivating Fearlessness and Compassion*. Boston: Shambhala, 2008.

———. *Living Beautifully with Uncertainty and Change*. Boston: Shambhala, 2012.

———. *The Places That Scare You: A Guide to Fearlessness in Difficult Times*. Boston: Shambhala, 2002.

Chodron, Thubten. *Working with Anger*. Ithaca, NY: Snow Lion, 2001.

Clooney, Francis J. *Comparative Theology: Deep Learning across Religious Borders*. Malden, MA: Wiley-Blackwell, 2010.

———, ed. *The New Comparative Theology: Interreligious Insights from the Next Generation*. London: T. & T. Clark, 2010.

Cobb, John B., Jr. *Beyond Dialogue: Toward a Mutual Transformation of Christianity and Buddhism*. 1982. Reprinted, Eugene, OR: Wipf & Stock, 1998.

———. "Beyond 'Pluralism.'" In *Christian Uniqueness Reconsidered: The Myth of a Pluralistic Theology of Religions*, edited by Gavin D'Costa, 81–95. Faith Meets Faith Series. Maryknoll, NY: Orbis, 1990.

———. *Transforming Christianity and the World: A Way beyond Absolutism and Relativism*. Edited and introduced by Paul F. Knitter. Faith Meets Faith Series. Maryknoll, NY: Orbis, 1999.

Cornille, Catherine. *The Im-possibility of Interreligious Dialogue*. New York: Crossroad, 2008.

———. *Many Mansions? Multiple Religious Belonging and Christian Identity*. Faith Meets Faith Series. 2002. Reprinted, Eugene, OR: Wipf & Stock, 2010.

Dean, Thomas, ed. *Religious Pluralism and Truth: Essays on Cross-Cultural Philosophy of Religion*. SUNY Series in Religious Studies. Albany: State University of New York Press, 1995.

D'Costa, Gavin, ed. *Christian Uniqueness Reconsidered: The Myth of a Pluralistic Theology of Religions*. Faith Meets Faith Series. Maryknoll, NY: Orbis, 1990.

———. *Christianity and World Religions: Disputed Questions in the Theology of Religions*. Malden, MA: Wiley-Blackwell, 2009.

Deegalle, Mahinda, ed. *Buddhism, Conflict, and Violence in Modern Sri Lanka*. Routledge Critical Studies in Buddhism. London: Routledge, 2006.

———. "JHU Politics for Peace and a Righteous State." In *Buddhism, Conflict, and Violence in Modern Sri Lanka*, edited by Mahinda Deegalle, 233–54. Routledge Critical Studies in Buddhism. London: Routledge, 2006.

Dhammika, Ven. S., trans. *The Edicts of King Asoka*. Kandy, Sri Lanka: The Buddhist Publication Society, 1993. Online: http://www.accesstoinsight.org/lib/authors/dhammika/wheel386.html/.

Dharmasiri, Gunapala. *A Buddhist Critique of the Christian Concept of God*. Antioch, CA: Golden Leaves, 1988.

Driver, Tom F. "The Case for Pluralism." In *The Myth of Christian Uniqueness: Toward a Pluralistic Theology of Religions*, edited by John Hick and Paul F. Knitter. Faith Meets Faith Series. 1987. Reprinted, Eugene, OR: Wipf & Stock, 2005.

Dunn, Richard S. *The Age of Religious Wars, 1559–1715*. 2nd ed. The Norton History of Modern Europe. New York: Norton, 1979.

Dupuis, Jacques. *Toward a Christian Theology of Religious Pluralism*. Maryknoll, NY: Orbis, 1998.

Dzogchen Ponlop, Rinpoche. *Penetrating Wisdom: The Aspiration of Samantabhadra*. Vancouver, BC: Siddhi, 2002.

Eck, Diana. *Encountering God: A Spiritual Journey from Boseman to Banares*. Boston: Beacon, 1993.

———. *A New Religious America: How a "Christian Country" Has Become the World's Most Religiously Diverse Nation*. New York: Harper & Row, 2001.

Eliade, Mircea. *The Sacred and the Profane: The Nature of Religion*. Harper Torchbooks. New York: Harper & Row, 1961.

Fronsdal, Gil, trans. *The Dhammapada*. Boston: Shambhala, 2005.

Fletcher, Jeannine Hill. *Monopoly on Salvation? A Feminist Approach to Religious Pluralism*. New York: Continuum, 2005.

Gampopa. *The Jewel Ornament of Liberation*. Translated by Herbert V. Guenther. Clear Light Series. Berkeley, CA: Shambhala, 1971.

———. *Gems of Dharma, Jewels of Freedom: The Clear and Authoritative, Classic Handbook of Mahayana Buddhism by the Great 12th century Tibetan Bodhisattva*. Translated by Ken and Katia Holmes. Fores, Scotland: Altea, 1995.

Garfield, Jay L. *The Fundamental Wisdom of the Middle Way: Nagarjuna's Mulamadhyamikakarika*. New York: Oxford University Press, 1995.

Geertz, Clifford A. "Religion as a Cultural System." In *Reader in Comparative Religion: An Anthropological Approach*, edited by William A. Lessa and Evon Z. Vogt, 167–78. 3rd ed. New York: Harper & Row, 1972. Reprinted in Geertz, *The Interpretation of Cultures*, 87–125. New York: Basic Books, 1973.

Gethin, Rupert, trans. *Sayings of the Buddha: New Translations from the Pali Nikayas*. Oxford World's Classics. Oxford: Oxford University Press, 2008.

Gilkey, Langdon. "Plurality and Its Theological Implications." In *The Myth of Christian Uniqueness: Toward a Pluralistic Theology of Religions*, edited by John Hick and Paul F. Knitter, 37–50. Faith Meets Faith Series. 1987. Reprinted, Eugene, OR: Wipf & Stock, 2005.

Girard, René. *Violence and the Sacred*. Translated by Patrick Gregory. Baltimore: Johns Hopkins University Press, 1977.

Grant, Patrick. *Buddhism and Ethnic Conflict in Sri Lanka*. SUNY Series in Religious Studies. Albany: State University of New York Press, 2009.

Greeley, Andrew, and Michael Hout. *The Truth about Conservative Christians: What They Think and What They Believe*. Chicago: University of Chicago Press, 2006.

Griffiths, Paul J. *Christianity through Non-Christian Eyes*. Faith Meets Faith Series. Maryknoll, NY: Orbis, 1990.

———. *Problems of Religious Diversity*. Exploring the Philosophy of Religion 1. Malden, MA: Blackwell, 2001.

Gross, Rita M. *Buddhism after Patriarchy: A Feminist History, Analysis, and Recon-struction of Buddhism.* Albany: State University of New York, 1993.

———. "Buddhist Contributions to the Civic and Conscientious Public Forums." In *Taking Religious Pluralism Seriously: Spiritual Politics on America's Sacred Ground,* edited by Barbara A. McGraw and Jo Renee Formicola, 215–34. Waco: Baylor University Press, 2005.

———. "Buddhist History for Buddhist Practitioners." *Tricycle: The Buddhist Review* 20/1 (2010) 83–85, 118–20.

———. "Buddhist Theology?" In *Buddhist Theology: Critical Reflections by Contem-porary Buddhist Scholars,* edited by Roger Jackson and John Makransky, 53–60. Curzon Critical Studies in Buddhism. London: Routledge Curzon, 2000.

———. "Excuse Me, but What's the Question? Isn't Religious Diversity Normal?" In *The Myth of Religious Superiority: Multifaith Explorations of Religious Pluralism,* edited by Paul F. Knitter, 75–87. Faith Meets Faith Series. Maryknoll, NY: Orbis, 2005.

———. *Feminism and Religion: An Introduction.* Boston: Beacon, 1996.

———. "Feminist Theology: Religiously Diverse Neighborhood or Christian Ghetto?" *Journal of Feminist Studies in Religion* 16/2 (2000) 73–78.

———. *A Garland of Feminist Reflections: Forty Years of Religious Exploration.* Berkeley: University of California Press, 2009.

———. "I Am Speechless: Thank You, Colleague Friends." *Buddhist–Christian Studies* 31 (2011) 89–99.

———. "How Clinging to Gender Subverts Enlightenment." *Enquiring Mind* 27/1 (2010) 18–19, 32.

———. "Prayer and Meditation." In *Christians Talk about Buddhist Meditation, Buddhists Talk about Christian Prayer,* edited by Rita M. Gross and Terry C. Muck. New York: Continuum, 2003.

———. "Why We Need to Know Our Buddhist History." Commentary (Editorial), *Buddha Dharma: The Practitioner's Quarterly* (Spring 2009) 7–8.

———, ed. *Beyond Androcentrism: New Essays on Women and Religion.* American Academy of Religion Aids for the Study of Religion 6. Missoula: Scholars, 1977.

Gross, Rita M., and Terry Muck, eds. *Buddhists Talk about Jesus, Christians Talk about the Buddha.* New York: Continuum, 2000.

———, eds. *Christians Talk about Buddhist Meditation, Buddhists Talk about Christian Prayer.* New York: Continuum, 2003.

Gross, Rita M., and Rosemary Radford Ruether. *Religious Feminism and the Future of the Planet: A Buddhist–Christian Conversation.* New York: Continuum, 2001.

Gunn, T. Jeremy, and John Witte, eds. *No Establishment of Religion: American's Original Contribution to Religious Liberty.* Oxford: Oxford University Press, 2012.

Habito, Ruben L. F. *Healing Breath: Zen Spirituality for a Wounded Earth.* Ecology and Justice Series. Maryknoll, NY: Orbis, 1996.

Herbert, David. *Religion and Civil Society: Rethinking Public Religion in the Contemporary World.* Ashgate Religion, Culture & Society Series. Aldershot, UK: Ashgate, 2003.

Harris, Elizabeth. "Buddhism and Post-War Reconciliation in Sri Lanka: The Use and Misuse of Symbolism." Paper presented at the American Academy of Religion meetings in San Francisco, CA, November 19–22, 2011.

Harris, Matthew L., and Thomas S. Kidd. *The Founding Fathers and the Debate over Religion in Revolutionary America: A History in Documents.* Oxford: Oxford University Press, 2012.

Heisig, James W., and John C. Maraldo, eds. *Rude Awakenings: Zen, the Kyoto School, & the Question of Nationalism.* Nanzan Studies in Religion and Culture. Honolulu: University of Hawaii Press, 1994.

Hick, John. *A Christian Theology of Religions: The Rainbow of Faiths.* Louisville: Westminster John Knox, 1995.

———. *Dialogues in the Philosophy of Religion.* Basingstoke, UK: Palgrave Macmillan, 2010.

———. *God and the Universe of Faiths.* New York: St. Martin's, 1973.

———. *God Has Many Names: Britain's New Religious Pluralism.* London: Macmillan, 1980.

———. *An Interpretation of Religion: Human Responses to the Transcendent.* 2nd ed. New Haven: Yale University Press, 2004.

———. "The Next Step beyond Dialogue." In *The Myth of Religious Superiority: Multifaith Explorations of Religious Pluralism,* edited by Paul F. Knitter, 3–12. Faith Meets Faith Series. Maryknoll, NY: Orbis, 2005.

———. *Philosophy of Religion.* 4th ed. Prentice-Hall Foundations in Philosophy Series. Englewood Cliffs, NJ: Prentice-Hall, 1990.

Hick, John, and Brian Hebblethwaite, eds. *Christianity and Other Religions: Selected Readings.* Philadelphia: Fortress, 1980.

Hick, John, and Paul F. Knitter, eds. *The Myth of Christian Uniqueness: Toward a Pluralistic Theology of Religions.* Faith Meets Faith Series. 1987. Reprinted, Eugene, OR: Wipf & Stock, 2005.

Heim, S. Mark. *Salvations: Truth and Difference in Religion.* Faith Meets Faith Series. Maryknoll, NY: Orbis, 1995.

His Holiness, the Dalai Lama XIV. *Beyond Religion: Ethics for a Whole World.* Boston: Houghton Mifflin Harcourt, 2011.

———. *The Good Heart: A Buddhist Perspective on the Teachings of Jesus.* Boston: Wisdom Publications, 1996.

———. "'Religious Harmony' and Extracts from *The Bodhgaya Interviews.*" In *Christianity through Non-Christian Eyes,* edited by Paul J. Griffiths, 162–70. Faith Meets Faith Series. Maryknoll, NY: Orbis, 1990.

———. *Toward a True Kinship of Faiths: How the World's Religions Can Come Together.* New York: Doubleday Religion, 2010.

Hood, Bruce. *The Self Illusion: How the Social Brain Creates Identity.* Oxford: Oxford University Press, 2012

Hopkins, Thomas J. *The Hindu Religious Tradition.* The Religious Life of Man. Belmont, CA: Dickenson, 1971.

Hutchison, William R. *Religious Pluralism in America: The Contentious History of a Founding Ideal.* New Haven: Yale University Press, 2003.

Ives, Christopher. *Imperial-Way Zen: Ichikawa Hakugen's Critique and Lingering Questions for Buddhist Ethics.* Honolulu: University of Hawaii Press, 2009.

Jerryson, Michael K., and Mark Juergensmeyer, eds. *Buddhist Warfare.* Oxford: Oxford University Press, 2010.

Jetsun Khandro, Rinpoche. Oral teachings given at Lotus Garden Retreat Center, Stanley, VA, August–September 2011.

Juergensmeyer, Mark. *Terror in the Mind of God: The Global Rise of Religious Violence.* Comparative Studies in Religion and Society 13. Berkeley: University of California Press, 2000.

Kabat-Zinn, Jon. *Full Catastrophe Living: Using the Wisdom of Your Body and Mind to Face Stress, Pain, and Illness.* New York: Random House, 1990.

Kaplan, Benjamin J. *Divided by Faith: Religious Conflict and the Practice of Toleration in Early Modern Europe.* Cambridge, MA: Belknap, 2007.

Kaufman, Gordon D. *God, Mystery, Diversity: Christian Theology in a Pluralistic World.* Minneapolis: Fortress, 1996.

Khan, Muqtedar. "Dalai Lama Condemns Islamic and Christian Practice of Conversions." Online: http://www.beliefnet.com/Faiths/Islam/2001/02/Dalai-Lama-Condemns-Islamic-And-Christian-Practice-Of-Conversions.aspx/.

Khyentse, Dzongsar Jamyang. *What Makes You Not a Buddhist?* Boston: Shambhala, 2007.

Kiblinger, Kim Beise. *Buddhist Inclusivism: Attitudes toward Religious Others.* Ashgate World Philosophies Series. Aldershot, UK: Ashgate, 2005.

Kim, Sebastian C. H. *In Search of Identity: Debates on Religious Conversion in India.* Oxford: Oxford University Press, 2003.

Kimball, Charles. *When Religion Becomes Evil.* San Francisco: HarperSanFrancisco, 2002.

Knitter, Paul F. "Inter-Religious Dialogue and Social Action." In *The Wiley-Blackwell Companion to Interreligious Dialogue*, edited by Catherine Cornille, 133–48. Wiley-Blackwell Companions to Religion. Hoboken, NJ: Wiley, 2013.

———. *Introducing Theologies of Religion.* Maryknoll, NY: Orbis, 2002.

———. *No Other Name? A Critical Survey of Christian Attitudes toward the World Religions.* American Society of Missiology Series 7. Maryknoll, NY: Orbis, 1985.

———. *One Earth, Many Religions: Multifaith Dialogue and Global Responsibility.* Maryknoll, NY: Orbis, 1995.

———, ed. *The Myth of Religious Superiority: Multifaith Explorations of Religious Pluralism.* Faith Meets Faith Series. Maryknoll, NY: Orbis, 2005.

———. "Rita Gross: Buddhist–Christian Dialogue about Dialogue." *Buddhist–Christian Studies* 31 (2011) 79–84.

———. "Toward a Liberation Theology of Religions." In *The Myth of Christian Uniqueness: Toward a Pluralistic Theology of Religions*, edited by John Hick and Paul F. Knitter, 178–200. 1987. Reprinted, Eugene, OR: Wipf & Stock, 2005.

———. *Without Buddha I Could Not Be a Christian.* Oxford: Oneworld, 2009.

Küng, Hans. *Global Responsibility: In Search of a New World Ethic.* New York: Crossroad, 1991.

Kyabgon, Traleg. *The Essence of Buddhism: An Introduction to Its Philosophy and Practice.* Shambhala Dragon Editions. Boston: Shambhala, 2001.

———. *Mind at Ease: Self-Liberation through Mahamudra Meditation.* Boston: Shambhala, 2004.

———. *The Practice of Lojong: Cultivating Compassion through Training the Mind.* Boston: Shambhala, 2007.

Lamotte, Etienne. *History of Indian Buddhism: From the Origins to the Saka Era.* Publications de l'Institut orientaliste de Louvain 36. Louvain-la-Neuve: Université catholique de Louvain, Institut orientaliste, 1988.

Larson, Gerald James. *India's Agony over Religion*. SUNY Series in Religious Studies. Albany: State University of New York Press, 1995.

Lindbeck, George A. *The Nature of Doctrine: Religion and Theology in a Postliberal Age*. 25th anniversary ed. Louisville: Westminster John Knox, 2009.

Levinson, Sanford. *Wrestling with Diversity*. Durham: Duke University Press, 2001.

Makransky, John. "A Buddhist Critique of and Learning from Christian Liberation Theology." Paper delivered at International Conference on Socially Engaged Buddhists and Christian Liberation Theology held at Union Theological Seminary, New York City, 2013.

Marty, Martin E. *When Faiths Collide*. Blackwell Manifestos. Malden, MA: Blackwell, 2005.

McDermott, Gerald R. *Can Evangelicals Learn from World Religions? Jesus, Revelation, and Religious Traditions*. Downers Grove, IL: InterVarsity, 2000.

McGraw, Barbara A. *Rediscovering America's Sacred Ground: Public Religion and Pursuit of the Good in a Pluralistic America*. SUNY Series in Religion and American Public Life. Albany: State University of New York Press, 2003.

McGraw, Barbara A., and Jo Renee Formicola, eds. *Taking Religious Pluralism Seriously: Spiritual Politics on America's Sacred Ground*. Waco: Baylor University Press, 2005.

McKim, Robert. *Religious Ambiguity and Religious Diversity*. Oxford: Oxford University Press, 2001.

McLaren, Brian D. *Why Did Jesus, Moses, the Buddha, and Mohammed Cross the Road? Christian Identity in a Multifaith World*. New York: Jericho, 2012.

McLeod, Ken. *Wake Up to Your Life: Discovering the Buddhist Path of Attention*. San Francisco: HarperSanFrancisco, 2001.

Michaels, Arno. *My Life after Hate*. Milwaukee: La Prensa de LAH, 2010.

Mipham, Sakyong, Rinpoche. *The Shambhala Principle: Discovering Humanity's Hidden Treasure*. New York: Harmony Books, 2013.

Monsma, Stephen V., and J. Christopher Soper, eds. *The Challenge of Pluralism: Church and State in Five Democracies*. 2nd ed. Lanham, MD: Rowman & Littlefield, 2009.

Murray, Bruce T. *Religious Liberty in America: The First Amendment in Historical and Contemporary Perspective*. Amherst: University of Massachusetts Press, 2008.

Nalanda Translation Committee. *The Heart Sutra*. Online: http://nalandatranslation. org/media/Heart-Sutra.pdf/.

Nandalike, Walter, editor-in-chief. *Daijiworld Media Pvt Ltd Mangalore*. Website. Online: http://www.daijiworld.com/news/news_disp.asp?n_id=156600/.

Nhat Hanh, Thich. *Anger: Wisdom for Cooling the Flames*. New York: Riverhead, 2002.

———. *Fear: Essential Wisdom for Getting through the Storm*. New York: HarperOne, 2012.

———. *Going Home: Jesus and Buddha as Brothers*. New York: Riverhead, 1999.

———. *Good Citizens: Creating Enlightened Society*. Berkeley, CA: Parallax, 2012.

———. *The Heart of the Buddha's Teaching*. New York: Broadway, 1998.

———. *Living Buddha, Living Christ*. New York: Riverhead, 1995.

———. *The Path of Emancipation: Talks from a 21-Day Mindfulness Retreat*. Berkeley, CA: Parallax, 2000,

Nussbaum, Martha. *The New Religious Intolerance: Overcoming the Politics of Fear in an Anxious Age*. Cambridge, MA: Belknap, 2012.

Obeyesekere, Gananath, and Frank Reynolds. *The Two Wheels of Dhamma: Essays on the Theravada Tradition in India and Ceylon*. Edited by Bardwell L. Smith.

American Academy of Religion Studies in Religion 3. Chambersburg, PA: American Academy of Religion, 1972.

Oldenberg, Hermann, trans. *Vinaya Texts.* 3 vols. 1881–85. Reprinted, N.p.: Forgotten Books, 2007.

O'Neill, Maura. *Mending a Torn World: Women in Interreligious Dialogue.* Faith Meets Faith Series. Maryknoll, NY: Orbis, 2007.

———. *Women Speaking, Women Listening: Women in Interreligious Dialogue.* Faith Meets Faith Series. Maryknoll, NY: Orbis, 1990.

Owen, J. Judd. *Religion and the Demise of Liberal Rationalism: The Foundational Crisis of the Separation of Church and State.* Chicago: University of Chicago Press, 2001.

Paden, William E. *Interpreting the Sacred: Ways of Viewing Religion.* Boston: Beacon, 1992.

———. *Religious Worlds: The Comparative Study of Religion.* Boston: Beacon, 1988.

Patel, Eboo. *Sacred Ground: Pluralism, Prejudice, and the Promise of America.* Boston: Beacon, 2012.

Paul, Thomas, ed. *Human Rights and Religious Conversion.* Delhi: Media House. 2002.

Peiris, Aloysius. *Fire and Water: Basic Issues in Asian Buddhism and Christianity.* Faith Meets Faith Series. Maryknoll, NY: Orbis, 1996.

———. *Love Meets Wisdom: A Christian Experience of Buddhism.* Faith Meets Faith Series. Maryknoll, NY: Orbis, 1988.

Phan, Peter C. *Being Religious Interreligiously: Asian Perspectives on Interfaith Dialogue.* Maryknoll, NY: Orbis, 2004.

Prothero, Stephen. *Religious Literacy: What Every American Needs to Know—and Doesn't.* New York: HarperCollins, 2008.

Quinn, Philip L., and Kevin Meeker, eds. *The Philosophical Challenge of Religious Diversity.* New York: Oxford University Press, 2000.

Race, Alan. *Christians and Religious Pluralism: Patterns in the Christian Theology of Religion.* Maryknoll, NY: Orbis, 1982.

Race, Fran. "Dalai Lama Urges Christians Not to Convert to Buddhism." *Modern Buddhism,* September 2006. Online: http://newbuddhist.com/discussion/1955/dalai-lama-urges-christians-not-to-convert-to-buddhism/.

Rambo, Lewis R. *Understanding Religious Conversion.* New Haven: Yale University Press, 1993.

Robinson, Richard, et al. *Buddhist Religions: A Historical Introduction* 5th ed. Religious Life in History. Belmont, CA: Wadsworth, 2005.

Robinson, Rowena, and Sathianathan Clark, eds. *Religious Conversion in India: Modes, Motivations, and Meanings.* New Delhi: Oxford University Press, 2003.

Samartha, Stanley J. "The Cross and the Rainbow." In *The Myth of Christian Uniqueness: Toward a Pluralistic Theology of Religions,* edited by John Hick and Paul F. Knitter, 69–88. 1987. Reprinted, Eugene, OR: Wipf & Stock, 2005.

Sanghrakshita, Bhikshu. *Ambedkar and Buddhism.* Glasgow: Windhorse, 1986 Online: http://www.sangharakshita.org/_books/Ambedkar_and_Buddhism.pdf/.

Schmidt-Leukel, Perry, ed. *Buddhism and Christianity in Dialogue: The Gerald Weisfeld Lectures 2004.* London: SCM, 2005.

———, ed. *Buddhism and Religious Diversity.* 4 vols. London: Routledge, 2013.

———. *Buddhist Attitudes to Other Religions.* St. Ottilien: EOS, 2008.

———. "Exclusivism, Inclusivism, Pluralism: The Tripolar Typology—Clarified and Reaffirmed." In *The Myth of Religious Superiority: Multifaith Explorations of*

Religious Pluralism, edited by Paul F. Knitter, 13–27. Faith Meets Faith Series. Mary-knoll, NY: Orbis, 2005.

———. *Transformation by Integration: How Inter-faith Encounter Changes Christianity*. London: SCM, 2009.

Schrobe, Richard. *Don't-Know Mind: The Spirit of Korean Zen*. Boston: Shambhala, 2004.

Schwartz, Regina M. *The Curse of Cain: The Violent Legacy of Monotheism*. Chicago: University of Chicago Press, 1997.

Seiko, Hirata. "Zen Buddhist Attitudes to War." In *Rude Awakenings: Zen, The Kyoto School and the Question of Nationalism*, edited by James W. Heisig and John C. Maraldo, 3–15. Nanzan Studies in Religion and Culture. Honolulu: University of Hawaii Press, 1994.

Selengut, Charles. *Sacred Fury: Understanding Religious Violence*. 2nd ed. Lanham, MD: Rowman & Littlefield, 2008.

Seneviratne, H. L. *The Work of Kings: The New Buddhism in Sri Lanka*. Chicago: University of Chicago Press, 1999.

Sernett, Milton C. "Religion and Group Identity: Believers as Behavers." In *Introduction to the Study of Religion*, edited by T. William Hall, 217–30. New York: Harper & Row. 1978.

Sharma, Arvind. *Problematizing Religious Freedom*. Studies in Global Justice 9. Dordrecht: Springer: 2012.

Simmer-Brown, Judith, and Fran Grace. *Meditation and the Classroom: Contemplative Pedagogy for Religious Studies*. SUNY Series in Religious Studies. Albany: State University of New York Press, 2011.

Smith, Christian. *Christian America? What Evangelicals Really Want*. Berkeley: University of California Press, 2000.

Smith, Wilfred Cantwell. "The Christian in Religiously Plural World." In *Christianity and Other Religions: Selected Readings*, edited by John Hick and Brian Hebblethwaite, 87–107. Philadelphia: Fortress, 1980.

———. *The Meaning and End of Religion*. Minneapolis: Fortress, 1991.

———. *Religious Diversity*. A Crossroad Paperback. New York: Crossroad, 1982.

———. *Towards a World Theology: Faith and the Comparative History of Religion*. Philadelphia: Westminster, 1981.

Smith-Christopher, Daniel L., ed. *Subverting Hatred: The Challenge of Nonviolence in Religious Traditions*. Boston: Boston Research Center for the 21st Century, 1998.

Spinner-Halev, Jeff. *Surviving Diversity: Religion and Democratic Citizenship*. Baltimore: Johns Hopkins University Press, 2000.

Stabile, Susan J. *Growing in Love and Wisdom: Tibetan Buddhist Sources for Christian Meditation*. Oxford: Oxford University Press, 2012.

Stark, Rodney. *One True God: Historical Consequences of Monotheism*. Princeton: Princeton University Press, 2001.

Steward, Robert B., ed. *Can Only One Religion Be True? Paul Knitter and Harold Netland in Dialogue*. Minneapolis: Fortress, 2013.

Stone, Jon R., ed. *The Essential Max Müller: On Language, Mythology, and Religion*. New York: Palgrave Macmillan, 2002.

Strong, John S. *The Legend of King Asoka: A Study and Translation of the Asokavadana*. Princeton Library of Asian Translations. Princeton: Princeton University Press, 1983.

Sucitto, Ajahn. *Turning the Wheel of Truth: Commentary on the Buddha's First Teaching.* Boston: Shambhala, 2010.

Suchocki, Marjorie Hewitt. *Divinity & Diversity: A Christian Affirmation of Religious Pluralism.* Nashville: Abingdon, 2003.

Sullivan, Winnifred Fallers. *The Impossibility of Religious Freedom.* Princeton: Princeton University Press, 2005.

——— et al., eds. *After Secular Law.* The Cultural Lives of Law. Stanford: Stanford University Press, 2011.

Swidler, Leonard, ed. *Toward a Universal Theology of Religions.* Faith Meets Faith Series. Maryknoll, NY: Orbis, 1988.

Tambiah, Stanley Jeyaraja. *Buddhism Betrayed? Religion, Politics and Violence in Sri Lanka.* Chicago: University of Chicago Press, 1992

———. *World Conqueror and World Renouncer: A Study of Buddhism and Polity in Thailand with a Historical Background.* Cambridge Studies in Social Anthropology 15. Cambridge: Cambridge University Press, 1976.

Tartakov, Gary. "B. K. Ambedkar and the Navayana Diksha." In *Religious Conversion in India: Modes, Motivations and Meanings* edited by Rowena Robinson and Sathanathan Clark, 192–215. Oxford: Oxford University Press, 2004.

Taylor, Charles. *A Secular Age.* Cambridge, MA: Belknap, 2007.

Thanissaro, Bhikkhu. "The Shape of Suffering: A Study of Dependent Co-arising." Online: http://www.dhammatalks.org/Archive/Writings/DependentCo-arising.pdf/.

Thrangu, Khabje Khenchen. *The Ninth Gyalwa Karmapa's "Pointing Out the Dharmakaya."* Auckland, NZ: Zhyisil, Chokyi Ghatsal, 2002.

Thomas, Cal. "Accepting Help Offered." *Eau Claire Leader Telegram*, Dec. 23, 2012, 3F.

Trungpa, Chogyam, Rimpoche. *Cutting through Spiritual Materialism.* Edited by John Baker and Marvin Casper. The Clear Light Series. Berkeley, CA: Shambhala, 1973.

———. *Shambhala: The Sacred Path of the Warrior.* Boston: Shambhala, 1988.

Trzebiatowska, Marta, and Steve Bruce. *Why Are Women More Religious Than Men?* Oxford: Oxford University Press, 2012

Tzu Chi Foundation. "Biography of Dharma Master Cheng Yen." Online: http://www. us.tzuchi.org/us/en/index.php?option=com_content&view=article&id=159%3Ai ntroduction&catid=81%3Aabout&Itemid=198&lang=en/.

Vatican Council II. "Declaration on the Relation of the Church to Non-Christian Religions." In *Christianity and Other Religions*, edited by John Hick and Brian Hebblethwaite, 81–86. Philadelphia: Fortress, 1980.

Vélez de Cea, J. Abraham. *The Buddha and Religious Diversity.* Routledge Studies in Asian Religion and Philosophy 6. New York: Routledge, 2013.

Victoria, Brian Daizen. *Zen at War.* 2nd ed. War and Peace Library. Lanham, MD: Rowman & Littlefield, 2006.

Volf, Miroslav. *Exclusion and Embrace: A Theological Exploration of Identity, Otherness, and Reconciliation.* Nashville: Abingdon, 1996.

Wallace, B. Alan. *The Attention Revolution: Unblocking the Power of the Focused Mind.* Boston: Wisdom Publications, 2006.

Walpola Rahula. *What the Buddha Taught.* An Evergreen Book. Rev. ed. New York: Grove Press, 1974.

Waldenfels, Hans. *Absolute Nothingness: Foundations for a Buddhist–Christian Dialogue.* Translated by J. W. Heisig. New York: Paulist, 1980.

Wentz, Richard E. *The Culture of Religious Pluralism*. Explorations. Boulder: Westview, 1998.

Wiggins, James B. *In Praise of Religious Diversity*. New York: Routledge, 1996.

World Council of Churches. "Christian Witness in a Multi-Religious World." Online: http://www.oikoumene.org/en/resources/documents/wcc-programmes/ interreligious-dialogue-and-cooperation/christian-identity-in-pluralistic- societies/christian-witness-in-a-multi-religious-world.html/.

Wood, Peter. *Diversity: The Invention of a Concept*. San Francisco: Encounter Books, 2003.

Wuthnow, Robert. *America and the Challenges of Religious Diversity*. Princeton: Princeton University Press, 2005.

Yang, Martin C. *A Chinese Village: Taitou, Shantung Province*. New York: Columbia University Press, 1945.

Yong, Amos. *Hospitality and the Other: Pentecost, Christian Practices, and the Neighbor*. Faith Meets Faith Series. Maryknoll, NY: Orbis, 2008.

Zagorin, Perez. *How the Idea of Religious Toleration Came to the West*. Princeton: Princeton University Press, 2003.

Subject and Names Index

Abhidharma Buddhism, 157

Absolute truth claims. *See* Exclusive
  truth claims

Aggression, 5, 181, 185, 308, 317
  military, 47, 314
  social action and, 132–34, 179, 187
  truth claims and, 64, 65, 179, 187

Ambedkar, B.R., 247–48

American Academy of Religion, 192,
  194, 197

Analogues for religion, science and
  history as, 115–17

Anatman (egolessness), 156

Anger, 131–34, 179, 185–87
  hatred *vs.*, 317
  self-righteous, 133–34, 185–86,
    317, 319–20

Appearances, 125, 128, 138
  interdependence of, 128

Art(s), religion and, 117

Ashoka, Emperor, 42–45, 237

"The Aspiration of Samantabhadra,"
  126–28

Awareness, 119, 127–28, 130, 181–82,
  186
  dualistic consciousness *vs.*, 127–28
  of space, 120
  of thoughts, 182, 187

Barbarian(s), 61

Barth, Karl, 91

Basic goodness, 99, 206, 315–16,
  327–29, 331, 334.
  See also Buddha-nature

Basic space, 120, 125–27, 211, 225

Being Peace (Nhat Hanh), 75

Beyond Religion (Dalai Lama), 10,
  173, 310, 318

Biblical interpretation, 292–93, 335

Buddha-nature, 99, 328–29, 316, 334

Buddha, the, 41, 49, 98, 105, 106–7,
  122–24, 279
  as leader, 42
  rebirth of, 123
  on teaching Dharma, 236, 319

Buddhahood, 126, 279

Buddhism after Patriarchy (Gross), 12

Buddhism, 10–11, 14, 23–26, 40–51,
  76, 77, 93, 108, 130, 202–3
  in Bhutan, 205–6, 225
  in China, 23, 26–27, 48, 237, 333
  Christianity and, 104, 141–45,
    157–58, 195–98, 275, 279, 306
  diversity of, 85–87
  enlightened society and, 307–8
  gender and, 12, 145, 202–4
  in Japan, 26, 45–47
  as means to end, 105–8
  politics and, 35, 40–51, 308
  beyond religion, 311
  in Sri Lanka, 45, 46, 49–51, 237
  truth claims in, 236, 242–43
  in West, 11, 86, 203–4, 228.
  See also Engaged Buddhism; indi-
    vidual forms by name

Buddhist Eightfold Path, 244, 312,
  315

Buddhist-Christian Studies Journal,
  306–7

Caste system (Indian), 246–48, 256
  conversion and, 246–48
Chauvinism:
  cultural, 203, 265
  religious, 82, 251, 266, 325, 327
Cheng, Yen, Dharma master, 280–81
A Chinese Village (Yang), 26–27
Christ, Carol P. (Goddess theologian),
  164, 299–300
Christian Uniqueness Reconsidered
  (Cobb), 142–43
"Christian Witness in Multi-Religious
  World," 240
Christianity, 3, 5, 23, 55–56, 66–69,
  96–97, 141–45, 168–69, 221–23
  Buddhism and, 104, 141–45,
    157–58, 195–98, 275, 279, 306
  in China, 26–27
  diversity within, 193–95
  European, 35–40, 51, 56
  exclusivism of, 4, 23, 56, 59, 67
  United States, 15, 34–35, 38, 146,
    161, 205, 208–9, 213–15,
    22–24.
  See also Conservatives;
    Fundamentalism
Church and state, 40–42, 205, 207,
  218–21
  separation of, 34–38, 40–42, 49,
    207–12, 216–20.
  See also Religion and politics
Claremont colleges/graduate schools,
  302–3, 305
Cobb-Abe group, 142, 196, 197–98
Cobb, John, 142–45
  on Christian uniqueness, 143–45
  on interfaith dialogue, 142, 277–78,
    280
Colonialism, 237, 246
  Buddhism and, 49, 308
Common Denominator (religious), 9,
  70–71, 259, 264, 276, 304
  human welfare as, 74–75, 79–80
  male dominance/sexism as, 98,
    190, 283
Comparative mirror [metaphor], 148,
  195, 253–66, 268, 278, 295
Comparative theology, 55, 58–59, 72,
  121

Compassion, 89, 94–96, 99, 133,
  145, 173, 241–42, 313–14, 316,
  318–21
  mindfulness practice and, 318–20
  as noninterference, 66, 133, 167,
    264, 291
  trickiness/pitfalls of 65, 133, 241,
    314
  wisdom and, 89
Confucianism, 26–27
Conscience, freedom of, 210
Consciousness, 83, 119, 132, 157, 162
  dualistic, 61, 127–28, 327–28
  thoughts and, 182
Conservatives (religious), 51, 59, 102,
  103, 138, 190, 214, 217, 219–23,
  228, 258, 268, 280
  dialogue with, 278, 305–7
  religious identity and, 289–90
  scripture and, 335.
  See also Fundamentalism
Contemplation, 100, 154, 183–84
  Buddhist, 310
  meditation and, 125, 130, 176
Contemplative education, 188
Contemplative practices. *See* Spiritual
  disciplines
Conversion, 16, 30, 56, 223, 226–33,
  244–48
  of Ashoka, 43
    Judaism and, 228
  missionary activity and, 226–30,
    235, 238–42, 244
  Muslims and, 228
  proselytizing *vs.*, 235
Conviction(s), 15, 65, 108–9, 137,
  160, 216, 253, 316
  psychology of, 166–69
Copernican revolution, religious
  diversity as, 5, 82, 84, 293
Cornille, Catherine, 271
Cosmotheandric experience (Panikkar), 73
Creedal belief(s), 77, 80, 87, 94
Culture(s), 203, 260, 265
  mono-, 149, 175, 231–32
  religion and, 167, 267–68, 292
  western, 65, 165, 331

Cutting Through Spiritual Materialism (Trungpa), 154

D'Costa, Gavin, 75
Dalai Lama, H.H. Tendzin Gyatso, 7, 10, 74, 78, 173, 188, 269–70, 325, 329, 332
  on active compassion, 280, 313–14, 316, 318
  on anger, 317
  on Buddhism, 325–26
  on conversion, on, 238–39, 272
  on enlightened society, 307, 309–10
    on ethical convergence, 311, 313, 315–16, 321, 337
  on interreligious exchange, 282
  on religious diversity, 337
Daoism, 26–27
Davidson, Richard, 188
Death, 123, 184, 308
  interdependence of birth and, 129
Debate, 273–74
Deity:
  external, 84, 309
    male languaging of, 98
  universal, 29–30.
  See also God
Dhamma, two wheels of, 41–43
Dhammapada, 317
Dharma:
  Buddhist, 242
  teachers of, 202–3
Dialogue, 5, 275–76
  beyond, 278
  conversion *vs.*, 272, 279
  debate *vs.*, 273–74
  exclusivism *vs.*, 59, 271–72, 278, 305–6
  proclamation *vs.*, 272–73, 283, 293
  purpose of, 275, 281
  women and, 196–203, 282.
  See also Interreligious dialogue
Discrimination, 207, 211, 220
  legal, 207, 211, 220
Diversity, 5–6, 167, 217
  compassion and, 167
  ethical, 217
  fear of, 260, 276

internal/external, 41, 82–83, 85–88, 161
  uniqueness and, 135, 140–41, 148–49.
  See also Religious diversity
Divine revelation, 102–3, 113
Doctrine(s), 91–94, 102, 104, 115
  evaluating, 100, 112
  as tools, 91–94, 100
  truth *vs.*, 92
Dualistic thinking, 61–62, 123, 161, 166–67, 187, 330, 335
  awareness *vs.*, 127
  as basis of exclusivism, 62
  as default, 327, 335
  gender theories as, 198–99
  social reform and, 133–34
  tetralemma vs., 123.
  See also Duality; Us/them mentality
Duality, 6, 61, 104, 115, 118–24, 126n.7, 327–28
  distinctiveness, *vs.*, 305
  identity and, 154–55, 290
  self/other, 6, 15, 118–22, 134, 327–28

Eck, Diana (on pluralism), 8, 58, 286
Education:
  contemplative, 188
    interreligious/diversity, 149, 251–58, 266–67, 302–3
  for ministry, 286–88.
  See also Religious studies
Ego, 154, 172
  as illusory, 155
  as separate self, 154, 328
Egolessness, 156, 177
Eliade, Mircea, 61
Empathy, practice of, 255, 257–58, 262, 266, 288
Emptiness (Skt. *shunyata*), 105, 124–25, 131
  Buddhist-Christian discussion of, 279
  as sacred ground, 211
  wisdom of, 107.
  See also Interdependence
Engaged Buddhism, 281, 307
  Christian influence on, 280–81

Enlightened society, 206, 307–9,
 311–16, 319, 329
basic goodness and, 331
Buddhist proposals for, 310–12
beyond religion, 310
Enlightenment, 87, 90, 99, 105–6,
 112, 329
 sun/clouds analogy, 329–30.
 See also Basic Goodness
Eternalism/nihilism, extremes of,
 123–24
Ethical responsibility, 7, 16, 252, 286,
 293
 religious studies as, 252, 268
Ethics:
 convergence of, 311, 313, 315–16,
 321, 337
 non-interference as, 133
 religion and, 6–7, 16, 74, 94–96,
 132–33, 173, 217–20, 293,
 304, 310–11, 314
 beyond religion, 310–11, 314–15.
 See also Ethical responsibility
Ethnoreligion(s), 22, 24–25, 38, 39,
 61, 230, 232, 233
 conversion and, 230, 233
 monotheism and, 31
Ethnocentrism, 292–93
European Enlightenment, 115
Exclusive truth claims, 21–23, 29–32,
 52, 59–66, 112–13, 224, 229–30,
 292–94
 aberrance of, 229, 291–93
 biblical interpretation as, 292–93,
 335
 dialogue with, 59, 271–72, 278,
 305–6.
 See also Exclusivism
Exclusivism, 4–5, 15, 21–23, 39, 100,
 136, 139, 160–67, 217–18, 300,
 328, 336
 basis of, 62, 171
 Buddhist, 23
 Christian, 56–59, 234
 ethnocentrism as, 292–93
 harm/danger of, 5, 34, 40, 52, 57,
 63–65, 94, 98, 137, 186–87,
 218

identity and, 60, 155
Islamic, 59, 234
legal discrimination and, 207, 211
politics and, 34–35, 42, 217
proselytizing and, 23, 231, 234
religious diversity *vs.*, 4, 24, 31, 82,
 218, 291–93
universal truth claims *vs.*, 31–32,
 52, 242

Faith, 168, 183
 revealed texts and, 29–30
Fear, 139, 174, 232, 287–88, 301–2,
 334
 Buddhist view of, 299–302
 of diversity, 260, 276
 meditation and, 301
 of Pterodactyls, 180
Feminism, 52, 120, 134, 163–66
 Buddhism and, 161
 cultural chauvinism of, 203
 religious diversity and, 15, 164–66,
 190–204
 religious language and, 170
 social change and, 309
"Feminist Theology as Theology of
 Religions" (Gross), 192–93
Feminist theology, 164, 191–97, 254,
 299–300
First Amendment Non-Establishment
 Clause, 208–10
Five *skandhas* (aggregates), 157, 162
Fletcher, Jeannine Hill, 165–66
Four kinds of wrong speech (Buddhist), 244
Four Noble Truths (Buddha's), 107–8,
 112, 122, 315
Freedom:
 education as, 51, 252
 from religion, 223, 226–27, 230
 of religion, 35, 208–10, 218–21,
 226, 230, 235
 of speech, 244
Fundamentalism, 222, 289–90
 as modern heresy, 115–16.
 See also Conservatives (religious)

Geertz, Clifford, definition of religion, 9
Gender issues, 12, 90, 145, 190–91, 198–205, 265
Generosity (Buddhist), 241–42
    threefold purity of, 241
Global ethic, 314–16
God, 103, 215, 314
    blaming, 263=64, 336
    hidden, 115
    relationship with, 96–97, 334
    "under," 215, 221.
    See also Ultimate Reality
Good Citizens: Creating Enlightened Society (Nhat Hanh), 307
Grasping, 179

Habitual patterns/tendencies, 130, 181, 188
    cultural, 167
Haguken, Ichikawa, 46
Harris, Elizabeth, 50
Heart Sutra, 107–8
Heresy, 37, 93
    fundamentalism as, 115–16
Hick, John, 4, 58, 60, 71, 77, 82, 96–97, 132, 270, 293
Hinduism, 27–31, 67–68, 77, 232–34, 246–48, 256–57
    Christianity and, 233–35
    diversity of, 27–28, 31, 233–34
    polytheism of, 28, 171, 257
History, discipline of, 7, 85, 115–17
    as analogue of religion, 115–17, 263
Holy war, 52, 314
Homosexuality, 211, 217, 219, 220
Hostility, religious, 290, 300
Human nature, 130, 331
    basic goodness as, 99.
    See also Buddha nature
Humanitarian aid, conversion and, 241.
    See also Missionary activities

Identity, 5–6, 15, 16, 153–66, 331
    beyond, 171–73
    composite, 6, 15, 134, 155–66, 176
    duality and, 154–55, 289–91
    group, 6, 154–55, 165, 289–91
    mistaken, 154
    oppositional, 155, 163, 168
    sexual, 163–65, 199.
    See also Religious identity; Self
Ignorance, 179
The Im-Possibility of Interreligious Dialogue (Cornille), 271
Imperial Way Buddhism (Japan), 47
The Impossibility of Religious Freedom (Sullivan), 209n.4, 219
"In God We Trust" (slogan), 146, 213, 214, 224
Inclusivism (fulfillment model), 57, 59, 66–69, 93, 139, 334–35
Individualism, 243, 308, 311
Injustice, 184–86
    anger reaction to, 110, 317
    Buddhist teachings on, 185
Inquisition, 36
Integrity, moral, 5–7, 16, 122, 251, 285, 310, 331
    compassion and, 7
Interbeing (Nhat Hanh), 128–30, 313, 315
Interdependence (dependent arising), 31–32, 111, 121–25, 128, 159, 241–43, 310
    of appearances, 128–29
    of culture/religion, 258
    impermanence and, 242–43
    nondual, 241
    of self/other, 11, 119–22, 124–28, 130, 134
    theisim and, 131.
    See also Emptiness; Interbeing
Interreligious dialogue, 7, 16, 73–74, 143, 191, 195–203, 269–80
    guidelines for, 272, 276–77
    kinds of, 281–82
    partnering for, 282–85
    purpose of, 273, 275
    sexism and, 283–84
    women and 282
Introducing Theologies of Religion (Knitter), 146
Islam, 23, 24, 39, 59, 67–68, 231–32, 256
    conversion and, 232

Jefferson, Thomas, 208–10
Jesus Christ:
   proclaiming, 272–73
   relevance of, 78–79, 93, 141–46,
      278–79
JHU (National Sinhala Heritage
   Party), 50–51
Journal of Feminist Studies in Religion,
   194
Judaism, 24, 30, 39, 228, 334
   monotheism of, 30

Kabat-Zinn, Jon, 188
Kalama Sutta, 99
Karma, 130, 184, 243, 280
Karmic patterns. *See* Habitual
   patterns
Khandro Rinpoche, Jetsun, 92, 167
Khyentse Rinpoche, Dzongsar, 105,
   106
Kimball, Charles, 51–52
Kindness, 95–96.
   See also Compassion
Knitter, Paul, 58, 66, 68, 69, 72, 73–78,
   104, 292, 300, 305, 306
   on religious language, 169–70
   on uniqueness/universality,
      141–42, 146
Küng, Hans, 69

Language:
   of analogy, 106, 108, 112–15
   beyond, 71–73, 87, 90, 102–5, 114,
      126, 184
   compassion *vs.* justice, 145
   duality and, 104
   emptiness of, 131
   as linear medium, 153, 169
   male, 78, 98
   of nonduality, 138
   nontheistic, 131
   "rights," 233.
   See also Religious language
Leadership (religious), 41–42, 164,
   193, 196–99, 286–88, 302
   enlightened, 312
   fear-based, 287–88, 302
Levi-Strauss, Claude, 83

Liberation theology (Christian), 74,
   76, 146, 280, 281
Listening:
   deep, 317
   skills, 276
Locke, John, 210

Madhyamika (Mahayana Buddhist),
   123, 125
   tetralemma, 123, 125
Mahayana Buddhism, 87–89, 93, 107,
   123, 125, 179
   scriptures, 102–3
   social concerns, 307–8
Makransky, John, on engaged Buddhism, 281
Male dominance, 90, 98, 120, 164,
   190, 197, 264–65, 283–84
McGraw, Barbara, 211–12
McLaren, Brian, 168–69, 289–90
McLeod, Ken, 7–8
Meditation practice, 122, 125, 130,
   147, 176–82, 188, 279, 301, 309,
   317–18
   non-sectarian, 318
   samatha, 177, 188
   vipashyana, 177.
   See also Mindfulness practices
Middle Way (Buddhist), 106–7,
   123–24
   eternalism/nihilism *vs.,* 123–24
Mind Life Institute, 188
Mind, 85, 115, 157, 179–80
   defilements of, 179
   fear-based, 287–88, 302
   "only don't know," 109, 185
   resting in nature of, 114
   training, 85, 174–89
   Mindfulness practices, 177–89,
      317–20
   Buddhism and, 317–20
   compassion and, 318–21
   scientific study of, 188
   stress reduction and, 188, 320.
   See also Spiritual disciplines
Ministry, training for, 286–88
Mipham Rinpoche, Sakyong, 330–31

Missionary activity, 3, 23, 59, 94, 95,
    168, 225–29, 238, 245–46
  Buddhism and, 45, 236–37, 241–42
  Christian interpretation of, 245–46
  colonialism and, 237, 246, 308
  conversion *vs.*, 226–30, 235,
    238–42, 244
  religious other and, 121–22
Monasticism, 279, 282
  Buddhist, 44, 86–87, 280, 308
  social action and, 282
Monopoly on Salvation? (Fletcher),
    166
Monotheism, 29–32, 80, 83, 121, 131,
    138
  exclusivism and, 29–32
  politics and, 30–31
  polytheism *vs.*, 77, 257
Moral obligations, 213–16.
  See also Ethical responsibility
Muck, Terry, 306–7
Müller, Max, 192, 254
Muslim(s), 39, 228, 256
  in America, 161, 232
  nation-states, 232
  women, 265
The Myth of Christian Uniqueness
    (Hick, Knitter), 74, 141–42, 143
The Myth of Religious Superiority
    (Knitter), 55n.1

Nagarjuna, 105, 106–7
National identity, religion and,
    205–16
Native American religions, 24, 25, 224
Navayana Buddhism, 247–48
Nhat Hanh, Thich, 128–29, 313–17
  on engaged Buddhism, 319–20
  on enlightened society, 307, 314–15
  on fear, 301–2
  on mindfulness training, 311,
    318–19
  on Right View, 312–13
No Establishment of Religion (Gunn,
    Witte), 209
No Other Name? (Knitter), 75, 169,
    293
Nonduality, 89, 121, 211

of absolute/relative truth, 126
  interdependence as, 121
  language of, 104, 138
  of self/other, 332
Noninterference, 235, 244
  compassion as, 66, 133, 167, 264,
    291
Nontheism, 84–85, 131, 177, 274, 311,
    318, 329

O'Connor, Sandra Day, 215
One True Faith, 4, 27, 60, 64, 72, 82,
    113, 137, 139–40, 187, 217, 244,
    295
  distinctiveness *vs.*, 305
  isolation and, 326–27
One True Poem, 117
Original sin, 98–99
Other(s), self and, 5–6, 11, 118–26,
    130–34, 153–55.
  See also Religious other

Paden, William, 258–59
Padmasambhava, 103
Panikkar, Raimon, 58, 72–73
Paramitas (transcendent virtues),
    89–90
Patel, Eboo, 288, 294, 299
Perennial Philosophy (Huxley), 72
Personal immortality, 157–58, 311
  non-self *vs.*, 274, 318
Plaskow, Judith, 164
Pledge of Allegiance, 35, 205, 215,
    221, 224
Pluralism (religious), 8–9, 58–60,
    69–80, 102, 291–92, 294, 304–5,
    334–35
  beyond, 311
  fear of, 139
  Hinduism and, 27–28
Politics, religion and, 14–16, 30–31,
    33–38, 40–52, 206–7, 212,
    216–21.
  See also Church and state
Prajna (wisdom), 90
Problematizing Religious Freedom
    (Sharma), 231

Proselytizing religions, 16, 167,
  230–35, 239
  non-, 167, 230–31, 233–35
Protestant Reformation, 34–40, 56,
  209, 308
Prothero, Stephen, 252–53
Public sphere, religion in, 216–18,
  223–25
Quran, 83–84

Race, Alan, 58
Rahner, Karl (inclusivist model),
  66–67
Rambo, Lewis R., 238, 245
Reality, nature of, 71–72, 90, 120, 125
  as "moon," 106, 113–15.
  See also Ultimate Reality
Received/revealed truths, 14, 29–30,
  32, 55, 96–97, 101–4, 113, 157–
  58, 193, 251–52
  Buddhist, 102–3
*Rediscovering America's Sacred
  Ground* (McGraw), 210
Religion(s), 8–9, 21–31, 43–44, 61, 67,
  149, 171, 191–94, 230, 252
  analogues for, 115–17, 263
  beyond, 310–11
  disestablishment of, 208–10
  ethics and, 6–7, 16, 74, 94–96,
    132–33, 173, 217–20, 293,
    304, 310–14
  male dominance of, 90, 98, 120,
    164, 190, 196–99, 264–65,
    283–84
  politics and, 14–16, 30–31, 33–38,
    40–52, 206–7, 212, 216–21
  proselytizing, 16, 167, 230–35, 239
  public sphere and, 216–18, 223–25
  sameness of, 130–31, 260
  theistic *vs.* nontheistic, 77, 98, 274
  usefulness of, 94, 105
  as works of art, 117, 263.
  See also Ethnoreligions; Universal-
    izing religions
Religious belonging, 14, 21, 24–27,
  29, 229–30
  four modes of, 24–29, 39

Religious diversity, 3–8, 17, 39–45,
  54, 79, 85, 92–94, 166, 174–75,
  189–203, 252, 261, 283–87, 330
  Buddhist analogies for, 86
  as Copernican revolution, 5, 82,
    84, 293
  exclusivism *vs.*, 4, 29, 31–32, 82,
    218
  feminism and, 15, 164, 190–204
  flourishing with, 5–6, 12–13, 52,
    63–64, 74, 79, 94–95, 100,
    136, 336
  modes of, 24–29, 31, 325
  as norm, 14, 40–41, 81–83, 176,
    207
  pluralism *vs.* 8–9
  "problem" of, 73, 93, 94, 189, 207,
    218, 231, 260
  spiritual disciplines and, 15, 174,
    320–21, 330–32, 336–37
  state and, 52, 206–8
Religious doctrine(s):
  evaluating, 100
  as tools, 94, 100
*Religious Feminism and the Future of
  the Planet* (Gross, Reuther), 196
Religious identity, 15, 60, 155–69
  changing, 160, 226–27
  national identity and, 50, 163,
    205–9.
  See also Conversion
Religious language, 14, 73, 169–71
  limits of, 101–5, 260
  as "love" language, 170
Religious other, 5–6, 14, 55–56, 65,
  85, 118, 121–22, 153, 166–67,
  330
  contact with, 331–36
Religious Right, 52.
  See also Conservatives;
    Fundamentalism
Religious studies, 55, 251–58, 266–68,
  286, 332
  in seminary, 267–68, 288
  teachers of, 255
  threefold agenda of, 255–58.
  See also Education for ministry
Reuther, Rosemary, 196

Right speech (Buddhist), 244
Right view (Buddhist), 87, 312
Rock Edicts of Ashoka, 43–45
Roman Catholic Church, 35–36, 57
  inclusivism of, 66
  Protestantism *vs.*, 35–36
  on sexual/ reproductive choice,
    216–21

The Sacred and the Profane (Eliade),
  61
Sacred ground, 210–12
  America's, 210–11
  space/silence, as, 211
Salvation, 23, 64, 76–77
monopoly on, 57, 63
Samartha, Stanley J., 58, 138, 140
Samatha (calm abiding) meditation,
  177, 188
San Francisco Zen Center, 237
Schmidt-Leukal, Perry, 58, 72, 77
Scholar-practitioner(s), 10, 13,
  161–62, 197, 276, 296, 298, 299
Science, 7, 115–17, 188
  as analogy for religion, 117, 263
  envy, 116
Secularity, 10, 177, 210, 212, 217, 221
  neutrality *vs.*, 212
Self (separate), 119–20, 126–28, 132,
  154, 159
  composite, 128–29, 156–57, 166
    ego as, 154
  interdependence of, 131, 153, 332
  and other, 6, 11, 119–28, 130–36,
    153–55
Self-discipline, 239, 263, 264, 330–31
Self-esteem, 329
Seminaries, 299, 302–3
  education in, 288, 294–303
  as weak link or lynch pin, 288, 299,
    302
Sexism, 76, 98, 120, 283–84, 292–93,
  336
  as common denominator, 98, 190,
    283
Shambhala (society),206, 307
Shambhala Training, 206, 307, 318,
  331, 337

*Shambhala: The Sacred Path of the
  Warrior* (Trungpa), 307
Sharma, Arvind, 231–35, 244
Shinto religion (Japanese), 26
Siddartha Gautama (Buddha), 41–42,
  179
Silence, 211, 215–16, 224–25, 319
  space and, 127, 211, 225
  truth in, 73, 94, 115, 127
Skillful methods (Skt. *upaya*), 87–90,
  92–94, 98–100
  enlightenment *vs.*, 105–6
  religion as, 96, 105–6
  wisdom and, 89–90, 96, 106.
  See also *Upaya*
Smith, Wilfred Cantwell, 97, 299
Social activism/change, 133–34, 280,
  319
  meditation and, 309, 319
Society for Buddhist-Christian Studies, 104, 198
Spiritual disciplines, 100, 122, 173–82,
  206, 317, 330–32
  activism and, 279, 309
  Buddhist, 11, 177, 183, 317–18
  individual/personal, 308–9, 311,
    319, 336
  Protestant Reformation and, 308–9
  religious diversity and, 15, 174,
    320–21, 330–32, 336–37.
  See also Mindfulness practices
Spirituality, endangered forms of, 246
Sri Lanka, Buddhism in, 45, 49–51
  Tamils *vs.*, 45, 49–50
State(s):
  multireligious, 52, 206–8
  neutrality of, 208–12
  as sacred ground, 210–12.
  See also Church and state
Stendahl, Krister, 169–70
Stress reduction, mindfulness-based,
  188, 320
Suffering, 150, 184
  easing, 310–11
  mistaken identity as, 154
Suzuki Roshi, Shunryu, 237

Tetralemma (Budddhist), 123, 125

Theism, 84–85, 87, 131, 274.
　See also Monotheism
Theology, 84, 96, 218
　as "story," 117
　woman and, 164.
　See also Feminist theology
Theology of religions (Christian), 55,
　　58–59, 66, 76, 121, 334
　topics for, 330
Theravada Buddhism, 42, 50–51
Thirty Years' War, 35
Threefold purity (Buddhist), 241
Tibetan Buddhism, 11, 23, 25, 48,
　　103, 274, 332–33
　debate in, 274
　terma tradition of, 103
　threefold analytic method of, 327
　See also Vajrayana Buddhism
Toward a True Kinship of Faiths (Dalai
　Lama), 74, 269, 337
Transformation, 94, 100, 135, 179
　Buddhist view of, 188
　through dialogue, 94, 145, 278,
　　280, 284
　personal/individual, 81, 176, 183,
　　309, 315–19, 336
Trungpa Rinpoche, Chögyam, 154,
　　206, 301, 318
　on dogma/theory, 312
　on ego, 328
　on enlightened society, 307, 312,
　　315–16, 329
　on individual change, 315–16, 18
Truth claims, 167–68, 328
　neutrality *vs.*, 266
　preference for, 336.
　See also Exclusive truth claims;
　　Inclusivism
Truth(s), 114, 136, 183, 262–64
　absolute/relative, 52, 126, 138
　doctrine *vs.*, 91–92, 115
　external, 336
　non-empirical, 116
　question of, 70–79, 92–96, 100,
　　112, 135–36, 149
　in silence, 73, 94, 115, 127
　usefulness *vs.*, 94, 105
Twelve *nidanas*, 159, 162.

　See also Interdependence
Two truths (Buddhist), 61–62, 202n13
Tzu Chi Foundation, 280–81

Ultimate Reality, 71, 84, 100, 103, 262
Union Theological Seminary, 302, 320
Uniqueness, 15, 148–49
　diversity and, 135, 140–41, 148–49
　of Jesus Christ, 141–46, 279
United States, Christianity in, 15, 38,
　　146, 161, 205, 208, 213–15
Unity/oneness:
　diversity *vs.*, 136–38, 148, 305
　nonduality *vs.*, 89, 138
Universal truth claims, 31–32
　Buddhist, 242–43
　exclusive truth claims *vs.*, 31–32,
　　52, 242
Universalizing religion(s), 22–25, 29,
　　230
　Buddhism as, 236
　missionary activity of, 230
Upaya (skillful methods), 87–90, 94
　doctrine as, 92
　paramitas as, 89–90
　for religious diversity, 98–100.
　See also Skillful methods
Us/them mentality (oppositional du-
　alism), 62, 118, 134, 166–68, 172,
　　287–88, 302, 330, 331, 334

Vajrayana Buddhism, 25, 115, 126,
　　169, 317.
　See also Tibetan Buddhism
Vatican II (Second Vatican Council),
　　55, 57, 66, 272
Vedic religions, 171
"Verses on the Middle Way" (Nagar-
　juna), 106–7
Victoria, Brian, 46–47
View(s), attachment to, 108–10
Vipashyana (clear seeing) meditation,
　　177

Wall of separation (Jefferson), 208–10,
　　216, 218–19
Wars of religion, 14, 47
　Buddhism and, 45–51

European, 34–40, 56, 64, 210
"What Evangelicals Want" (Smith), 222–23
When Religion Becomes Evil (Kimball), 51–52
Wisdom, 89–90, 107
  compassion and, 89
  skillful methods and, 89–90, 96, 106
Without Buddha I Could Not Be A Christian (Knitter), 75, 145–46
Womanspirit Rising (Christ and Plaskow), 164
Women:
  "othering" of, 120
  presence/absence of, 202
  religion and, 15, 76, 146–47, 161, 163–66, 170, 175, 190–204, 264–65

teachers of Dharma, 202–3
Words and concepts, 101–6, 111–17, 136, 176, 183
  fundamentalism and, 115–16
  truth *vs.*, 94.
  See also Language
World Council of Churches, 66, 200
Worldview(s), 136, 148
Wuthnow, Robert, 286–87, 291

Yang, Martin C., 26

Zen at War (Victoria), 46
Zen Buddhism, 47, 106, 109, 185n.5, 237